THE EXODUS AND ADVENT MOVEMENTS

IN TYPE AND ANTITYPE

Elder Taylor G. Bunch

Published by
Return of the Latter Rain Publishers
returnofthelatterrain@gmail.com

Page Design by Emily Duffield
Cover design by Emily Duffield

Originally published in 1937 by the author.

ISBN: 978-1-945933-15-8

Elder Taylor G. Bunch

TABLE OF CONTENTS

FOREWORD

In 1924, nine years after the death of Ellen White, the Ministerial Association Advisory Council voted to have Elder A. G. Daniells—former General Conference President of 22 years—arrange a compilation of Ellen White's writings on the subject of justification by faith. As Daniells began his "exhaustive research," he was "amazed and awed at the solemn obligation resting" upon him. His study of the subject of righteousness by faith from the writings of Ellen White, led him to the "settled conviction" that her instruction presented two aspects: "primarily, the great amazing fact that *by faith in the Son of God sinners may receive the righteousness of God*; and secondarily, the purpose and providence of God in sending the specific message of receiving the righteousness of God by faith to His people assembled in General Conference in the city of Minneapolis, Minnesota, in the year 1888."[1]

Yet, as Daniells surveyed the thirty-eight years since the Minneapolis message began, he was led to the sorrowful conclusion: "How sad, how deeply regrettable, it is that this message of righteousness in Christ should, at the time of its coming, have met with opposition on the part of earnest, well-meaning men in the cause of God! *The message has never been received, nor proclaimed, nor given free course as it should have been in order to convey to the church the measureless blessings that were wrapped within it.*"[2]

Such a history of events led Daniells to lament; "O that we had all listened as we should to both warning and appeal as they came to us in that seemingly strange, yet impressive, way at the Conference of 1888! What uncertainty would have been removed, *what wanderings and defeats and losses would have been prevented!* What light and blessing and triumph and progress would have come to us!"[3]

One individual strongly influenced by reading Daniells' book was Taylor G. Bunch. Born in Oregon in 1885, Bunch had attended law school and then felt the call to make the gospel ministry his lifework. He would go on to serve as pastor

---

1. A. G. Daniells, *Christ Our Righteousness* (Washington, D.C.: Review and Herald Pub. Assn., 1926), p. 5, 6-7; emphasis original.
2. *Ibid.*, p. 47; emphasis supplied.
3. *Ibid.*, p. 47; emphasis supplied.

of some of the largest Seventh-day Adventist churches in the United States. While pastoring in South Lancaster and Takoma Park, he lectured regularly in the Religion Departments of Columbia Union College and Atlantic Union College, where he also served for five years as the head of the Department of Religion. For seven years he had charge of the Department of Religion at Loma Linda University. He also served as president of three conferences, Southern Oregon, Idaho, and Michigan, between the years of 1913 and 1947. During his long and active ministry, he authored more than 20 books, going to his rest in 1969.[4]

In 1928, only two years after A. G. Daniells' *Christ Our Righteousness* was published, Taylor Bunch published a small 45-page pamphlet of his own, titled: *Forty Years in the Wilderness in Type and Antitype*. In his pamphlet, Bunch presented the parallels between the Seventh-day Adventist Church and the children of Israel in their journey from Egypt to Canaan, as described in the Bible and the writings of Ellen White. Bunch's *Forty Years in the Wilderness* went into more detail than Daniells had in *Christ Our Righteousness*, regarding Adventist history. Bunch recognized that righteousness by faith was the foundational message being proclaimed at the 1888 Minneapolis Conference, and that the Lord was beginning to pour out His Spirit as the Loud Cry message of Christ and His righteousness sounded throughout the land during the years following 1888. Bunch also recognized that just as Moses, Caleb, and Joshua were criticized and murmured against during the rebellion on the borders of Canaan, so modern Israel responded in a similar manner to the messengers that God had sent.

But even in the year 1928, Taylor Bunch saw hope for the near future, believing that the Lord was once again drawing attention to how He had led in the past and the message He had sent. We do not know how many of Taylor Bunch's pamphlets were circulated among Adventists, since they were self-published, but it is clear that the topic of the comparison between ancient Israel and the Advent movement was one to which he often returned.

With the help of his wife, Taylor Bunch presented the fall and spring Weeks of Prayer at Pacific Union College during the 1930-1931 school year. Here he presented the subject matter from his pamphlet to the student body. A report in the pages of the *Review*, described how Elder and Mrs. Bunch worked "tireless in their efforts to reach every individual member of our college with the gospel of salvation." The interests in the meetings never waned as the "unusually attentive audience of students, teachers, and brethren and sisters from the village" listened each day. Some observers indicated that they "were beginning to catch a faint glimpse of the experience spoken of by the prophet Joel

4. Adapted from: Don F. Neufeld, ed., *Seventh-day Adventist Encyclopedia*, vol. 10, rev. ed. (Washington, D.C.: Review and Herald Pub. Assn., 1976), p. 203.

in chapter, 2, verse 28," regarding the outpouring of God's spirit in latter rain power.[5]

The descriptions given in the *Review* of the revival at Pacific Union College, both during and following the Week of Prayer, were of a very similar nature to the revivals that took place in Battle Creek and other Colleges in the 1890s:[6]

> The spirit of confession and prayer took possession of the school to a marked degree. Although a comparatively large number of regular prayer bands already existed among the students, volunteer bands composed of two or three members each sprang into existence for the purpose of interceding in behalf of the unconverted. No one was forgotten. The backslidden and the indifferent were visited, and many were in this manner brought to the foot of the cross. The hours of the night were, in some instances, turned into seasons of heart searching and prayer, and victories were gained. Both teachers and students feel that this Week of Prayer was indeed a refreshing from the Lord. A new determination to prepare for the coming of the Lord has taken possession of the large majority at Pacific Union College and in the immediate community.[7]

Taylor Bunch also wrote an article following the two Weeks of Prayer, affirming that "the Lord came very near during these occasions, and by His Spirit witnessed to the timeliness of the Laodicean message. Special emphasis was placed upon the remedy for the Laodicean condition, and the results that will follow a personal application and acceptance of the counsel of the True Witness." Bunch also described how revival continued through the Weeks of Prayer, and "the spirit of repentance and confession gave evidence of the genuineness of the revival that swept through the school." Once again, in descriptions similar to the revivals of the 1890s, Bunch stated that "no appeal was made to human emotions, but as the Saviour was uplifted in the beauty of His imputed and imparted righteousness, the Holy Spirit came in and touched the sacred emotions of the heart. The notes of praise and the unusual ring of joy and victory in the testimonies, bore evidence of early-rain experiences, and gave promise of a permanent work of grace in the lives of many there."[8] Truly the "most precious message" from the 1888 era had not lost its power, even when presented to a new generation of young people.

---

5. Joseph M. Peterson, "Week of Prayer at Pacific Union College," *The Advent Review and Sabbath Herald*, May 21, 1931, p. 24.
6. For an account of the revivals that took place following the 1888 Conference, see; Ron Duffield, *The Return of the Latter Rain*, vol. 1, chapters 8 & 9; and *Wounded in the House of His Friends*, chapters 2 through 8.
7. Joseph M. Peterson, "Week of Prayer at Pacific Union College," *The Advent Review and Sabbath Herald*, May 21, 1931, p. 24-25.
8. Taylor G. Bunch, "Pacific Union College," *The Advent Review and Sabbath Herald*, May 21, 1931, p. 25.

Six years later in 1937, while pastoring the Battle Creek Tabernacle, Taylor Bunch presented a similar series of 36 sermons during the Sabbath afternoon vesper services, on the parallels between ancient and modern Israel in the Exodus and Advent movements. Bunch would later self-published his sermon notes in book form under the title, *The Exodus and Advent Movement in Type and Antitype*, for "the special accommodation of those who heard them, and also because of requests from ministers and other gospel workers who desire them."[9]

In this longer "series of studies," Bunch was able to go into more detail regarding Adventist history than A. G. Daniells had in his book *Christ our Righteousness*, and in his own booklet *Forty Years in the Wilderness*, written nine years before. Throughout the series Bunch would point his readers to the abundant evidence of God's desire to bring the Advent movement to their heavenly Canaan home. But Bunch also pointed his readers to the Advent history that must be reviewed and understood before the fulfillment of their long-awaited hopes could be realized:

> Since 'we are repeating the history of that people,' we too must get a vision of the past just before our pilgrim journey is ended. Just before the end the Advent people will review their past history and see it in a new light. We must study and understand the antitypes of the two Kadesh-Barnea experiences of ancient Israel and profit by the mistakes of our fathers especially during the 1888 crisis. We must acknowledge and confess the mistakes of our fathers and see to it that we do not repeat them and thus further delay the final triumph of the Advent Movement.
>
> The history of the past must be reviewed and studied in the light of these mistakes and their consequence in a long delay of the coming of Christ. Such a vision will explain many puzzling questions and will greatly strengthen our faith in the divine leadership of the Advent Movement. It is for this purpose that this series of studies are being given and published.[10]

It is our prayer that the republishing of Taylor Bunch's *The Exodus and Advent Movements in Type and Antitype*, will once again spark an interest in "the way the Lord has led us, and His teaching in our past history."

Ron Duffield
May 2019

---

9. Taylor G. Bunch, *The Exodus and Advent Movements in Type and Antitype* (Denton, NC: Barnes Printing, 2019), p. 13.
10. Ibid. (2019), p. 326.

NOTE FROM EDITORS

The book you hold in your hands is a reformatted edition of Taylor G. Bunch's sermon notes for his thirty-six-part series on the parallels between ancient and modern Israel in the Exodus and Advent movements. The editors have strictly followed the original manuscript except in the following ways: Many of the chapters and main headings in Taylor Bunch's sermon notes began with a scriptural reference, which he no doubt read as part of his discourse. These texts have been written out in full from the King James Version, the translation that Taylor Bunch most likely quoted from. All other references for quoted Scripture, the writings of Ellen G. White, and other quotes from various authors, have been removed from the main text of the manuscript and placed in footnotes. Large quotations, especially those from the writings of Ellen G. White, have been indented and broken up into paragraphs according to the original reference. Lastly, in order to help with the flow of the sermon notes, short editorial comments have been added throughout the book. In all such instances editorial comments have been put in {brackets}. Other than these listed additions and changes, this book remains unchanged from Bunch's original manuscript.

The Editors
May 2019

PREFACE

This series of thirty-six sermons on the parallels between ancient and modern Israel in the Exodus and Advent movements were delivered during the Sabbath afternoon vesper services in the Battle Creek Tabernacle. They are being published in this form for the special accommodation of those who heard them, and also because of requests from ministers and other gospel workers who desire them. This series is of special value in meeting apostates and divergent movements, and in establishing Seventh-day Adventists in "the faith which was once delivered unto the saints."

The Author

1

PURPOSE OF THE SERIES

Certainty of Truth

Luke 1:1-4: "Forasmuch as many have taken in hand to set forth in order a declaration of those things which are most surely believed among us, Even as they delivered them unto us, which from the beginning were eyewitnesses, and ministers of the word; It seemed good to me also, having had perfect understanding of all things from the very first, to write unto thee in order, most excellent Theophilus, That thou mightest know the certainty of those things, wherein thou hast been instructed."

We are living in a world of uncertainty where there is nothing sure but God and His truth. If we pass safely through the perils of the last days we must know individually the certainties of the foundations of our faith. Satan is now making his last and fiercest attack on the remnant against whom he is furiously angry.[1]

As we near the end of the conflict Satan will make his supreme and most desperate effort to shake our confidence in the word of God and the message of salvation for this time. Under this attack many will lose faith and cast away their confidence. Just before the return of Jesus many will get off on side issues and allow themselves to be sidetracked from the main line of the message. We can only reach our destination by keeping on the main line.[2]

A Sure Foundation

2 Timothy 2:15-19: "Study to show thyself approved unto God, a workman that needeth not to be ashamed, rightly dividing the word of truth. But shun profane and vain babblings: for they will increase unto more ungodliness. And their word will eat as doth a canker: of whom is Hymenaeus and Philetus; Who concerning the truth have erred, saying that the resurrection is past already; and overthrow the faith of some. Nevertheless the foundation of God standeth sure, having this seal, The Lord knoweth them that are his. And, Let every one that nameth the name of Christ depart from iniquity."

1. Revelation 12:12.
2. Hebrews 10:35-39.

{In Weymouth's Translation it says:}[3]

"Yet God's solid foundation stands unmoved, bearing this inscription, 'The Lord knows those who really belong to Him' and this also, 'Let everyone who names the name of the Lord renounce all wickedness.'"[4]

The seal that makes the foundation sure is God's acknow-ledgment that we are His because we have departed from all iniquity. A "seal" is defined as "that which authenticates, confirms, ratifies, makes stable; that which effectually secures." That which makes the foundation of God's church-temple secure and stable and effectually secures all who build on it, is victory over sin through faith in Christ. These alone are acknowledged as His and in them He is well pleased. A mere knowledge of the truth is not enough to constitute a sure foundation. Many who have such a knowledge are apostatizing and their character-buildings are crashing before the storm.

The Bulwarks of Zion

Psalm 48:12-14: "Walk about Zion, and go round about her: tell the towers thereof. Mark ye well her bulwarks, consider her palaces; that ye may tell it to the generation following. For this God is our God for ever and ever: he will be our guide even unto death."

The time has come when every believer in the threefold message should walk about Zion and count her towers, mark well her bulwarks, and consider her strongholds to see if they will stand the strain of the coming storm. This is the purpose of this series of studies when we can together make this examination.

{Ellen White writes:}

> A good character must be built up brick by brick, everyday growing in proportion to the effort put forth.....A storm is arising that will wrench and test the spiritual foundation of everyone to the utmost. Therefore avoid the sand-bed; hunt for the rock. Dig deep; lay your foundation sure. Build, oh build for eternity. Build with tears and heart-felt prayers.[5]

Both builders had a knowledge of the word and therefore it is not the amount of known truth but of obeyed truth that constitutes the sure and safe foundation.

---

3. Editorial Note: In order to help with the flow of the sermon notes, short editorial comments have been added throughout the book. In all such instances editorial comments have been put in {brackets}.
4. 2 Timothy 2:19 (Weymouth Translation).
5. Ellen White, *Testimonies for the Church*, vol. 5 (1889), p. 129, 130. See Matthew 7:24-27; Luke 6:47-49.

Present Truth

2 Peter 1:10-13,16,19: "Wherefore the rather, brethren, give diligence to make your calling and election sure: for if ye do these things, ye shall never fall: For so an entrance shall be ministered unto you abundantly into the everlasting kingdom of our Lord and Saviour Jesus Christ. Wherefore I will not be negligent to put you always in remembrance of these things, though ye know them, and be established in the present truth. Yea, I think it meet, as long as I am in this tabernacle, to stir you up by putting you in remembrance; ...For we have not followed cunningly devised fables, when we made known unto you the power and coming of our Lord Jesus Christ, but were eyewitnesses of his majesty. ...We have also a more sure word of prophecy; whereunto ye do well that ye take heed, as unto a light that shineth in a dark place, until the day dawn, and the day star arise in your hearts:"

Every generation has had its message of present truth for that time and the eternal destiny of those who heard it depended upon their attitude toward it. This was true of the Antediluvians and the message of Noah; of Sodom and Gomorrah and the message of Lot; of Nineveh and the message of Jonah; of ancient Israel and the message of Elijah; of the Jewish nation and the threefold message of John the Baptist, Christ and the apostles. It is equally true of the threefold message of Revelation 14 which is present truth for this generation.

> Different periods in the history of the church have each been marked by the development of some special truth, adapted to the necessities of God's people at that time. Every new truth has made its way against hatred and opposition; and those who were blessed with its light were tempted and tried.[6]

Personal Knowledge

{In the *Testimonies for the Church*, vol. 5 we are told:}

> As real spiritual life declines, it has ever been the tendency to cease to advance in the knowledge of the truth. Men rest satisfied with the light already received from God's word, and discourage any further investigation of the Scriptures. They become conser-vative, and seek to avoid discussion.
>
> ...when no new questions are started by investigation of the Scriptures, when no difference of opinion arises which will set men to searching the Bible for themselves, to make sure that they have the truth, there will be many now, as in ancient times, who will hold to tradition, and worship they know not what.
>
> I have been shown that many who profess to have a knowledge of present

6. Ellen White, *Great Controversy* (1911), p. 609.

> truth, know not what to believe. They do not know the evidences of their faith...When the time of trial shall come, there are men now preaching to others, who will find, upon examining the positions they hold, that there are many things for which they can give no satisfactory reason...
>
> ...Precious light has come, appropriate for this time. It is Bible truth, showing the perils that are right upon us. This light should lead us to a diligent study of the Scriptures, and a most critical examination of the positions which we hold. God would have all the bearings and positions of truth thoroughly and perseveringly searched, with prayer and fasting...
>
> ...We should present sound arguments, that will not only silence our opponents, but will bear the closest and most searching scrutiny...
>
> Whatever may be man's intellectual advancement, let him not for a moment think that there is no need of thorough and continuous searching of the Scriptures for greater light.[7]

Books of Parallels

The Bible is a book of parallel events and movements; of types and their antitypes. This makes the Bible an up-to-date Book from Genesis to Revelation to the very close of human history. Thus "all Scripture is profitable for doctrine, for reproof, for correction, for instruction in righteousness." [8]

Adam, the first man, was a type of Christ, the second Adam; Enoch and Elijah were types of those who will be translated when Jesus comes; Moses was a type of those who will be resurrected at the second advent; Noah and his message were typical of the messengers and message of the second advent; so also were the messages of Elijah and John the Baptist.

Jezebel was a type of the papacy; ancient Egypt, of spiritual darkness and the bondage of sin; and ancient Babylon, of Satan's false and counterfeit system of religion to the close of time. The earthly sanctuary with its apartments, furniture, service, and priesthood, were typical of the heavenly temple and the atoning ministration of Christ.

Ancient and Modern Israel

One of the greatest parallels consisting of types and antitypes is found in what we call the Exodus and Advent movements of ancient and modern Israel. The Lord delivered ancient Israel from the bondage of Egypt and led them through the wilderness into the earthly Canaan, or the "promised land." The exodus from Egypt and the experiences of Israel were typical of the gathering of modern Israel out of the darkness of modern Egypt and spiritual Babylon to lead them into the heavenly Canaan.

7. Ellen White, *Testimonies for the Church*, vol. 5 (1889), p. 706-708.
8. 2 Timothy 3:16.

These are the two greatest religious movements of all history. Both arose in fulfillment of prophecy and accomplished their work in harmony with a divine purpose and move forward under the leadership of the God of heaven.

Parallel Movements

Jeremiah 16:14-16, 19: "Therefore, behold, the days come, saith the LORD, that it shall no more be said, The LORD liveth, that brought up the children of Israel out of the land of Egypt; But, The LORD liveth, that brought up the children of Israel from the land of the north, and from all the lands whither he had driven them: and I will bring them again into their land that I gave unto their fathers. Behold, I will send for many fishers, saith the LORD, and they shall fish them; and after will I send for many hunters, and they shall hunt them from every mountain, and from every hill, and out of the holes of the rocks… O LORD, my strength, and my fortress, and my refuge in the day of affliction, the Gentiles shall come unto thee from the ends of the earth, and shall say, Surely our fathers have inherited lies, vanity, and things wherein there is no profit."

Jeremiah 23:5-8: "Behold, the days come, saith the LORD, that I will raise unto David a righteous Branch, and a King shall reign and prosper, and shall execute judgment and justice in the earth. In his days Judah shall be saved, and Israel shall dwell safely: and this is his name whereby he shall be called, THE LORD OUR RIGHTEOUSNESS. Therefore, behold, the days come, saith the LORD, that they shall no more say, The LORD liveth, which brought up the children of Israel out of the land of Egypt; But, The LORD liveth, which brought up and which led the seed of the house of Israel out of the north country, and from all countries whither I had driven them; and they shall dwell in their own land."

The deliverance from Egypt and its bondage was the greatest event in the history of ancient Israel and they were never to forget it. It was to be commemorated by the Passover, the Feast of Tabernacles and other memorials. But the time will come when God's people will experience another and greater deliverance upon which they will place the emphasis rather than upon the exodus from Egypt. Modern Israel is to be delivered from the bondage of sin and gathered from "all lands" and from "the ends of the earth."

The Remnant

Isaiah 11:10-12, 16: "And in that day there shall be a root of Jesse, which shall stand for an ensign of the people; to it shall the Gentiles seek: and his rest shall be glorious. And it shall come to pass in that day, [that] the Lord shall set his hand again the second time to recover the remnant of his people, which shall be left, from Assyria, and from Egypt, and from Pathros, and from Cush, and from Elam, and from Shinar, and from Hamath, and from the islands of the sea. And he shall set up an ensign for the nations, and shall assemble the outcasts of Israel, and gather together the dispersed of Judah from the four corners of the earth. ...And there shall be an highway for the remnant of his people, which shall be left, from Assyria; like as it was to Israel in the day that he came up out of the land of Egypt."

The second advent movement had its real beginning in apostolic days but was brought to a standstill by the great apostasy or "falling away." The purpose of God's message today is to finish the gospel commission which the apostles so nobly began. This movement includes "the remnant of His people" gathered out of all the world "like as" the gathering of ancient Israel out of Egypt. The last great gathering is "from the islands of the sea" and from "the four corners of the earth." It is spoken of as the "second time" which indicates that there have been two movements of the same kind, one being a type of the other. The second is fulfilled only in the final world message described in Revelation 14:6-14.

Song of Moses

Revelation 15:2, 3: "And I saw as it were a sea of glass mingled with fire: and them that had gotten the victory over the beast, and over his image, and over his mark, and over the number of his name, stand on the sea of glass, having the harps of God. And they sing the song of Moses the servant of God, and the song of the Lamb, saying, Great and marvellous are thy works, Lord God Almighty; just and true are thy ways, thou King of saints."

Why will the Advent people repeat the same song sung by ancient Israel to celebrate their deliverance unless they go through a similar experience? "That song does not belong to the Jewish nation alone. It points forward to the destruction of all the foes of righteousness, and the final victory of the Israel of God."[9]

{Conway in *Pulpit Commentary* writes:}

> This scene is another reminder, but of many more, that in the history of Israel may be read, in symbol, the story of the Christian church.[10]

Only those in the Advent movement who have passed through the experience of the Exodus movement can sing the song commemorating their triumph.

9. Ellen White, *Patriarchs and Prophets* (1890), p. 289.
10. Conway in *Pulpit Commentary*.

2
ANCIENT AND MODERN ISRAEL PARALLELED

Type and Antitype

1 Corinthians 10:1-11: "Moreover, brethren, I would not that ye should be ignorant, how that all our fathers were under the cloud, and all passed through the sea; And were all baptized unto Moses in the cloud and in the sea; And did all eat the same spiritual meat; And did all drink the same spiritual drink: for they drank of that spiritual Rock that followed them: and that Rock was Christ. But with many of them God was not well pleased: for they were overthrown in the wilderness. Now these things were our examples, to the intent we should not lust after evil things, as they also lusted. Neither be ye idolaters, as were some of them; as it is written, The people sat down to eat and drink, and rose up to play. Neither let us commit fornication, as some of them committed, and fell in one day three and twenty thousand. Neither let us tempt Christ, as some of them also tempted, and were destroyed of serpents. Neither murmur ye, as some of them also murmured, and were destroyed of the destroyer. Now all these things happened unto them for ensamples: and they are written for our admonition, upon whom the ends of the world are come."

This language is clear and the application unmistakable. Verse 11 is the key text because it explains the reason for those which precede it. The experiences of God's people under the Exodus movement were typical of those under the Advent movement. The history of ancient Israel was recorded "for our admonition, upon whom the ends of the world are come."[1]

After quoting the above Scripture God's servant wrote: "The experience of Israel, referred to in the above words of the apostle, and as recorded in the 105th and 106th Psalm, contain lessons of warnings that the people of God in these last days especially need to study. I urge that these chapters be read at least once every week."[2]

Not All Recorded

Jesus said and did many things which the Holy Spirit did not have recorded in

1. 1 Corinthians 10:11.
2. Ellen White, *Testimonies to Ministers and Gospel Workers* (1923), p. 89.

the four gospels.[3] Just so there were many things which happened to ancient Israel during their deliverance from Egypt and their journey to the promised land which the Holy Spirit did not have recorded in the books of Exodus, Leviticus, Numbers and Deuteronomy.

Our text tells us that only those things were recorded which "happened to them for ensamples"[4] ("types"—Margin) of the experiences of the people of God "upon whom the ends of the world are come." Not all that "happened" was typical, but all that was "written." If all that took place during those 40 years had been recorded it would require a great library to contain it. Everything written in the Scriptures regarding the Exodus movement contains lessons for us.

Meaning of Type

2 Corinthians 10:11: "Now all these things happened unto them for ensamples: and they are written for our admonition, upon whom the ends of the world are come."

{If we take a look at the phrase "for examples" in other translations we better understand the meaning as shown below:}

"By way of example" — R.V.
"By way of figure." — R.V. Margin.
"But these things occurred to them typically." — Emphatic Diaglott.
"All this kept happening to them with a figurative meaning." — Weymouth.

Type is defined as "a figure, emblem or symbol; a symbol or figure of something to come; a pattern." Figure is defined as something "to prefigure; to foreshow; to represent by typical or figurative resemblance; a pattern, emblem, type, image, or imitation."

A type is a literal representation of a spiritual fact. Baptism is called "a figure"[5] of the resurrection the first Adam "the figure of Him who was to come",[6] that is the second Adam. "In Adam we have a type of Him whose coming was still future."[7] The earthly sanctuary and its services and priesthood are said to be "a figure"[8] of the heavenly sanctuary and ministration of Christ.

Never Identical

Types and antitypes are never identical but only similar. In fact there must be

3. John 20:30, 31; 21:25.
4. 1 Corinthians 10:11.
5. 1 Peter 3:21.
6. Romans 5:14.
7. Romans 5:14 (Weymouth Translation).
8. Hebrews 9:8, 9, 24.

differences in many respects.

> As there must be a similarity or analogy between the type and the antitype, so there is also a diversity of dissimilitude between them. It is not in the nature of the types and antitypes that they should agree in all things; else, instead of similitude, there would be identity. Hence the apostle, while making Adam a type of Christ, yet shows how infinitely the latter excelled the former (1 Corinthians 15:47). So the priests of old were types of Christ, though He infinitely excelled them.[9]

The same author mentioned as examples of "Actions Typical", "the deliverance out of Egypt, passage of the Red Sea, sojourn in the wilderness, passage over Jordan, entrance into Canaan, and restoration from Babylon."

The Two Movements

In the type and antitype as represented by the Exodus and Advent movements there are of necessity many differences. In the first a nation of people in one group was delivered and taken out of a single nation and led through a literal wilderness to the literal Canaan, while in the antitype God's people are gathered out of all the nations on earth in a great spiritual movement and are led through a spiritual wilderness to the heavenly Canaan.

In paralleling these two religious movements we must use the same reasons and good judgment as in the study of all types and antitypes which are never identical in their details. The lamb was a type of Christ, the Lamb of God, but they are far from being identical.

Another Scripture

Ezekiel 20:33-38: "As I live, saith the Lord GOD, surely with a mighty hand, and with a stretched out arm, and with fury poured out, will I rule over you: And I will bring you out from the people, and will gather you out of the countries wherein ye are scattered, with a mighty hand, and with a stretched out arm, and with fury poured out. And I will bring you into the wilderness of the people, and there will I plead with you face to face. Like as I pleaded with your fathers in the wilderness of the land of Egypt, so will I plead with you, saith the Lord GOD. And I will cause you to pass under the rod, and I will bring you into the bond of the covenant: And I will purge out from among you the rebels, and them that transgress against me: I will bring them forth out of the country where they sojourn, and they shall not enter into the land of Israel: and ye shall know that I am the LORD."

Just as the Lord led Israel out of Egypt "with a mighty hand, and with a stretched

9. *Popular and Critical Bible Encyclopedia*, article "Type."

arm, and with fury poured out," so the Lord will gather the remnant of His people out of all "the countries wherein ye are scattered, with a mighty hand, and with a stretched out arm, and with fury poured out." This doubtless refers to the plagues of Egypt and the seven last plagues.

We are to be brought "into the wilderness of the people" and pled with "face to face" "like as" the Lord brought ancient Israel into the wilderness and pled with them "face to face." The Lord will cause modern Israel to pass under the rod or be numbered and will bring them under the bond of the new covenant.

Just as the Lord "purged" the Exodus movement by shaking out the rebels, so He will purge modern Israel of its rebels by "shaking" or "spewing" them out. In those two parallel movements the Lord does not call the faithful out in order to purify the church but He purges or shakes out the rebels.

Spirit of Prophecy

{We see the same idea expressed in the Spirit of Prophecy:}

> The apostle Paul plainly states that the experience of the Israelites in their travels has been recorded for the benefit of those living in this age of the world, those upon whom the ends of the world are come. We do not consider that our dangers are any less than those of the Hebrews, but greater. There will be temptations to jealousies and murmurings, and there will be outspoken rebellion, as are recorded of ancient Israel.[10]
>
> The history of the wilderness life of Israel was chronicled for the benefit of the Israel of God to the close of time. The record of God's dealings with the wanderers of the desert in all their marchings to and fro, in their exposure to hunger, thirst, and weariness, and in the striking manifestations of His power for their relief, is fraught with warning and instruction for His people in all ages. The varied experience of the Hebrews was a school of preparation for their promised home in Canaan. God would have His people in these days review with a humble heart and teachable spirit the trials through which ancient Israel passed, that they may be instructed in preparation for the heavenly Canaan.[11]

Repeating History

> I have been shown that the spirit of the world is fast leavening the church. You are following the same path as did ancient Israel.[12]

---

10. Ellen White, *Testimonies for the Church*, vol. 3 (1875), p. 358.
11. Ellen White, *Patriarchs and Prophets* (1890), p. 293.
12. Ellen White, *Testimonies for the Church*, vol. 5 (1889), p. 75.

The sin of ancient Israel was in disregarding the expressed will of God and following their own way according to the leadings of unsanctified hearts. Modern Israel is fast following in their footsteps and the displeasure of the Lord is as surely resting upon them.[13]

Satan's snares are laid for us as verily as they were laid for the children of Israel just prior to their entrance into the land of Canaan. We are repeating the history of that people.[14]

Same Disobedience

The same disobedience and failure which were seen in the Jewish church have characterized in a greater degree the people who have had this great light from heaven in the last message of warning. Shall we let the history of Israel be repeated in our experience?[15]

I was pointed back to ancient Israel. But two of the adults of the vast army that left Egypt entered the land of Canaan. Their dead bodies were strewn in the wilderness because of their transgressions. Modern Israel are in greater danger of forgetting God and being led into idolatry than were His ancient people. Many idols are worshiped, even by professed Sabbathkeepers...

...The sins and iniquities of rebellious Israel are recorded and the picture presented before us as a warning, that if we imitate their example of trans-gressions, and depart from God, we shall fall as surely as did they. "Now all these things happened unto them for ensamples; and they are written for our admonition, upon whom the ends of the world are come."[16]

Objectionable Features

We are inclined to feel that only the good features of the Exodus movement were typical of experiences in the Advent movement. But their mistakes and failures and apostasies are also recorded for our benefit.

I question whether genuine rebellion is ever curable. Study in Patriarchs and Prophets the rebellion of Korah, Dathan and Abiram. This rebellion was extended, including more than two men. It was led by two hundred and fifty princes of the congregation, men of renown. Call rebellion by its right name, and then consider that the experience of the ancient people of God with all its objectionable features was faithfully chronicled to pass

13. *Ibid.*, p. 94.
14. Ellen White, *Testimonies for the Church*, vol. 5 (1889), p. 160.
15. *Ibid.*, p. 456.
16. Ellen White, *Testimonies for the Church*, vol. 1 (1868), p. 609.

into history. The Scripture declares, "These things were written for our admonition upon whom the ends of the world are come."[17]

Personal Application

The history of the church in any period is a reflection of the experiences of the individual members. Church history is made by the personal experiences of the majority of its members. This series of studies on the Exodus of ancient Israel will accomplish but little good unless we apply the lessons to our individual lives. The experiences of ancient Israel are replete with warnings, reproofs and admonitions that are invaluable to us as individuals. If we fail to make a personal application this series will have been given in vain.

Individual Accountability

We will be held accountable as individuals, for sin is always an individual matter. We sometimes speak of group or national sins but they are simply the sins of the majority of the individuals who make up the group or nation. The appeal of the apostle Paul to those "upon whom the ends of the world are come", is, that as individuals we profit by the mistakes of the individuals who made up the Exodus movement.[18]

"Notice the constant forgetfulness, ingratitude, and failure of Israel. 'In tracing the progress of Israel in the wilderness, I read the history of my own heart and life.'"[19] Let us endeavor to do the same during this series.

17. Leaflet Series, "Apostasies", Number 3.
18. 1 Corinthians 10:1-11.
19. Saphir in "The Lord's Prayer", p. 319.

3

THE TWO MOVEMENTS IN PROPHECY

Time Prophecy

The Exodus movement was based on a definite time prophecy given 422 years before it began.[1] The 400 years include the time of their sojourn in Canaan as pilgrims and strangers in a strange country, after Abraham returned from his first journey into Egypt, and the Lord renewed to him the promise that Palestine would be given to him and his seed forever.[2]

This is made clear in the Samaritan Pentateuch rendering of Exodus 12:40, 41. "In the land of Egypt and in the land of Canaan." There is no contradiction even in the Authorized Version for at that time Egypt was the ruling power of the world and Canaan was a part of the Egyptian Empire. It was part of "the land of Egypt."

Journey Into Egypt

The exodus out of Egypt indicates a former ingress into Egypt. This took place when Jacob and his sons moved into Egypt because of the famine. While they sojourned in the land of Goshen they multiplied and became a great tribe or nation. But their mingling with the heathen Egyptians was detrimental to their own religion.

There came a great apostasy or "falling away" from the faith of their fathers, the faith once delivered to Abraham, Isaac and Jacob. In their contact with the pagan gods and false worship of the Egyptians they lost their knowledge of the true God and His truth. They gradually adopted heathen customs and finally worshiped heathen gods and forgot the God of their fathers.

Sun-Worship

While the Egyptians worshiped many gods, their chief god was the sun. In fact all other gods were various manifestations of the sun-god and his creative power in nature. In "defiling themselves with the idols of Egypt" they worshiped "the host of heaven."[3]

1. Genesis 15:12-16.
2. See Genesis 13.
3. Ezekiel 20:5-8; Acts 7:39-42.

When the children of Israel forgot the Creator and began to worship the creature, they also ceased to celebrate the sign of the true God and the memorial of His creative power, the Sabbath. As the true Sabbath gradually lost its significance to them they gradually adopted its counterfeit, the sign of idolatry and the memorial of sun-worship.

The Solar Holiday

The Egyptians dedicated the first day of the week to their first or chief god, Amon Ra, —the sun. Since the king of Egypt was the chief pontiff of their religion and the high-priest of sun-worship, he took the dynastic title of Pharaoh which is the Hebrew rendering of Ph Ra—the sun. The Sun's Day finally became known as Sunday, "the wild solar holiday of all pagan times."[4]

{Morer writes:}

> It is not to be denied but we borrow the name of this day from the ancient Greeks and Romans, and we allow that the old Egyptians worshiped the sun, and as a standing memorial of their veneration, dedicated this day to him. And we find by the influence of their example, other nations, and among them the Jews themselves, doing him homage.[5]

Became Semi-Pagans

By the end of the fourth generation the Israelites were in such dense darkness and idolatry that they were but little better than the Egyptians themselves. They were at least semi-pagans with but little left of the faith and practice of Abraham, Isaac, and Jacob. The Exodus movement was therefore a reformation to lead Israel back to the knowledge of the true God; back to "the faith once delivered to the saints."[6]

Started on Time

The Lord through Abraham not only foretold the length of time His people would remain in the bondage and affliction of Egypt, but also the time and generation when they would be delivered and the Exodus would begin. He also predicted that the affliction and persecution would be the worst just before the deliverance.

Pointing to this great time prophecy, Moses doubtless told the afflicted Israelites that deliverance was not only near but that "this generation shall not pass, till all these things be fulfilled."[7] The generation did not pass without seeing the time prophecy fulfilled and the Israelites on their way out of Egypt toward the promised land. The

---

4. *The North British Review*, vol. 18, p. 409.
5. Morer, *Dialogues on the Lord's Day*, p. 22, 23.
6. Jude 1:3.
7. Luke 21:32.

time was so long that doubtless many were tempted to "cast away their confidence" and give up all hope of deliverance.

Why the Delay?

Genesis 15:16: "But in the fourth generation they shall come hither again: for the iniquity of the Amorites is not yet full."

{If we look at Genesis 15:16 in other translations we see:}

> "For the guilt of the Amorites is not yet full."— Moffatt.
> "When the sins of the Amorites will be complete." — Fenton.

The Amorites were the most powerful and distinguished of the Canaanitish nations and is here used to represent them all. The nations in possession of the promised land must be given time to repent before they could be dispossessed by the Israelites. This is the chief reason why the Lord led Israel through the wilderness instead of the direct route so the inhabitants of Canaan could hear of their coming under the leadership of the God of heaven and of His mighty works in their behalf, so that they would repent of their sins and be saved. It was their last opportunity and had they accepted it they would have been spared and remained forever with the Israelites in their own land.

Probation Closed

Instead of welcoming the Israelites as the people of God they fiercely attacked them and this was the last act of resistance and rebellion which sinned away their day of grace and closed their probation. They began their attacks soon after Israel crossed the Red Sea and did not even wait till they reached the borders of Canaan. They harassed Israel all along their journey, cutting off the feeble and infirm.

Their final destruction was an act of mercy on the part of God. Their "iniquity was full" and there was no room for mercy. {Of this Ellen White writes:}

> The Amalekites had long been high-handed sinners, and their crimes had cried to God for vengeance, yet His mercy had still called them to repentance; but when the men of Amalek fell upon the wearied and defenseless ranks of Israel, they sealed their doom.[8]

The Antitype

Modern Israel had a pure faith in apostolic days. It was the faith of Abraham, Isaac and Jacob.[9] Every false and pagan plant that was not of divine origin had been rooted

8. Ellen White, *Patriarchs and Prophets* (1890), p. 300.
9. Galatians 3:6-9; John 8:39.

out of God's garden or church.[10] But there came a gradual apostasy or "falling away" from the "faith of Jesus" and the apostles.[11]

The church gradually adopted worldly customs and practices and finally drifted so far into Egyptian or pagan darkness that the "light of the world" was extinguished in the "Dark Ages." Modern Israel went down into modern Spiritual Babylon and became so conformed to her customs and doctrines that the mark of distinction almost disappeared. They lost their Christian characteristics and became at best semi-Christian and semi-pagan.

The Sabbath

The apostolic church in its pure faith was loyal to God and His law. They worshiped the Creator and observed the memorial of His creation, the Sabbath. In Babylon they gradually lost sight of the Creator and became worshipers of creature-gods. They, therefore, forgot the Sabbath of Christ and the apostles, and adopted the heathen day of the sun, or Sunday.

{In his book, *Versteendniss des Neue Testament*, Dr. H. Kunkel wrote:}

> The taking over of Sunday by the early Christians is, to my mind, an exceedingly important symptom that the early church was directly influenced by a spirit that does not originate in the gospel, nor in the Old Testament, but in a religious system foreign to it.[12]

This foreign religious system from whence Sunday came is paganism as represented by Babylon.

A Compromise

> The Gentiles were an idolatrous people, who worshiped the sun, and Sunday was their most sacred day. Now, in order to reach the people in this new field, it seems but natural, as well as necessary, to make Sunday the day of rest of the church. At this time it was necessary for the church to either adopt the Gentile's day, or else to have the Gentiles change their day. To change the Gentile's day would have been an offense and a stumbling-block to them. The church could naturally reach them better by keeping their day.[13]

They had so far departed from the faith of the apostles that they would rather

10. Matthew 15:13.
11. 2 Thessalonians 2:2-7.
12. Dr. H. Kunkel, in *Versteendniss des Neue Testament*, p. 76.
13. Wm. Frederick, *Three Prophetic Days*, pp. 169, 170.

offend God than their heathen neighbors.

Time Prophecy

Seven time-prophecies, some of which were made more than 500 years before Christ, gave the time God's people would remain in the darkness and bondage of spiritual Babylon, and also the time when their exodus back to Zion would begin.[14] For 1260 prophetic days or literal years, the church would be subject to the authority of the "beast" under the papal head, and would be afflicted and persecuted. The most bitter persecutions came near the end of the period.[15]

While the reformation began before the end of the 1260 year period of papal supremacy the Advent movement proper, which was to call God's people all the way out of Babylon, did not start till about 30 years after the close of the time prophecy. This is significant in the light of the fact that while the preparation for the exodus of ancient Israel began before the close of the 400 years, the movement itself did not leave Egypt till 30 years after the close of the predicted period of their bondage.[16]

Began on Time

Daniel 8:13, 14: "Then I heard one saint speaking, and another saint said unto that certain saint which spake, How long shall be the vision concerning the daily sacrifice, and the transgression of desolation, to give both the sanctuary and the host to be trodden under foot? And he said unto me, Unto two thousand and three hundred days; then shall the sanctuary be cleansed."

Revelation 14:6-14: "And I saw another angel fly in the midst of heaven, having the everlasting gospel to preach unto them that dwell on the earth, and to every nation, and kindred, and tongue, and people, Saying with a loud voice, Fear God, and give glory to him; for the hour of his judgment is come: and worship him that made heaven, and earth, and the sea, and the fountains of waters.

"And there followed another angel, saying, Babylon is fallen, is fallen, that great city, because she made all nations drink of the wine of the wrath of her fornication. And the third angel followed them, saying with a loud voice, If any man worship the beast and his image, and receive his mark in his forehead, or in his hand, The same shall drink of the wine of the wrath of God, which is poured out without mixture into the cup of his indignation; and he shall be tormented with fire and brimstone in the presence of the holy angels, and in the presence of the Lamb: And the smoke of their torment ascendeth up for ever and ever: and they have no rest day nor night, who worship the beast and his image, and whosoever receiveth the mark of his name. Here is the patience of the saints: here are they that keep the commandments

---

14. See Daniel 7:25; Revelation 11:2, 3.
15. Mathew 24:20, 21.
16. Exodus 12:40, 41.

of God, and the faith of Jesus.

"And I heard a voice from heaven saying unto me, Write, Blessed are the dead which die in the Lord from henceforth: Yea, saith the Spirit, that they may rest from their labours; and their works do follow them. And I looked, and behold a white cloud, and upon the cloud one sat like unto the Son of man, having on his head a golden crown, and in his hand a sharp sickle."

The Investigative judgment and the Advent movement were to begin and did begin at the same time, at the end of the 2300 years. The Advent movement arose in fulfillment of time prophecy and started on time. While the proclamation of the second advent message started several years before the close of the 2300 years, the movement proper in its threefold aspect, as described in Revelation 14, did not start till the very year 1844, when a company of Adventists began to observe the Sabbath. That was the beginning of a world movement that has now reached almost every part of the globe.

A Reformation

The Advent movement is a reformation to bring God's people out of Babylon and all the way back to the faith and practice of Christ and the apostles, "the faith once delivered to the saints." It is the closing phase of the Reformation which began in the 16th century and which prepares a people for the second advent of Christ. Victory must be gained over all the customs and practices of Babylon so that God's people are a separate people.[17]

Full Cup of Iniquity

The probation of the world cannot close so that the saints can "inherit the earth" and occupy the territory of the modern nations, until they have filled up the cup of their iniquity. This is one reason for the delay in the fulfillment of God's promises to the Advent people. They cannot have possession of the promised land (this earth in its redeemed state) until the inhabitants of the earth have rejected the last call and sinned away their day of grace.

> With unerring accuracy, the Infinite One still keeps an account with all nations. While his mercy is tendered, with calls to repentance, His account will remain open; but when the figures reach a certain amount which God has fixed, the ministry of His wrath commences. The account is closed. Divine patience ceases. There is no more pleading of mercy in their behalf.[18]

17. Revelation 18:1-5; 2 Corinthians 6:14-18.
18. Ellen White, *Testimonies for the Church*, vol. 5 (1889), p. 208.

The Records Closed

{In volume 5 of the *Testimonies* we read:}

> God keeps a reckoning with the nations. Through every century of this world's history, evil workers have been treasuring up wrath against the day of wrath; and when the time fully comes that iniquity shall have reached the stated boundary of God's mercy, His forbearance will cease. When the accumulated figures in heaven's record books shall mark the sum of transgression complete, wrath will come, unmixed with mercy, and then it will be seen what a tremendous thing it is to have worn out the divine patience. This crisis will be reached when the nations shall unite in making void God's law.[19]

---

19. Ellen White, *Testimonies for the Church*, vol. 5 (1889), p. 524. See also *Prophets and Kings*, p. 535.

4

THE LAW AND THE SABBATH

Purpose of Exodus

Exodus 4:22, 23; 9:1: "And thou shalt say unto Pharaoh, Thus saith the LORD, Israel is my son, even my firstborn: And I say unto thee, Let my son go, that he may serve me: and if thou refuse to let him go, behold, I will slay thy son, even thy firstborn." "Then the LORD said unto Moses, Go in unto Pharaoh, and tell him, Thus saith the LORD God of the Hebrews, Let my people go, that they may serve me."

The Israelites could no longer serve God and remain in Egypt. Obedience to God made it imperative that they leave Egypt. While in bondage they were serving man instead of God and were therefore guilty of idolatry.[1] In serving the Egyptians they were actually serving and worshiping the beast or dragon.[2] Not "a" but "the great dragon" and there is but one.

Egypt was the first of the seven heads of the great red dragon and the beast of Revelation 12, 13 and 17, which represents Satan's earthly kingdom in all its phases since the deluge. The purpose of Israel's deliverance from Egyptian bondage is again stated in Psalm 105:43, 45; Deuteronomy 6: 21-25.

The Antitype

God is calling His people out of modern Egypt or Babylon for the same purpose.[3] We give glory to God and serve Him by obeying Him, and obedience is worship.[4]

The language of the last message indicates that the people of God in Babylon are giving glory to another besides the Creator. They are serving and thus worshiping man and are therefore guilty of idolatry.[5] "For it indicates a certain man."[6] In serving the man at the head of the beast power they are worshiping the beast and the dragon,

1. Exodus 1:13, 14; 14:5, 12.
2. Ezekiel 29:2, 3.
3. Revelation 14:6,7; 18:1-5.
4. Romans 6:16.
5. Revelation 13:4, 8, 18.
6. Revelation 13:18 (Weymouth Translation).

which primarily represents Satan and secondarily his kingdom. Satan is called a "man" because he is a created being with no right to receive worship. He is primarily "the man of sin" who sits in the temple of God to receive worship as God and the whole world does him homage. He is the "god of this world."

Satan's Throne

Revelation 2:13: "I know thy works and where thou dwellest, even where Satan's seat is: and thou holdest fast my name, and hast not denied my faith, even in those days wherein Antipas was my faithful martyr, who was slain among you, where Satan dwelleth."

{If we look at other translations of this phrase "where Satan dwelleth" we see:}

> "Satan's throne is there." — Weymouth Translation
> "Where the throne of the adversary is." — Emphatic Diaglott.

"Where God's throne should have been, Satan placed his throne. The world laid its homage, as a willing offering, at the feet of the enemy."[7] Satan's throne and headquarters in this world over which he rules is in Babylon and he is the king of Babylon. God's people cannot serve Him and remain in Babylon and so the call is given,

"Come out of her, My people."[8] They are God's people and are called out to obey His law.[9] This exodus from modern Babylon will include all of the honest in heart, for they are the people of God. "Every truly honest soul will come to the light of the truth."[10]

Majority in Babylon

{In the book the *Great Controversy* we read:}

> And in what religious bodies are the great part of the followers of Christ now to be found? Without doubt, in the various churches professing the Protestant faith.[11]
>
> Notwithstanding the spiritual darkness and alienation from God that exist in the churches which constitute Babylon, the great body of Christ's true followers are still to be found in their communion. …
> Revelation 18 points to the time when the people of God still in Babylon

---

7. Ellen White, *Testimonies for the Church*, vol. 6 (1901), p. 236.
8. Revelation 18:2, 3.
9. Revelation 12:17; 14:12; 22:14.
10. Ellen White, *Great Controversy* (1911), p. 522.
11. *Ibid.*, p. 383.

will be called upon to separate from her communion ... Then the light of truth will shine upon all whose hearts are open to receive it, and all the children of the Lord that remain in Babylon will heed the call, 'Come our of her, My people.'[12]

Sign of Allegiance

Moses and Aaron tried to teach the Israelites to observe the Sabbath in Egypt.[13] Resting on the Sabbath made Pharaoh angry and he issued a decree that made Sabbath keeping impossible in Egypt. The other commands of the law of God could be more easily observed. The test came on the Sabbath commandment, and Sabbathkeeping brought oppressive legislation and persecution. Israel was called out of Egypt that they might observe the Sabbath and obey God's whole law. To Israel the Sabbath became the test of obedience and the sign of allegiance.[14] This happened a month before the law was given at Sinai.

When the law was proclaimed from the mount, the Sabbath was placed in the very center, there being 146 words on each side of the statement, "Seventh day is the Sabbath." Dr. Adam Clarke said that the law was first spoken from Sinai on the Sabbath and that Pentecost was a memorial of that event. The law was placed in the center of the ark, the ark in the center of the holy of holies of the sanctuary, which was in the midst of the priestly tribe, which was in the midst of the camp of Israel, and the Lord placed Israel in the center of the world.

Memorial of Creation

To Israel the Sabbath was the memorial of creation and its observance the celebration of the birthday of the world.[15] It is a part of the everlasting covenant and a sign between the Creator and His people forever.[16] It was also the sign that they had been delivered from the idolatry of Egypt and that they were worshiping the true God who was distinguished from all false gods because of His power to create.[17] Since only the Creator can redeem, and it requires creative power to recreate, the Sabbath is also the sign of holiness or redemption from sin.[18]

Sabbath in Advent Movement

Isaiah 56:1: "Thus saith the LORD, Keep ye judgment, and do justice: for my salvation is near to come, and my righteousness to be revealed."

---

12. *Ibid.*, p. 390.
13. Exodus 5:4-14.
14. Exodus 16:4, 22, 23.
15. See Exodus 20:8-11.
16. Exodus 31:15-17.
17. Ezekiel 20:20.
18. Ezekiel 29:11, 12; Isaiah 56:2.

When does this text apply?

Hebrews 9:28: "So Christ was once offered to bear the sins of many; and unto them that look for him shall he appear the second time without sin unto salvation."

1 Peter 1:4, 5: "To an inheritance incorruptible, and undefiled, and that fadeth not away, reserved in heaven for you, Who are kept by the power of God through faith unto salvation ready to be revealed in the last time."

In Isaiah 56:2-8 is described the gathering of Sabbath-keepers just before the coming of Christ. This gathering under the advent movement includes every "man" who "keepeth the Sabbath from polluting it, and keepeth his hand from doing any evil." It also includes 12 the "sons of the stranger" and the "eunuchs that keep my Sabbaths." Not only does this call include the "outcasts of Israel" but "others" which embraces "all people" for the Lord declares that His house "shall be called an house of prayer for all people." In the advent movement the Sabbath must be the outward sign of a godly character and separation from all evil. It is the outward sign of the character of God.

Seal of the Law

Isaiah 8:16, 17, 20: "Bind up the testimony, seal the law among my disciples. And I will wait upon the LORD, that hideth his face from the house of Jacob, and I will look for him. ...To the law and to the testimony: if they speak not according to this word, it is because there is no light in them."

Revelation 7:1-4; 14:1,5: "And after these things I saw four angels standing on the four corners of the earth, holding the four winds of the earth, that the wind should not blow on the earth, nor on the sea, nor on any tree. And I saw another angel ascending from the east, having the seal of the living God: and he cried with a loud voice to the four angels, to whom it was given to hurt the earth and the sea, Saying, Hurt not the earth, neither the sea, nor the trees, till we have sealed the servants of our God in their foreheads. And I heard the number of them which were sealed: and there were sealed an hundred and forty and four thousand of all the tribes of the children of Israel." "And I looked, and, lo, a Lamb stood on the mount Sion, and with him an hundred forty and four thousand, having his Father's name written in their foreheads....And in their mouth was found no guile: for they are without fault before the throne of God."

The Sabbath command makes authentic the whole law since it is the only one of the ten that identifies the Lawgiver. Its observance therefore is the test of obedience to the whole law.[19] True Sabbath-keeping shows that the law of God is written in the heart

19. James 2:10-12.

and that we are under the New Covenant.[20] Because the Sabbath is the sign of loyalty to the Creator, and a sign of holiness in those who keep it, its observance stirs up the wrath of the dragon and he persecutes.[21]

Religious laws will eventually become so oppressive that the sentence of death will be visited upon the violators. It isn't so difficult to observe the other nine commandments in modern Babylon but it is impossible to keep the Sabbath and remain where the opposition is so bitter and the persecution so great. "As God called the children of Israel out of Egypt, that they might keep His Sabbath, so He calls His people out of Babylon, that they may not worship the beast nor his image." [22]

A Separate People

Nehemiah 10:28: "And the rest of the people, the priests, the Levites, the porters, the singers, the Nethinims, and all they that had separated themselves from the people of the lands unto the law of God, their wives, their sons, and their daughters, every one having knowledge, and having understanding;"

The Sabbath has always made its observers a separate and distinct people from the world. "He that observes the Sabbath aright holds the history of that which it celebrates to be authentic. He therefore believes in the creation of the first man; in the creation of a fair abode for man in the space of six days; in the primeval and absolute creation of the heavens and the earth, and as a necessary antecedent to all this, in the Creator, who at the close of His latest creative effort, rested on the seventh day.

The Sabbath thus becomes a sign by which the believers in a historical revelation are distinguished from those who have allowed these great facts to fade from their remembrance."[23]

Why God Chose Israel

Deuteronomy 7:6-9: "For thou art an holy people unto the LORD thy God: the LORD thy God hath chosen thee to be a special people unto himself, above all people that are upon the face of the earth. The LORD did not set his love upon you, nor choose you, because ye were more in number than any people; for ye were the fewest of all people: But because the LORD loved you, and because he would keep the oath which he had sworn unto your fathers, hath the LORD brought you out with a mighty hand, and redeemed you out of the house of bondmen, from the hand of Pharaoh king of Egypt. Know therefore that the LORD thy God, he is God, the

20. Hebrews 8:10.
21. See 2 Timothy 3:12; Revelation 12:17; 13:15-17, 18.
22. *An Appeal to our Ministers and Conference Committees*, p. 16, Written Feb. 18, 1892.
23. James G. Murphy, quoted from an editorial in *The Moody Bible Institute Monthly*, November 1930.

faithful God, which keepeth covenant and mercy with them that love him and keep his commandments to a thousand generations."

Israel was not selected from among the nations of the world because of their numbers, for they were "the fewest of all people." Yet there were several millions of them. They were chosen because their hearts were more inclined toward the law of God than any other people. Their obedience made them a holy nation, a peculiar people, separate and distinct from all the world. Likewise the advent people are a "little flock" compared to the other religious movements and are therefore called "the remnant," but because of their obedience to their Creator and His laws, they also are a "peculiar people" and a "holy nation."[24] Because they are different from the world they will be hated and persecuted.[25]

Sabbath Breaking

While the children of Israel had the true Sabbath they were often unfaithful and lax in its observance.[26] "During the entire forty years in the wilderness, the people were every week reminded of the sacred obligation of the Sabbath, by the miracle of the manna.

Yet even this did not lead them to obedience. Though they did not venture upon so open and bold transgression as had received such signal punishment (as the man who defied God by gathering sticks on the Sabbath) yet, there was great laxness in the observance of the fourth commandment."[27] The disastrous results of laxness in Sabbath keeping in the later history of Israel are related in Jeremiah 17:24-27, and Nehemiah 13:17, 18.

Modern Israel

Since we are following in the footsteps of ancient Israel we are in danger of the same laxness in Sabbath observance, and of this danger we are warned.

> We must be guarded lest the lax practices that prevail among Sunday-keepers shall be followed by those who profess to observe God's holy rest-day. The line of demarcation is to be made clear and distinct between those who bear the mark of God's kingdom and those who bear the sign of the kingdom of rebellion.
>
> Far more sacredness is attached to the Sabbath than is given it by many professed Sabbath-keepers. The Lord has been greatly dishonored by those who have not kept the Sabbath according to the commandment,

24. 1 Peter 2:9.
25. John 16:18-20.
26. Ezekiel 20:12-20.
27. Ellen White, *Patriarchs and Prophets* (1890), p. 409.

either in the letter or in the spirit. He calls for a reform in the observance of the Sabbath…

…We are to understand its spiritual bearing upon all the transactions of life. All who regard the Sabbath as a sign between them and God, showing that He is the God who sanctifies them, will represent the principles of His government. They will bring into daily practice the laws of His kingdom. Daily it will be their prayer that the sanctification of the Sabbath will rest upon them. Every day they will have the companionship of Christ, and will exemplify the perfection of His character.[28]

We should each Sabbath reckon with our souls to see whether the week that has ended has brought spiritual gain or loss. It means eternal life to keep the Sabbath holy unto the Lord.[29]

---

28. Ellen White, *Testimonies for the Church*, vol. 6 (1901), p. 353.
29. *Ibid.*, p. 356.

5

THE JUDGMENTS OF GOD

Wrath of God

The persecution of God's people in Egypt brought upon the persecutors the wrath of God which was manifested in ten plagues which were poured out just before the deliverance of Israel.[1] These plagues were not only to punish the persecutors but to prove that the God of Israel was mightier than the gods of the Egyptians. Pharaoh was the supreme pontiff, or the Pontifex Maximus of the pagan religion of Egypt.

All idolatrous nations attributed their success in war to the superiority of their gods over those of their enemies. Pharaoh challenged the God of the Hebrews.[2] The Egyptians had doubtless taunted the Israelites regarding the weakness of their God because He was not able to deliver them from bondage. They boasted that their gods had brought victory and prosperity to the nation.

God's Answer

God's answer to the challenge of Pharaoh was the ten plagues which were punishments of the gods of Egypt.[3] Each plague was designed by the Lord to destroy the confidence of the Egyptians in the power and protection of their gods, and to reveal to them the Creator as the God of the Hebrews; that even the creature-objects of their worship were under His control.

{Ellen White wrote:}

> The Lord would give the Egyptians an opportunity to see how vain was the wisdom of their mighty men, how feeble the power of their gods, when opposed to the commands of Jehovah. He would punish the people of Egypt for their idolatry, and silence their boasting of the blessing received from their senseless deities. God would glorify His own name, that other nations might hear of His power and tremble at His mighty acts, and that His people might be led to turn from their idolatry and

1. Exodus 3:20.
2. Exodus 5:2, 3.
3. Exodus 12:12; Numbers 33:4.

render Him pure worship.[4]

The First Miracle

Exodus 7:8-12: "And the LORD spake unto Moses and unto Aaron, saying, When Pharaoh shall speak unto you, saying, Show a miracle for you: then thou shalt say unto Aaron, Take thy rod, and cast it before Pharaoh, and it shall become a serpent. And Moses and Aaron went in unto Pharaoh, and they did so as the LORD had commanded: and Aaron cast down his rod before Pharaoh, and before his servants, and it became a serpent. Then Pharaoh also called the wise men and the sorcerers: now the magicians of Egypt, they also did in like manner with their enchantments. For they cast down every man his rod, and they became serpents: but Aaron's rod swallowed up their rods."

When Moses and Aaron appeared in the court of Pharaoh claiming to be the spokesmen of the God of the Hebrews, he demanded a miracle as the evidence of their office. Miracles are the usual credentials of a prophet or a messenger of God.

The magicians of Egypt, as agents of Satan, performed counterfeit miracles to prove their claim. Their rods were doubtless charmed and stiffened serpents which looked like rods. This was a common trick of the magicians of Egypt.[5] They were jugglers and tricksters of the first class and their "miracles" were counterfeits and "lying wonders" as are all of Satan's miracles. Only God can create.[6]

The greatest tricksters of the world today are found in Cairo, Egypt. The final result of the test proved the superiority of Israel's God. When God began to work for the deliverance of His people, Satan performs miracles to deceive the Egyptians and to counter the work of God for the salvation of His people.[7]

The First Plague

Exodus 7:15-25: "Get thee unto Pharaoh in the morning; lo, he goeth out unto the water; and thou shalt stand by the river's brink against he come; and the rod which was turned to a serpent shalt thou take in thine hand. And thou shalt say unto him, The LORD God of the Hebrews hath sent me unto thee, saying, Let my people go, that they may serve me in the wilderness: and, behold, hitherto thou wouldest not hear. Thus saith the LORD, In this thou shalt know that I am the LORD: behold, I will smite with the rod that is in mine hand upon the waters which are in the river, and they shall be turned to blood. And the fish that is in the river shall die, and the river shall stink; and the Egyptians shall loathe to drink of the water of the river. And

4. Ellen White, *Patriarchs and Prophets* (1890), p. 263.
5. See *Descriptions de l'Egypte*, vol. 1, p. 159.
6. 2 Thessalonians 2:9.
7. See Ellen White, *Patriarchs and Prophets* (1890), p. 264-265.

the LORD spake unto Moses, Say unto Aaron, Take thy rod, and stretch out thine hand upon the waters of Egypt, upon their streams, upon their rivers, and upon their ponds, and upon all their pools of water, that they may become blood; and that there may be blood throughout all the land of Egypt, both in vessels of wood, and in vessels of stone. And Moses and Aaron did so, as the LORD commanded; and he lifted up the rod, and smote the waters that were in the river, in the sight of Pharaoh, and in the sight of his servants; and all the waters that were in the river were turned to blood. And the fish that was in the river died; and the river stank, and the Egyptians could not drink of the water of the river; and there was blood throughout all the land of Egypt. And the magicians of Egypt did so with their enchantments: and Pharaoh's heart was hardened, neither did he hearken unto them; as the LORD had said. And Pharaoh turned and went into his house, neither did he set his heart to this also. And all the Egyptians digged round about the river for water to drink; for they could not drink of the water of the river. And seven days were fulfilled, after that the LORD had smitten the river."

The Egyptians considered the Nile as sacred, and Pharaoh probably went out to it each morning to worship it as a god (Keil). It was known as "the Nile-god" and was identified with Ammon-Ra. It was said to be "self-created" and was sometimes called "the Father of all the gods" and "the chief of the waters." The whole nation depended on the River Nile for their water supply and the very existence of the kingdom was dependent on its yearly overflow. "The beneficent Nile, the very life of the state of the people."[8]

It is only natural therefore that a pagan people who worshipped the powers of nature should make a god of this great river. Even many of the creatures that lived in its waters were considered sacred and were objects of worship. The Egyptians bathed in and drank its waters with reverence and with delight believing them to have healing virtues.

Universal

This first plague covered "all the land of Egypt." The "streams" doubtless refer to the branches of the Nile in its delta of which there were seven according to Herodotus. The "rivers" probably refer to the canals, the "ponds" to the natural and artificial lakes and reservoirs and cisterns. A partial remedy was found in digging for clear water in the sand or no one could have lived through the seven days the plague continued.

The death of the fish of the river cut off one of their chief food supplies. According to Birch the Egyptians lived to a large extent on fish.[9] This was one reason that the river was worshipped. That which they looked upon as their greatest benefactor was turned into a curse.

---

8. Stanley.
9. *Egypt from the Earliest Times*, p. 45.

The Plague of Frogs

Exodus 8:1-6: "And the LORD spake unto Moses, Go unto Pharaoh, and say unto him, Thus saith the LORD, Let my people go, that they may serve me. And if thou refuse to let them go, behold, I will smite all thy borders with frogs: And the river shall bring forth frogs abundantly, which shall go up and come into thine house, and into thy bedchamber, and upon thy bed, and into the house of thy servants, and upon thy people, and into thine ovens, and into thy kneadingtroughs: And the frogs shall come up both on thee, and upon thy people, and upon all thy servants. And the LORD spake unto Moses, Say unto Aaron, Stretch forth thine hand with thy rod over the streams, over the rivers, and over the ponds, and cause frogs to come up upon the land of Egypt. And Aaron stretched out his hand over the waters of Egypt; and the frogs came up, and covered the land of Egypt."

Frogs were regarded as sacred by the Egyptians because they lived in the River Nile and were considered the emblem of creative power. One of their gods was called "Heka," and was a frog-headed goddess. The description of these frogs is identical with a species in Egypt today called the "Rana Mosaica," doubtless so named for that very reason. They are very loathsome creatures that crawl instead of hop and which croak constantly.

During the plague they were everywhere and couldn't be killed because they are sacred. They even entered the "ovens" or baking pans. In Egypt the young frogs come out of the Nile in September, and are sometimes so numerous as to be a menace even today. There are historical records of communities where frogs became such a menace that the people had to flee the country to escape them.

The Third Plague

Exodus 8:16-18: "And the LORD said unto Moses, Say unto Aaron, Stretch out thy rod, and smite the dust of the land, that it may become lice[10] throughout all the land of Egypt. And they did so; for Aaron stretched out his hand with his rod, and smote the dust of the earth, and it became lice in man, and in beast; all the dust of the land became lice throughout all the land of Egypt. And the magicians did so with their enchantments to bring forth lice, but they could not: so there were lice upon man, and upon beast."

Many Bible students believe that the weight of authority is in favor of rendering the original word, "kinnim," "gnats" or "mosquitoes." Geikie says the original word means various kinds of poisonous insects. Herodotus, Philo, Wilkinson and others tell of the great mosquito pest of Egypt, especially in the fall, usually in October, when the receding waters of the Nile leaves pools of water over the lowlands. They also annoy the beasts.

---

10. Greek Septuagint: "Mosquitoes." Fenton Translation: "Gad-flies"

Kalisch wrote of the mosquitoes in Egypt:

> Mosquitoes molest especially beasts as oxen and horses, flying into their eyes and nostrils, driving them to madness and fury, and sometimes even torturing them to death.

Sir Samuel Baker tells of a tick in Egypt that lives in the sand and is about the size of a grain of sand in its natural state but swells up while sucking blood, and "is the greatest enemy of man and beast."

Blow at Idolatry

This plague was a severe blow to Egyptian idolatry for while it lasted no act of worship could be performed.

{Gleik wrote:}

> No one could approach the altars of Egypt upon whom so impure an insect harbored, and the priests, to guard against the slightest risk of contamination, wore only lined garments, and shaved their heads and bodies every day.[11]

{And Herodotus wrote that it was:} "Every third day."[12]

The first two plagues came from the water and the third came from the earth which was also worshipped. The magicians who had imitated the first two plagues now give up the contest and acknowledge their defeat.

The Plague of Flies

Exodus 8:20-24: "And the LORD said unto Moses, Rise up early in the morning, and stand before Pharaoh; lo, he cometh forth to the water; and say unto him, Thus saith the LORD, Let my people go, that they may serve me. Else, if thou wilt not let my people go, behold, I will send swarms of flies[13] upon thee, and upon thy servants, and upon thy people, and into thy houses: and the houses of the Egyptians shall be full of swarms of flies, and also the ground whereon they are. And I will sever in that day the land of Goshen, in which my people dwell, that no swarms of flies shall be there; to the end thou mayest know that I am the LORD in the midst of the earth. And I will put a division between my people and thy people: to morrow shall this sign be. And the LORD did so; and there came a grievous swarm of flies into the

11. Gleik.
12. Herodotus.
13. Psalmist: "Divers sorts of flies." Margin: "A mixture of noisome beasts." Greek Septuagint: "The dog-fly."

house of Pharaoh, and into his servants' houses, and into all the land of Egypt: the land was corrupted by reason of the swarm of flies."

Psalm 105:31: "He spake, and there came divers sorts of flies, and lice in all their coasts."

This is not the common housefly but a species that constituted a terrible affliction in Egypt.[14] They may have included a kind of beetle which at times appear in the Nile in great numbers and "inflict very painful bites with their jaws; gnaw and destroy clothes, household furniture, leather, and articles of every kind, and even consume or render unavailable all eatables."[15] They sometimes drive people out of their houses and they devastate the crops.

Beetles were sacred to Ra, the sun-god, and one form of Ra was a man with a beetle head. The Egyptian fly-god, Beelzebub was reverenced as the protector from ravenous swarms of insects which infested the land at certain seasons. This plague demonstrated the impotence of the fly-god to protect the Egyptians, and Pharaoh begged Moses and Aaron to entreat Jehovah to remove the curse.

Israel Protected

Beginning with the fourth plague the land of Goshen was severed from the rest of Egypt and Israel was protected. The first three were universal and the seven last of the ten fell upon the Egyptians only.[16] "The severance is a new feature, and one distinguishing the latter from the former plagues."[17] The swarms of flies of diverse sorts "filled the houses and swarmed upon the ground, so that 'the land was corrupted by reason of the swarm of flies.' These flies were large and venomous; and their bite was extremely painful to man and beast. As had been foretold, this visitation did not extend to the land of Goshen."[18]

The Fifth Plague

Exodus 9:1-7: "Then the LORD said unto Moses, Go in unto Pharaoh, and tell him, Thus saith the LORD God of the Hebrews, Let my people go, that they may serve me. For if thou refuse to let them go, and wilt hold them still, Behold, the hand of the LORD is upon thy cattle which is in the field, upon the horses, upon the asses, upon the camels, upon the oxen, and upon the sheep: there shall be a very grievous murrain.[19] And the LORD shall sever between the cattle of Israel and the cattle of Egypt: and there shall nothing die of all that is the children's of Israel. And the LORD

14. Philo.
15. Kalisch.
16. Exodus 8:22, 23; 9:6, 26; 10:23.
17. *Pulpit Commentary.*
18. Ellen White, *Patriarchs and Prophets* (1890), p. 266.
19. Moffatt : "A deadly pest"

appointed a set time, saying, To morrow the LORD shall do this thing in the land. And the LORD did that thing on the morrow, and all the cattle of Egypt died: but of the cattle of the children of Israel died not one. And Pharaoh sent, and, behold, there was not one of the cattle of the Israelites dead. And the heart of Pharaoh was hardened, and he did not let the people go."

The fifth plague was a "grievous murrain" upon the livestock of the Egyptians. This judgment was aimed at the entire system of Egyptian brute-worship as representatives of the sun, moon, and stars. They worshipped the sacred bull, Apis, the calf, Nmevis, and also heifers, rams, goats, and other animals. In those days wealth was reckoned mostly in livestock. The Israelites were especially a pastoral people and the severance of the land of Goshen was an evidence to Pharaoh that it was a divine judgment demonstrating the superiority of Jehovah over the gods of Egypt.

The Sixth Plague

Exodus 9:8-11: "And the LORD said unto Moses and unto Aaron, Take to you handfuls of ashes of the furnace, and let Moses sprinkle it toward the heaven in the sight of Pharaoh. And it shall become small dust in all the land of Egypt, and shall be a boil breaking forth with blains upon man, and upon beast, throughout all the land of Egypt. And they took ashes of the furnace, and stood before Pharaoh; and Moses sprinkled it up toward heaven; and it became a boil breaking forth with blains upon man, and upon beast. And the magicians could not stand before Moses because of the boils; for the boil was upon the magicians, and upon all the Egyptians."

The boils of the sixth plague broke out in blains or blisters. This is doubtless what is referred to in Deuteronomy 28:27, as "the botch of Egypt" which caused an itching sensation and was incurable. It may have been something like elephantiasis or the black leprosy.

In Egypt there were several altars on which human sacrifices were offered in time of plague and disease, the victim being burned alive. The ashes were gathered by the priests and thrown into the air and wherever they fell they were supposed to stop the ravages of the disease by propitiating Typhon, or the "Evil Principle."

{Geikie, speaking of the human sacrifices of the Egyptians, wrote:}

> The victims after being burned alive on the high altar, their ashes were scattered in the air by the priests in the belief that they would avert evil from all parts whither they were blown.[20]

The furnace was the emblem of the bitter slavery and sufferings of the Hebrews

20. Geikie.

in Egypt.[21] This act of Moses in sprinkling the ashes toward heaven in the sight of Pharaoh indicated that the plague came as the result of the cruel bondage which consumed the Israelites in the furnace of affliction. Fire is the greatest of all germ destroyers and the Lord demonstrated His power by producing disease germs from the ashes or "soot of the furnace."

The Seventh Plague

Exodus 9:22-34: "And the LORD said unto Moses, Stretch forth thine hand toward heaven, that there may be hail in all the land of Egypt, upon man, and upon beast, and upon every herb of the field, throughout the land of Egypt. And Moses stretched forth his rod toward heaven: and the LORD sent thunder and hail, and the fire ran along upon the ground; and the LORD rained hail upon the land of Egypt. So there was hail, and fire mingled with the hail, very grievous, such as there was none like it in all the land of Egypt since it became a nation. And the hail smote throughout all the land of Egypt all that was in the field, both man and beast; and the hail smote every herb of the field, and brake every tree of the field. Only in the land of Goshen, where the children of Israel were, was there no hail.

"And Pharaoh sent, and called for Moses and Aaron, and said unto them, I have sinned this time: the LORD is righteous, and I and my people are wicked. Entreat the LORD (for it is enough) that there be no more mighty thunderings and hail; and I will let you go, and ye shall stay no longer. And Moses said unto him, As soon as I am gone out of the city, I will spread abroad my hands unto the LORD; and the thunder shall cease, neither shall there be any more hail; that thou mayest know how that the earth is the LORD's. But as for thee and thy servants, I know that ye will not yet fear the LORD God. And the flax and the barley was smitten: for the barley was in the ear, and the flax was bolled. But the wheat and the rie were not smitten: for they were not grown up. And Moses went out of the city from Pharaoh, and spread abroad his hands unto the LORD: and the thunders and hail ceased, and the rain was not poured upon the earth. And when Pharaoh saw that the rain and the hail and the thunders were ceased, he sinned yet more, and hardened his heart, he and his servants."

This plague was a severe hail storm mingled with electricity and thunder. An electric storm often comes with hail. The cattle and people who were unprotected were wounded and many killed. The flax and barley crops, which were almost ready for the sickle, were destroyed. They matured in March while the wheat and rye harvests came more than a month later. Flax was used in making garments and according to Herodotus, the Egyptians preferred them to clothing made from any other material.[22]

The Eighth Plague

Exodus 10:1-15: "And the LORD said unto Moses, Go in unto Pharaoh: for I have

21. Genesis 15:17; Deuteronomy 4:20.
22. See Psalms 105:32, 33.

hardened his heart, and the heart of his servants, that I might show these my signs before him: And that thou mayest tell in the ears of thy son, and of thy son's son, what things I have wrought in Egypt, and my signs which I have done among them; that ye may know how that I am the LORD. And Moses and Aaron came in unto Pharaoh, and said unto him, Thus saith the LORD God of the Hebrews, How long wilt thou refuse to humble thyself before me? let my people go, that they may serve me. Else, if thou refuse to let my people go, behold, to morrow will I bring the locusts into thy coast: And they shall cover the face of the earth, that one cannot be able to see the earth: and they shall eat the residue of that which is escaped, which remaineth unto you from the hail, and shall eat every tree which groweth for you out of the field: And they shall fill thy houses, and the houses of all thy servants, and the houses of all the Egyptians; which neither thy fathers, nor thy fathers' fathers have seen, since the day that they were upon the earth unto this day. And he turned himself, and went out from Pharaoh. And Pharaoh's servants said unto him, How long shall this man be a snare unto us? let the men go, that they may serve the LORD their God: knowest thou not yet that Egypt is destroyed?

"And Moses and Aaron were brought again unto Pharaoh: and he said unto them, Go, serve the LORD your God: but who are they that shall go? And Moses said, We will go with our young and with our old, with our sons and with our daughters, with our flocks and with our herds will we go; for we must hold a feast unto the LORD. And he said unto them, Let the LORD be so with you, as I will let you go, and your little ones: look to it; for evil is before you. Not so: go now ye that are men, and serve the LORD; for that ye did desire. And they were driven out from Pharaoh's presence.

"And the LORD said unto Moses, Stretch out thine hand over the land of Egypt for the locusts, that they may come up upon the land of Egypt, and eat every herb of the land, even all that the hail hath left. And Moses stretched forth his rod over the land of Egypt, and the LORD brought an east wind upon the land all that day, and all that night; and when it was morning, the east wind brought the locusts. And the locusts went up over all the land of Egypt, and rested in all the coasts of Egypt: very grievous were they; before them there were no such locusts as they, neither after them shall be such. For they covered the face of the whole earth, so that the land was darkened; and they did eat every herb of the land, and all the fruit of the trees which the hail had left: and there remained not any green thing in the trees, or in the herbs of the field, through all the land of Egypt."

The plague of locusts is also described in Psalm 105:34, 35: "He spake, and the locusts came, and caterpillars, and that without number, and did eat up all the herbs in their land, and devoured the fruit of their ground.." They destroyed everything in the vegetable kingdom that was left by the hail.[23]

Many writers tell how locusts bark the trees after stripping them of the leaves:

23. See Joel 2:3, 5.

> Over an area of 1,800 square miles the whole surface might literally be said to be covered with them.[24]

> When their swarms appear everything green vanishes instantaneously from the fields, as if a curtain were rolled up; the trees and plants stand leafless, and nothing is seen but naked boughs and stalks."[25]

During 1932 in South Africa swarms of locust 500 miles wide and 1500 miles long devastated portions of the country.

Enter Houses

Exodus 10:6: "They shall fill thy houses."

{Morier writes:}

> They entered the inmost recesses of the houses, were found in every corner, stuck to our clothes, and infested our food.[26]

{And Burckhardt adds:}

> They overwhelm the province of Nedjd sometimes to such a degree that, having destroyed the harvest, they penetrate by thousands into the private dwellings, and devour whatsoever they can find, even the leather of the water vessels.[27]

The Egyptian windows were lattice-work and made it easy for the locusts to enter.

Came With East Wind

Exodus 10:13: "And Moses stretched forth his rod over the land of Egypt, and the LORD brought an east wind upon the land all that day, and all that night; and when it was morning, the east wind brought the locusts."

Inroads of locusts are not common in Egypt and they come from other countries and usually from Arabia in Asia to the East. North Arabia is noted for its locusts and they generally travel with the wind. A French traveler in Egypt wrote of a swarm of locusts visiting Egypt and they came with an East wind. Verse 14 tells us that the plague covered "all the land of Egypt."

---

24. Barrow.
25. Volney.
26. Morier in *Second Journey*, p.100.
27. Burckhardt, "Notes," vol. 2, p. 90.

Egypt was about 520 miles long and only about 20 miles wide in the delta. Swarms of locusts much larger than this have been described by travelers in different countries. According to verse 19 the locusts departed out of Egypt with a West wind. They left as suddenly as they came which is a characteristic of these insects.

This judgment was directed at Serapis, whose office was to protect the country from locusts. Forty-two temples had been erected in honor of this deity. At the command of Moses the locusts came and at his command they departed and Serapis was powerless.

The Ninth Plague

Exodus 10:21-23: "And the LORD said unto Moses, Stretch out thine hand toward heaven, that there may be darkness over the land of Egypt, even darkness which may be felt. And Moses stretched forth his hand toward heaven; and there was a thick darkness in all the land of Egypt three days: They saw not one another, neither rose any from his place for three days: but all the children of Israel had light in their dwellings."

The ninth plague was the darkness that could be felt. Egypt was sometimes visited during the vernal equinox by the "Wind of the Desert" which was sometimes accompanied by weird darkness caused by clouds of sand and dust which was worse than "the most gloomy night." They could not see one another during this plague. "While it lasts no man rises from his place; men and beasts hide themselves; the inhabitants of towns and villages shut themselves up in their houses in underground apartments or vaults."[28]

These visitations of darkness usually last two or three days. The darkness could be "felt" indicating the intensity and oppressiveness of the darkness when the air was filled with sand and dust. There was light in the dwellings of the Israelites. This plague was directed at Isis and Osiris representing the sun and moon who were supposed to control the light and the elements. Jehovah in this plague summons nature to proclaim Him the true God.

The Last Plague

Exodus 12:12: "For I will pass through the land of Egypt this night, and will smite all the firstborn in the land of Egypt, both man and beast; and against all the gods of Egypt I will execute judgment: I am the LORD."

Exodus 12:29-32: "And it came to pass, that at midnight the LORD smote all the firstborn in the land of Egypt, from the firstborn of Pharaoh that sat on his throne unto the firstborn of the captive that was in the dungeon; and all the firstborn of

28. Note from the editors: There is no reference in the original text.

cattle. And Pharaoh rose up in the night, he, and all his servants, and all the Egyptians; and there was a great cry in Egypt; for there was not a house where there was not one dead. And he called for Moses and Aaron by night, and said, Rise up, and get you forth from among my people, both ye and the children of Israel; and go, serve the LORD, as ye have said. Also take your flocks and your herds, as ye have said, and be gone; and bless me also."

The slaying of the first-born of man and beast was the most terrible of the ten plagues. The first-born of both man and beast were given special privileges and were considered sacred. Pharaoh in his palace was more or less protected personally from the other plagues, but this one entered the royal palace and slew the crown-prince and heir to the throne. It caused Pharaoh to acknowledge the defeat of his gods by a superior God before whose power he yields. He tells Israel to go and asks for a parting blessing.[29]

The Antitype

The wrath of God will be poured out upon wicked Babylon because of her persecutions of the remnant and for her idolatry in worshipping the beast and his image instead of God.[30] As in Egypt God's wrath will be manifested in plagues which will be poured out just before the final deliverance of modern Israel.[31] They will be similar to those of Egypt. "The plagues upon Egypt when God was about to deliver Israel, were similar in character to those more terrible and extensive judgments which are to fall upon the world just before the final deliverance of God's people."[32]

Seven Last Plagues

Revelation 16:1-21: "And I heard a great voice out of the temple saying to the seven angels, Go your ways, and pour out the vials of the wrath of God upon the earth. And the first went, and poured out his vial upon the earth; and there fell a noisome and grievous sore upon the men which had the mark of the beast, and upon them which worshipped his image. And the second angel poured out his vial upon the sea; and it became as the blood of a dead man; and every living soul died in the sea. And the third angel poured out his vial upon the rivers and fountains of waters; and they became blood. And I heard the angel of the waters say, Thou art righteous, O Lord, which art, and wast, and shalt be, because thou hast judged thus. For they have shed the blood of saints and prophets, and thou hast given them blood to drink; for they are worthy. And I heard another out of the altar say, Even so, Lord God Almighty, true and righteous are thy judgments.

"And the fourth angel poured out his vial upon the sun; and power was given

29. Exodus 12:32.
30. Revelation 14:8-11; 16:19.
31. Revelation 15:1, 6-8; 16:1; 18:4-6.
32. Ellen White, *Great Controversy* (1890), p. 627, 628.

unto him to scorch men with fire. And men were scorched with great heat, and blasphemed the name of God, which hath power over these plagues: and they repented not to give him glory. And the fifth angel poured out his vial upon the seat of the beast; and his kingdom was full of darkness; and they gnawed their tongues for pain, And blasphemed the God of heaven because of their pains and their sores, and repented not of their deeds. And the sixth angel poured out his vial upon the great river Euphrates; and the water thereof was dried up, that the way of the kings of the east might be prepared. And I saw three unclean spirits like frogs come out of the mouth of the dragon, and out of the mouth of the beast, and out of the mouth of the false prophet. For they are the spirits of devils, working miracles, which go forth unto the kings of the earth and of the whole world, to gather them to the battle of that great day of God Almighty.

"Behold, I come as a thief. Blessed is he that watcheth, and keepeth his garments, lest he walk naked, and they see his shame. And he gathered them together into a place called in the Hebrew tongue Armageddon. And the seventh angel poured out his vial into the air; and there came a great voice out of the temple of heaven, from the throne, saying, It is done. And there were voices, and thunders, and lightnings; and there was a great earthquake, such as was not since men were upon the earth, so mighty an earthquake, and so great. And the great city was divided into three parts, and the cities of the nations fell: and great Babylon came in remembrance before God, to give unto her the cup of the wine of the fierceness of his wrath. And every island fled away, and the mountains were not found. And there fell upon men a great hail out of heaven, every stone about the weight of a talent: and men blasphemed God because of the plague of the hail; for the plague thereof was exceeding great."

7 Last Plagues are:

1. A noisome and grievous sore.
2. The sea turned to blood and the death of its creatures.
3. The rivers and fountains become blood.
4. The sun scorches men with great heat.
5. The seat of the beast filled with darkness "and they gnaw their tongues for pain."
6. The Armageddon war.
7. The great earthquake and heavy hail that leaves the whole world desolate.[33]

The plagues on Egypt were of brief duration probably falling within a year. The seven last plagues will also be of brief duration.[34]

Not Universal

Ellen White wrote of the seven last plagues:

33. Jeremiah 4:23-27.
34. Revelation 18:8, 10, 19.

> These plagues are not universal, or the inhabitants of the earth would be wholly cut off. Yet they will be the most awful scourges that have ever been known to mortals. All the judgments upon men, prior to the close of probation, have been mingled with mercy … But in the final judgments, wrath is poured out unmixed with mercy.[35]

Test of the True God

The plagues of Egypt proved to Pharaoh and the Egyptians that their gods were false and that Jehovah was the true God.[36] "The nation had worshipped Pharaoh as a representative of their god; but many were now convinced that he was opposing himself to One who made all the powers of nature the ministers of His will."[37] The seven last plagues will convince the wicked that the God of the remnant is the true and only God.[38]

The purpose of the seven last plagues, like those of Egypt, is to expose the sin of creature worship and prove to all that the Creator is the true and only God. The plagues cause every knee to bow and every tongue to confess the true God whom the persecuted saints have worshipped 'even unto death.' Those who worship the beast will find that the beast cannot protect them but the very object of their worship is smitten by the plagues.

Plagues Cause Confession

The plagues caused the Egyptians to confess their guilt.[39] Even the magicians acknowledged that "This is the finger of God."[40] Thus will the seven last plagues humble the wicked and cause them to confess their guilt and acknowledge that God is with the despised remnant.[41] "Every knee shall bow and every tongue confess."[42]

{Ellen White wrote:}

> Men whom the world has worshipped for their talents and eloquence now see things in their true light. They realize what they have forfeited by transgression, and they fall at the feet of those whose fidelity they have despised and derided, and confess that God has loved them.[43]

---

35. Ellen White, *Great Controversy* (1890), p. 628, 629.
36. Exodus 5:2; 7:17, 22; 8:19; 9:14.
37. Ellen White, *Patriarchs and Prophets* (1890), p. 271, 272.
38. Revelation 19:1-2; Ezekiel 38:16, 18-23; 39:1-8.
39. Exodus 9:27; 10:16, 17.
40. Exodus 8:19.
41. Isaiah 49:23; 60:14, 15; Revelation 3:9, 10.
42. See Isaiah 45:23; Romans 14:11.
43. Ellen White, *Great Controversy* (1911), p. 655. See also *Early Writings*, p. 124.

Israel Protected

Just as ancient Israel in Egypt escaped the seven last of the ten plagues, so will modern Israel escape the seven last of the plagues that fall on modern Babylon.[44] The statement "seven last plagues" indicates that there will be others before them that will be universal. We do not know whether there will be just three or more of these universal plagues. The Influenza epidemic was a plague and so was the world war. But the seven last will fall upon the wicked only.

44. Psalm 91:1-11; Isaiah 33:14-16.

6

THE MIDNIGHT DELIVERANCE

The Passover

Exodus 12:3-14: "Speak ye unto all the congregation of Israel, saying, In the tenth day of this month they shall take to them every man a lamb, according to the house of their fathers, a lamb for an house: And if the household be too little for the lamb, let him and his neighbour next unto his house take it according to the number of the souls; every man according to his eating shall make your count for the lamb. Your lamb shall be without blemish, a male of the first year: ye shall take it out from the sheep, or from the goats: And ye shall keep it up until the fourteenth day of the same month: and the whole assembly of the congregation of Israel shall kill it in the evening. And they shall take of the blood, and strike it on the two side posts and on the upper door post of the houses, wherein they shall eat it. And they shall eat the flesh in that night, roast with fire, and unleavened bread; and with bitter herbs they shall eat it. Eat not of it raw, nor sodden at all with water, but roast with fire; his head with his legs, and with the purtenance thereof. And ye shall let nothing of it remain until the morning; and that which remaineth of it until the morning ye shall burn with fire. And thus shall ye eat it; with your loins girded, your shoes on your feet, and your staff in your hand; and ye shall eat it in haste: it is the LORD'S passover. For I will pass through the land of Egypt this night, and will smite all the firstborn in the land of Egypt, both man and beast; and against all the gods of Egypt I will execute judgment: I am the LORD. And the blood shall be to you for a token upon the houses where ye are: and when I see the blood, I will pass over you, and the plague shall not be upon you to destroy you, when I smite the land of Egypt. And this day shall be unto you for a memorial; and ye shall keep it a feast to the LORD throughout your generations; ye shall keep it a feast by an ordinance for ever."

Escape from the tenth and last plague of Egypt was possible only to the Israelites who sprinkled the blood of the slain lamb on the door-posts of their dwellings. As the angel of death passed through the land of Egypt he passed over the homes of those who had the sign of the blood.

As far as the record goes, this is the only thing ever required of the Israelites to protect themselves from the plagues. Because their homes were passed over and their firstborn protected the deliverance was called the Passover and under divine direction a memorial was instituted to commemorate the event.

Mark of God

Exodus 12:13: "And the blood shall be to you for a token upon the houses where ye are: and when I see the blood, I will pass over you, and the plague shall not be upon you to destroy you, when I smite the land of Egypt."

The sprinkled blood on the door-posts was a token of redemption, a sign of God's ownership, a pledge of security, and a mark of obedience. This mark secured the safety of those who exhibited it from the wrath and judgments of God. Deliverance from bondage and the last plague depended on their faith in the sprinkled blood which was symbolic of the blood of Christ, the Lamb of God.

The angel of death passed over every home that had the mark of God's approval and protection. His avenging sword was unsheathed in every other household in the land. The mark was an outward sign of obedience and showed that the inmates were worshipers of the true God and were obedient to His will.

The Antitype

Ezekiel 9:1-9: "He cried also in mine ears with a loud voice, saying, Cause them that have charge over the city to draw near, even every man with his destroying weapon in his hand. And, behold, six men came from the way of the higher gate, which lieth toward the north, and every man a slaughter weapon in his hand; and one man among them was clothed with linen, with a writer's inkhorn by his side: and they went in, and stood beside the brazen altar. And the glory of the God of Israel was gone up from the cherub, whereupon he was, to the threshold of the house. And he called to the man clothed with linen, which had the writer's inkhorn by his side; And the LORD said unto him, Go through the midst of the city, through the midst of Jerusalem, and set a mark upon the foreheads of the men that sigh and that cry for all the abominations that be done in the midst thereof. And to the others he said in mine hearing, Go ye after him through the city, and smite: let not your eye spare, neither have ye pity: Slay utterly old and young, both maids, and little children, and women: but come not near any man upon whom is the mark; and begin at my sanctuary.

"Then they began at the ancient men which were before the house. And he said unto them, Defile the house, and fill the courts with the slain: go ye forth. And they went forth, and slew in the city. And it came to pass, while they were slaying them, and I was left, that I fell upon my face, and cried, and said, Ah Lord GOD! wilt thou destroy all the residue of Israel in thy pouring out of thy fury upon Jerusalem? Then said he unto me, The iniquity of the house of Israel and Judah is exceeding great, and the land is full of blood, and the city full of perverseness: for they say, The LORD hath forsaken the earth, and the LORD seeth not."

The angels of death here represent the seven last plagues and only those who have the mark of God will be delivered. This mark is an outward sign of the character of

God which is imparted by faith in the sprinkled blood of the Lamb of God. It indicates that all sin has been washed away in the cleansing blood of Christ.

Of them the Revelator says: "These are they which came out of great tribulation, and have washed their robes, and made them white in the blood of the Lamb."[1] The marking angel in Ezekiel's vision is followed by the angels of death who pass over those who have the protecting mark. This mark is a sign of their allegiance to the true God and insures their deliverance from the seven last plagues and from the bondage and persecutions of Babylon.

The Sabbath

Exodus 20:12, 20: "Moreover also I gave them my sabbaths, to be a sign between me and them, that they might know that I am the LORD that sanctify them. And hallow my sabbaths; and they shall be a sign between me and you, that ye may know that I am the LORD your God."

Revelation 7:1-3: "And after these things I saw four angels standing on the four corners of the earth, holding the four winds of the earth, that the wind should not blow on the earth, nor on the sea, nor on any tree. And I saw another angel ascending from the east, having the seal of the living God: and he cried with a loud voice to the four angels, to whom it was given to hurt the earth and the sea, Saying, Hurt not the earth, neither the sea, nor the trees, till we have sealed the servants of our God in their foreheads."

The Sabbath is the sign of the Creator or the true God, and also of redemption or sanctification. It is the outward sign of a character that has been cleansed from all sin by the blood of Christ.[2] The Sabbath is therefore the sign of the sprinkled blood of Christ that alone can sanctify and make us holy. It is the seal or mark that secures the receivers from the weapons of the slaughter angels representing the wrath of God.

{In *Pulpit Commentary* it says:}

> It is a sign of ownership, a mark of possession, a pledge of security, a badge of service, a token of redemption.[3]

{And Seiss remarks that:}

> This sealing secures the safety of the sealed ones as the judgment of the great day goes over the nations.[4]

---

1. Revelation 7:14.
2. Isaiah 56:2.
3. *Pulpit Commentary.*
4. Seiss.

Delivered at Midnight

Exodus 11:4: "And Moses said, Thus saith the LORD, About midnight will I go out into the midst of Egypt:"

Exodus 12:29: "And it came to pass, that at midnight the LORD smote all the firstborn in the land of Egypt, from the firstborn of Pharaoh that sat on his throne unto the firstborn of the captive that was in the dungeon; and all the firstborn of cattle."

The deliverance of Israel under the Exodus from Egypt took place at midnight during the last plague. The preparation necessary was to have the blood sprinkled on the door-posts and to have everything packed up and ready to move. They were to be dressed with their sandals on their feet and their staves in their hands.[5]

Exactly at midnight the angel of death to the Egyptians and of deliverance to the Israelites passed through the land. There arose a wail of woe from the Egyptians and a shout of deliverance from the people of God. The hosts of Israel had been organized for the journey and all preparations had been made. The 430 years were ended and the prophetic movement started from Egypt to Canaan, from bondage to freedom.

The Death Sentence

Exodus 14:5-31: "And it was told the king of Egypt that the people fled: and the heart of Pharaoh and of his servants was turned against the people, and they said, Why have we done this, that we have let Israel go from serving us? And he made ready his chariot, and took his people with him: And he took six hundred chosen chariots, and all the chariots of Egypt, and captains over every one of them. And the LORD hardened the heart of Pharaoh king of Egypt, and he pursued after the children of Israel: and the children of Israel went out with an high hand. But the Egyptians pursued after them, all the horses and chariots of Pharaoh, and his horsemen, and his army, and overtook them encamping by the sea, beside Pihahiroth, before Baalzephon.

"And when Pharaoh drew nigh, the children of Israel lifted up their eyes, and, behold, the Egyptians marched after them; and they were sore afraid: and the children of Israel cried out unto the LORD. And they said unto Moses, Because there were no graves in Egypt, hast thou taken us away to die in the wilderness? wherefore hast thou dealt thus with us, to carry us forth out of Egypt? Is not this the word that we did tell thee in Egypt, saying, Let us alone, that we may serve the Egyptians? For it had been better for us to serve the Egyptians, than that we should die in the wilderness. And Moses said unto the people, Fear ye not, stand still, and see the salvation of the LORD, which he will show to you to day: for the Egyptians whom ye have seen to day, ye shall see them again no more for ever. The LORD shall fight for you, and ye shall hold your peace.

5. Exodus 12:11-13.

"And the LORD said unto Moses, Wherefore criest thou unto me? speak unto the children of Israel, that they go forward: But lift thou up thy rod, and stretch out thine hand over the sea, and divide it: and the children of Israel shall go on dry ground through the midst of the sea. And I, behold, I will harden the hearts of the Egyptians, and they shall follow them: and I will get me honour upon Pharaoh, and upon all his host, upon his chariots, and upon his horsemen. And the Egyptians shall know that I am the LORD, when I have gotten me honour upon Pharaoh, upon his chariots, and upon his horsemen.

"And the angel of God, which went before the camp of Israel, removed and went behind them; and the pillar of the cloud went from before their face, and stood behind them: And it came between the camp of the Egyptians and the camp of Israel; and it was a cloud and darkness to them, but it gave light by night to these: so that the one came not near the other all the night. And Moses stretched out his hand over the sea; and the LORD caused the sea to go back by a strong east wind all that night, and made the sea dry land, and the waters were divided. And the children of Israel went into the midst of the sea upon the dry ground: and the waters were a wall unto them on their right hand, and on their left.

"And the Egyptians pursued, and went in after them to the midst of the sea, even all Pharaoh's horses, his chariots, and his horsemen. And it came to pass, that in the morning watch the LORD looked unto the host of the Egyptians through the pillar of fire and of the cloud, and troubled the host of the Egyptians, And took off their chariot wheels, that they drave them heavily: so that the Egyptians said, Let us flee from the face of Israel; for the LORD fighteth for them against the Egyptians.

"And the LORD said unto Moses, Stretch out thine hand over the sea, that the waters may come again upon the Egyptians, upon their chariots, and upon their horsemen. And Moses stretched forth his hand over the sea, and the sea returned to his strength when the morning appeared; and the Egyptians fled against it; and the LORD overthrew the Egyptians in the midst of the sea. And the waters returned, and covered the chariots, and the horsemen, and all the host of Pharaoh that came into the sea after them; there remained not so much as one of them. But the children of Israel walked upon dry land in the midst of the sea; and the waters were a wall unto them on their right hand, and on their left. Thus the LORD saved Israel that day out of the hand of the Egyptians; and Israel saw the Egyptians dead upon the sea shore. And Israel saw that great work which the LORD did upon the Egyptians: and the people feared the LORD, and believed the LORD, and his servant Moses."

The final deliverance of the Israelites took place at the Red Sea as they passed out of the dominion of Egypt. Here they were delivered from the sentence of death which was the final act in the drama of their Egyptian pilgrimage. Pharaoh's decree was that they be brought back into bondage or destroyed.[6] God's people were apparently in a trap with no human possibility of escape. The outlook from their viewpoint

6. Exodus 15:9.

seemed hopeless. They must either return to Egypt to a more cruel bondage or face the sentence of death. It was a test of faith and the deliverance was sudden and unexpected. The Lord opened up the Red Sea and led them to freedom.

Also at Midnight

Exodus 14:19, 20: "And the angel of God, which went before the camp of Israel, removed and went behind them; and the pillar of the cloud went from before their face, and stood behind them: And it came between the camp of the Egyptians and the camp of Israel; and it was a cloud and darkness to them, but it gave light by night to these: so that the one came not near the other all the night."

The deliverance at the Red Sea took place at night. All night they were protected by a guard of angels between them and the enemy. According to verses 24, 25, the Egyptians were destroyed during the morning watch which came between two in the morning and sunrise. Since several millions of men, women and children had to make the journey with all their belongings including live-stock, it doubtless required several hours to make the passage. The Red Sea at this point is estimated to have been at least one mile and probably five miles wide or even more. The 600 chariots of Pharaoh with perhaps 100,000 soldiers were in the midst of the passage in the morning watch. This would make the opening of the Red Sea for their deliverance about midnight.

The Distance

George Stanley Faber declares that:

> The tongue of the Red Sea at that place is about twelve miles broad....In the time of Diodorus it was three fathoms[7] deep.

George Rawlinson wrote:

> The space may have been one of considerable width. The Israelites entering upon it, perhaps about midnight, accomplished the distance, which may not have exceeded a mile, with all their belongings, in the course of five or six hours, the pillar of fire withdrawing itself, as the last Israelites entered the sea-bed, and retiring after them like a rearguard. Thus protected, they made the transit in safety, and morning saw them encamped upon the shores of Asia.

Death-Sentence Reversed

The sentence of death decreed upon the Israelites returned upon the heads of the

7. (18 feet).

Egyptians.[8] The enemies of God's people were all destroyed and the Israelites were delivered from them forever. "There remained not so much as one of them."[9] In connection with the destruction of the Egyptians, there took a place a terrific storm accompanied by thunder, lightning and earthquakes.[10]

{Josephus writes:}

> Showers of rain came down from the sky, and dreadful thunders and lightning, with flashes of fire; thunderbolts also were darted upon them; nor was there anything wont to be sent by God upon men as indications of His wrath, which did not happen upon this occasion.[11]

Song of Deliverance

Exodus 15:1-27: "Then sang Moses and the children of Israel this song unto the LORD, and spake, saying, I will sing unto the LORD, for he hath triumphed gloriously: the horse and his rider hath he thrown into the sea. The LORD is my strength and song, and he is become my salvation: he is my God, and I will prepare him an habitation; my father's God, and I will exalt him.

"The LORD is a man of war: the LORD is his name. Pharaoh's chariots and his host hath he cast into the sea: his chosen captains also are drowned in the Red sea. The depths have covered them: they sank into the bottom as a stone. Thy right hand, O LORD, is become glorious in power: thy right hand, O LORD, hath dashed in pieces the enemy. And in the greatness of thine excellency thou hast overthrown them that rose up against thee: thou sentest forth thy wrath, which consumed them as stubble. And with the blast of thy nostrils the waters were gathered together, the floods stood upright as an heap, and the depths were congealed in the heart of the sea. The enemy said, I will pursue, I will overtake, I will divide the spoil; my lust shall be satisfied upon them; I will draw my sword, my hand shall destroy them. Thou didst blow with thy wind, the sea covered them: they sank as lead in the mighty waters.

"Who is like unto thee, O LORD, among the gods? who is like thee, glorious in holiness, fearful in praises, doing wonders? Thou stretchedst out thy right hand, the earth swallowed them. Thou in thy mercy hast led forth the people which thou hast redeemed: thou hast guided them in thy strength unto thy holy habitation. The people shall hear, and be afraid: sorrow shall take hold on the inhabitants of Palestina. Then the dukes of Edom shall be amazed; the mighty men of Moab, trembling shall take hold upon them; all the inhabitants of Canaan shall melt away. Fear and dread shall fall upon them; by the greatness of thine arm they shall be as still as a stone; till thy people pass over, O LORD, till the people pass over, which thou hast purchased.

---

8. Exodus 14:24-30.
9. Exodus 14:28.
10. Psalm 77:15-20.
11. Josephus, *Antiquity of the Jews,* vol. 2, p.16.

Thou shalt bring them in, and plant them in the mountain of thine inheritance, in the place, O LORD, which thou hast made for thee to dwell in, in the Sanctuary, O Lord, which thy hands have established.

"The LORD shall reign for ever and ever. For the horse of Pharaoh went in with his chariots and with his horsemen into the sea, and the LORD brought again the waters of the sea upon them; but the children of Israel went on dry land in the midst of the sea. And Miriam the prophetess, the sister of Aaron, took a timbrel in her hand; and all the women went out after her with timbrels and with dances. And Miriam answered them, Sing ye to the LORD, for he hath triumphed gloriously; the horse and his rider hath he thrown into the sea.

"So Moses brought Israel from the Red sea, and they went out into the wilderness of Shur; and they went three days in the wilderness, and found no water. And when they came to Marah, they could not drink of the waters of Marah, for they were bitter: therefore the name of it was called Marah. And the people murmured against Moses, saying, What shall we drink?

"And he cried unto the LORD; and the LORD showed him a tree, which when he had cast into the waters, the waters were made sweet: there he made for them a statute and an ordinance, and there he proved them, And said, If thou wilt diligently hearken to the voice of the LORD thy God, and wilt do that which is right in his sight, and wilt give ear to his commandments, and keep all his statutes, I will put none of these diseases upon thee, which I have brought upon the Egyptians: for I am the LORD that healeth thee. And they came to Elim, where were twelve wells of water, and threescore and ten palm trees: and they encamped there by the waters."

With their own eyes the Israelites witnessed the destruction of their enemies and saw their dead bodies along the shore. Josephus declared that an eastward wind with the tide carried the bodies of the Egyptians to the eastern shore where the hosts of Israel could see them and that Moses stripped them of their armor and weapons to equip his own army.[12]

The song of deliverance is called "the song of Moses" because it was doubtless composed by him to commemorate the event and to celebrate their triumph. The song is divided into two parts. Verses 1-12 celebrate the deliverance that had just been experienced. Verses 13-18 are prospective of the results that were to come in the future because of the Red Sea deliverance. Verses 19-21 give us the sequel to the song, giving its historic background and the part Miriam played in the celebration.

The Antitype

Modern Israel will likewise experience a twofold deliverance from the power and wrath of modern Babylon. The first deliverance is from the sentence of death and the second from the world itself at the second advent.[13] This text enumerates four

12. Josephus, *Antiquity of Judah*, vol. 2., p. 16.

13. Daniel 12:1, 2.

important events: (1) The close of probation, (2) the plagues of time of trouble, (3) the deliverance of God's people, and (4) the special resurrection. The final sentence of death is predicted in Revelation 13:15. Deliverance from this sentence will come before the partial resurrection and therefore before the second coming of Christ and the final deliverance out of the world.

No Apparent Escape

Like Israel of old at the Red Sea, God's remnant people will apparently be trapped with no possibility of escape. They must either yield their allegiance to God and return to Babylon or be killed.

{Ellen White writes:}

> When the protection of human laws shall be withdrawn from those who honor the law of God, there will be in different lands, a simultaneous movement for their destruction. As the time appointed in the decree draws near, the people will conspire to root out the hated sect. It will be determined to strike in one night a decisive blow, which shall utterly silence the voice of dissent and reproof.[14]

> It was an hour of fearful, terrible agony to the saints. Day and night they cried unto God for deliverance. To outward appearance, there was no possibility of escape.[15]

Guard of Angels

Just as a company of mighty angels stood guard between the Israelites and the Egyptians all through the night of their trial and deliverance, so modern Israel while under sentence of death will be protected by angel messengers.[16]

{In *Great Controversy* we read:}

> Could men see with heavenly vision, they would behold companies of angels that excel in strength stationed about those who have kept the word of Christ's patience. With sympathizing tenderness, angels have witnessed their distress, and have heard their prayers. They are waiting the word of their Commander to snatch them from their peril....
>
> ...Though a general decree has fixed the time when commandment keepers may be put to death, their enemies will in some cases anticipate the decree, and before the time specified, will endeavor to take their lives.

14. Ellen White, *Great Controversy* (1911), p. 635.
15. Ellen White, *Early Writings* (1882), p. 283.
16. Isaiah 4:5, 6; Psalm 91.

But none can pass the mighty guardians stationed about every faithful soul.

{And in *Early Writings* we see that} "As the saints left the cities and villages, they were pursued by the wicked, who sought to slay them. ... Angels of God shielded the saints." This is what happened in the flight of ancient Israel from Egypt.

Delivered at Midnight

All laws go into effect at midnight and this will be true of the law with the death-penalty. Therefore the deliverance of God's people from the wrath and power of modern Babylon will take place at midnight.

{In the same way we see that} "It is at midnight that God manifests His power for the deliverance of His people."[17] "It was at midnight that God chose to deliver His people."[18]

Then follows a description of their deliverance, of the special resurrection, and later of the coming of Christ and the general resurrection of the righteous. It seems evident that the final deliverance from the world at the coming of Christ takes place at night and probably at midnight. It may be during the same night as the deliverance from the sentence of death although there is a train of events between the two that may take more time.

Death Sentence Reversed

The wicked will never be permitted to execute their sentence of death against the righteous, but God will execute His death-sentence against them.[19] There will not be one wicked person left. The righteous will behold the destruction of their enemies.[20] Protected by guardian angels from the wrath and devices of their enemies, the faith and patient endurance of God's people are finally rewarded. Like the Israelites at the Red Sea they witness the vengeance of God upon their persecutors, and see them rewarded with the very sentence of death they had expected to execute upon the righteous.

An Awful Storm

In connection with the deliverance of God's people and the destruction of the wicked there will be a great rainstorm with hail stones, thunder, lightning, and a great earthquake.[21]

---

17. Ellen White, *Great Controversy* (1911), p. 636.
18. Ellen White, *Early Writings* (1882), p. 285.
19. Revelation 14:9-11; 18:5-8; 19:19-21.
20. Psalm 91:3-8.
21. See Jeremiah 4:24-27; Ezekiel 38:19-22; Revelation 16:17-21.

{Ellen White was shown:}

> There is a mighty earthquake. ... The mountains shake like a reed in the wind, and ragged rocks are scattered on every side. There is a roar as of a coming tempest. The sea is lashed into fury. There is heard the shriek of the hurricane, like the voice of demons upon a mission of destruction. The whole earth heaves and swells like the waves of the sea. Its surface is breaking up. Its very foundations seem to be giving way. Mountain chains are sinking. Inhabited islands disappear. The seaports that have become like Sodom for wickedness, are swallowed by the angry waters. ... Great hailstones are doing their work of destruction. The proudest cities of the earth are laid low. ...
>
> ...Fierce lightnings leap from the heavens, enveloping the earth in a sheet of flames. Above the terrific roar of thunder, voices, mysterious and awful, declare the doom of the wicked.[22]

This is what happened in the destruction of the Egyptians at the Red Sea only the latter is on a world-wide scale.

Song of Deliverance

Revelation 15:2-4: "And I saw as it were a sea of glass mingled with fire: and them that had gotten the victory over the beast, and over his image, and over his mark, and over the number of his name, stand on the sea of glass, having the harps of God. And they sing the song of Moses the servant of God, and the song of the Lamb, saying, Great and marvellous are thy works, Lord God Almighty; just and true are thy ways, thou King of saints. Who shall not fear thee, O Lord, and glorify thy name? for thou only art holy: for all nations shall come and worship before thee; for thy judgments are made manifest."

Just as triumphant Israel on the shores of the Red Sea celebrated their deliverance in song, so the delivered advent people will repeat the same song on the sea of glass because they have gone through the same experiences.[23] God's people rejoice over their enemies who, "like a great millstone" "cast" "cast into the sea", go down to rise no more forever.[24]

In connection with the descriptions of the final deliverance and song of victory the same terms and illustrations are used as are found in the Exodus description of ancient Israel's experience and the song of Moses sung at the Red Sea. As Miriam, the prophetess of the exodus movement led in the song-celebration at the Red Sea,

---

22. Ellen White, *Great Controversy* (1911), p. 637-638.
23. "By the sea of glass." (R.V.)
24. Revelation 18:20, 21; 19:1-3.

it may be that the song of triumph of the remnant of Israel who go through the final crisis will be led by the Prophetess of the Advent movement. At least it seems appropriate that it should be so. The song of triumph is the song of the Lamb. Jesus, the Lamb of God, won His victory in the Garden of Gethsemane about midnight. His midnight victory made possible our midnight deliverance.

7

THE MIXED MULTITUDE

Not All Israelites

Exodus 12:37, 38: "And the children of Israel journeyed from Rameses to Succoth, about six hundred thousand on foot that were men, beside children. And a mixed multitude went up also with them; and flocks, and herds, even very much cattle."

"With them": indicates that they were not of them and were therefore not Israelites.

{If we look at some different translations we see:}

> A great mixture — Margin.
> Many strangers. — Fenton.

Who were these "strangers" who composed the "mixed multitude" and why did they join the movement?

{Ellen White writes in *Patriarchs and Prophets*:}

> In this multitude were not only those who were actuated by faith in the God of Israel, but also a far greater number who desired only to escape from the plagues or who followed in the wake of the moving multitudes, merely from excitement and curiosity. This class was ever a hindrance and a snare to Israel.[1]

Many of them were doubtless Egyptians, and others a mixture of the Hamitic and Semitic races as the result of inter-marriage.

Selfish Motive

With a few exceptions this multitude was controlled by a selfish motive. Because of the terrible judgments of God upon the enemies of His people they thought it was safer to cast their lot with the Israelites. Not only did they desire to escape the

1. Ellen White, *Patriarchs and Prophets* (1890), p. 281.

plagues, but they had heard the glowing accounts of the promised land as a country "flowing with milk and honey, which is the glory of all lands."[2] They wanted to share with Israel in the inheritance of Canaan and inhabit cities already built and eat the fruit of vineyards and orchards already planted.

Trouble Makers

The mixed multitude who traveled with Israel but were never of Israel, caused most of the trouble along the way to the promised land. They were the authors of most of the apostasies and rebellions that delayed the entrance of Israel into the promised land forty years.

{Again Ellen White writes:}

> The mixed multitude that came up with the Israelites from Egypt were a source of continual temptation and trouble. They professed to have renounced idolatry, and to worship the true God; but their early education and training had molded their habits and characters, and they were more or less corrupted with idolatry and with irreverence for God. They were oftenest the ones to stir up strife, and were the first to complain, and they leavened the camp with their idolatrous practices and their murmurings against God.[3]

The Complainers

The mixed multitude were critical especially of the leadership of the Exodus movement. They were chronic complainers and nothing suited them. They were overthrown in the wilderness and not permitted to enter the promised land because "they despised the pleasant land" and "believed not" God's word.[4]

{In Patriarchs and Prophets we see:}

> After three days' journey, open complaints were heard. These originated with the mixed multitude, many of whom were not fully united with Israel, and were continually watching for some cause of censure. The complainers were not pleased with the direction of the march, and they were continually finding fault with the way in which Moses was leading them, though they well knew that he, as well as they, were following the guiding cloud. Dissatisfaction is contagious and it soon spread in the encampment.[5]

---

2. Exodus 20:6.
3. Ellen White, *Patriarchs and Prophets* (1890), p. 408.
4. Psalm 106:24-26.
5. Ellen White, *Patriarchs and Prophets* (1890), p. 337.

Their bitter criticism of the leadership of the movement, which they wanted to lead, led them to start offshoot movements of which there were many, all of which soon came to naught.

Sinai Apostasy

The first great apostasy of the Exodus movement was at Mount Sinai.[6] This apostasy took place while Moses was up in the Mount and originated with the mixed multitude.

> While Moses was absent, it was a time of waiting and suspense to Israel....
>
> During this period of waiting, there was time for them to meditate upon the law of God which they had heard, and to prepare their hearts to receive the further revelations that He might make to them. They had none too much time for this work; and had they been thus seeking a clearer understanding of God's requirements, and humbling their hearts before Him, they would have been shielded from temptation. But they did not do this, and they soon became careless, inattentive, and lawless. Especially was this the case with the mixed multitude. They were impatient to be on their way to the land of promise,-the land flowing with milk and honey...There were some who suggested a return to Egypt, but whether forward to Canaan or backward to Egypt, the masses of the people were determined to wait no longer for Moses. Feeling their helplessness in the absence of their leader, they returned to their old superstitions. The 'mixed multitude' had been the first to indulge murmurings and impatience, and they were the leaders in the apostasy that followed.[7]

Complained of Diet

Numbers 11:4-6, 10: "And the mixed multitude that was among them fell a lusting: and the children of Israel also wept again, and said, Who shall give us flesh to eat? We remember the fish, which we did eat in Egypt freely; the cucumbers, and the melons, and the leeks, and the onions, and the garlic: But now our soul is dried away: there is nothing at all, beside this manna, before our eyes.

"Then Moses heard the people weep throughout their families, every man in the door of his tent: and the anger of the LORD was kindled greatly; Moses also was displeased."

The mixed multitude did not like the health reform principles the Lord had given the Exodus movement and they lusted for the diet they had in Egypt. They reminded the Israelites of what they had to eat while in Egypt and they too began to complain

6. Exodus 32:1-6.
7. Ellen White, *Patriarchs and Prophets* (1890), p. 315-316.

of the food God had given them.

> Again they began to clamor for flesh to eat. Though abundantly supplied with manna, they were not satisfied. The Israelites, during their bondage in Egypt, had been compelled to subsist on the plainest and simplest food; but the keen appetite induced by privation and hard labor had made it palatable. Many of the Egyptians, however, who were now among them, had been accustomed to a luxurious diet; and these were the first to complain.[8]

The "mixed multitude" were therefore composed of Egyptians who were "among" the Israelites.

On Outskirts of Camp

Numbers 2:2, 17: "Every man of the children of Israel shall pitch by his own standard, with the ensign of their father's house: far off about the tabernacle of the congregation shall they pitch.

"Then the tabernacle of the congregation shall set forward with the camp of the Levites in the midst of the camp: as they encamp, so shall they set forward, every man in his place by their standards."

Deuteronomy 23:7, 8: "Thou shalt not abhor an Edomite; for he is thy brother: thou shalt not abhor an Egyptian; because thou wast a stranger in his land. The children that are begotten of them shall enter into the congregation of the LORD in their third generation."

{Ellen White writes:}

> The mixed multitude that had accompanied Israel from Egypt were not permitted to occupy the same quarters with the tribes, but were to abide upon the outskirts of the camp, and their offspring were to be excluded from the community until the third generation.[9]

> On one occasion, the son of an Israelitish woman and of an Egyptian, one of the mixed multitude that had come up with Israel from Egypt, left his own part of the camp and entered that of the Israelites, claimed the right to pitch his tent there. This the divine law forbade him to do, the descendants of an Egyptian being excluded from the congregation until the third generation. A dispute arose between him and an Israelite, and the matter being referred to the judges was decided against the offender.[10]

---

8. Ellen White, *Patriarchs and Prophets* (1890), p. 377.
9. *Ibid.* p. 375.
10. *Ibid.* p. 377.

The Advent Movement

1 Corinthians 10:5-11: "But with many of them God was not well pleased: for they were overthrown in the wilderness. Now these things were our examples, to the intent we should not lust after evil things, as they also lusted. Neither be ye idolaters, as were some of them; as it is written, The people sat down to eat and drink, and rose up to play. Neither let us commit fornication, as some of them committed, and fell in one day three and twenty thousand. Neither let us tempt Christ, as some of them also tempted, and were destroyed of serpents. Neither murmur ye, as some of them also murmured, and were destroyed of the destroyer. Now all these things happened unto them for ensamples: and they are written for our admonition, upon whom the ends of the world are come."

The advent movement faces the same temptations and dangers and is therefore cursed with a mixed multitude. Who are they? They must be the murmurers, complainers, critics, idolaters, fornicators, and the worldly element who are always lusting for the things of the world and the flesh-pots of Babylon. They are the unconverted and the half-converted who have the theory of the truth without the experience of righteousness. They are Babylonians or at best are only half Christian and half worldling; half Israelite and half Egyptian. They follow the Lord "afar off" and remain on the outskirts of the camp.

This worldly element is always seeking to bring into the church worldly pleasures and worldly policies. It seems impossible for them to distinguish between right and wrong; between what is proper and improper for a Christian. Their spirituality is at a low ebb and their standards are trailing in the dust.

Menace to Movement

The mixed multitude in modern Israel have kept the movement wandering around in the wilderness of sin. They have kept back the blessings of the early and latter rain and have delayed the coming of Christ. They are the leaders and followers in the offshoots and apostasies of which there have been many and will be many more. They commit the abominations in the church over which the faithful will be sighing and crying when the seal of God is impressed. They are the "foolish virgins" and the "evil servants" who "say in their hearts, My Lord delayeth His coming," and therefore they become careless and worldly. They are a menace to the progress of the movement and must be kept on the outskirts of the camp and not allowed to control the church of make up or dominate its leadership. They are indeed a "great mixture" of "strangers" in Zion.

A Multitude

This worldly and murmuring element is not small. It constitutes a multitude. Half of the ten virgins representing the advent people were of this "foolish" class. Speaking of the cause of the low spiritual ebb in the church the servant of the Lord wrote:

{In the Spirit of Prophecy we see written concerning this:}

> And what has caused this alarming condition? Many have accepted the theory of the truth, who have had no true conversion.[11]
>
> I have been shown that there must be a great awakening among the people of God. Many are unconverted whose names are on our church books.[12]
>
> Soon God's people will be tested by fiery trials, and the great proportion of those who now appear to be genuine and true will prove to be base metal.[13]
>
> When multitudes of false brethren are distinguished from the true, then the hidden ones will be revealed to view, and with hosannas range under the banner of Christ.[14]

Why Join Movement?

Why do these unconverted people join the Advent Movement and why do they stay in it and even try to control it? Because they are convinced of the theory of the truth of the advent message, and hope to sweep into the kingdom with it and thus partake of the benefits and privileges of "the inheritance of the saints in light." They have been thrilled with the descriptions of the Heavenly Canaan and want to share in its joys and glories. They have also heard about the seven last plagues and are anxious to escape them. They are controlled by selfish motives and while they are in the movement their hearts and interests are centered in the world or Egypt.

Purged by Shaking

The Exodus movement was purged by the shaking out of the rebels who made this mixed multitude.[15] The Lord did not send a message declaring that the church had become Babylon and that the faithful must be called out into a new movement under a new leadership. He cleansed the movement by shaking out the rebels. Not one of the rebels were permitted to enter Canaan.[16] The final purging came at Baal-Peor on the banks of the Jordan when 24,000 of the mixed multitude were eliminated.[17]

> The judgments visited upon Israel for their sin at Shittim destroyed the

11. Ellen White, *Testimonies for the Church*, vol. 5 (1889), p. 218.
12. Ellen White, *Review and Herald*, August 13, 1889.
13. Ellen White, *Testimonies for the Church*, vol. 5 (1889), p. 136.
14. *Ibid*, p. 81.
15. Ezekiel 20:35-38.
16. Numbers 14:22-24; 32:11-15.
17. See Numbers.25 and 26.

survivors of the vast company, who, nearly forty years before, had incurred the sentence, 'They shall surely die in the wilderness.'[18]

The Antitype

The Advent movement will be cleansed and purified in the same way: —by the shaking out of the mixed multitude. The Lord will never send a message declaring that the church has fallen and is therefore rejected and become Babylon. We are told that those who get such a burden are not of God but are under satanic inspiration. It is for this reason that all offshoots and apostasies in the past have come to naught and all those of the present and future must likewise ignominiously fail. These false movements however are blessings in disguise because they constitute a part of the sifting process by which the chaff and rubbish of the mixed multitude are shaken out.

{Ellen White, wrote:}

> God will arouse His people; if other means fail, heresies will come in among them, which will sift them, separating the chaff from the wheat.

The apostasies and offshoots from the Advent movement are composed of "chaff" and they call only "chaff" out of our midst. They are therefore rendering the Advent movement a valuable service.

Spiritual Reformation

Nehemiah 13:3: "Now it came to pass, when they had heard the law, that they separated from Israel all the mixed multitude."

The Advent movement will be cleansed by a great spiritual revival and reformation brought by the preaching of the Laodicean message. This purifying message shakes out the worldly and rebellious.[19]

The purpose of all spiritual reformations is to separate the false from the true; and wheat from the chaff; the mixed multitude from the true Israel. As soon as the shaking has accomplished its work and the church is purified, the latter rain will fall the work will be quickly finished and cut short in righteousness.

> Then a multitude not of their faith, seeing that God is with His people, will unite with them in serving the Redeemer."[20]

---

18. Ellen White, *Patriarchs and Prophets* (1890), p. 456.
19. See Ellen White, *Early Writings* (1882), p. 270.
20. Ellen White, "The Perils and Priveleges of the Last Days," *Review and Herald*, February 25, 1902, par 16; in A.G. Danielles, *Christ our Righteousness*, p. 123. See also Ellen White, *Testinmonies for the Church*, vol. 5 p. 80-82.

The Loyal

Only the faithful and loyal, who, like Joshua and Caleb "had another spirit in them" and "wholly followed the Lord", will enter the Heavenly Canaan.[21]

{Ellen White writes:}

> Those who come up on every point, and stand every test, be the price what it may, have heeded the counsel of the True Witness, and they will receive the latter rain, and thus be fitted for translation.[22]

21. Rev.14:1-5, 12; 22:14.
22. Ellen White, *Testimonies for the Church*, vol. 1 (1868), p. 186, 187. See also vol. 5, p. 214, 216.

8

DIVINE LEADERSHIP

The Guiding Pillar

Exodus 13:21, 22: "And the LORD went before them by day in a pillar of a cloud, to lead them the way; and by night in a pillar of fire, to give them light; to go by day and night: He took not away the pillar of the cloud by day, nor the pillar of fire by night, from before the people."

Nehemiah 9:12: "Moreover thou leddest them in the day by a cloudy pillar; and in the night by a pillar of fire, to give them light in the way wherein they should go."

The pillar of cloud by day and fire by night was the outward and visible sign of the divine leadership of the Exodus movement. It hovered over the camp when they rested, and went before them when they marched. Israel kept their eyes on the cloudy chariot and it indicated when they should march and which way they should go. That Christ was the occupant of the cloudy and fiery chariot is evident from several texts:

1 Corinthians 10:1-4: "Moreover, brethren, I would not that ye should be ignorant, how that all our fathers were under the cloud, and all passed through the sea; And were all baptized unto Moses in the cloud and in the sea; And did all eat the same spiritual meat; And did all drink the same spiritual drink: for they drank of that spiritual Rock that followed them: and that Rock was Christ."

Isaiah 63:8, 9, 12: "For he said, Surely they are my people, children that will not lie: so he was their Saviour. In all their affliction he was afflicted, and the angel of his presence saved them: in his love and in his pity he redeemed them; and he bare them, and carried them all the days of old." "That led them by the right hand of Moses with his glorious arm, dividing the water before them, to make himself an everlasting name?"

Nehemiah 9:6-15: "Thou, even thou, art LORD alone; thou hast made heaven, the heaven of heavens, with all their host, the earth, and all things that are therein, the seas, and all that is therein, and thou preservest them all; and the host of heaven worshippeth thee. Thou art the LORD the God, who didst choose Abram, and broughtest him forth out of Ur of the Chaldees, and gavest him the name of Abraham; And foundest his heart faithful before thee, and madest a covenant with him to give the land of the Canaanites, the Hittites, the Amorites, and the Perizzites, and the Jebusites, and the Girgashites, to give it, I say, to his seed, and hast performed thy words; for thou art righteous:

"And didst see the affliction of our fathers in Egypt, and heardest their cry by the Red sea; And showedst signs and wonders upon Pharaoh, and on all his servants, and on all the people of his land: for thou knewest that they dealt proudly against them. So didst thou get thee a name, as it is this day. And thou didst divide the sea before them, so that they went through the midst of the sea on the dry land; and their persecutors thou threwest into the deeps, as a stone into the mighty waters.

"Moreover thou leddest them in the day by a cloudy pillar; and in the night by a pillar of fire, to give them light in the way wherein they should go. Thou camest down also upon mount Sinai, and spakest with them from heaven, and gavest them right judgments, and true laws, good statutes and commandments: And madest known unto them thy holy sabbath, and commandedst them precepts, statutes, and laws, by the hand of Moses thy servant: And gavest them bread from heaven for their hunger, and broughtest forth water for them out of the rock for their thirst, and promisedst them that they should go in to possess the land which thou hadst sworn to give them."

It was Christ who led and preserved the Exodus movement, and the pillar was the visible sign of His presence and leadership. It was Christ who furnished Israel with both physical and spiritual food; who gave the law and all the instructions concerning the sanctuary and its services.

The Advent Movement

Christ is likewise the Leader of modern Israel in the Advent movement.[1] Those who sin in this movement are tempting Christ the Leader. God's remnant people are likewise guided and protected by a pillar of cloud and fire, or light.[2]

> I saw a covering that God was drawing over His people to protect them in the time of trouble; and every soul that was decided on the truth, and was pure in heart, was to be covered with the covering of the Almighty.[3]

What is the light that guides, and the covering and shield that protects God's remnant people on their journey to the heavenly Canaan?[4] "I am the Light of the world," said Jesus.

The Visible Sign

1. 1 Corinthians 10:9, 11.
2. Isaiah 4:5, 6; 49:1-12, 22, 23.
3. Ellen White, *Early Writings* (1882), p. 34.
4. Psalm 91:1-4; 9-12; Psalm 119:105; Proverbs 6:22, 23; John 1:4, 9, 10.

The outward and visible sign that modern Israel is under divine leadership is their obedience to the Law and the Scriptures.[5] The Sabbath as the seal of the law and the mark of loyalty to the true God, is the sign of sanctification.[6]

{In *Testimonies for the Church* we read:}

> There is a great similarity between our history and that of the children of Israel. God led His people from Egypt into the wilderness, where they could keep His law and obey His voice....
>
> So, at this time, there is a people whom God has made the depositaries of His law. To those who obey them, the commandments of God are as a pillar of fire, lighting and leading the way to eternal salvation.[7]

Christ is the living Law and Word

{Ellen White writes concerning the word of God:}

> Every chapter and every verse of the Bible is a communication from God to man. ... If studied and obeyed, it would lead God's people as the Israelites were led, by the pillar of cloud by day, and the pillar of fire by night.[8]

The Human Agent

Hosea 12:13: "And by a prophet the LORD brought Israel out of Egypt, and by a prophet was he preserved."

The Exodus movement was led and preserved by Christ through the human instrumentality of Moses, His prophet and spokesman. Moses was assisted by Aaron and Miriam.[9] The movement would have gone to pieces on many different occasions had it not been for the spirit of prophecy that held it together. Without this divine gift the Israelites never would have left Egypt, and after leaving Egypt they never could have reached Canaan but would have returned to Egyptian bondage. Abraham, Isaac and Jacob had the gift of prophecy, but this gift was withdrawn during the time Israel was in bondage and darkness because they had forgotten God and His law.[10]

Character of Moses

Numbers 12:3: "(Now the man Moses was very meek, above all the men which were upon the face of the earth.)"

---

5. Isaiah 20; 1 John 2:3, 4.
6. Ezekiel 20:12, 20.
7. Ellen White, *Testimonies for the Church*, vol. 4 (1881), p. 27.
8. Ellen White, *Patriarchs and Prophets* (1890), p. 504.
9. Psalm 77:20; Micah 6:4.
10. Proverbs 29:18; Lamentations 2:9.

Meekness is one of the chief qualifications for leadership and has characterized all of God's prophets.[11] Moses did not seek leadership. Esteeming others better and more qualified than themselves has always been the attitude of those whom God chooses to do special service for Him. But Moses did not shirk responsibility. He was afraid that Israel would not believe him or accept him as their prophet and leader.[12]

Israel was soon convinced that Moses was chosen of God to be His spokesman and their leader. As the end of the prophetic period was approaching, the Lord began to prepare His agencies for the deliverance of His people. Moses was born on time and trained for the task.[13] The forty years as a shepherd in the Land of Midian was an important part of his preparation to shepherd Israel for forty years in the same wilderness.

One-Prophet Movement

Not "by prophets", but "by a Prophet" was Israel led and preserved during their journey from Egypt to the borders of the promised land. Moses, the prophet of the Exodus movement, died a short time before Israel entered Canaan. Before his death, Moses was given a vision of the promised land including the new earth.[14]

{Of this vision we read:}

> And now a panoramic view of the land of promise was presented to him. Every part of the country was spread out before him, not faint and uncertain in the dim distance, but standing out clear, distinct, and beautiful to his delighted vision. In this scene it was presented, not as it then appeared, but as it would become, with God's blessing upon it, in possession of Israel. He seemed to be looking upon a second Eden.[15]
>
> Still another scene opens to his view, the earth freed from the curse, lovelier than the fair land of promise so lately spread out before him. There is no sin, and death cannot enter. There the nations of the saved find their eternal home. With joy unutterable, Moses looks upon the scene, the fulfillment of a more glorious deliverance than his brightest hopes have ever pictured. Their earthly wanderings forever past, the Israel of God have at last entered the goodly land.[16]

Moses also saw the deliverance under the Advent movement in that last vision.

11. Exodus 3:10, 11; 4:10-14.
12. Exodus 4:1, 29-31.
13. Acts 7:17-22.
14. Deuteronomy 34:1-4.
15. Ellen White, *Patriarchs and Prophets* (1890), p. 472.
16. *Ibid.*, p. 477.

Burden of Moses

Moses was afraid that the younger generation who had not witnessed the power of God in the beginning of the movement would fail to recognize its divine leadership all along the way.

> Before relinquishing his position as the visible leader of Israel, Moses was directed to rehearse to them the history of their deliverance from Egypt and their journeyings in the wilderness, and also to recapitulate the law spoken from Sinai. When the law was given, but few of the present generation were old enough to comprehend the awful solemnity of the occasion.[17]

> After the public rehearsal of the law, Moses completed the work of writing all the laws, the statutes, and the judgments which God had given him, and all the regulations concerning the sacrificial system. The book containing these was placed in charge of the proper officers, and was for safe-keeping deposited in the side of the ark. Still the great leader was filled with fear that the people would depart from God. In a most sublime and thrilling address he set before them the blessings that would be theirs on condition of obedience, and the curses that would follow upon transgression.[18]

Before Moses died he was given all the instruction needed to take the Children of Israel into the promised land and establish them there. He wrote out this instruction and Joshua simply carried it out as the appointed leader of Israel.[19]

Test of Prophetic Gift

Deuteronomy 13:1-5: "If there arise among you a prophet, or a dreamer of dreams, and giveth thee a sign or a wonder, And the sign or the wonder come to pass, whereof he spake unto thee, saying, Let us go after other gods, which thou hast not known, and let us serve them; Thou shalt not hearken unto the words of that prophet, or that dreamer of dreams: for the LORD your God proveth you, to know whether ye love the LORD your God with all your heart and with all your soul. Ye shall walk after the LORD your God, and fear him, and keep his commandments, and obey his voice, and ye shall serve him, and cleave unto him. And that prophet, or that dreamer of dreams, shall be put to death; because he hath spoken to turn you away from the LORD your God, which brought you out of the land of Egypt, and redeemed you out of the house of bondage, to thrust thee out of the way which the LORD thy God commanded thee to walk in. So shalt thou put the evil away from the midst of thee."

---

17. Ellen White, *Patriarchs and Prophets* (1890), p. 463.
18. *Ibid.*, p. 466.
19. Deuteronomy 34:9, 10.

The Lord told ancient Israel how to test the claim to the gift of prophecy. The performing of a miracle or the fulfilling of a prediction do not in themselves constitute sufficient evidence. The magicians of Pharaoh performed signs and the Witch of Endor foretold the death of Saul. Through conjecture based on his knowledge of the past, through the wonders of modern science, and because of his ability to carry out his own predictions or plans, Satan through his human mediums and false prophets is able to perform wonders and reveal future events. God alone can actually see the future. The only safe test is the life and teachings of the prophet. Both must be in harmony with the word and character of God. God chooses "holy men" to speak for Him. And yet His prophets have all been human beings subject to all the mistakes and frailties of mankind. They must get the victory and develop characters in the same way that others do.[20] Deuteronomy 18:9-15 is a timely warning for both ancient and modern Israel.

In Advent Movement

1 Corinthians 1:6-8:"Even as the testimony of Christ was confirmed in you: So that ye come behind in no gift; waiting for the coming of our Lord Jesus Christ: Who shall also confirm you unto the end, that ye may be blameless in the day of our Lord Jesus Christ."

1 Corinthians 12:1-28: "Now concerning spiritual gifts, brethren, I would not have you ignorant. Ye know that ye were Gentiles, carried away unto these dumb idols, even as ye were led. Wherefore I give you to understand, that no man speaking by the Spirit of God calleth Jesus accursed: and that no man can say that Jesus is the Lord, but by the Holy Ghost.

"Now there are diversities of gifts, but the same Spirit. And there are differences of administrations, but the same Lord. And there are diversities of operations, but it is the same God which worketh all in all. But the manifestation of the Spirit is given to every man to profit withal.

"For to one is given by the Spirit the word of wisdom; to another the word of knowledge by the same Spirit; To another faith by the same Spirit; to another the gifts of healing by the same Spirit; To another the working of miracles; to another prophecy; to another discerning of spirits; to another divers kinds of tongues; to another the interpretation of tongues: But all these worketh that one and the selfsame Spirit, dividing to every man severally as he will.

"For as the body is one, and hath many members, and all the members of that one body, being many, are one body: so also is Christ. For by one Spirit are we all baptized into one body, whether we be Jews or Gentiles, whether we be bond or free; and have been all made to drink into one Spirit. For the body is not one member, but many. If the foot shall say, Because I am not the hand, I am not of the body; is it therefore not of the body? And if the ear shall say, Because I am not the eye, I am not of the body;

20. James 5:17.

is it therefore not of the body? If the whole body were an eye, where were the hearing? If the whole were hearing, where were the smelling? But now hath God set the members every one of them in the body, as it hath pleased him.

"And if they were all one member, where were the body? But now are they many members, yet but one body. And the eye cannot say unto the hand, I have no need of thee: nor again the head to the feet, I have no need of you. Nay, much more those members of the body, which seem to be more feeble, are necessary: And those members of the body, which we think to be less honourable, upon these we bestow more abundant honour; and our uncomely parts have more abundant comeliness. For our comely parts have no need: but God hath tempered the body together, having given more abundant honour to that part which lacked: That there should be no schism in the body; but that the members should have the same care one for another.

"And whether one member suffer, all the members suffer with it; or one member be honoured, all the members rejoice with it. Now ye are the body of Christ, and members in particular. And God hath set some in the church, first apostles, secondarily prophets, thirdly teachers, after that miracles, then gifts of healings, helps, governments, diversities of tongues."

Ephesians 4:8-11: "Wherefore he saith, When he ascended up on high, he led captivity captive, and gave gifts unto men. (Now that he ascended, what is it but that he also descended first into the lower parts of the earth? He that descended is the same also that ascended up far above all heavens, that he might fill all things.) And he gave some, apostles; and some, prophets; and some, evangelists; and some, pastors and teachers;"

Revelation 12:17: "And the dragon was wroth with the woman, and went to make war with the remnant of her seed, which keep the commandments of God, and have the testimony of Jesus Christ."

Revelation 19:10: "And I fell at his feet to worship him. And he said unto me, See thou do it not: I am thy fellowservant, and of thy brethren that have the testimony of Jesus: worship God: for the testimony of Jesus is the spirit of prophecy."

The gift of prophecy played an important part in the apostolic church. But during the "falling away" the spirit of prophecy with all the gifts of the Spirit gradually diminished in their operations. During the middle ages of darkness and apostasy the gift of prophecy was divinely bestowed only occasionally and then temporarily.

With the dawn of the Reformation, spiritual gifts began to return. At times the Lord gave visions and dreams to Savonarola, Wycliffe, Luther, Huss, Jerome, John Wesley, and other godly reformers to help them through emergencies. But not until the Advent message started and began to bring a people all the way back to the faith once delivered to the saints, including obedience to all the commandments of God, did the Lord place the gift upon a permanent prophet in the Church.

The Instrument Chosen

In 1842 the gift of prophecy was given to J.B. Finley, a godly young man who believed the advent message. He was given a vision to prepare the church for the disappointment, and because he did not understand its meaning he refused to follow instructions to relate it.

Later in the same year the same vision was given to William Foy, a young Baptist who was preparing for the ministry. For the same reason he refused to relate it to the Advent people. The vision was contrary to their teachings and expectations regarding the future and he was sure they would not believe him.

Early in 1844 the same vision was given to Hazen Foss who was instructed to relate it so as to prepare the Adventists for the bitter disappointment soon to take place. He too refused and the Lord told him that the gift would be given to "the weakest of the weak." It was bestowed upon Ellen G. Harmon, who at the age of 17 was given the same vision which she faithfully related.

Her Experience

{Of her experience Ellen White writes:}

> After I came out of this vision, I was exceedingly troubled. My health was very poor, and I was but seventeen years old. I knew that many had fallen through exaltation, and I knew that if I in any way became exalted, God would leave me, and I should surely be lost. I went to the Lord in prayer and begged Him to lay the burden on someone else. It seemed to me that I could not bear it. I lay upon my face a long time, and all the light I could get was, 'Make known to others what I have revealed to you.' In my next vision I earnestly begged of the Lord, that, if I must go and relate what He had shown me, He would keep me from exaltation. Then He showed me that my prayer was answered, and if I should be in danger of exaltation His hand should be laid upon me, and I should be afflicted with sickness.[21]

The prophet of the Advent movement was as meek and humble as Moses. Just as Moses was afraid to tell Israel that the Lord had appeared to him, so the instrument chosen to be God's spokesman in these days hesitated to relate her vision to modern Israel.

But One Prophet

"By a prophet" has modern Israel been led and preserved, not by "prophets". Mrs.

21. Ellen White, *Early Writings* (1882), p. 20-21.

Ellen G. White was the prophet of the advent movement for 71 years and still is through her written testimonies. In harmony with the type there will doubtless be no other regular prophet and indeed there is no need of one. Like Moses she died on the borders of the heavenly Canaan without enjoying the privilege of translation, but before her death all the instruction for the entire journey of the advent people was written out in detail.

While the gift will doubtless be temporarily given to various persons during the very closing days to help God's people through emergencies and crises, there is really no need for another regular prophet.[22] The duty of the leaders now is to carry out the instruction given in such abundance. Before her death God's servant was given visions of the heavenly Canaan to cheer on the Advent people to the end of their pilgrimage. She was promised a part in the inheritance.

Led and Preserved

This movement would have gone to pieces long ago had it not been for the guidance of God through the gift of prophecy. Through this means the plans of Satan for the disrupting of the movement have been disclosed, and his false doctrines and deceptions have been revealed. In times of crisis, instruction has come to guide the church safely through, and time has abundantly demonstrated that the instruction was of divine origin. Through this gift perplexing problems have been solved and hidden truths revealed. Our success or failure as individuals or as a church depends upon our attitude toward the instruction given through this medium.

Satan's Anger

Revelation 12:17: "And the dragon was wroth with the woman, and went to make war with the remnant of her seed, which keep the commandments of God, and have the testimony of Jesus Christ."

{In Weymouth's translation the phrase "wroth" is translated as} "Furiously angry." [23] From Satan's viewpoint there is every reason why he should hate the gift of prophecy in the church and persecute the prophet. He always has. Through this means the Lord reveals his most secret plans against the church.[24] Through this gift the Lord leads and preserves His church, and obedience to the instruction of God through His prophets brings prosperity.[25]

The bitterest attacks made against the Advent movement have been and will continue to be against the Spirit of Prophecy. These attacks will grow more frequent and

---

22. See Joel 2:28-30.
23. Revelation 12:17 (Weymouth's Translation)..
24. See 2 Kings 6:8-17.
25. 2 Chronicles 20:20.

fierce as we near the end. Every effort will be made to undermine faith and confidence in this gift and the instruction given through it.

Meets the Test

The most modern of all of God's prophets meets all the tests of a true prophet.[26] This shows that there will be prophesying in the remnant of God's church that will stand the test of proof and investigation, and that this gift will be instrumental in perfecting a people for translation. Wherever there is the false there must be the true. Satan never counterfeits what does not exist. There will be many false prophets in the last days.[27]

The test of a true prophet is not on the basis of appearance or miracles, or even the fulfillment of predictions. The important questions are, first, does the life of the prophet harmonize with the Scriptures? And second, are the instructions in harmony with the law and the testimony of the other prophets? When Canright was making his attacks against Sister White and her writings he was publicly asked if he thought anyone would be saved who followed the example of her life and obeyed the instructions of her writings. His answer was, "Yes".

A Human Being

No prophet of God was ever fully accepted as a prophet by all the members of the church to whom they ministered. It always has been true that, "a prophet is not without honor, but in his own country, and among his own kin, and in his own house."[28]

The great prophet Elijah "was a man subject to like passions as we are" and so were all the other prophets including Sister White. The bestowing of the gift of prophecy or any of the other spiritual gifts does not insure perfection. A prophet, like an apostle, pastor, teacher, or evangelist, must develop character in the same way as the humblest member of the church. Having a gift of the Spirit does not insure perfection or victory over sin. It does add to one's responsibility to live a careful Christian life.

When the Lord selected Ellen G. Harmon, she was "the weakest of the weak," both physically and intellectually and then He demonstrated what He could do through such a weak instrument.[29] We must learn to take our eyes off of the weak human instrument and fix them upon the divine gift. The human instrument was subject to the mistakes and frailties of human flesh, but the gift itself is divine and therefore infallible.

26. 1 Thessalonians 5:19-23.
27. Matthew 24:24; 2 Thessalonians 2:9-12; Revelation 13:13, 14; 16:14.
28. Mark 6:4.
29. See 1 Corinthians 1:27-29.

Reason Necessary

{In the Spirit of Prophecy we see:}

> If man had kept the law of God, as given to Adam after his fall, preserved by Noah, and observed by Abraham, there would have been no necessity for the ordinance of circumcision. And if the descendants of Abraham had kept the covenant, of which circumcision was a sign, they would never have been seduced into idolatry, nor would it have been necessary for them to suffer a life of bondage in Egypt; they would have kept God's law in mind, and there would have been no necessity for it to be proclaimed from Sinai, or graven upon tables of stone. And had the people practiced the principles of the ten commandments, there would have been no need of the additional directions given to Moses.[30]

In other words, most of the instruction to ancient Israel through the gift of prophecy would have been unnecessary if they had faithfully obeyed the law and the instructions previously given.

In Advent Movement

The same is true today. The Spirit of Prophecy among God's remnant people does not reveal additional light but calls us back to the neglected Scriptures.

> If you had made God's word your study, with a desire to reach the Bible standard and attain to Christian perfection, you would not have needed the Testimonies....
>
> ...The written Testimonies are not to give new light, but to impress vividly upon the heart the truths of inspiration already revealed. ... Additional truth is not brought out; but God has through the Testimonies simplified the great truths already given, and in His own chosen way brought them before the people, to awaken and impress the mind with them, that all may be left without excuse.[31]

Further Testimony

{In the book, *Life Sketches*, we read:}

> I referred them to ancient Israel. God gave them His law; but they would not obey it. He then gave them ceremonies and ordinances, that in the performance of these, God might be kept in remembrance. They were so prone to forget Him and His claims upon them, that it was necessary to keep their minds stirred up to realize their obligations to obey

---

30. Ellen White, *Patriarchs and Prophets* (1890), p. 364.
31. Ellen White, *Life Sketches* (1915), p. 198-199.

and honor their Creator. Had they been obedient, and loved to keep God's commandments, the multitude of ceremonies and ordinances would not have been required. If the people who now profess to be God's peculiar treasure would obey His requirements, as specified in His word, special testimonies would not be given to awaken them to their duty, and impress upon them their sinfulness and fearful danger in neglecting to obey the word of God. Consciences have been blunted, because light has been set aside, neglected and despised.[32]

32. Ellen White, *Life Sketches* (1915), p. 200-201.

9

ORGANIZATION AND FINANCES

Exodus Movement

The Exodus Movement was throughly organized. Exodus 12:17; 13:18: "And ye shall observe the feast of unleavened bread; for in this selfsame day have I brought your armies out of the land of Egypt: therefore shall ye observe this day in your generations by an ordinance for ever.

"But God led the people about, through the way of the wilderness of the Red sea: and the children of Israel went up harnessed out of the land of Egypt."

{If we look at the margin of Exodus 13:18 and Numbers 10, we see:}

> By five in a rank.[1]
> According to their armies.[2]

They were organized after the pattern of an army, the most thorough of all human organizations. Moses had been the commander-in-chief of the armies of Egypt and was therefore well trained for organizing and handling large bodies of people. There were doubtless between two and four millions of men, women and children who left Egypt, besides their vast herds of domestic animals, and it would have been impossible to lead them on such a journey without the discipline and organization of an army.

Further Organization

The organization of the movement was further perfected as the needs required.[3] Who was Jethro who gave this counsel?

Exodus 18:1, 12: "When Jethro, the priest of Midian, Moses' father in law, heard of all that God had done for Moses, and for Israel his people, [and] that the LORD had brought Israel out of Egypt;

"And Jethro, Moses' father in law, took a burnt offering and sacrifices for God: and

1. Margin.
2. Numbers 10:18.
3. Exodus18:13-26.

Aaron came, and all the elders of Israel, to eat bread with Moses' father in law before God."

He was a priest of God. The Israelites had seven groups of rulers or leaders over as many divisions. Moses was the general human leader of the entire movement, which was divided into the twelve tribal divisions with their respective leaders or princes. These were sub-divided into bodies of thousands, hundreds, fifties, tens and fives, with their respective leaders. The organization was so complete that when Balaam saw the camp of Israel in such perfect order, "according to their tribes", that the "spirit of the Lord came upon him" and he blessed those he had come to curse.[4]

Without this perfect organization the Exodus Movement would have utterly failed of its purpose and would have been helpless against its enemies. Organization saved the movement from going to pieces when the different apostasies and offshoots tried to wreck it or lead it back to Egypt.

Spirit of Prophecy

{The Spirit of Prophecy gives the following summary of the organization of ancient Israel:}

> The government of Israel was characterized by the most thorough organization, wonderful alike for its completeness and its simplicity. The order so strikingly displayed in the perfection and arrangement of all God's created works was manifest in the Hebrew economy. God was the center of authority and government, the sovereign of Israel. Moses stood as their visible leader, by God's appointment, to administer the laws in His name. From the elders of the tribes a council of seventy was afterwards chosen to assist Moses in the general affairs of the nation. Next came the priests, who consulted the Lord in the sanctuary. Chiefs, or princes, ruled over the tribes. Under these were 'captains over thousands, and captains over hundreds, and captains over fifties, and captains over tens'; and lastly, officers who might be employed for special duties.[5]

Advent Movement

In 1 Corinthians 12 the church is symbolized by the human body with the head representing Christ, its Leader, and the various members symbolizing the divisions of the church into working bodies. The human body is the most perfect symbol of organization known, even exceeding that of an army. It represents the most perfect unity and cooperation down to the smallest and humblest members which are said to be "necessary".

4. Numbers 24:2.
5. Ellen White, *Patriarchs and Prophets* (1890), p. 374. See Deuteronomy 1:15.

One of the spiritual gifts enumerated in verse 28 is "governments" or "directors". {If we look at other translations of the spiritual gift of government we see it translated as:}

Powers of organization — Weymouth
Capacity to govern— C.N.T.
Administrators— Moffatt.

In Romans 12:8, "he that ruleth" is rendered "the President" in the Twentieth Century New Testament. In Ephesians 2:19-23 the church is represented as a building "fitly framed together". No one part of a building can stand alone. Although there are pillars and timbers holding more important positions than others, all are necessary to make a complete building.

Similar to Israel

The organization of the Advent Movement is strikingly similar to that of the Exodus Movement and there has been no effort to imitate it either. The President of the General Conference corresponds to the position of Moses, the princes of the twelve tribal divisions to the presidents of the division conferences of which there are twelve, the captains over thousands to the presidents of union conferences, the captains over hundreds to the presidents of local conferences, the captains over fifties to the pastors of churches, the captains over tens to the leaders of departments in the church, and the groups "five in a rank" to the band organizations in the church and the classes in the Sabbath School.

Order in Heaven

Order is said to be heaven's first law. The universe is well organized. Among the stars there is perfect order, system and organization. The angels are formed into companies with leaders. Christ is "the Great Prince" and "the Captain of the Lord's Host." He declared that "legions of angels were under His command.

{Ellen White wrote:}

> God is a God of order. Everything connected with heaven is in perfect order; subjection and thorough discipline mark the movements of the angelic host. Success can only attend order and harmonious action. God requires order and system in His work now no less than in the days of Israel.[6]

Evil Hosts Organized

While Satan would like to see God's work disorganized, and uses his agents to at-

6. Ellen White, *Patriarchs and Prophets* (1890), p. 376.

tempt to accomplish this purpose, he believes in a thorough organization for his own forces and government.

> O how Satan would rejoice if he could succeed in his efforts to get in among this people, and disorganize the work at a time when thorough organization is essential, and will be the greatest power to keep out spurious uprisings, and to refute claims not endorsed by the word of God. We want to build the lines evenly, that there shall be no breaking down of the system of organization and order that has been built up by wise, careful labor.[7]

Of course organization is a power for evil if not under the control of God.

> Organizations, institutions, unless kept by the power of God, will work under Satan's dictation to bring men under the control of men; and fraud and guile will bear the semblance of zeal for truth, and for the advancement of the kingdom of God.[8]

Financial System

Organization calls for a financial system to operate it. The chief source of revenue for the church is the tithe. The tithing system largely financed the Exodus Movement.[9] The tithe is on the same basis as the Sabbath. Both are "holy unto the Lord." The Creator reserves one seventh of our time and one tenth of our income. The first is a recognition that He is the Creator of all things, and the second that He is the Owner of all things.[10] The purpose of the tithe is given in Numbers 18:21-26.

Because of the principle involved in tithe paying, the priest paid tithe on the tithe they received.[11] The tithe had to be paid into the recognized treasury to be distributed by the appointed treasurers.[12] No person was permitted to make his own decision as to where the tithe should be paid and how it should be used. If it was wrongly used by the priests they had to bear the responsibility and not those who paid it. It belongs to the Lord and must go into His treasury.[13]

Not a New System

The tithing system was not new as it was God's plan in the days of Abraham, Isaac,

7. Ellen White, *Testimonies for the Church*, vol. 9 (1909), p. 258.
8. Ellen White, *Testimonies for Ministers and Gospel Workers* (1923), p. 494.
9. Leviticus 27:30-32.
10. Psalm 24:1.
11. Nehemiah 10:38.
12. Nehemiah 13:10-13.
13. Malachi 3:8-10.

and Jacob.[14] Like many other truths and institutions the tithing system was lost sight of during the sojourn of Israel in Egypt. A recognition that God is the Owner as well as the Creator must be a part of every reformation.

The tithe is numbered among the first-fruits and if it is faithfully paid it will be followed by a fruitful harvest.[15] Both temporal and spiritual blessings are promised. Unfaithfulness brings a withering curse because it is declared to be robbery. It is that form of robbery known as embezzlement because it is a breach of trust.

Many Offerings

In ancient Israel there were also many different free-will offerings for various purposes. The tithe is not an offering because it belongs to God. It is estimated that the Israelites gave from one fifth to one fourth of their income in tithes and offerings. The first-fruits of everything were given to the Lord. Every special spiritual, temporal or physical blessing was celebrated with a thank-offering.

Since the plan of salvation was laid in sacrifice there is a very close relation between giving and spirituality. Prosperity in health and the temporal blessings of life depend more than we realize upon soul prosperity.[16] In Deuteronomy 16:16,17 we are given the true basis of giving. This is the basis on which the tithe is paid. If all would do this there would be plenty of means in the treasury.

A Liberal People

Israel was the most liberal of all ancient peoples. Their liberality in free-will offerings for the building of the sanctuary is a good demonstration of their spirit.[17] The offerings must be made "willingly" and be love-gifts from the heart. the Lord refuses to accept gifts grudgingly made. Since they had been a race of slaves, where did they get their wealth?

Genesis 15:13, 14: "And he said unto Abram, Know of a surety that thy seed shall be a stranger in a land that is not theirs, and shall serve them; and they shall afflict them four hundred years; And also that nation, whom they shall serve, will I judge: and afterward shall they come out with great substance."

They came out of Egypt "with great substance." The Exodus Movement was a tremendous undertaking. A nation of several millions of people must be rooted up, led through a barren country, and transplanted in a new territory after destroying thirty nations each stronger than they. It looked like a super-human task and it was. But

14. Genesis 14:18-20; 28:20-22.
15. Proverbs 3:9,10; Malachi 3:8-12.
16. 3 John 2.
17. Exodus 25:1-8; 35:21, 22; 36:5-7.

God was the Leader and nothing is impossible with Him.

Wealth of Egyptians

Exodus 11:2, 3: "Speak now in the ears of the people, and let every man borrow of his neighbour, and every woman of her neighbour, jewels of silver, and jewels of gold. And the LORD gave the people favour in the sight of the Egyptians. Moreover the man Moses was very great in the land of Egypt, in the sight of Pharaoh's servants, and in the sight of the people."

Exodus 12:35, 36: "And the children of Israel did according to the word of Moses; and they borrowed of the Egyptians jewels of silver, and jewels of gold, and raiment: And the LORD gave the people favour in the sight of the Egyptians, so that they lent unto them such things as they required. And they spoiled the Egyptians."

"Borrow" is a very unfortunate translation and gives a wrong impression. The Revised Version says "ask" as does also the Douay. {Or as Moffatt translates it:} "They let the people have what they asked for." The meaning is to solicit, beseech, and almost demand as it if was the duty of the Egyptians to give. {And in Fenton's translation it puts it:} "Demand."

It was their duty as they owed their very lives to the Israelites. Joseph had saved the nation from ruin. The wealth of the Egyptians not only belonged to the Lord but they had gotten rich through the slave labor of the Israelites.

> The Egyptians had made slaves of the children of Israel, when they were not slaves, and the Egyptians were not entitled to their labor. They had only allowed the children of Israel a sustenance, and had enriched themselves with the labor which they had extorted from them.[18]

The Israelites only asked for what rightly belonged to them, their just wages. It was not a loan, or even a gift, but a debt. They received "such things as they required".

Wrong Translation

{Of this George Rawlison writes:}

> It is plain that the gold and silver articles and the raiment, were free-will gifts, which the Egyptians never expected to see again, and which the Hebrews asked and took, but in no sense 'borrowed'. Hengstenberg and Kurtz have shown clearly that the primary meaning of the words translated 'borrowed' and 'lent' is 'asked' and 'granted' and that the sense of 'borrowing' and

18. Ellen White, *Spiritual Gifts*, vol. 3 (1878), p. 191.

'lending' is only to be assigned to them when it is required by the context.[19]

Because of their misconception of the meaning of these texts the Mormons believe that it is proper to borrow of their Gentile neighbors and never repay or return that which they borrowed. Others do the same thing without the pretext of Scriptural backing. A neglect to return or repay that which is borrowed is a form of stealing.

Secret of Success

All the Israelites took part in this ingathering campaign and every man asked his neighbor, and every woman her neighbor and those that sojourned "in her house". Every man solicited "his friend". They were on friendly terms with their neighbors. "The Lord gave them favor in the sight of the Egyptians",[20] and their gifts were willing and liberal. Most of the wealth was in jewels and vessels of gold and silver, and in raiment. Much of this was put to a wrong use especially by the "mixed multitude".

They used them for adornment and from the jewels the golden calf was made at Mount Sinai.[21] The offerings for the building of the sanctuary were mostly jewels and vessels of Gold and Silver solicited from the Egyptians.

The Advent Movement

The world-wide work of modern Israel is supported largely by the tithing system.

1 Corinthians 9:13, 14: "Do ye not know that they which minister about holy things live of the things of the temple? and they which wait at the altar are partakers with the altar? Even so hath the Lord ordained that they which preach the gospel should live of the gospel."

"Even so" indicates the same means or system. The Lord instituted the tithing system and it therefore cannot be improved upon by human inventions. Christ placed His approval upon tithe paying and named it as one of the Christian duties.[22] It is just as necessary to recognize God as the Owner now as in the days of ancient Israel. The Melchizedek priesthood was supported by the tithe and that priesthood is unchangeable.[23] The priesthood of Christ is after the same order. All Christians are children of Abraham and will therefore "do the works of Abraham".[24]

One of the works of Abraham was to pay tithe to support the Melchizedek priesthood which is continued in the priesthood of Christ. This is not a new system but a

19. George Rawlison, *Pulpit Commentary.*
20. Exodus 11:2-3.
21. Exodus 32:1-4.
22. Matthew 23:23.
23. Hebrews 7:1-3,24.
24. Galatians 3:29; John 8:39.

return to what was lost when the church went into Babylon where is was supplanted by many foolish and man-made substitutes. Tithe paying is a part of the reformation that prepares a people for the second advent of Christ.

Many Offerings

Besides the tithe it requires many annual, monthly and weekly free-will offerings to finance the great undertaking of a world-movement. Only the offerings that are made freely and cheerfully are acceptable to the Lord.[25] No gift should ever be made grudgingly or because of pressure. Force or high pressure methods are out of place in God's work, and begging and undue urging should never be permitted.

{Ellen White writes:}

> There may sometimes have been too much urging for means. But when the light and love of Jesus illuminates the hearts of His followers, there will be no occasion for urging or begging their money or their service. … They will with cheerful heart and unswerving fidelity render to God the things that are His. The Lord will not accept an offering that is made unwillingly, grudgingly.[26]

Most Liberal People

Seventh-day Adventists have the reputation of being the most liberal people in the world. The tithe and offerings per capita for home and foreign work exceeds that of other religious bodies. We are constantly held up as worthy examples in liberal giving.

> If the Methodist Episcopal Church had given as much per capita for all church expenses as the Seventh-day Adventist gave, she would have paid $163,175,261 in a single year instead of $47,074,301, or enough to take care of all her church expenses and $116,100,960 to apply on her Centenary subscription, thus paying in a single year the whole five year quota.[27]

This is a sample of many such comparisons.

No Cause for Boasting

{Yet, Ellen White writes:}

> The work of God, which should be going forward with ten-fold its present strength and efficiency, is kept back, like a spring season held by the chilling blast of winter, because some of God's professed people are appro-

25. 2 Corinthians 9:6,7.
26. Ellen White, Testimonies for the Church, vol. 5 (1889), p. 285.
27. *World Survey of the Interchurch World Movement*, Foreign Volume, p. 184.

priating to themselves the means that should be dedicated to His service. Because Christ's self-sacrificing love is not interwoven into the life practices, the church is weak where it should be strong. By its own course it has put out its light, and robbed millions of the gospel of Christ.[28]

The True Witness declares, 'I know thy works'. ... They profess to believe that Jesus is coming; but their works deny their faith. Every person will live out all the faith he has. False-hearted professor, 'Jesus knows thy works'. He hates your stinted offerings, your lame sacrifices.[29]

Covenant by Sacrifice

Psalm 50:3-5: "Our God shall come, and shall not keep silence: a fire shall devour before him, and it shall be very tempestuous round about him. He shall call to the heavens from above, and to the earth, that he may judge his people. Gather my saints together unto me; those that have made a covenant with me by sacrifice."

We do not yet know much about real sacrifice. {In the Spirit of Prophecy we read:}

I looked to see who of those who professed to be looking for Christ's coming, possessed a willingness to sacrifice offerings to God or their abundance. I could see a few humble poor ones, who like the poor widow, were stinting themselves, and casting in their mite. Every such offering is accounted to God as precious treasure. But those who are acquiring means, and adding to their possessions, are far behind. They do comparatively nothing to what they might. They are withholding, and robbing God, for they are fearful that they shall come to want. They dare not trust God. This is one of the reasons that, as a people, we are so sickly, and so many are falling into their graves.[30]

Wealth of Gentiles

Isaiah 60:1-16: "Arise, shine; for thy light is come, and the glory of the LORD is risen upon thee. For, behold, the darkness shall cover the earth, and gross darkness the people: but the LORD shall arise upon thee, and his glory shall be seen upon thee. And the Gentiles shall come to thy light, and kings to the brightness of thy rising.

"Lift up thine eyes round about, and see: all they gather themselves together, they come to thee: thy sons shall come from far, and thy daughters shall be nursed at thy side. Then thou shalt see, and flow together, and thine heart shall fear, and be enlarged; because the abundance of the sea shall be converted unto thee, the forces of the Gentiles shall come unto thee. The multitude of camels shall cover thee, the

---

28. Ellen White, *Review and Herald*, October 13, 1896.
29. Ellen White, *Testimonies for the Church*, vol. 1 (1868), p. 195.
30. *Ibid.*, vol. 2 (1871), p. 189-199.

dromedaries of Midian and Ephah; all they from Sheba shall come: they shall bring gold and incense; and they shall show forth the praises of the LORD. All the flocks of Kedar shall be gathered together unto thee, the rams of Nebaioth shall minister unto thee: they shall come up with acceptance on mine altar, and I will glorify the house of my glory.

"Who are these that fly as a cloud, and as the doves to their windows? Surely the isles shall wait for me, and the ships of Tarshish first, to bring thy sons from far, their silver and their gold with them, unto the name of the LORD thy God, and to the Holy One of Israel, because he hath glorified thee. And the sons of strangers shall build up thy walls, and their kings shall minister unto thee: for in my wrath I smote thee, but in my favour have I had mercy on thee. Therefore thy gates shall be open continually; they shall not be shut day nor night; that men may bring unto thee the forces of the Gentiles, and that their kings may be brought. For the nation and kingdom that will not serve thee shall perish; yea, those nations shall be utterly wasted.

"The glory of Lebanon shall come unto thee, the fir tree, the pine tree, and the box together, to beautify the place of my sanctuary; and I will make the place of my feet glorious. The sons also of them that afflicted thee shall come bending unto thee; and all they that despised thee shall bow themselves down at the soles of thy feet; and they shall call thee, The city of the LORD, The Zion of the Holy One of Israel. Whereas thou hast been forsaken and hated, so that no man went through thee, I will make thee an eternal excellency, a joy of many generations. Thou shalt also suck the milk of the Gentiles, and shalt suck the breast of kings: and thou shalt know that I the LORD am thy Saviour and thy Redeemer, the mighty One of Jacob."

This will happen during the latter rain after the church has been awakened by the Laodicean message and is clothed in the glory of Christ's righteousness.

> God has an abundance in our world, and He has placed His goods in the hands of all, both the obedient and the disobedient. He is ready to move upon the hearts of worldly men, even idolaters, to give of their abundance for the support of His work; and He will do this soon as His people learn to approach these men wisely and to call their attention to that which it is their privilege to do. If the needs of the Lord's work were set forth in a proper light before those who have means and influence, these men might do much to advance the cause of present truth.[31]

But the Lord will never bring to us the wealth of the Gentiles until we learn to sacrifice to the limit of our ability.

Under the Latter Rain

The promised gift of the Holy Spirit "brings all other blessings in its train". Under

31. Ellen White, *Southern Watchman*, March 15, 1904.

the early rain the believers gave all their possessions and there was no lack of means. Joseph and Nicodemus and other wealthy men gave all their wealth. There was no necessity for urging or campaigning for means to support the work nor will there be under the latter rain. "God is not straitened for men or means."[32] He is not restricted, for the wealth of the world is His and He can get it when He wants it. He can multiply means as Christ multiplied the loaves and fishes in the feeding of the multitude.

{In the *Desire of Ages* we read:}

> The means in our possession may not seem to be sufficient for the work; but if we will move forward in faith, believing in the all-sufficient power of God, abundant resources will open before us. If the work be of God, He Himself will provide the means for its accomplishment.[33]

---

32. Ellen White, *Testimonies for the Church*, vol. 5 (1889), p. 224.
33. Ellen White, *Desire of Ages* (1898), p. 370.

10

HEALTH REFORM

Purpose of Exodus

The purpose of the Exodus of ancient Israel was to bring them back to the faith and practice of Abraham, Isaac and Jacob. While in Egypt they had learned to eat the abominations of the heathen and had forgotten the diet restrictions and regulations practiced by their fathers. Health reform was an important part of the movement out of Egypt. The use of the flesh foods that the Lord had pronounced unclean and an "abomination".[1] This was not a new restriction as the division had been made before the flood and these divine regulations were carefully observed by the faithful after the flood.

The Original Diet

In the beginning the Creator gave to all His creatures the food that was for their best good. The diet of man was restricted to the highest types of all foods, —grains, nuts and fruits.[2] After the entrance of sin which cursed the ground and made it necessary for man to live by the sweat of his face, the Lord added the herbs or vegetables to his diet.[3] This amended diet is therefore God's ideal for His people during the reign of sin.

Toward this ideal the Lord endeavored to lead Israel and is also attempting to lead modern Israel. In the Paradise restored the original diet will be fully restored. Those who are prepared for translation will be all the way back to the amended diet and therefore but one step from the original plan.

The Apostasy

As man's rebellion against God increased, all restrictions were broken down and the human family began to imitate the savage beasts in devouring their fellow-creatures. Sinful men were not satisfied to get their food directly from the vegetable kingdom; they turned cannibals and began to eat the flesh of the lower animals. Then in an effort to check the apostasy, the Lord made a division between the animals. He se-

1. See Leviticus 11; Deuteronomy 14.
2. Genesis1:29, 30; 2:16.
3. Genesis 3:17-19.

lected the most healthful and designated them as "clean" with permission to eat them, and all others as "unclean" and positively unfit for food and even an "abomination".

But this second barrier was soon broken down by the rebels and the apostasy continued until every living creature in the animal kingdom is used for food. Men even began to eat their fellow men.

The Reformation

The purpose of the gospel is to restore what was lost through sin; to bring man back to his original state. The steps in rebellion and apostasy must all be retraced by those who enter the Paradise restored. When the gospel reaches the most degraded human beings, cannibalism ceases. Then they eliminate from their diet the unclean abominations forbidden in the Scriptures. When the reformation is completed under the Advent Movement which prepares a people to enter the Heavenly Canaan, the steps in diet reform will have all been taken except the last which is for the perfect sinless state.

Angel's Food

In an attempt to lead Israel back toward the original diet, the Lord gave them manna.[4] In Psalm 78:23-25, the manna is called "angel's food" and the "corn of heaven." {Or in the margin:} "The bread of the mighty."

It was the food used by the angels and unfallen beings, the best food in the universe. There was nothing on earth to equal it. It contained more of the vital food elements than any food known to man. The nature of the manna is described in Exodus 16:31, and Numbers 11:7, 8. Coriander seed is the seed of a plant that grows wild in Palestine and neighboring countries and is cultivated and sold in the United States. It is pleasant to the taste and smell and is white "as the color of bdellium".

Israel Not Satisfied

But the Israelites had such perverted appetites as the result of their sojourn in Egypt that they were not satisfied even with the food of angels.[5] They were tired of the manna and lusted for the flesh-pots of Egypt which included even the unclean meats. This rebellion against the health principles of the Exodus Movement was started by the "mixed multitude".

The Lord did not give them what they lusted and cried for but sent them the cleanest of all clean flesh, — wild quails.[6] While three quarts of manna was sufficient for each person per day, they were so gluttonous for flesh that the least number of quails

4. Exodus 16:2-4,25.
5. Numbers 11:4-6.
6. Numbers 11:10-14, 31-33.

gathered by one person was ten homers or from 80 to 100 bushels. It was their gluttony that made the Lord so angry. They were so ravenous for flesh that they hardly took time to cook it.[7] The Lord gave them their request only to teach them a lesson. Their lust, gluttony and disobedience brought leaness to their souls.

Spirit of Prophecy

{The Spirit of Prophecy tells us:}

> God gave the people that which was not for their highest good because they persisted in desiring it; they would not be satisfied with those thing that would prove a benefit to them. Their rebellious desires were gratified, but they were left to suffer the result. They feasted without restraint, and their excesses were speedily punished. 'The Lord smote the people with a very great plague.' Large numbers were cut down by burning fevers, while the most guilty among them were smitten as soon as they tasted the food for which they had lusted.[8]

> They loathed the food given them and wished themselves back in Egypt, where they could sit by the flesh-pots. They preferred to endure slavery, and even death, rather than to be deprived of flesh. God granted their desire, giving them flesh, and leaving them to eat till their gluttony produced a plague, from which many of them died.[9]

Sin of Gluttony

Deuteronomy 21:18-21: "If a man have a stubborn and rebellious son, which will not obey the voice of his father, or the voice of his mother, and that, when they have chastened him, will not hearken unto them: Then shall his father and his mother lay hold on him, and bring him out unto the elders of his city, and unto the gate of his place; And they shall say unto the elders of his city, This our son is stubborn and rebellious, he will not obey our voice; he is a glutton, and a drunkard. And all the men of his city shall stone him with stones, that he die: so shalt thou put evil away from among you; and all Israel shall hear, and fear."

> The word of God places the sin of gluttony in the same catalogue with drunkenness. So offensive was this sin in the sight of God that He gave directions to Moses that a child who would not be restrained on the point of appetite, but would gorge himself with anything his taste might crave, should be brought by his parents before the rulers of Israel, and should be stoned to death. The condition of the glutton was considered hopeless. He

---

7. Psalm 78:17, 18, 26-31; 106:14, 15.
8. Ellen White, *Patriarchs and Prophets* (1890), p. 382.
9. Ellen White, *Counsels on Health* (1923), p. 111.

> would be of no use to others, and was a curse to himself. No dependence could be placed upon him in anything. His influence would be ever contaminating others, and the world would be better without such a character; for his terrible defects would be perpetuated.[10]

This sin is very prevalent today and is no less serious than in the days of ancient Israel. Modern parents make bit little or no effort to keep their children from gorging themselves. Over-eating or surfeiting is one of the sins of the last days.[11]

True Basis of Health

Exodus 15:26: "And said, If thou wilt diligently hearken to the voice of the LORD thy God, and wilt do that which is right in his sight, and wilt give ear to his commandments, and keep all his statutes, I will put none of these diseases upon thee, which I have brought upon the Egyptians: for I am the LORD that healeth thee."

Deuteronomy 7:5-15: "But thus shall ye deal with them; ye shall destroy their altars, and break down their images, and cut down their groves, and burn their graven images with fire. For thou art an holy people unto the LORD thy God: the LORD thy God hath chosen thee to be a special people unto himself, above all people that are upon the face of the earth. The LORD did not set his love upon you, nor choose you, because ye were more in number than any people; for ye were the fewest of all people: But because the LORD loved you, and because he would keep the oath which he had sworn unto your fathers, hath the LORD brought you out with a mighty hand, and redeemed you out of the house of bondmen, from the hand of Pharaoh king of Egypt.

"Know therefore that the LORD thy God, he is God, the faithful God, which keepeth covenant and mercy with them that love him and keep his commandments to a thousand generations; And repayeth them that hate him to their face, to destroy them: he will not be slack to him that hateth him, he will repay him to his face. Thou shalt therefore keep the commandments, and the statutes, and the judgments, which I command thee this day, to do them. Wherefore it shall come to pass, if ye hearken to these judgments, and keep, and do them, that the LORD thy God shall keep unto thee the covenant and the mercy which he sware unto thy fathers: And he will love thee, and bless thee, and multiply thee: he will also bless the fruit of thy womb, and the fruit of thy land, thy corn, and thy wine, and thine oil, the increase of thy kine, and the flocks of thy sheep, in the land which he sware unto thy fathers to give thee. Thou shalt be blessed above all people: there shall not be male or female barren among you, or among your cattle. And the LORD will take away from thee all sickness, and will put none of the evil diseases of Egypt, which thou knowest, upon thee; but will lay them upon all them that hate thee."

---

10. Ellen White, *Counsels on Health* (1923), p. 71.
11. Luke 21:34.

Health depends upon obedience to the laws of God both moral and physical. Obedience to the laws of nature alone is not sufficient. The greatest factor in healthful living is a spiritual experience. It is just as impossible to have perfect health by obedience to natural laws or by biologic living, as it is to gain salvation by human obedience to moral law. Faith and works must be combined in obtaining health as well as in obtaining salvation. A good Christian experience is of first importance in health reform. Combined with our obedience to health principles there must be a divine miracle working power within. This was the secret of the health of the Israelites. "There was not one feeble person among their tribes."[12]

The Advent Movement

1 Corinthians10:6, 11: "Now these things were our examples, to the intent we should not lust after evil things, as they also lusted." "Now all these things happened unto them for ensamples: and they are written for our admonition, upon whom the ends of the world are come."

The apostolic church observed the rules of health and diet restrictions. When the church went into Babylon they learned to eat all of the abominations of the heathen or Babylonians. The purpose of the Advent Movement is to call God's people out of Babylon and bring them back to the faith and practice of Christ and the apostles. The remnant will not eat unclean meats.[13] As we near the end of the journey and prepare to enter the heavenly Canaan, the Lord will endeavor to lead his people back to the original diet which they will have in Eden restored. His ideal for His people now is the diet as amended to meet the condition of sin.

Antitype of Manna

{Ellen White writes:}

> The light that God has given and will continue to give on the food question is to be His people today what the manna was to the children of Israel. The manna fell from heaven, and the people were told to gather it, and prepare it to be eaten. So in the different countries of the world, light will be given to the Lord's people, and health foods suited to these countries will be prepared. … In grains, fruits vegetables, and nuts are to be found all the food elements that we need.[14]
>
> If we will come to the Lord in simplicity of mind, He will teach us how to prepare wholesome food free from the taint of flesh meat.[15]

---

12. Psalm 105:37; Deuteronomy 8:4.
13. Isaiah 66:15-17; Ezekiel 22:26.
14. Ellen White, *Medical Ministry* (1932), p. 267.
15. *Ibid.*

A Broad Subject

Health reform is a big subject covering far more than our diet.[16] "Whatsoever" is all-inclusive. It includes exercise, recreation, work, rest, sleep and dress. While health reform is closely related to our spiritual life it is not the gospel.[17]

> The health reform is closely connected with the work of the third message, yet it is not the message. Our preachers should teach the health reform, yet they should not make this the leading theme in the place of the message.[18]

We cannot eat our way into heaven for that would be salvation by works. However, the way we eat may keep us out of the kingdom. Those who enter the family of God will eat, drink, dress and act as do the other members of His family. These things do not make them citizens of the heavenly kingdom, but they are evidences that they are citizens. Citizenship is a gift from God while conduct is an evidence of that relationship.

Will Produce Health

True health reform will produce health. Good health or better health is the evidence that the reform is genuine, and ill health that it is unbalanced. The good health of the Israelites testified that their health principles were sound and scientific. The good health of those who are ready for translation will demonstrate that the health principles of the Advent Movement are based upon the soundest reason.[19]

Adventists are to be "preserved" in spirit and soul and body." There is a close relation between a strong body and a strong mind and spirit.[20] We can not have a clear mind without a healthy body. In an army every effort is made to keep the soldiers in the best health possible. It is one of the most important elements in the morale of fighting men. Athletes know that success depends upon temperance of the strictest type. They abstain from everything that injures them physically.

Dangers of Extreme

{Of the dangers of extremes we read in the Spirit of Prophecy:}

> We would caution those who are extremists not to raise a false standard, and then endeavor to bring everybody to it.[21]

---

16. 1 Corinthians 10:31.
17. Romans 14:17, 18.
18. Ellen White, *Testimonies for the Church*, vol. 1 (1868), p. 559.
19. 1 Thessalonians 5:23.
20. 1 Corinthians 9:24-27; Philippians 3:18-20.
21. Ellen White, *Testimonies for the Church*, vol. 2 (1871), p. 375.

> Men go to an extreme in one direction and if not corrected, go to an extreme in the opposite direction.[22]

There are people who are extreme by nature and are never balanced on any subject. A great deal of counsel has been given us on this subject, especially along the lines of health reform.

{And again:}

> But we should be very cautious not to advance too fast, lest we be obliged to retrace our steps. In reforms, we would better come one step short of the mark than to go one step beyond it. And if there is error at all, let it be on the side next to the people.[23]

Here we are instructed to be guided by principle and the "shun the extremes." We are told that those who are the least informed are often the most rigid and that the effect of their mistakes reforms "is seen in their own ill-health."

Dangers of Laxness

On the other hand, we are warned against laxness which is the other extreme of fanaticism.

> We need now the sword of the Lord to cut to the very soul and marrow of fleshly lusts, appetites and passions.[24]

> The question of how to preserve the health is one of primary importance. …
>
> God demands that the appetites be cleansed, and that self-denial be practiced in regard to those things which are not good. This is a work that will have to be done before His people can stand before Him a perfected people..[25]

> It is impossible for those who indulge the appetite to attain to Christian perfection.[26]

> True temperance teaches us to dispense entirely with everything hurtful and to use judiciously that which is healthful. There are few who re-

22. Ellen White, *Testimonies to Ministers and Gospel Workers* (1923), p. 314.
23. Ellen White, *Testimonies for the Church*, vol. 3 (1875), p. 21. See also *Ministry of Healing* (1905), p. 318-319.
24. *Ibid.*, vol. 8, p. 315.
25. *Ibid.*, vol. 9, p. 153.
26. *Ibid.*, vol. 2, p. 400.

alize as they should how much their habits of diet have to do with their health, their character, their usefulness in this world, and their eternal destiny. The appetite should ever be in subjection to the moral and intellectual powers. The body should be servant to the mind, and not the mind to the body.[27]

Relation to Spiritual Health

2 John 1:2 "For the truth's sake, which dwelleth in us, and shall be with us for ever."

The health of the body depends upon the health of the soul. Spiritual healing must come first because it is as much more important than physical healing as eternal life is more important than temporal life.[28] We are told that when we fully do God's will, "then shall thy light break forth as the morning, and thine health shall spring forth speedily."[29]

> When the gospel is received in its purity and power, it is a cure for the maladies that originated in sin. ... The love which Christ diffuses through the whole being is a vitalizing power. Every vital part— the brain, the heart, the nerves—it touches with healing. ... It frees the soul from the guilt and sorrow, the anxiety and care, that crush the life forces. With it come serenity and composure. It implants in the soul joy that nothing earthly can destroy,—joy in the Holy Spirit—health-giving, life-giving joy. ... If human beings would open the windows of the soul heavenward, in appreciation of the divine gifts, a flood of healing virtue would flow in.[30]

Under Latter Rain

The call for a spiritual revival and a spiritual reformation is the most important of all roads to health reform. This is the message that will bring the latter rain of spiritual and physical healing. Then there will not be a feeble one among God's true people. Divine miracle-working power will cooperate with obedience to the laws of health, producing a people "to be wondered at" in health and wisdom, even as were Daniel and his companions in ancient Babylon.

{Ellen White writes:}

> In physical strength and beauty, in mental vigor and literary attainment, they stood unrivaled. The erect form, the firm, elastic step, the fair countenance, the undimmed senses, the untainted breath—all were so many cer-

27. Ellen White, *Patriarchs and Prophets* (1890), p. 562.
28. Psalm 103:3.
29. See Isaiah 58:1-11; Malachi 4:2.
30. Ellen White, *Ministry of Healing* (1905), p. 115-116.

tificates of good habits, insignia of the nobility with which nature honors those who are obedient to her laws.[31]

31. Ellen White, *Patriachs and Prophets* (1890), p. 485.

11

THE SYMBOL OF RIGHTEOUSNESS

A Reformation

The Exodus Movement was a reformation as has been every great religious awakening or movement to lead God's people out of the world. On coming out of Egypt, the Israelites had many things to learn and many to unlearn. For generations they had been influenced by heathen customs and practices until the lines of demarcation was almost indistinguishable. Placing themselves under Divine leadership called for a complete reformation touching every phase of life. They must learn to eat, drink, dress and act in harmony with their holy calling and heavenly citizenship.

A Sign

Citizenship in an earthly nation is a favor bestowed by the government and is not obtained on the basis of conformity to its laws and customs. However, the person who receives the gift of citizenship will demonstrate his sincerity by obedience to the laws and customs of the nation of his adoption. Likewise membership in the family of God is possible only through the new birth, and citizenship in the heavenly kingdom is a divine gift.

These blessings and privileges are not obtained through conformity to the divine regulations regarding the diet, dress, language and customs of the saints of God. But those who become members of the family of God and citizens of the kingdom of God will give evidence of the relationship and demonstrate their sincerity by cheerfully conforming to all the restrictions and regulations and customs of the family and kingdom to which they belong.

Symbolic Garments

Moses was divinely instructed to make "holy garments" for Aaron and his sons who ministered in holy office.[1] These holy garments were to be sanctified with the priests who wore them. The penalty for rendering these sacred garments was death.[2]

These priestly garments were not only symbolic of the sacred office, but also represented the righteousness of Christ, the High Priest of the heavenly sanctuary. These sacred garments were to be made "for glory and beauty." This was not only because

1. Exodus 28:1,2; Leviticus 8:30.
2. Leviticus 10:6; 21:10.

they represented the beautiful robe of Christ's righteousness and were thus the symbol of His character, but also as an example to all Israel to teach them to avoid carelessness in dress and to clothe themselves in a neat and becoming manner.

Divine Comment

{In the Testimonies, Ellen White writes:}

> The idolatry of dress is a moral disease. It must not be taken over into the new life. In most cases, submission to the gospel requirements will demand a decided change in dress. There should be no carelessness in dress. For Christ's sake, whose witnesses we are, we should seek to make the best of our appearance. In the tabernacle service, God specified every detail concerning the garments of those who ministered before him. Thus we are taught that he has a preference in regard to the dress of those who serve Him. Very specific were the directions given in regard to Aaron's robes for his dress was symbolic. In all things we are to be representatives of Him. Our appearance in every respect should be characterized by neatness, modesty, and purity....The words of Scripture in regard to dress should be carefully considered. We need to understand that which the Lord of heaven appreciates in even the dressing of the body. All who are in earnest in seeking for the grace of Christ will heed the precious words of instruction inspired by God. Even the style of the apparel will express the truth the truth of the gospel.[3]

Sign of Character

But the Lord did not confine His dress regulations to the priests. He gave instructions that regulated the dress of every member of the movement. Their dress must distinguish them from the world and be an outward sign that they were children of God.[4]

After quoting this text the prophet of the Advent Movement wrote:

> Here God expressly commanded a very simple arrangement of dress for the children of Israel for the purpose of distinguishing them from the idolatrous nations around them. As they looked upon their peculiarity of dress, they were to remember that they were God's commandment keeping people, and that He had wrought in a miraculous manner to bring them from Egyptian bondage to serve Him, to be a holy people unto Him...An Israelite was known to be such as soon as seen, for God through simple means distinguished him as His.[5]

---

3. Ellen White, *Testimonies for the Church*, vol. 6 (1901), p. 96.
4. Numbers 15:37-41.
5. Ellen White, *Testimonies for the Church*, vol. 1 (1868), p. 524.

Dress Restrictions

Deuteronomy 22:5,11: "The woman shall not wear that which pertaineth unto a man, neither shall a man put on a woman's garment: for all that do so are abomination unto the LORD thy God. Thou shalt not wear a garment of divers sorts, as of woollen and linen together."

It is very evident that the Lord intended that His people should be distinguished from the world by their clothing. Women should not appear manish in their wearing apparel or men effeminate. This distinction should especially be seen in the hairdress.[6] The modern custom among women of bobbing their hair is dangerously near the border-line of disobedience to God's instructions regarding a clear distinction between the appearance of men and women. The boyish or manish bob is clearly a divinely forbidden custom. Many other customs in modern dress are breaking down the distinguishing marks identifying the opposite sexes and are thus contributing to the modern laxity in moral standards.

Ornaments Forbidden

Exodus 33:5, 6: "For the LORD had said unto Moses, Say unto the children of Israel, Ye are a stiffnecked people: I will come up into the midst of thee in a moment, and consume thee: therefore now put off thy ornaments from thee, that I may know what to do unto thee. And the children of Israel stripped themselves of their ornaments by the mount Horeb."

These ornaments were solicited from the Egyptians to finance the movement and not to wear.[7] Their decking themselves with jewelry was the sign of their apostasy. The golden calf was made from jewelry and in worshiping it they worshiped their heathen ornaments which in their originals were pagan gods, images of the sun, moon and stars. The holy women among the Israelites did not adorn themselves with these Egyptian ornaments.[8]

The Lord faithfully chronicles events and customs regardless of whether they are right or wrong. It is just as unreasonable to use the example of persons mentioned in the Bible as an excuse for wearing rings, including wedding rings, as it is for the Mormons to get their belief in polygamy from the example of Abraham, Jacob, David and Solomon.

Rings and bracelets were originally images of the sun, moon and stars, which were worshiped as pagan gods, and the making and wearing of them violated the second commandment.

---

6. 1 Corinthians 11:14, 15.
7. Exodus 12:35, 36.
8. 1 Peter 3:3-5.

Belong to Babylon

Isaiah 47:1-3: "Come down, and sit in the dust, O virgin daughter of Babylon, sit on the ground: there is no throne, O daughter of the Chaldeans: for thou shalt no more be called tender and delicate. Take the millstones, and grind meal: uncover thy locks, make bare the leg, uncover the thigh, pass over the rivers. Thy nakedness shall be uncovered, yea, thy shame shall be seen: I will take vengeance, and I will not meet thee as a man."

{If we look at other translations:}

> Remove the veil. — R.V.
> Bare the shoulder. — Doray.
> Shave your tresses and strip off your robe. Bare your legs; strip yourselves bare, exposing your shame. — Fenton.

Here is a picture of the nudist tendency in modern Babylon. How sad that these immodest heathen customs are imitated by many of the daughters of Zion.[9] The distinction that should exist between Christians and the worldlings in their outward appearance is illustrated by the attire and appearance of the two symbolic women of Revelation 12, and 17. The first represents the bride or church of Christ, and the second the bride or church of Satan. In Jeremiah 4:30 the "daughter of Babylon" is described as clothed "with crimson", and decked "with ornaments of gold", and her face rent "with painting." The bride of Christ is simply, becomingly and modestly attired with no artificial make-up or loud colors or gilded ornaments.

Gospel Standard

1 Timothy 2:8-10: "I will therefore that men pray every where, lifting up holy hands, without wrath and doubting. In like manner also, that women adorn themselves in modest apparel, with shamefacedness and sobriety; not with broided hair, or gold, or pearls, or costly array; But (which becometh women professing godliness) with good works."

{In Weymouth's translations it says:}

> I would have the women dress becomingly, with modesty and self-control, not with plaited hair or gold or pearls or costly clothes, but - as befits women making a claim to godliness - with the ornaments of good works.[10]

A converted person will show the evidence of his godly character in his outward appearance.

9. Isaiah 3:16-25.
10. 1 Timothy 2:8-10 Weymouth's Translation.

{Ellen White writes:}

> Cleanse the fountain, and the streams will be pure. If the heart is right, your words, your dress, your acts, will all be right.[11]

The dress that symbolizes the character of righteousness of Christ will be becoming and attractive.

> We are not to feel it our duty to wear a pilgrim"s dress of just such a color, just such a shape, but neat, modest apparel, that the Word of inspiration teaches us we should wear. If our hearts are united with Christ's heart, we shall have a most intense desire to be clothed with His righteousness. Nothing will be put upon the person to attract attention, or to create controversy.[12]

These statements are reasonable and lay down fundamental principles.

Vitally Important

{If we look at several Spirit of Prophecy we see:}

> Satan invented the fashions.[13]

> Obedience to fashion is pervading our Seventh-day Adventist churches, and is doing more than any other power to separate our people from God. I have been shown that our church rules are very deficient. All exhibitions of pride in dress, which is forbidden in the word of God, should be sufficient reason for church discipline. If there is a continuance, in the face of warnings and appeals and entreaties, to still follow the perverse will, it may be regarded as proof that the heart is in no way assimilated to Christ. Self, and only self, is the object of adoration and one such professed Christian will lead many away from God. There is a terrible sin upon us as a people, that we have permitted our church members to dress in a manner inconsistent with their faith. We must arise at once, and close the door against the allurements of fashion. Unless we do this, our churches will become demoralized.[14]

Methodist Church

In 1913 Bishop Foster of the Methodist church said:

---

11. Ellen White, *Testimonies for the Church*, vol. 1 (1868), p. 158.
12. Ellen White, *Testimonies to Ministers and Gospel Workers* (1923), p. 130, 131.
13. Ellen White, *Testimonies for the Church*, vol. 4 (1881), p. 629.
14. *Ibid.*, p. 547, 648.

> The church of God is today courting the world. Its members are trying to bring it down to the level of the ungodly...Do not Methodists, in violation of God's word and their own discipline, dress as extravagantly and fashionably as any other class? Do not the ladies and often the wives and daughters of the ministry, put on gold and pearls and costly array? Would not the plain dress insisted upon by John Wesley, Bishop Asbury, and worn by Hester Ann Rogers, Lady Huntington and others equally distinguished, be now regarded in Methodist circles as fanaticism? can any one on going into a Methodist church in any of our chief cities distinguish the attire of the communicants from that of the theater and ball-goer?. ... How true that the Methodist discipline is a dead letter. ... Its rules forbid the wearing of gold or pearls or costly array. Yet no one ever thinks of disciplining its members for violating them. They forbid the reading of such books and the taking of such diversions as do not minister to godliness, yet the church itself goes to shows and frolics and festivals and fairs, which destroy the spiritual life of the young as well as the old. The extent to which this is now carried on is appalling. The spiritual death it carries in its train will only be known when the millions it has swept into hell stand before the judgment.[15]

God's Remnant People

The people of the Advent Movement who go through to the kingdom will be clothed with the beautiful garments of Christ's righteousness, the wedding robe that prepares them for the coming Bridegroom and "the marriage of the Lamb."[16] In Isaiah 52:1 this character-robe is called "beautiful garments", and in Ephesians 5:25-27 it is said to be without "spot, or wrinkle, or any such thing"; but it is "holy and without blemish." The dress and appearance of the Advent people will be an index to a character like that of their expected Lord.

> God will have a people separate and distinct from the world. And as soon as any have a desire to imitate the fashions of the world, that they do not immediately subdue, just so soon God ceases to acknowledge them as His Children. They are the children of the world and of darkness.[17]

The Royal Robe

{Ellen White writes:}

> In dress, as in all things else, it is our privilege to honor our Creator. He desires our clothing to be not only neat and healthful, but appropri-

15. Quoted from the *Review and Herald*, October 2, 1913.
16. Revelation 19:7, 8.
17. Ellen White, *Testimonies for the Church*, vol. 1 (1868), p. 137.

ate and becoming. A person's character is judged by his style of dress. A refined taste, a cultivated mind, will be revealed in the choice of simple and appropriate attire. Chaste simplicity in dress, when united with modest demeanor, will go far toward surrounding a young woman with that atmosphere of sacred reserve which will be her shield from a thousand perils....It is right to love beauty and to desire it; but God desires us to love and to seek first the highest beauty, —that which is imperishable. ... Let the youth and the little children be taught to choose for themselves that royal robe woven in heaven's loom, —the fine linen, clean and white, which all the holy ones of earth will wear.

This robe, Christ's own spotless character, is freely offered to every human being. But all who receive it will receive and wear it here...This apparel will make them beautiful and beloved here, and will hereafter be their title of admission to the palace of the King.[18]

18. Ellen White, *Education* (1903), p. 248, 249.

12

THE SIN OF FALSE WITNESSING

Sermon Text:

Exodus 20:16: "Thou shalt not bear false witness against thy neighbour."

The decalogue contains ten commands which are the ten fundamental principles embracing "the whole duty of man." On these ten precepts "hang all the law and the prophets." The Law is an abridged edition of the Bible, and the Bible is an unabridged edition of the Law. The Scriptures are an unfolding of the principles enunciated in the Ten Commandments. Therefore the Decalogue is the standard of right conduct and will be the rule of judgment.[1] Our words and actions must be in harmony with the law because we will be judged by the law. The ninth commandment is the only one of the ten that deals directly with our words.

Death Penalty

The transgression of any of the commands of God's law is divinely designated as "sin" and "the wages of sin is death." "The soul that sinneth it shall die" is heaven's decree. The penalty for sin is not the ordinary death; it is eternal death. The penalty therefore for bearing false witness against another is eternal death. The seriousness of a crime is measured or determined by the severity of the penalty. The death sentence always indicates a terrible crime. Bearing false witness must be a terrible thing from heaven's viewpoint. In human law, false witnessing is a crime known as "perjury" and carries with it a heavy penalty.

"Love" is declared to be "the fulfilling of the law", and the measure of love is contained in the statement: "Thou shalt love they neighbor as thyself." The person who reaches this standard will not bear false witness against another because he would not bear false witness against himself. He treats his neighbor as he treats himself and as he would like to have his neighbor treat him. He obeys the Golden Rule. This is the standard demanded by the law.[2]

1. Ecclesiastes 12:13, 14; James 2:8-12.
2. Matthew 7:12.

False Report

Exodus 23:12: "Six days thou shalt do thy work, and on the seventh day thou shalt rest: that thine ox and thine ass may rest, and the son of thy handmaid, and the stranger, may be refreshed."

{If we look at several translations we see:}

> Receive — Margin.
> Take up — R.V.
> You must never repeat a baseless rumor — Moffatt.

This command is a further explanation of the ninth commandment of the Decalogue. It forbids originating a false report, or repeating one that is brought to us, or even receiving or believing it. This would be "talebearing" which is expressly forbidden in Leviticus 19:16. "You shall not go up and down slandering people."[3] A "tale-bearer" is defined as "a meddling informer; mischief-maker; scandalmonger." He is a news-carrier who delights to pass on information of the rumor-variety without any inquiry as to whether or not it is true. Tale-bearers find but little satisfaction in repeating rumors that reflect another's honor or brings him credit. Their specialty is rumors of the scandalous and slandering variety.

The Severe Penalty

Deuteronomy 19:15-21: "One witness shall not rise up against a man for any iniquity, or for any sin, in any sin that he sinneth: at the mouth of two witnesses, or at the mouth of three witnesses, shall the matter be established. If a false witness rise up against any man to testify against him that which is wrong; Then both the men, between whom the controversy is, shall stand before the LORD, before the priests and the judges, which shall be in those days; And the judges shall make diligent inquisition: and, behold, if the witness be a false witness, and hath testified falsely against his brother; Then shall ye do unto him, as he had thought to have done unto his brother: so shalt thou put the evil away from among you. And those which remain shall hear, and fear, and shall henceforth commit no more any such evil among you. And thine eye shall not pity; but life shall go for life, eye for eye, tooth for tooth, hand for hand, foot for foot."

This is a divine rule given to guide the Hebrew judges in dealing with falsewitnessing and false-witnesses. It is another application of the Golden Rule. It will be done unto us as we do unto others. What we mete out to others will be meted out to us; as we judge we will be judged.

False witnesses were to be given the same penalty as would have been visited upon

3. Moffatt.

the accused if the accusation had been true. If the penalty was death, the false witness must suffer death. The purpose of this severe penalty was to stamp out this terrible evil from among God's people. It was to cause people to think before they speak. If this penalty against falsewitnesses could be visited upon transgressors today what a change it would soon bring about.

Diligent Inquisition

Before a person has a right to sit in judgment upon another because of a report or rumor, he must make "diligent inquisition" as to whether or not the report is true. Its truthfulness must be established by more than one witness. There must be at least two witnesses to corroborate the report before we have a right to form our own opinion or render a decision if that is our prerogative. No person ever has a right to pass on or report a rumor about another until he has run down the matter and found out by diligent inquiry that it is true and then he must report only to the proper persons who will be able to correct the wrong. In this matter we all stand guilty before God. But genuine Christianity demands that victory be gained over this grievous sin.

Duty to Report

But while there is a terrible penalty against bearing false witness, we cannot altogether ignore reports and rumors which reflect on the character of our neighbor or brother and bring reproach upon God's work. If the report is untrue we have a duty to help stop the circulation of the report. We will do this if we love the neighbor as we love ourselves.

If the report is true we have an obligation to help the neighbor or brother correct the wrong and if it is not done the matter must reported to the proper persons. It is a sin to overlook and wink at wrongs which should be known and corrected by the proper authorities. The standard must not be lowered. The person who knows that another is a criminal and does not report it becomes a partaker in the crime. This is true also regarding sins. Leviticus 5:1. We must not be guilty of helping a sinner to keep his sins covered.

Universal Sin

The sin of false witnessing has not been confined to any specific age or generation. It is the universal sin of all ages.[4] Five of the seven sins that God especially abominates are different forms of false witnessing.[5] Because this sentence is not executed as soon as the sin is committed has made tale-bearers bold in their character-assassinating work.[6] The sentence for talebearing is again stated in Proverbs 21:28. Complete victory over this sin is one of the qualifications for entrance into the heavenly

4. Proverbs 6:16-19.
5. Proverbs 19:5.
6. Ecclesiastes 8:11.

Canaan.[7] It was necessary in the apostolic church to warn against this terrible evil.[8] False witnessing is an evidence of idleness; that the persons do not have enough to do to keep themselves busy so they seek to attend of other people's business.

The Advent Movement.

Zephaniah 3:8, 9, 13, 20: "Therefore wait ye upon me, saith the LORD, until the day that I rise up to the prey: for my determination is to gather the nations, that I may assemble the kingdoms, to pour upon them mine indignation, even all my fierce anger: for all the earth shall be devoured with the fire of my jealousy. For then will I turn to the people a pure language, that they may all call upon the name of the LORD, to serve him with one consent.

"The remnant of Israel shall not do iniquity, nor speak lies; neither shall a deceitful tongue be found in their mouth: for they shall feed and lie down, and none shall make them afraid.

"At that time will I bring you again, even in the time that I gather you: for I will make you a name and a praise among all people of the earth, when I turn back your captivity before your eyes, saith the LORD."

{If we take a look at other translations:}

> A pure lip. — Margin.
> A clean speech. — Moffatt.
> Telling no lies, uttering no fraud. — Moffatt.

The application of these texts to God's remnant people cannot be questioned. Those who receive the latter rain and have part in the final gathering under the loud cry will have a pure language and a clean speech. Their language will be free from slang and the "foolish talking" and unclean and filthy jesting mentioned in Ephesians 5:3-5, as being unbecoming to saints. The victory of the remnant will be so complete that they will not "do iniquity, nor speak lies; neither shall a deceitful tongue be found in their mouth." There will be no false witnesses among them; no talebearers or gossipers. The perfect control of speech will be the evidence of their perfection of character.[9]

No Guile

Revelation 14:5: "And in their mouth was found no guile: for they are without fault before the throne of God."

Guile means the same as "deceit." The remnant will be like Jesus in this respect.

---

7. Psalm 15:1-3. Margin.
8. 2 Thessalonians 3:11, 12; 1 Timothy 5:13.
9. James 3:2.

"Neither was any deceit found in His mouth."[10] Guile also has the meaning of "ferment" or "fermentation" because that which produces fermentation is called "guile." A tongue filled with guile or deceit causes fermentation in the church. It spoils the sweet spirit that prevailed and produces bitterness. It causes fermentation. Here too, complete victory over lying and false witnessing is the evidence of their perfection.

{Looking at several translations of this verse in Revelation 14 we see:}

> And no lie has ever been found upon their lips; they are faultless. — Weymouth's.
>
> In their mouth no falsehood was found; they are spotless. — Fenton.
>
> And on their lips no lie was ever detected; they are stainless. — Moffatt.

Three times the Revelator declares that no liars will enter into the celestial city or the kingdom of glory.

Unruly Tongues

{Ellen White writes:}

> It pains me to say that there are unruly tongues among church members. There are false tongues that feed on mischief. There are sly, whispering tongues. There are tattling, impertinent meddling, adroit quizzing. Among the lovers of gossip some are actuated by curiosity, others by jealousy, many by hatred against those through whom God has spoken to reprove them. All these discordant elements are at work. Some conceal their real sentiments, while others are eager to publish all they know, or even suspect, of evil against another.[11]

We are told that these gossipers make trifling and unpremeditated remarks that are "unworthy of notice" and view the faults of others "through Satan's magnifying glass" and ponder and repeat them "until molehills becomes mountains."[12]—Ibid., p. 95.

Terrible Indictment

{In *Testimonies to Ministers* we read the following:}

> Wrong prevails, man is made an offender for a word, and suspicion, distrust, jealousy, evil-surmising, evil speaking, and injustice reproduce themselves even in connection with the cause of God....The persecution

---

10. Isaiah 53:9.
11. Ellen White, *Testimonies for the Church*, vol. 5 (1889), p. 94.
12. *Ibid.*, p. 95.

that is carried on among churchmembers is a most terrible thing. It is true that some have committed errors, and made mistakes, but it is equally true that these errors and mistakes are not nearly as grievous in the sight of God as is the harsh and unforgiving spirit of those who are criticizers and censors. Many of these who are free to pass judgment on others, are committing errors which, although not made manifest, are tainted with deadly evil that is corrupting their spiritual life. ... Many are making manifest that they are not controlled by the Spirit of Christ, but by another spirit. The attributes they display are as unlike the attributes of Christ as are the characteristics of Satan.[13]

Called Traitors

{Ellen White writes:}

If Satan can employ professed believers to act as accusers of the brethren, he is justly pleased; for those who do this are just as truly serving him as was Judas when he betrayed Christ, although they may be doing it ignorantly. Satan is no less active now than in Christ's day, and those who lend themselves to do his work will be manifest in spirit. Floating rumors are often the destroyers of unity among brethren. There are some who watch with open mind and ears to catch flying scandal. They gather up little incidents which may be trifling in themselves, but which are repeated and exaggerated until a man is made an offender for a word.[14]

Cannibalism

{Spirit of Prophecy tells us:}

We think with horror of the cannibal who feasts on the still warm and trembling flesh of his victim; but are the results of even this practice more terrible than are the agony and ruin caused by misrepresenting motive, blackening reputation, dissecting character?[15]

How many families season their daily meals with doubt and questionings. They dissect the characters of their friends, and serve them up as a dainty dessert. A precious bit of slander is passed around the board to be commented upon, not only by adults, but by the children. ... The names of God's chosen servants have been handled with disrespect, and in some cases with absolute contempt, by certain persons whose duty it is to uphold them.[16]

---

13. Ellen White, *Testimonies to Ministers and Gospel Workers* (1923), p. 186.
14. *Ibid.*, p. 504, 505.
15. Ellen White, *Education* (1903), p. 235.
16. Ellen White, *Testimonies for the Church*, vol. 4 (1881), p. 195.

No wonder it is impossible for ministers and other church workers to help the children in some homes. Their confidence in church leaders has been destroyed by gossip.

Refuse to Hear

{Ellen White writes:}

> Speak evil of no man. Hear evil of no man. If there be no hearers, there will be no speakers of evil. If anyone speaks evil in your presence, check him. Refuse to hear him though his manner be ever so soft, and his accents mild. He many profess attachment, and yet throw out covert hints and stab the character in the dark. Resolutely refuse to hear, though the whisperer complains of being burdened till he speak. Burdened indeed with a cursed secret which separateth very friends. Go, burdened one, and free yourselves from your burden in God's appointed way. First go tell your brother his fault between you and him alone.[17]

> Gossipers and news-carriers are a terrible curse to neighborhoods and churches.[18]—Ibid., p.466.

How quickly this method would close the mouths of gossipers and tale-bearers. Another good plan is to ask them to write it down and sign their names to it. Still another is to insist that the person involved be call in to hear the story.

Complete Victory

Those who receive the latter rain and are translated will be complete victors over this terrible evil. Dan was a back-biter and no Danites will enter the kingdom of heaven. "He that will love life, and see good days, let him refrain his tongue from evil, and his lips that they speak no guile. Let him eschew evil and do good; let him seek peace and ensue it. For the eyes of the Lord are over the righteous, and His ears are open unto their prayers."[19]

---

17. Ellen White, *Testimonies for the Church*, vol. 2 (1871), p. 54.
18. *Ibid.*, p. 446.
19. Psalm 34:12-15.

13

MARRIAGE AND DIVORCE

Marriage to Unbelievers

Deuteronomy 7:2-6: "And when the LORD thy God shall deliver them before thee; thou shalt smite them, and utterly destroy them; thou shalt make no covenant with them, nor show mercy unto them: Neither shalt thou make marriages with them; thy daughter thou shalt not give unto his son, nor his daughter shalt thou take unto thy son. For they will turn away thy son from following me, that they may serve other gods: so will the anger of the LORD be kindled against you, and destroy thee suddenly. But thus shall ye deal with them; ye shall destroy their altars, and break down their images, and cut down their groves, and burn their graven images with fire. For thou art an holy people unto the LORD thy God: the LORD thy God hath chosen thee to be a special people unto himself, above all people that are upon the face of the earth."

The book of Deuteronomy is a series of addresses given by Moses on the banks of the Jordan just before his death and just before Israel entered the promised land. He gives two reasons why Israelites should not intermarry with unbelieving nations. First such marriages would turn them away from following the true God, and second, they would soon cease to be a distinct and holy people. So great was this danger that Joshua gave the same warning in his farewell sermon just before his death.[1] Joshua declared that the results of such marriages would be fatal to their prosperity and spirituality and even their national existence.

The Reformation

The future history of Israel showed the need of these warnings although they were forgotten, especially during the Babylonian captivity. On the return to the promised land, Ezra carried on a reformation in which he demanded obedience to God's instruction through Moses and Joshua.[2] This shows how terrible the sin of mixed marriages is in the sight of God. The people responded to the call for a reformation and the camp was cleansed of an evil that was bringing upon them "the fierce wrath

1. Joshua 23:1-13.
2. Ezra 9:1-6, 10-12, 15.

of God."[3] But only 12 years later the reformation had to be resumed by Nehemiah who used severe measures to convince the Israelites of the terrible nature of sin of intermarriage.[4] This was a part of the reformation which included proper Sabbath observance and faithfulness in tithe paying.[5]

Still Dangerous

The passing of time has not lessened the danger of God's people intermarrying with unbelievers.[6] Our very message is to announce that "Babylon is fallen, is fallen. ... Come out of her my people."[7] And yet in the face of all the warnings of Scripture and the sad lesson of the past, thousands of modern Israelites are going into modern Babylon to find their life companions.

This is a very serious step and one of three things must eventually happen. Either the Christian will give up his or her faith and go with the unconverted companion into the world and be lost, or the worldly companion will become a Christian, or there must eventually be a sad separation. In only a small percent of such unions is the unconverted and worldly companion won to the church. Two persons cannot be happy unless they are agreed and can walk together. It is essential to a happy home that the husband and wife be mated physically, intellectually, morally and spiritually, and of the four, spiritual agreement is the most important.

Sign of the End

Genesis 6:2, 5: "That the sons of God saw the daughters of men that they were fair; and they took them wives of all which they chose. And God saw that the wickedness of man was great in the earth, and that every imagination of the thoughts of his heart was only evil continually."

Matthew 24:37-39: "But as the days of Noe were, so shall also the coming of the Son of man be. For as in the days that were before the flood they were eating and drinking, marrying and giving in marriage, until the day that Noe entered into the ark, And knew not until the flood came, and took them all away; so shall also the coming of the Son of man be."

{Ellen White writes:}

> We are living in the last days when the mania upon the subject of marriage constitutes one of the signs of the near coming of Christ. God is not

3. Ezra 10:1-14.
4. Nehemiah 13:23-27.
5. Nehemiah 13:10-22.
6. 2 Corinthians 6:14-18.
7. Revelation 18:1-4.

> consulted in these matters....There is not one marriage in one hundred that results happily, that bears the sanction of God, and places the parties in a position better to glorify Him. The evil consequences of poor marriages are numberless. They are contracted from impulse. A candid review of the matter is scarcely thought of and consultation with those of experience is considered old-fashioned. Impulse and unsanctified passion exist in the place of pure love. Many imperil their own souls, and bring the curse of God upon them, by entering into the marriage relation merely to please the fancy.[8]

Marriage is often considered a joke and not half the study and thought given it as to a business partnership or even a business contract.

Worldly Alliances

{In *Testimonies for the Church* we read again:}

> It is a dangerous thing to form a worldly alliance. Satan well knows that the hour that witnesses the marriage of many young men and women closes the history of their religious experience and usefulness. They are lost to Christ. They may for a time make an effort to live a Christian life; but all their strivings are made against a steady influence in the opposite direction. Once is was a privilege and a joy to speak of their faith and hope; but they become unwilling to mention the subject, knowing that the one with whom they have linked their destiny takes no interest in it. As the result, faith in the precious truth dies out of the heart, and Satan insidiously weaves about them a web of skepticism. ... Those who profess the truth trample on the will of God in marrying unbelievers; they lose His favor, and make bitter work for repentance.[9]

If those contemplating such a step could only hear some of the heart-breaking confessions that are being made to church leaders, it would warn them of the fearful consequences of going contrary to God's instruction.

Forfeit Protection

> Though the companion of your choice was in all other respects worthy, yet he has not accepted the truth for this time; he is an unbeliever, and you are forbidden of heaven to unite yourself with him. You cannot without peril to your soul, disregard the divine injunction. ... You cannot see behind the scenes, and discern the snares that Satan is laying for your soul. ... To connect with an unbeliever is to place yourself on Satan's

8. Ellen White, *Testimonies for the Church*, vol. 4 (1881), p. 503-504.
9. *Ibid.*, p. 504. 505.

> ground. You grieve the Spirit of God and forfeit His protection. Can you afford to have such terrible odds against you in fighting the battle for everlasting life? You may say, "but I have given my promise, and shall I now retract it?" I answer, if you have made a promise contrary to the Scriptures, by all means retract it without delay, and in humility before God repent of the infatuation that led you to make so rash a pledge. Far better to take back such a promise, in the fear of God, than keep it, and thereby dishonor your Maker.[10]

High Moral Standard

Deuteronomy 23:14, 17; 22:20, 21: "For the LORD thy God walketh in the midst of thy camp, to deliver thee, and to give up thine enemies before thee; therefore shall thy camp be holy: that he see no unclean thing in thee, and turn away from thee. ... There shall be no whore of the daughters of Israel, nor a sodomite of the sons of Israel.

"But if this thing be true, [and the tokens of] virginity be not found for the damsel: Then they shall bring out the damsel to the door of her father's house, and the men of her city shall stone her with stones that she die: because she hath wrought folly in Israel, to play the whore in her father's house: so shalt thou put evil away from among you."

Under the Exodus movement unfaithfulness to the marriage vow was especially severely dealt with.[11] Has God changed or lowered His standard in this matter?[12] If the Lord pronounced the sentence of death upon those guilty of adultery, surely the church can do nothing less than disfellowship them. This is absolutely necessary to the preservation of the purity of the church. This is the standard under the Advent Movement and it should be maintained without fear or favor.

> Cleanse the camp of this moral corruption, if it takes the highest men in the highest positions. God will not be trifled with. Fornication is in our ranks, I know it, for it has been shown me to be strengthening and extending its pollutions. ... Cleanse the camp, for there is an accursed thing in it.[13]

> The time has come for earnest and powerful efforts to rid the church of the slime and filth which is tarnishing her purity.[14]

On page 434 we are told that any woman who permits undue attention and famil-

10. Ellen White, *Testimonies for the Church*, vol. 5 (1889), p. 364, 365.
11. Deuteronomy 22:22.
12. Ecclesiastes 8:11.
13. Ellen White, *Testimonies to Ministers and Gospel Workers* (1923), p. 427, 428.
14. *Ibid.*, p. 450.

iarities from any man other than her husband "is an adulteress and harlot."

Divorce Permitted

Divorce was not only divinely permitted in the Exodus Movement but is absolutely necessary to the protection of the marriage institution. Only one ground for divorce, however, was recognized.

Deuteronomy 24:1-4: "When a man hath taken a wife, and married her, and it come to pass that she find no favour in his eyes, because he hath found some uncleanness in her: then let him write her a bill of divorcement, and give it in her hand, and send her out of his house. And when she is departed out of his house, she may go and be another man's wife. And if the latter husband hate her, and write her a bill of divorcement, and giveth it in her hand, and sendeth her out of his house; or if the latter husband die, which took her to be his wife; Her former husband, which sent her away, may not take her again to be his wife, after that she is defiled; for that is abomination before the LORD: and thou shalt not cause the land to sin, which the LORD thy God giveth thee for an inheritance."

{In Moffatt translation is says:}

> If she goes and marries another man.[15]

There is no divine permission for her to remarry, because she is the guilty party, but if she does remarry and then gets a divorce, the first husband has no right to remarry her.

{Fenton translation says:}

> She shall not be allowed to return to the first who divorced her, to be married as his wife, after she has sinned, for that would be loathsome in the presence of the Ever-Living.[16]

This is equivalent to saying that no person has the right to marry the guilty party who also has no right to remarry. It also indicates that it is a sin to continue living with a husband or wife who is guilty of adultery, unless, of course, there is a thorough repentance and reformation.

New Testament

The New Testament maintains exactly the same standards, for the Scriptures constitute one Book with one standard. The entire Bible came from the same source and

15. Deuteronomy 24:1-4 Moffatt.
16. *Ibid.*, Fenton.

cannot contradict itself. Jesus did not lift the standard any higher. He only "magnified" the law and the Old Testament Scriptures so that we can grasp their true spiritual significance.

This is illustrated in Matthew 5:21, 22, 27, 28, 31, 32: "Ye have heard that it was said by them of old time, Thou shalt not kill; and whosoever shall kill shall be in danger of the judgment: But I say unto you, That whosoever is angry with his brother without a cause shall be in danger of the judgment: and whosoever shall say to his brother, Raca, shall be in danger of the council: but whosoever shall say, Thou fool, shall be in danger of hell fire. ... Ye have heard that it was said by them of old time, Thou shalt not commit adultery: But I say unto you, That whosoever looketh on a woman to lust after her hath committed adultery with her already in his heart. ... It hath been said, Whosoever shall put away his wife, let him give her a writing of divorcement: But I say unto you, That whosoever shall put away his wife, saving for the cause of fornication, causeth her to commit adultery: and whosoever shall marry her that is divorced committeth adultery."

Jesus does not raise the standard of the writings of Moses; he only explains their real meaning and significance. It was Christ who gave the instruction through Moses and He is only explaining His own Word. It is not true that Moses permitted divorce on unscriptural grounds, and it is also not true that Christ did not permit divorce on any grounds. The standard is the same in both ancient and modern Israel in both the Old and New Testament.

The statement of Christ is repeated in Matthew 19:9: "And I say unto you, Whosoever shall put away his wife, except it be for fornication, and shall marry another, committeth adultery: and whoso marrieth her which is put away doth commit adultery." Divorce and remarriage are divine rights on the part of the innocent party only.

Marriage Tie Broken

Adultery by either husband or wife breaks the marriage tie as completely as if the marriage had never been consummated.[17] "Or do you not know that a man who has do with a prostitute is one with her in body? For God says, 'The two shall become one.'"[18] (Wey). This explains what Jesus meant when he said that when a man and woman are joined in marriage "the two shall become one flesh."

Therefore when either of them commit adultery; the marriage tie is broken and the guilty party becomes one flesh with another. This is one meaning of the statement, "what God has joined together let no man put asunder." Husbands and wives are commanded not to permit another man or woman to come between them and put them asunder by breaking the marriage tie.

---

17. 1 Corinthians 6:15-18.
18. *Ibid.*, Weymouth's.

Innocent Party

If the innocent party continues to live with a companion who is living in adultery and who has thus become one flesh with another, he or she also becomes guilty of immorality. Of course if the guilty party truly repents and confesses the wrong and shows evidence of bringing forth fruit meet for repentance, the innocent party may exercise forgiveness and take the transgressor back. However, this decision can be made only by the one who has remained loyal to the marriage tie, and if there is evidence that the repentance is not genuine and that the sin will be repeated, he or she has the right before God to make the separation permanent and to obtain a divorce. There is no other way to protect the sacredness of the marriage institution.

The person who obtains a divorce on the only grounds recognized in the Scriptures, has just as much right to remarry as to marry in the first place and is undeserving of criticism when he or she chooses to exercise this right.

Advent Movement

This is the standard of the Advent Movement. See "Church Manual" on "Marriage and Divorce." With those who accept the truth and come out of the world, we believe that the Lord accepts them where he finds them and forgives the past in which are many things that cannot be undone. An attempt to fix up the past would in many instances do more harm than good by adding sin to sin. Whatever the past life has been, if there is evidence of genuine repentance and of a consistent Christian life we must conclude that God has forgiven and accepted those whom Christ is able and anxious to "save to the uttermost."

The genuine Christian in the church will never snub such or harass them with gossip but will treat them as they would be treated. Jesus declared that the publicans and harlots had a better chance of entering the kingdom than the hypocritical and self righteous Pharisees. There is nothing that more effectually disqualifies a person for the kingdom of heaven like the spirit of intolerance. The spirit of Christ and Christians is that of love, forbearance and forgiveness.

A Godly Example

The relation between Christ and His church, and Christ and His individual followers, is represented in the Scriptures by the marriage relation. We are united to Christ by the cords of love which produce loyalty. Sin cuts the tie that binds us to Christ and if persistently and continuously indulged in will eventually lead to a divorce or separation. Any kind of disloyalty or unfaithfulness to Christ including "the friendship of the world" is declared to be spiritual adultery.[19] Christ is not bound to continue in union with a harlot. The very thought is repulsive. Therefore, Christ Himself has set

19. James 4:4.

the example of divorce on the ground of adultery.[20] Nothing short of this high standard of purity and loyalty is in keeping with the character of Christ, who is "of purer eyes than to behold evil," and to "look on iniquity." The Lord intends that His people shall maintain the same high standards in purity and morality.

20. See Ezekiel 23:1-5; Isaiah 50:1; Jeremiah 3:8.

14

THE SPIRIT OF REVERANCE

Sermon Text:

Hebrews 12:28, 29: "Wherefore we receiving a kingdom which cannot be moved, let us have grace, whereby we may serve God acceptably with reverence and godly fear: For our God is a consuming fire."

"May offer service well-pleasing to God with reverence and awe."[1] Another well authenticated rendering is, "With godly caution and fear." The reason given for this kind of service and worship is because "our God is a consuming fire." Our text declares that the only service that is pleasing or acceptable to God is that which is inspired by awe and reverence and godly fear. Therefore He refuses to accept worship that is offered in irreverence and disrespect.

> The holiness and glory of God, the power and the curse of sin, our own utter weakness and the terrible danger of the multitudes around us, call every Christian to offer his service to God with godly fear and awe.[2] The Holiest of All, Andrew Murray.

Reverence Defined

"Fear mingled with respect and esteem; veneration, honor, adoration." "A feeling of profound respect, often mingled with awe and affection." As with love, reverence or respect is based on acquaintance and knowledge. A person who is not reverent in his attitude toward God and sacred things demonstrates his ignorance. He is not acquainted with God and therefore does not love and respect Him or His possessions. This is indicated in Proverbs 9:10: "The fear of the LORD is the beginning of wisdom: and the knowledge of the holy is understanding."

{The Moffatt translates this verse as:} "The first thing in knowledge is reverence for the Eternal; to know the Deity is what knowledge means."[3] The person who is not controlled by the spirit of true reverence does not know God, regardless of how or-

1. Hebrews 12:28 R.V.
2. Andrew Murray, *The Holiets of All.*
3. Proverbs 9:10 Moffatt.

thodox he is in belief and practice and how well acquainted he is with the Scriptures. Reverence is the test of a genuine Christian experience.

Fruit of Discipline.

Hebrews 12:5-11: "And ye have forgotten the exhortation which speaketh unto you as unto children, My son, despise not thou the chastening of the Lord, nor faint when thou art rebuked of him: For whom the Lord loveth he chasteneth, and scourgeth every son whom he receiveth. If ye endure chastening, God dealeth with you as with sons; for what son is he whom the father chasteneth not? But if ye be without chastisement, whereof all are partakers, then are ye bastards, and not sons.

"Furthermore we have had fathers of our flesh which corrected us, and we gave them reverence: shall we not much rather be in subjection unto the Father of spirits, and live? For they verily for a few days chastened us after their own pleasure; but he for our profit, that we might be partakers of his holiness. Now no chastening for the present seemeth to be joyous, but grievous: nevertheless afterward it yieldeth the peaceable fruit of righteousness unto them which are exercised thereby."

The only children who respect and reverence their parents are those who, like Jesus, "learned obedience by the things which He suffered." The parents who wisely enforce obedience on their children will receive loving and voluntary reverence in return. In the end we always respect those who have the highest standards and live up to them.

The breakdown of discipline in the home has caused a corresponding breakdown of discipline in the church. For this reason the modern generation has but little respect for their parents, and reverence for God and holy things has almost disappeared from the earth. The irreverent attitude of even professed Christians is appalling. They seem to think that God has changed and is less strict and particular than He used to be; therefore they presume on His mercy.

Exodus Movement

During the bondage in Egypt the children of Israel almost entirely lost their knowledge of God, and therefore their reverence for Him. Through precepts and judgments the Lord taught them reverence and godly fear. It was a hard lesson to learn to approach God and all the sacred things connected with His service in a spirit of holy awe and reverential fear. The first lesson had to be learned by Moses, the leader of the Exodus Movement, for his example would indicate the measure of reverence expected of the people.

Moses got a new vision of God and the reverence with which He should be approached and worshiped in the experience of the burning bush at Mount Horeb.[4] What suddenly made that ground holy? It had been trampled underfoot for genera-

4. Exodus 3:1-6.

tions by irreverent and godless heathen tribesmen. The presence of God makes any person or any thing holy. There is no other source of holiness. The Lord said to Israel: "Ye shall be holy: for I the Lord your God am holy."[5]

All Leaders

The Lord was very strict in His requirements for the leaders of the Exodus Movement respecting reverence, and very severe in dealing with their exhibitions of irreverence.[6] The reason for this terrible judgment against irreverence is given in verses 10,11. The Lord told the Israelites that the ark of the covenant was holy and that they must not touch it lest they die. Staves were placed in the sides of the ark to carry it by and then only by holy men. As clear as this instruction was it had to be enforced by two terrible judgments. (2 Sam. 6:2-7; 1 Samuel 6:19, 20). 50,070 were slain for looking in the ark.

All Israel

The greatest lesson on reverence for all Israel was given at Mount Sinai in connection with the giving of the law.[7] Our text declares that we should serve God with "with reverence and godly fear" because "our God is a consuming fire." This statement has direct reference to the giving of the law which was the greatest of all exhibitions of God's majesty and glory. True reverence leads us to approach God with clean bodies, clean clothes, and clean characters. Just as people who are unholy in character and filthy in their habits feel unclean in the presence of saints, so all physical, mental and moral uncleanness should make us feel uncomfortable when we come into the presence of God. Reverence demands cleanliness, both physical and spiritual.

The Sanctuary

Leviticus 19:30: "Ye shall keep my sabbaths, and reverence my sanctuary: I am the LORD."

This command is repeated for emphasis in Leviticus 26:2. Every part of the sanctuary was holy, even the court, the only part the congregation could enter. Only holy priests could enter the holy place but not until a special atonement was made for their sins and they were clothed in garments that were spotlessly clean.

The high priest only could enter the holy of holies and then only once a year after very careful preparation. His body and clothes must be scrupulously clean and his soul free from every stain of sin. The holiness of the place increases as we approach the presence of God. The temple of Solomon, which was built under divine direction, had many chambers of various degrees of holiness. One apartment was the most

---

5. Leviticus 19:2; Psalm 89:6, 7.
6. Leviticus 10:1-7.
7. Exodus 19:10-24; 24:17.

holy place because it represented the immediate presence of God.

Holy Men

Through precept and judgments the Lord also taught ancient Israel to respect and reverence the holy men who served in holy office, whether in the sanctuary or in positions of leadership in the movement. "Thou shalt not revile the judges, nor curse the ruler of they people."[8] When Paul quoted this text he said: Thou shalt not speak evil of the ruler of thy people." (Acts 23:5). To enforce this lesson the Lord visited terrible judgments upon Korah, Dathan, and Abiram, and their followers (Numbers 16).

Advent Movement

1 Corinthians 10:11: "Now all these things happened unto them for ensamples: and they are written for our admonition, upon whom the ends of the world are come."

Many have become bold in irreverence, because the Lord does not immediately execute His sentences against transgressors.[9] In His dealings with ancient Israel the Lord demonstrated what His attitude is toward every sin in every age, because His standards never change. The Lord and everything connected with His worship are just as holy and should be treated with as much reverence as in days of old. The passing millenniums have made no difference in the attitude of the angels as they enter into the presence of the Creator. They still tread softly and bow their knees and veil their faces as they enter His courts, crying "Holy, holy, holy."

A Prophecy

Ezekiel 22:26: "Her priests have violated my law, and have profaned mine holy things: they have put no difference between the holy and profane, neither have they showed difference between the unclean and the clean, and have hid their eyes from my sabbaths, and I am profaned among them."

{Or as it is put in several different translations:}

> Making no difference between the sacred and the secular — Moffatt.
>
> They do not distinguish between the consecrated and the common. — Fenton.

Many even in the Advent Movement seem to find it impossible to distinguish between the holy and the secular, the sacred and the common. They seem to have lost their spirituality to such an extent that they have lost all sense of reverence for holy things. Their sense of right and wrong seems to be so blunted and their vision so dimmed that they treat the holy and secular almost alike with no clear line of de-

8. Exodus 22:28.
9. Ecclesiastes 8:11.

marcation between them. Their great need is a spiritual revival and a genuine conversion, for only deeply spiritual people can be truly reverential and they only can distinguish between the holy and the profane.

Sacred Things

God's name is holy and should be spoken with the utmost respect and reverence. "Holy and reverend is His name".[10] God's Sabbath is holy and therefore should be treated differently than the common, secular days of the week.[11] The penalty for profaning the Sabbath is still death. Reverence for the Sabbath demands that it be used for a different purpose than ordinary days. A part of true Sabbath keeping is to meet with God's people in "holy convocation".[12] Those who do not attend divine worship on the Sabbath when it is possible to do so are showing disrespect for God and irreverence for His Sabbath. Some of the things that profane the Sabbath are enumerated in Isaiah 58:13. The tithe is also holy. It is God's money and not our own and is declared to be "holy unto the Lord".[13] It should never be put to a secular, common use.

Holy Services

Religious services are called "holy convocations" because they are gatherings of "holy people" who meet in a holy house to worship a holy God who is present by His Holy Spirit and holy angels. We come together to study God's holy Word from His holy Book. Therefore divine services are different from all other gatherings and the distinction should be clearly recognized and defined. They should be attended with feelings of reverence and godly fear.

When we enter the house of God to listen to His holy word, we should give careful heed to the instruction in Ecclesiastes 5:1, 2. God's house should be treated in a different manner than we treat an ordinary house, and His Book should never be handled as an ordinary, secular book. Even the song books containing the hymns used for praise and worship are sacred. Most of the songs are based on scriptural statements and were written by men and women more or less divinely inspired.

Spirit of Prophecy

{In the Spirit of Prophecy we read:}

> To the humble, believing soul, the house of God on earth is the gate of heaven. ... From the sacredness which was attached to the earthly sanctuary. Christians may learn how they should regard the place where the Lord meets with His people. There has been a great change, not for the

---

10. Psalm 111:9.
11. Exodus 31:14-17.
12. Leviticus 23:3.
13. Leviticus 27:30-32.

better, but for the worse, in the habits and customs of the people in reference to religious worship. The precious, sacred things which connect us with God, are fast losing hold upon our minds and hearts, and are being brought down to the level of common things. ... When the worshipers enter the place of meeting, they should do so with decorum, passing quietly to their seats. ... Common talking, whispering and laughing should not be permitted in the house of worship either before or after service. Ardent, active piety should characterize the worshipers. ... If when the people come into the house of worship, they have genuine reverence for the Lord, and bear in mind that they are in His presence, there will be a sweet eloquence in silence. The whispering and laughing and talking which might be without sin in a common business place, should find no sanction in the house where God is worshiped.[14]

Dignified Solemnity

{And again we read:}

All the service should be conducted with solemnity and awe; as if in the visible presence of the Master of assemblies. When the word is spoken, you should remember that you are listening to the voice of God through His delegated servant. Listen attentively. Sleep not for one instant, because by this slumber you may lose the very words that you need most....Sometimes a little child may so attract the attention of the hearers that the precious seed does not fall into good ground and bring forth fruit. Sometimes young men and women have so little reverence for the house of worship of God that they keep up a continual communication with each other during the sermon. Could these see the angels of God looking upon them, and marking their doings, they would be filled with shame, with abhorrence of themselves.[15]

Close of Service

{And in the same book we read the following quotes:}

When the benediction is pronounced, all should still be quiet, as if fearful of losing the peace of Christ. Let all pass out without jostling or loud talking, feeling that they are in the presence of God, that His eye is resting upon them, and they must act as in His visible presence. Let there be no stopping in the aisles to visit or gossip, thus blocking them up so that others cannot pass out. The precincts of the church should be invested with a sacred reverence. It should not be made a place to meet old friends and

14. Ellen White, *Testimonies for the Church*, vol. 5 (1889), p. 491, 492.
15. *Ibid.*, p. 493.

visit and introduce common thoughts and worldly business transactions. … God and angels have been dishonored by the careless, noisy laughing and shuffling of feet heard in some places.[16]

Reverence Almost Extinct

No wonder our churches are feeble and do not have that deep, earnest piety in their borders that they should have. Our present habits and customs, which dishonor God and bring the sacred and heavenly down to the level of the common are against us. We have a sacred, testing, sanctifying truth; and if our habits and practices are not in accordance with the truth, we are sinners against great light and are proportionately guilty. It will be far more tolerable for the heathen in the day of God's retributive justice than for us. … It is too true that reverence for the house of God has become almost extinct. Sacred things and places are not discerned; the holy and exalted are not appreciated. … We have reason even to be more thoughtful and reverential in our worship than had the Jews. But an enemy has been at work to destroy our faith in the sacredness of Christian worship.[17]

Discipline Needed

Nearly all need to be taught how to conduct themselves in the house of God. Parents should not only teach, but command their children to enter the sanctuary with sobriety and reverence. … This matter has been sadly neglected. Its importance has been overlooked and as the result, disorder and irreverence have become prevalent, and God has been dishonored…. In the minds of many, there are no more sacred thoughts connected with the house of God than with the most common place. Some will enter the place of worship with their hats on, in soiled, dirty clothes. Such do not realize that they are to meet with God and holy angels. There should be a radical change in this matter all through our churches. Ministers themselves need to elevate their ideas, to have finer susceptibilities in regard to it. It is a feature of the work that has been sadly neglected. Because of the irreverence in attitude, dress, and deportment, and lack of a worshipful frame of mind, God has often turned His face away from those assembled for His worship.[18]

---

16. Ellen White, *Testimonies for the Church*, vol. 5 (1889), p. 494.
17. *Ibid.*, p. 495, 496.
18. *Ibid.*, p. 496-499.

15

THE SACREDNESS OF VOWS

Sermon Text:

Psalm 76:11: "Vow, and pay unto the LORD your God: let all that be round about him bring presents unto him that ought to be feared."

> Come, vow and pay the Lord your God. … Bring gifts to honor Him —Fenton.[1]

> For thou hearest my vows, O God, thou grantest the desire of reverent men. And I will ever sing the praise, paying my vows through all my days — Moffatt.

A vow is a "pledge"; it is "a solemn promise especially to God; and engagement solemnly entered into, to adopt a certain course of life, pursue a definite end, observe some moral precept, or surrender oneself to a higher life of holiness." Such a vow is made by every person who becomes a Christian. When we take on the name of Christ we solemnly promise to be like Christ. When we experience the new birth we enter into a pledge to live the new life. It is our duty to make such vows and it is also our duty to sacredly keep them.

Exodus Movement

Deuteronomy 23:21-23: "When thou shalt vow a vow unto the LORD thy God, thou shalt not slack to pay it: for the LORD thy God will surely require it of thee; and it would be sin in thee. But if thou shalt forbear to vow, it shall be no sin in thee. That which is gone out of thy lips thou shalt keep and perform; even a freewill offering, according as thou hast vowed unto the LORD thy God, which thou hast promised with thy mouth."

Here we are told that it is a sin to make a vow unto the Lord and not pay it. This includes oral vows "promised with thy mouth." The Lord made every effort to teach the Israelites that their promises to both God and man should be sacredly kept. If men or women vowed to devote themselves to the service of the Lord, they were

---

1. (Psalm 61:5, 8).

obliged to adhere strictly to His service, according to the conditions of the vow. The same was true when they pledged their children to a sacred service as in the case of Hannah and Samuel.[2] Samuel was her only child and it was a great sacrifice to give him up to the service of the temple from his early boyhood days, but if she had failed, the nation would have been deprived of the service of one of the greatest prophets and judges who ever lived. Hannah fulfilled her vow.

Money Vows

Numbers 30:1, 2: "And Moses spake unto the heads of the tribes concerning the children of Israel, saying, This is the thing which the LORD hath commanded. If a man vow a vow unto the LORD, or swear an oath to bind his soul with a bond; he shall not break his word, he shall do according to all that proceedeth out of his mouth."

Then follows instruction that the money vows or pledges made by children are void unless ratified by express or tacit consent of their parents. If the father holds his peace when he hears the vow of his child, his silence confirms the pledge and it is binding. If he immediately disallows the pledge the vow is void and the Lord releases the son or daughter from paying it. The same is true regarding the vows of married women without the knowledge and consent of their husbands. When he learns of the vow of his wife he can confirm it by his silence or annul it by disallowing it. In the case of a disallowed pledge the promise is "And the Lord will forgive her," that is, releases her from the vow.

Sacred Obligation

The Scriptures make it plain that vows made to the Lord are sacred and therefore binding and payment should not be deferred or put off.[3] The vow should be performed while the sense of the obligation is still fresh and strong in our minds lest the lapse of time should lead us to repent of the promise or even deny that the pledge was made. The reason given why this should not be done is because the Lord has no pleasure in fools; that is "hypocritical and perfidious persons, who, when they are in distress, make liberal vows, and when the danger is past neglect and break them, and so discover the highest folly in thinking to mock and deceive the All-seeing and Almighty God."[4]

Vows of Loyalty

Most vows of loyalty are made when we are in serious trouble or are facing grave danger. For this reason there is a temptation to forget the vow as soon as the danger is over and the deliverance accomplished. But these vows are also binding and obligatory. "I will go into thy house with burnt offerings: I will pay thee my vows, which my

2. 1 Samuel 1:9-11, 22, 28.
3. Ecclesiastes 5:4-6.
4. Cruden.

lips have uttered, and my mouth has spoken, when I was in trouble."[5] When the men who manned the ship on which Jonah was fleeing from duty had cast him overboard, "then the men feared the Lord exceedingly and offered a sacrifice unto the Lord, and made vows."[6]

Whether the vows were kept or not we are not told. While Jonah was in the belly of the whale he remembered his broken pledges and unpaid vows and promised to pay them if God would deliver him.[7] God delivered him and Jonah kept his promise and through him the Lord saved a great and wicked city from destruction.

Avoid Rash Vows

Because even the vows made while we are in trouble are binding we should be very careful lest in a time of emotional excitement or sudden fear or passion we rash vows which may be difficult of virtually impossible of fulfillment. A vow should be made deliberately and calmly with the knowledge that we have the power to perform it. If the fulfillment of a financial vow is uncertain it is perfectly proper to make the pledge conditional upon the continuance of the present income, or upon the expectation of money to be received. It is not wrong to make vows, in fact it is our duty to make them. The admonition is to recognize their sacred and binding nature and be careful. Legitimate and rational vows made in the face of danger are often ignored after the danger is over.

Jacob's Vow

Genesis 28:20-22: "And Jacob vowed a vow, saying, If God will be with me, and will keep me in this way that I go, and will give me bread to eat, and raiment to put on, So that I come again to my father's house in peace; then shall the LORD be my God: And this stone, which I have set [for] a pillar, shall be God's house: and of all that thou shalt give me I will surely give the tenth unto thee."

Jacob was in serious trouble and only God could help him. He had deceived his father and virtually stolen his brother's birthright from whose wrath he was now fleeing. In his helplessness he cast himself on the Lord and the Lord had given him a remarkable dream revealing to him the plan of redemption in the image of a ladder. In recognition of God's ownership of all things, Jacob vowed that he would faithfully return to Him the tenth, the tithe. Jacob kept his promise and the Lord gave him what he asked for and more too. His character was transformed as the result of his experience with the angel at the brook; he was reconciled to his angry brother, and became the father of the twelve tribes of Israel. The promise to Jacob included the new earth.[8]

---

5. Psalm 66:13,14.
6. Jonah 1:16.
7. Jonah 2:1-9.
8. See Genesis 31:13.

Our Vow

Every Sabbath Adventists should make the same vow Jacob made. All will, who get a clear view of the plan of salvation and who recognize God as the owner of all things. All who observe the Sabbath and thus recognize God as the Creator should also pay tithe and recognize Him as the possessor of the heavens and earth. The Lord will honor such a vow with rich blessings in this life and with an inheritance in the earth made new.

One of the greatest promises in the Bible is made to faithful tithe payers.[9] Most of you have made that vow and have been fulfilling it and can testify that the Lord's promise is good. Let me urge all others to make such a vow and then faithfully keep it. Begin now to recognize God as the owner of all things and therefore the dispenser of all the blessings of life.

Vow of Zacchaeus

Luke 19:1-10: "And Jesus entered and passed through Jericho. And, behold, there was a man named Zacchaeus, which was the chief among the publicans, and he was rich. And he sought to see Jesus who he was; and could not for the press, because he was little of stature. And he ran before, and climbed up into a sycamore tree to see him: for he was to pass that way. And when Jesus came to the place, he looked up, and saw him, and said unto him, Zacchaeus, make haste, and come down; for to day I must abide at thy house. And he made haste, and came down, and received him joyfully. And when they saw it, they all murmured, saying, That he was gone to be guest with a man that is a sinner.

"And Zacchaeus stood, and said unto the Lord; Behold, Lord, the half of my goods I give to the poor; and if I have taken any thing from any man by false accusation, I restore him fourfold. And Jesus said unto him, This day is salvation come to this house, forsomuch as he also is a son of Abraham. For the Son of man is come to seek and to save that which was lost."

{The Weymouth's translation of Luke 19:8 says:}

> Here and now, Master, I give half my property to the poor, and if I have unjustly exacted money from any man, I pledge to repay to him four times the amount.

Zacchaeus made this vow to Jesus in the presence of the multitude who were murmuring because Jesus was accepting the hospitality of one they considered a "notorious sinner." Restitution is one of the chief evidences of genuine conversion; it is one of the fruits meet for repentance. When genuine Christianity begins, all dishonesty ends. Zacchaeus kept his vow although it left him a poor man in material wealth, but

9. Malachi 3:7-12.

immensely rich in happiness and spiritual treasure. Poverty of soul is a far greater calamity than material poverty. Getting what our depraved appetites and passions lust for at the price of dishonesty brings "Leaness to the soul." The price is too great for such meager results.

All Obligation Are Vows

There are those who are unwilling to make even conditional pledges to the support of the church when they are constantly making vows to their fellow men. Every financial obligation and promise is a vow. This includes the monthly rent or payments on a contract and all other weekly, monthly or yearly payments or obligations, such as telephone, light, water, gas, coal, grocery and other bills. We cannot do business without making promises or vows to our fellow men and it is proper that we should do so providing we pay them and refuse to enter into any arrangement that we cannot live up to. This is where the instruction of Deuteronomy 23:21-23 and Ecclesiastes 5:4-6 especially applies. Why should we be so willing to make so many vows for our own benefit and then refuse to make pledges to finance God's cause? Such a course is inconsistent and unfair to others who are bearing the burdens in a business like manner.

Wages are Vows

Leviticus 19:13: "Thou shalt not defraud thy neighbour, neither rob him: the wages of him that is hired shall not abide with thee all night until the morning."

Deuteronomy 24:14,15: "Thou shalt not oppress an hired servant that is poor and needy, whether he be of thy brethren, or of thy strangers that are in thy land within thy gates: At his day thou shalt give him his hire, neither shall the sun go down upon it; for he is poor, and setteth his heart upon it: lest he cry against thee unto the LORD, and it be sin unto thee."

Jeremiah 22:13: "Woe unto him that buildeth his house by unrighteousness, and his chambers by wrong; that useth his neighbour's service without wages, and giveth him not for his work."

These Scriptures show that all who employ others for any kind of service and promise payment at a certain time are bound by the sacred obligations of a vow or pledge which should be strictly kept. A person has no right to employ another or others unless they are able to pay their wages. If there is any uncertainty about the time of payment it should be made known to the person employed before he begins his services. This is strict Christian honesty and should be carefully adhered to by all Christians.

Other Vows

A genuine Christian should faithfully live up to his or her marriage vows: "Do you covenant to live together in the relation of husband and wife, forsaking all others, promise to love, cherish and protect each other in sickness and in health; clinging to each other in adversity as well as in prosperity until death shall separate you?" Are you husbands and wives strictly loyal to that marriage vow which is sacred and binding? Your baptismal vow is sacred and binding. In it you promised to forsake the world and all its foolishness and follies and cling to Christ alone till death. Those who are baptized into this movement thereby vow to be loyal to the principles and teachings of the message, which is God's special message for this time. Are you loyal, or are you drifting and breaking your baptismal vows?

Condition of Eternal Life

Ezekiel 33:15, 16: "If the wicked restore the pledge, give again that he had robbed, walk in the statutes of life, without committing iniquity; he shall surely live, he shall not die. None of his sins that he hath committed shall be mentioned unto him: he hath done that which is lawful and right; he shall surely live."

Only those who make full restitution for dishonest dealings and who "restore the pledge" or pay their vows to both God and man are promised eternal life. The seriousness of breaking a promise or pledge is illustrated in the experience of Ananias and Sapphira.[10] They pledged the entire proceeds of a piece of property and then withheld part of the price and the Lord visited upon them terrible judgments for refusing to pay their vow. The last days are to be characterized by laxity in paying vows and meeting obligations. It is a generation of "liars" and "truce breakers" or covenant breakers. They do not keep their promises.

Spirit of Prophecy

{Ellen White writes:}

> At stated periods, in order to preserve the integrity of the law, the people (of Israel) were interviewed as to whether they had faithfully performed their vows or not. A conscientious few made returns to God of about one-third of all their income for the benefit of religious interests and for the poor. ... There must be an awakening among us as a people upon this matter. There are but few men who feel conscious-stricken if they neglect their duty in beneficence. But few feel remorse of soul because they are daily robbing God. ... There are many neglected vows and unpaid pledges, and yet how few trouble their minds over the matter; how few feel guilt of this violation of duty. We must have new and deeper convictions on this subject. The conscience must be aroused, and the matter receive earnest attention; for an account must be rendered to God in the last day, and His claims must be settled.[11]

---

10. Acts 5:1-11.
11. Ellen White, *Testimonies for the Church*, vol. 4 (1881), p. 467, 468.

Sacred and Binding

Although no visible marks of God's displeasure follow the repetition of the sin of Ananias and Sapphira now, yet the sin is just as heinous in the sight of God, and will as surely be visited upon the transgressor in the day of judgment; and many will feel the curse of God even in this life. When a pledge is made to the cause, it is a vow made to God, and should be sacredly kept. In the sight of God it is no better than sacrilege to appropriate to our own use that which has been once pledged to advance His sacred work.

When a verbal or written pledge has been made in the presence of our brethren, to give a certain amount, they are the visible witnesses of a contract made between ourselves and God. The pledge is not made to man, but to God, and is as a written note given to a neighbor. No legal bond is more binding upon the Christian for the payment of money, than a pledge made to God.

Persons who thus pledge to their fellow-men, do not generally think of asking to be released from their pledges. A vow made to God, the giver of all favors, is of still greater importance; then why should we seek to be released from our vows to God? Will man consider his promise less binding because made to God? Because his vow will not be put to trial in courts of justice, is it less valid? Will a man who professes to be saved by the blood of the infinite sacrifice of Jesus Christ "rob God?" Are not his vows and his actions weighed in the balances of justice in the heavenly courts?

Let us join the Psalmist in saying: "My praise shall be of thee in the great congregation: "I will pay my vows before them that fear Him."[12] "I will pay my vows unto the Lord now in the presence of all His people."[13]

12. Psalm 22:25.
13. Psalm 116:18.

16

THE JOURNEY FROM EGYPT

Date of Exodus

Exodus 12:40-41: "Now the sojourning of the children of Israel, who dwelt in Egypt, was four hundred and thirty years. And it came to pass at the end of the four hundred and thirty years, even the selfsame day it came to pass, that all the hosts of the LORD went out from the land of Egypt."

The marginal date for the Exodus from Egypt is 1491 B.C. According to Exodus 13:4 it was the month of Abib, the first month of the ecclesiastical year of the Hebrews; afterwards called Nisan, and corresponding to our March, or part of April. The Passover lamb was killed the evening of the 14th, or rather "between the two evenings."[1] On the 15th at midnight the Israelites were delivered and left Rameses in Egypt for the promised land.[2] Archeological discoveries have confirmed the Biblical chronology regarding the date of the Exodus.[3]

A Short Journey

Exodus 13:17-18: "And it came to pass, when Pharaoh had let the people go, that God led them not through the way of the land of the Philistines, although that was near; for God said, Lest peradventure the people repent when they see war, and they return to Egypt: But God led the people about, through the way of the wilderness of the Red sea: and the children of Israel went up harnessed out of the land of Egypt."

It was only a short journey from Egypt to Canaan by the most direct route. A splendid highway ran up the coast through the country of the Philistines and the distance was not over 250 miles, or about a month's journey. A few years ago two men in airship traveled from the land of Goshen in Egypt to the banks of the Jordan near Jericho in less than two hours. Because of their lack of faith the children of Israel were not prepared to make the journey by the shortest route. {Of this Ellen White wrote:}

---

1. Exodus 12:6, margin.
2. Numbers 33:3.
3. Sir Charles Martson, *New Bible Evidence*, p. 151.

> Had they attempted to pass through Philistia, their progress would have been opposed; for the Philistines, regarding them as slaves escaping from their masters, would not have hesitated to make war on them. The Israelites were poorly prepared for an encounter with that powerful and warlike people. They had little knowledge of God and little faith in Him, and they would have become terrified and disheartened.[4]

The Long Delay

The shortest and easiest way is not always the best way. Sometimes the longest and most difficult journey is the safest, surest and best in the end. But the Lord never intended that there would be such a long delay and that the short journey should require more than forty years.

It was not His good pleasure that they should wander so long in the wilderness. He would have brought them immediately to the promised land, had they submitted, and loved to be led by Him; but because they so often grieved Him in the desert, He sware in His wrath that they should not enter into His rest, save two who wholly followed Him.[5]

This is speaking of the Lord's plan to lead Israel into the promised land by way of Kadesh-Barnea which would have required but a few months time from Egypt to Canaan. There were at least four different routes and they traveled the longest one.

The Lord's Plan

The Lord never intended that Israel should fight their way into the promised land or conquer it by warfare. The victory was to be theirs by faith. He promised to fight their battles for them and to drive out the inhabitants of the promised land with hornets, hailstones and plagues.[6]

{Ellen White writes:}

> It was not God's will to deliver His people by warfare, as Moses thought, but by His own mighty power, that the glory might be ascribed to Him alone.[7]
>
> The Lord had never commanded them to go up and fight. It was not His purpose that they should gain the land by warfares, but by strict obedience to His commands.[8]

---

4. Ellen White, *Patriarchs and Prophets* (1890), p. 282.
5. Ellen Whtie, *Testimonies for the Church*, vol. 1 (1868), p. 281.
6. Exodus 23:27-28.
7. Ellen White, *Patriarchs and Prophets* (1890), p. 247.
8. *Ibid.*, p. 392.

A School

The Israelites must learn the needed lessons in the school of affliction and experience before they could be given possession of the promised land.

The varied experience of the Hebrews was a school of preparation for their promised home in Canaan. God would have His people in these days review with a humble heart and teachable spirit the trials through which ancient Israel passed, that they may be instructed in their preparation for the heavenly Canaan.[9]

It was to teach them the needed lessons of faith and trust in His leadership that the Lord led them in a circuitous route by "the way of the wilderness of the Red Sea."[10]

The First Lesson

The first lesson in faith was learned at the Red Sea.[11] The deliverance from the Egyptian army and the passage through the Red Sea was possible only by faith. "By faith they passed through the Red Sea as by dry land; which the Egyptians assaying to do were drowned."[12] What is faith?[13] There was no evidence of deliverance in sight; in fact the outlook seemed hopeless. But the Lord said, "Go forward", and they took Him at His word regardless of the seemingly impassible barrier before them. All of God's commands are enablings. When He says "Go" it is our duty to obey and His to open the way so we can go.[14]

Test of Faith

{Ellen White writes:}

> He might have saved them in any other way but He chose this method in order to test their faith and strengthen their trust in Him. The people were weary and terrified, yet if they had held back when Moses bade them advance, God would never have opened the path for them. It was "by faith" that "they passed through the Red Sea as by dry land." In marching down to the very water, they showed that they believed the word of God as spoken by Moses. They did all that was in their power to do, and then the mighty One of Israel divided the sea to make a path for their feet.[15]

The Israelites staked all on God's word and were not disappointed. All nations heard of their deliverance and of the destruction of their enemies, and the nations of the promised land trembled.

---

9 Ellen White, *Patriarchs and Prophets* (1890), p. 293.

10. Exodus 13:18.

11. Exodus 14:10-15.

12. Hebrews 1:29.

13. Hebrews 11:1.

14. Hebrews 11:7-8.

15. Ellen White, *Patriarchs and Prophets* (1890), p. 290.

The Advent Movement

The test of faith at the Red Sea at the beginning of the Exodus Movement has an antitype in the 1844 experience at the beginning of the Advent Movement.

> The history of ancient Israel is a striking illustration of the past experience of the Adventists body. God led His people in the Advent Movement, even as He led the children of Israel from Egypt. In the great disappointment their faith was tested as was that of the Hebrews at the Red Sea. Had they still trusted to the guiding hand that had been with them in their past experience, they would have seen of the salvation of God. If all who had labored unitedly in the work in 1844 had received the third angel's message and proclaimed it in the power of the Holy Spirit, the Lord would have wrought mightily with their efforts. A flood of light would have been shed upon the world. Years ago the inhabitants of the earth would have been warned, the closing work completed, and Christ would have come for the redemption of His people.[16]

A Short Journey

It is evident from this statement that the Lord intended that the journey of the Advent Movement should also be a short one. The Lord never intended that there should be such a long delay in the coming of Christ.

It was not the will of God that Israel should wander forty years in the wilderness. He desired to lead them directly to the land of Canaan, and establish them there, a holy, happy people. But "they could not enter in because of unbelief." Because of their backsliding and apostasy, they perished in the desert, and others were raised up to enter the promised land. In like manner, it was not the will of God that the coming of Christ should be so long delayed, and His people should remain so many years in this world of sing and sorrow. But unbelief separated them from God.[17]

The Lord's Plan

If ancient Israel had maintained the same faith by which they crossed the Red Sea the Lord would have quickly led them into the promised land and attempted to do so. There was a highway running in a northeasterly direction near where they crossed the Red Sea that would have saved them scores of miles. Instead they were led south through the great wilderness of sin and of Sinai where they must learn more lessons which were necessary before they could enter Canaan.

Likewise if the Advent people had manifested the same faith after the disappointment as they did before, the Lord would have given them the latter rain and the work

---

16. Ellen White, *Great Controversy* (1911), p. 457-458.
17. *Ibid.*, p. 458.

would soon have been finished and they would have entered the heavenly Canaan. This was God's plan but He was unable to carry it out because of their lack of faith.

Cause of Failure

That there was a long delay in the triumph of the Exodus Movement because of the unbelief of the people is certain. That there has also been a long delay in the triumph of the Advent Movement for the same cause is just as evident.

Hebrews 3:17-18: "But with whom was he grieved forty years? was it not with them that had sinned, whose carcases fell in the wilderness? And to whom sware he that they should not enter into his rest, but to them that believed not?"

Hebrews 4:1: "Let us therefore fear, lest, a promise being left us of entering into his rest, any of you should seem to come short of it."

Matthew 25:1-10: "Then shall the kingdom of heaven be likened unto ten virgins, which took their lamps, and went forth to meet the bridegroom. And five of them were wise, and five were foolish. They that were foolish took their lamps, and took no oil with them: But the wise took oil in their vessels with their lamps. While the bridegroom tarried, they all slumbered and slept. And at midnight there was a cry made, Behold, the bridegroom cometh; go ye out to meet him. Then all those virgins arose, and trimmed their lamps. And the foolish said unto the wise, Give us of your oil; for our lamps are gone out. But the wise answered, saying, Not so; lest there be not enough for us and you: but go ye rather to them that sell, and buy for yourselves. And while they went to buy, the bridegroom came; and they that were ready went in with him to the marriage: and the door was shut."

Hebrews 10:35-39: "Cast not away therefore your confidence, which hath great recompense of reward. For ye have need of patience, that, after ye have done the will of God, ye might receive the promise. For yet a little while, and he that shall come will come, and will not tarry. Now the just shall live by faith: but if any man draw back, my soul shall have no pleasure in him. But we are not of them who draw back unto perdition; but of them that believe to the saving of the soul."

These texts clearly indicate a delay in the coming of Christ because of a lack of faith on the part of the Advent people. This is definitely stated in the above quotation from the spirit of prophecy which continues as follows:

> As they refused to do the work which He had appointed them, others were raised up to proclaim the message. In mercy to the world, Jesus delays His coming, that sinners may have an opportunity to hear the warning, and find in Him a shelter before the wrath of God shall be poured out.[18]

18. Ellen White, *Great Controversy* (1911), p. 458

The failure of the church gives more time and opportunity to the world to hear the warning message and repent.

Exhibitions of Faith

Hebrews 11:29-30: "By faith they passed through the Red sea as by dry land: which the Egyptians assaying to do were drowned. By faith the walls of Jericho fell down, after they were compassed about seven days."

In the great faith-chapter, inspiration recognized but two exhibitions of faith in the Exodus Movement that were worthy of record; they came at the beginning and the end of the journey. How different would have been the history of Israel if they had kept the faith that delivered them at the Red Sea.

Likewise the two greatest exhibitions of faith in the Advent Movement come at the beginning and end of the journey, or during the movement's early and latter rains. The 1844 message and experience was a great demonstration of faith. Those pioneer Adventists staked all on the word of God. Because of their confidence in the 2300 year prophecy they braved a scoffing world with an unpopular message. Many demonstrated their faith by leaving their crops in the fields unharvested because they expected Jesus to come at the end of the prophetic period. Showers of spiritual blessings attended the preaching of the message. It was the early rain of the Advent Movement and it is evident that the Lord intended that it should swell into the loud cry under the latter rain which will close Christ's work in the heavenly sanctuary and His work on earth.

Spirit of Prophecy

> Of all the great religious movements since the days of the apostles, none have been more free from human imperfections and the wiles of Satan than was that of the autumn of 1844. Even now, after the lapse of many years, all who shared in that movement and who have stood firm upon the platform of truth, still feel the holy influence of that blessed work, and bear witness that it was of God.[19]

Another exhibition of great faith will bring the latter rain at the close of the movement.

> The Advent Movement of 1840-44 was a glorious manifestation of the power of God; the first angel's message was carried to every mission station in the world, and in some countries there was the greatest religious interest which has been witnessed in any land since the Reformation of the sixteenth century; but these are to be exceeded by the mighty movement

19. *Ibid.*, p. 401.

> under the last warning of the third angel.[20]
>
> The power which stirred the people so mightily in the 1844 movement will again be revealed. The third angel's message will go forth, not in whispered tones, but with a loud voice.[21]

These two spiritual baptisms are doubtless symbolized by the crossing of the Red Sea and the crossing of the Jordan at the beginning and end of the Exodus Movement.[22]

Red Sea to Sinai

{Sir William Dawson writes:}

> In so far as the journey of the Hebrews from the Red Sea to Sinai is concerned, little remains to be done with reference to the geographical details. The admirable work of the Ordinance Survey has forever settled all questions respecting the Mount of the Law and the way tither. It has done more than this; for the accurate labors of the scientific surveyors, while they have dissipated multitudes of theories formed by unscientific travelers, have vindicated in the most remarkable manner the truthfulness of the narratives in Exodus and Numbers. Every scientific man who reads the reports of the survey and studies its maps, must agree with the late Professor Palmer that they "afford satisfactory evidence of the contemporary character of the narrative." They prove, in short, that the narrator must have personally traversed the country and must have been a witness of the events he narrates. More than this they show that the narrative must have been a sort of daily journal, written from time to time as the events proceeded.[23]

Historical Evidence

George Stanley Faber, in his Horae Mosaicae Vol. 1, p. 186-195 {and} 247-253, gives this historical evidence that the Exodus Movement was a fact and not a fiction as many of the critics have contended.

Manetho, the high priest of Heliopolis during the reign of Ptolemy Philadelphus who flourished about twelve centuries after the Exodus, at the request of the king wrote three volumes in which he told the story of the foreign shepherds who came to Egypt and had a territory assigned to them on the east side of the River Nile. They increased very rapidly from a small beginning. They neither adored the gods

---

20. Ellen White, *Great Controversy* (1911), p. 611.
21. Ellen White, *Testimonies for the Church,* vol. 5 (1889), p. 252.
22. 1 Corinthians 10:1-2.
23. Sir William Dawson, *Popular and Critical Bible Encyclopedi*

of the country nor abstained from the animals which were accounted sacred. Under the authority of Osarsiph, a priest of Osiris, the name of the leader of these foreign shepherds was changed to Moses. Proving dangerous to the Egyptians government because he planned a revolution, these foreigners were all expelled from the country by Amonophis, who pursued them with his army to the borders of Syria.

Other Records

The story of the nation of the Jews in Egypt and the Exodus Movement was also recorded by Lysimachus, the general of Alexander. He told how Moses as the leader of the Israelites led them through the wilderness and after much suffering and many hardships they finally emerged from the desert and seized the land of Judea.

Diodorus Siculus, a Roman historian of the first century, also recorded the story of the Exodus. Tacitus, another Roman historian, declared that,

> most authors agree, that a cutaneous disorder spreading through Egypt, King Bocchoris consulted with the oracles of Hammon how to obtain relief; and the answer was, that he should purge his kingdom by expelling the Jews, who were a race of men hateful to the gods.[24] Justin, another Roman writer, tells how the Jews fled Egypt under the leadership of Moses and carried with them the sacred utensils of the Egyptians who followed in pursuit and were compelled to return home because of a violent storm.[25]

Eusebius' Account

According to Artapanus, the Heliopolitans gave the following account:

> The King of Egypt, as soon as the Jews had departed from his country, pursued them with an immense army, bearing along with him the consecrated animals. But Moses having by the divine command struck the waters with his rod, they parted asunder, and afforded a passage free to the Israelites. The Egyptians attempted to follow them, when fire suddenly flashed in their faces; and the sea, returning to its channel, brought an universal destruction upon their army.[26]

Archeological Discoveries

The recent discoveries of archeologists have completely confirmed almost every detail of the sojourn of the Israelites in Egypt and their Exodus to the land of Canaan. The evidence of the archeological records is so complete that a denial of the historicity of the events would be a demonstration of the ignorance of the most flagrant type.

---

24. Tacitus, *Hist. Liv.*, v.c. 3, p.
25. See Just. Hist. Phil. lib.xxxvi.c.2.
26. Eusebius, *Praep. Evang.*, lib. ix, p. 27.

Melvin G. Kile summed up the result of these discoveries in the statement:

> The substantiation of the credibility of the Biblical narrative is complete."[27]

27. Melvin G. Kile, *The Deciding Voice of the Monuments in Biblical Criticism.*

17

THE LAW AND THE SANCTUARY

The Bitter Waters

Exodus 15:22-27: "So Moses brought Israel from the Red sea, and they went out into the wilderness of Shur; and they went three days in the wilderness, and found no water. And when they came to Marah, they could not drink of the waters of Marah, for they were bitter: therefore the name of it was called Marah. And the people murmured against Moses, saying, What shall we drink? And he cried unto the LORD; and the LORD showed him a tree, which when he had cast into the waters, the waters were made sweet: there he made for them a statute and an ordinance, and there he proved them, And said, If thou wilt diligently hearken to the voice of the LORD thy God, and wilt do that which is right in his sight, and wilt give ear to his commandments, and keep all his statutes, I will put none of these diseases upon thee, which I have brought upon the Egyptians: for I am the LORD that healeth thee. And they came to Elim, where were twelve wells of water, and threescore and ten palm trees: and they encamped there by the waters."

On the way from the Red Sea to the Mount of the Law, the children of Israel experienced a disappointment which may have been typical of the bitter disappointment of the Advent people in 1844. At the waters of Marah, or "bitterness",[1] the Lord showed Moses "a tree, which when he had cast into the waters, the waters were made sweet."

In like manner, to the disappointed Adventists was divinely shown "a reed like unto a rod", by which they were to measure or study the sanctuary. The measuring rod by which they were to study the heavenly sanctuary and its services was the Mosaic tabernacle and its typical services. As the result of the discovery of the great sanctuary truth revealing the mediatorial work of Christ and the glad tidings of salvation through His priestly ministration, the bitter waters were sweetened and the disappointment was turned into rejoicing.[2]

Purpose of Exodus

1. Margin.
2. See Revelation 10:8-11; 11:1.

Psalm 105:43, 45: "And he brought forth his people with joy, and his chosen with gladness: That they might observe his statutes, and keep his laws. Praise ye the LORD."

For this reason a necessary preparation for entrance into the promised land was the giving of the law, the standard of God's righteousness and the constitution of His government. Moses therefore led Israel directly from the waters of Marah to the Mount of the Law. The Law and Sinai, however, are ineffectual without Christ and Calvary. Therefore with the giving of the law there must also be a revelation of the plan of salvation that redeems from the curse or condemnation of the law.

While camped at the base of Mount Sinai the Lord not only gave to Israel the Law with special emphasis on the Sabbath, but He also revealed to them the Sanctuary and its services which pictured the whole plan of redemption in types and symbols, all of which was a revelation of Christ, His atoning sacrifice on the cross of Calvary, and His mediatorial ministration in the heavenly sanctuary. All of this was necessary to prepare Israel to enter Canaan, and explains why the Lord led His people on the circuitous route through the Sinai Peninsula instead of directly by way of the Philistines.

Mount of the Law

Mount Sinai is a granite peak in a range of mountains and is 7,370 feet high. At its base is a large plain on which the millions of Israel camped for a number of months while they were learning the lessons of the law and sanctuary. It was the best camping sight in the Sinai Peninsula. Four living streams flow from the base of the mountain and besides there are a number of springs. There was also an abundance of pasture for their flocks and herds. On the entire journey it was the most ideal place for a long stay.

The place was well known to Moses as it was his principal camping ground during the forty years he was in charge of Jethro's sheep. On its slopes he had seen the burning bush and had received the commission to deliver Israel. To him the Lord said: "When thou hast brought forth the people out of Egypt, ye shall serve God upon this mountain."[3]

Giving of the Law

Exodus 19:14-25: "And Moses went down from the mount unto the people, and sanctified the people; and they washed their clothes. And he said unto the people, Be ready against the third day: come not at your wives. And it came to pass on the third day in the morning, that there were thunders and lightnings, and a thick cloud upon the mount, and the voice of the trumpet exceeding loud; so that all the people that was in the camp trembled.

"And Moses brought forth the people out of the camp to meet with God; and they

3. Exodus 3:12.

stood at the nether part of the mount. And mount Sinai was altogether on a smoke, because the LORD descended upon it in fire: and the smoke thereof ascended as the smoke of a furnace, and the whole mount quaked greatly. And when the voice of the trumpet sounded long, and waxed louder and louder, Moses spake, and God answered him by a voice. And the LORD came down upon mount Sinai, on the top of the mount: and the LORD called Moses up to the top of the mount; and Moses went up.

"And the LORD said unto Moses, Go down, charge the people, lest they break through unto the LORD to gaze, and many of them perish. And let the priests also, which come near to the LORD, sanctify themselves, lest the LORD break forth upon them. And Moses said unto the LORD, The people cannot come up to mount Sinai: for thou chargedst us, saying, Set bounds about the mount, and sanctify it. And the LORD said unto him, Away, get thee down, and thou shalt come up, thou, and Aaron with thee: but let not the priests and the people break through to come up unto the LORD, lest he break forth upon them. So Moses went down unto the people, and spake unto them."

This was one of the most important and spectacular events of all history. The Israelites had to spend three day in making most careful preparation for the giving of the law. Their bodies, clothes and camp had to be thoroughly cleansed and their sins confessed and forgiven. Christ Himself was the lawgiver.[4]

> Christ was not only the leader of the Hebrews in the wilderness, —the angel in whom was the name of Jehovah, and who, veiled in the cloudy pillar, went before the host, - but it was He who gave the Law to Israel. Amid the awful glory of Sinai, Christ declared in the hearing of all the people the ten precepts of His Father's law. It was He who gave to Moses the law engraved upon the tables of stone.[5]

Dr. Adam Clarke declared that the law was spoken on the Sabbath and that the festival of Pentecost was a memorial of that event. It was a great Sabbath service with Christ as the speaker, the Law as the sermon, and the millions of Israel as the congregation.

Need of Modern World

The Sinai message is one of the greatest needs of the modern lawless generation. William T. Ellis, writing from the summit of Mount Sinai on June 11, 1919, said:

> Day after day, in this morning air of crystalline clearness, from heights whence one may see fierce and blinding sandstorms raging on the desert

4. Isaiah 33:22; James 4:12.
5. Ellen White, *Patriarchs and Prophets* (1890), p. 366.

below, I have pondered the basic problems of this, our time. With all the honesty of soul I possess I have sought to see straight into the causes and character of conditions. Turn whichever way I will, follow whatever set of conditions I can call to mind, I find myself led straight up to the Mount of the Law. Here is the answer to every question. Things have gone wrong because nations and people have departed from this law. They will never go right until nations and people have the clarity of vision and the courage to return to the keeping of the ten words spoken on Sinai. ... They are, so far as I can see from this height of solitude and contemplation, the only way out.

A Reign of Law

There can be no throne or kingdom without law. The Decalogue is the fundamental law of Christ's kingdom, which is a reign of law.

> The reign of Christ is a reign of law. Law is an essential feature of all government, human and divine. The kingdom of our Master is entered by submission to law, and the enjoyment of its privileges is conditioned upon obedience to law. What mean then, those Scriptures which affirm that by the deeds of the law shall no flesh be justified, and that Christ took the law out of the way, nailing it to the cross? From such passages, some have apparently derived the impression that Sinai, as symbolizing law, has disappeared as effectually as if some Hercules had plucked it up by the roots and hurled it into the midst of the sea, and that the reign of Christ is more a reign of license than of law. In other words, we are told that grace has supplanted law. This is not so.[6]

Law Alone Not Sufficient

Romans 8:1-4: "There is therefore now no condemnation to them which are in Christ Jesus, who walk not after the flesh, but after the Spirit. For the law of the Spirit of life in Christ Jesus hath made me free from the law of sin and death. For what the law could not do, in that it was weak through the flesh, God sending his own Son in the likeness of sinful flesh, and for sin, condemned sin in the flesh: That the righteousness of the law might be fulfilled in us, who walk not after the flesh, but after the Spirit."

{In Weymouth's Translation, it puts it this way:}

> For what was impossible to the Law–powerless as it was because it acted through frail humanity–God effected. Sending His own Son in a body like that of sinful human nature and as a sacrifice for sin, He pronounced sentence upon sin in human nature; in order that in our case the require-

6. Rev. C.M. Gordon, *Australian Christian*, June 4, 1908.

ments of the Law might be fully met. For our lives are not regulated by our earthly, but by our spiritual natures.[7]

The purpose of the gospel is to bring men into conformity to God's law, which is the standard of His righteousness and will be the rule of His judgment. For this reason the sanctuary and its services were given to Israel in connection with the law. I

t revealed the way of escape from sin, the transgression of the law, and from the sentence of eternal death, the penalty for the violation of the law. It gave them a vision of Christ and Calvary. It revealed to them how the law could be transferred from the tables of stone to the fleshy tables of the heart to become the ruling principles of their lives.

The law and the gospel were both given to Israel at the Mount of God; the law, to reveal to them their sins, and the gospel, to take away their sins and free them from the sentence of eternal death.

Law and Grace

{The Reverend C.M. Gordan wrote:}

> The moral law, written on perishable tables of stone and confirmed by the thunders of Sinai, is now written on the imperishable tables of the heart and confirmed by the thunders of Calvary. The grace that came by Jesus Christ does not destroy the moral aspect of the law which was delivered to Israel through Moses, but fulfills it, reconfirms it, and enforces it with new motives, sublimer sanctions, and added insistence. Therefore, no subject of the government of Christ dare continue in sin that grace may abound. Grace thunders against sin as loudly, or even more loudly, than does law. The difference between law and grace is this: The law has no mercy; grace has mercy. The law has no Saviour; grace provides a Saviour. ... But let it never be forgotten that, while we can not be saved by the law without grace, no more can we be saved by grace without law. While we cannot be saved by morality without Christianity, no more can we be saved by Christianity without morality. In Christianity a wonderful thing has taken place; justice and mercy have celebrated their nuptials; law and grace have kissed each other; Sinai and Calvary have embraced each other.[8]

Righteousness of Christ

The Lord entered into the old covenant with Israel at Mount Sinai in order to teach them the impossibility of man's attaining to righteousness by obedience to the law

7. Romans 8:1-4, Weymouth's Translation.
8. Rev. C.M. Gordon, *Australian Christian,* June 4, 1908.

written on stone. This was necessary before they were willing to enter into the new covenant "established upon better promises," which write the same law in the heart and mind.[9]

Obedience to the law is righteousness, "for all they commandments are righteousness."[10] But human obedience to a law written only on stone is self-righteousness and is insufficient to give salvation.[11] The law must be written in the heart by the indwelling of Christ, the living law. When Christ lives out His life of perfect obedience in us we have the righteousness of Christ which brings salvation from sin and death.[12]

The Advent Movement

The Lord might have finished His work during the great Reformation had His people discovered and walked in all the light. More light was needed to prepare them to enter all the light. More light was needed to prepare them to enter the heavenly Canaan, but the Reformation came to a standstill and they formed their creeds and refused to advance in revealed truth.

Then came the message of the second advent with its greater light and attended by the outpouring of the Holy Spirit in the 1844 movement. But still the people of God were not all the way back to the faith and practice of the apostolic church. The law and the Sabbath, with the heavenly sanctuary and its services, had been trampled underfoot and buried beneath the rubbish of the papal apostasy for more than twelve centuries.

They must again be revealed to God's people as an essential preparation for the coming of Christ and entrance into His kingdom of glory. According to Daniel 8:12-14 this revelation would come at the close of the 2300 years, or in 1844, when the continual ministration of Christ in the true sanctuary would be made known.

The Discovery

As the result of the disappointment, the long lost and hidden truths concerning the law and the sanctuary were uncovered and brought to light.[13] Like Israel at Mount Sinai, the Advent people studied the sanctuary and its services in obedience to the divine command:

> Rise, and measure God's Sanctuary— and the altar—and count the worshipers who are in it.[14]

---

9. Hebrews 8:6-10.
10. Deuteronomy 6:25; Psalm 119:172.
11. Matthew 5:20.
12. Isaiah 51:7; Galatians 2:20.
13. See Revelation 10; 11:1.
14. Revelation 11:1 Weymouth's Translation.

Our pioneers discovered that the law was God's standard of righteousness, and the rule of His judgment which had already begun in heaven, and for which they were unprepared because they had been trampling under foot the Sabbath. They were led to the Mount of the Law for a vision of the majesty and glory of the character of God, and then through the sanctuary light they were brought to Calvary to have their sins washed away in the blood of the Lamb.

We are told that if they had fully entered into the experience of the imputed and imparted righteousness of Christ they would have received the latter rain and would soon have complete the work and entered the heavenly Canaan by translation.

A Revelation of Christ

{Ellen White writes:}

> The great plan of redemption, as revealed in the closing work for these last days, should receive close examination. The scenes connected with the sanctuary above should make such an impression upon the minds and hearts of all that they may be able to impress others. All need to become more intelligent in regard to the work of the atonement, which is going on in the sanctuary above. When this grand truth is seen and understood, those who hold it will work in harmony with Christ to prepare a people to stand in the great day of God, and their efforts will be successful. By study, contemplation, and prayer, God's people will be elevated above common, earthly thoughts and feelings, and will be brought into harmony with Christ and His great work of cleansing the sanctuary above from the sins of the people. Their faith will go with Him into the sanctuary, and the worshipers on earth will be carefully reviewing their lives, and comparing their characters with the great standard of righteousness. ...
>
> They must assimilate the word of God, and reflect the divine attributes. ... Christ must be abiding in us, and we in Him, in order to do work for God.[15]

If the Israelites had learned the lessons of the sanctuary and its services they would have been led directly into the promised land. If the Advent people had received the experience of righteousness by faith as taught by the sanctuary and its services they would have quickly entered the heavenly Canaan.

15. Ellen White, *Testimonies for the Church*, vol. 5 (1889), p. 575-576.

18

THE REBELLION AT KADESH-BARNEA

Sojourn at Horeb

The long sojourn at Mount Horeb was to enable the Israelites to learn the needed lessons taught by the law, and by the sanctuary and its services by which was revealed to them the whole plan of salvation. During these months they also perfected their organization for the remainder of the journey and for entrance into the promised land.

{Ellen White writes in *Patriarchs and Prophets* of this incident:}

> Nearly a year was spent in the encampment at Sinai. Here their worship had taken more definite form, the laws had been given for the government of the nation, and a more efficient organization had been effected preparatory to their entrance into the land of Canaan. The government of Israel was characterized by the most thorough organization, wonderful alike for its completeness and its simplicity.[1]

Heaven-sent Message

Deuteronomy 1:6-8: "The LORD our God spake unto us in Horeb, saying, Ye have dwelt long enough in this mount: Turn you, and take your journey, and go to the mount of the Amorites, and unto all the places nigh thereunto, in the plain, in the hills, and in the vale, and in the south, and by the sea side, to the land of the Canaanites, and unto Lebanon, unto the great river, the river Euphrates. Behold, I have set the land before you: go in and possess the land which the LORD sware unto your fathers, Abraham, Isaac, and Jacob, to give unto them and to their seed after them."

The Lord never intended that His people should settle down content on what light and experience they have. They must ever move forward. The time had come for Israel to leave the Mount of the Law and enter the promised land. The cheering message that they were to leave their desert camp and go directly into the promised land brought great rejoicing to the hosts of Israel.

1. Ellen White, *Patriarchs and Prophets* (1890), p. 374.

Many had complained because of the long delay and were impatient to be on their way to "the land flowing with milk and honey." The distance from Mount Horeb to Kadesh-Barnea near the borders of Canaan was less than 150 miles, or only an "eleven days journey."[2] During this journey they learned many valuable lessons.

A Desolate Country

This journey took the Israelites through a desolate country, a "no man's land", but the bright prospects ahead cheered them on.

> A distance of only eleven days' journey lay between Sinai and Kadesh, on the borders of Canaan; and it was with the prospect of speedily entering the goodly land that the hosts of Israel resumed their march, when the cloud at last gave the signal for an onward movement....
>
> As they advanced the way become more difficult. Their route lay through stony ravine and barren waste. All around them was the great wilderness,—'a land of deserts and of pits', 'a land that no man passed through , and where no man dwelt.' The rocky gorges, far and near, were thronged with men, women, and children, with beasts and wagons, and long lines of flocks and herds. Their progress was necessarily slow and toilsome.[3]

Open Complaint

Under the severe trials and difficulties men and women reveal their true characters. This experience was doubtless necessary to disclose to view and sift out the mixed multitude in order that the movement could soon triumph.

> After three days' journey, open complaints were heard. These originated with the mixed multitude, many of whom were not fully united with Israel, and were continually watching for some cause of censure. The complainers were not pleased with the direction of the march, and they were continually finding fault with the way in which Moses was leading them, though they well knew that he, as well as they, were following the guiding cloud. Dissatisfaction is contagious, and it soon spread in the encampment.[4]

Health Reform

It was during this experience that the Israelites were given further lessons in health reform, another necessary preparation for the promised land. The open complaining, which started with the mixed multitude, included expressed dissatisfaction with the diet the Lord had prescribed for them.

---

2. Deuteronomy 1:2.
3. Ellen White, *Patriarchs and Prophets* (1890), p. 376-377.
4. *Ibid.*, p. 377.

> Again they began to clamor for flesh to eat. Though abundantly supplied with manna, they were not satisfied.[5]

The Lord sent them quail and because of their gluttony a plague destroyed thousands of the leaders in the disaffection and "sent leanness" to the souls of all who manifested a rebellious and lustful spirit. This was a very striking and impressive lesson of the danger of lusting for flesh and complaining of the divinely given diet.[6]

Criticism of Leaders

Another lesson given to Israel during this journey was in regard to the danger of criticizing God's appointed leaders. Miriam became jealous of the Ethiopian wife of Moses and Aaron joined in severely criticizing Moses. Their complaints against his marriage led them to also criticize and even question his divine appointment as a prophet and a leader. The terrible judgment visited upon Miriam demonstrated the Lord's displeasure with those who unjustly criticize His appointed and anointed leaders.

> God had chosen Moses, and had put His Spirit upon him; and Miriam and Aaron by their murmurings were guilty of disloyalty, not only to the their appointed leader, but to God Himself. … The manifestation if the Lord's displeasure was designed to be a warning to all Israel, to check the growing spirit of discontent and insubordination.[7]

This experience delayed the progress of the march towards Kadesh for seven days.

Kadesh-Barnea

Deuteronomy 1:19-21: "And when we departed from Horeb, we went through all that great and terrible wilderness, which ye saw by the way of the mountain of the Amorites, as the LORD our God commanded us; and we came to Kadeshbarnea. And I said unto you, Ye are come unto the mountain of the Amorites, which the LORD our God doth give unto us. Behold, the LORD thy God hath set the land before thee: go up and possess it, as the LORD God of thy fathers hath said unto thee; fear not, neither be discouraged."

The book of Deuteronomy was written on the banks of the Jordan and the marginal dates reveal the time of the writing instead of when the recorded events took place. The marginal date in Numbers for the encampment at Kadesh is 1490 B.C. This was less then two years after the Israelites had left Egypt. They were now on the very borders of the Promised Land with Kadesh-Barnea as the gateway. It is evident that the

---

5. *Ibid.*
6. See Numbers 11.
7. Ellen White, *Patriarchs and Prophets* (1890), p. 384-395. See Numbers 12.

Lord's purpose was to lead them directly into their promised inheritance.

> They were now in sight of the hills of Canaan. A few days' march would bring them to the borders of the promised land. They were but a little distance from Edom, which belonged to the descendants of Esau, and through which lay the appointed route to Canaan.[8]

The Twelve Spies

Instead of going directly in to possess the Land of promise under divine leadership, Israel's faith wavered, and they proposed that a committee be chosen and sent in to see if the land was really what the Lord had said it was, and to see if they were able to conquer and possess it.[9] The request originated with the people and not with God.

> Eleven days after leaving Mount Horeb the Hebrew hosts encamped at Kadesh, in the wilderness of Paran, which was not far from the borders of the promised land. Here it was proposed by the people that spies be sent up to survey the country.[10]

This very proposal was an evidence that the Israelites did not believe God nor trust His leadership through the gift of prophecy. The Lord gave them their request and a prince was chosen from each of the twelve tribes to make up the investigating committee.[11]

A Glowing Report

The spies were gone forty days and returned with a glowing account of the promised land, and they brought back samples of its fruit. The committee was unanimous in their descriptions of the glories of the land, and they declared that it was all that the Lord had promised. It was "an exceeding good land."

This report backed by the evidence of the samples of fruit filled the whole camp with joy and rejoicing. "The people rejoiced that they were to come into possession of so goodly a land, and they listened intently as the report was brought to Moses, and not a word escaped them.

> We came into the land wither thou sentest us", the spies began, 'and surely it floweth with milk and honey, and this is the fruit of it.' The people were enthusiastic; they would eagerly obey the voice of the Lord, and go up at once to possess the land.[12]

---

8. Ellen White, *Patriarchs and Prophets* (1890), p. 413-414.
9. Deuteronomy 1:19-22.
10. Ellen White, *Patriarchs and Prophets*, (1890), p. 387.
11. See Numbers 13.
12. Ibid., p. 387-388.

A Divided Report

But after describing the glories of the land, the committee divided in their estimation of the possibility of their being able to conquer and possess it. Ten of the twelve men began to describe the walled cities as impregnable fortresses, and the inhabitants of the land as giants, and declared that it would be impossible for the Israelites to conquer the country. They left God entirely out of their reckoning as if He was not their Leader.

Caleb and Joshua tried to counteract the evil influence of this report and urged the people to go up at once and possess the land, saying; "for we are well able to overcome it."[13]

Effect on Camp

The effect of the exaggerated report of the ten was to change the rejoicing into weeping.[14]

{Ellen White writes of the effect of the report:}

> Now the scene changed. Hope and courage gave place to cowardly despair, as the spies uttered the sentiments of their unbelieving hearts, which were filled with discouragement prompted by Satan. Their unbelief cast a gloomy shadow over the congregation, and the mighty power of God, so often manifested in behalf of the chosen nation, was forgotten. … They left God out of the question, and acted as though they must depend solely on the power of arms. In their unbelief they limited the power of God, and distrusted the hand that had hitherto safely guided them.[15]

Caleb and Joshua

Caleb and Joshua made another desperate effort to turn the tide of unbelief and rebellion.[16] They said: "If the Lord delight in us, then He will bring us into this land, and give it to us." They begged them not to rebel, but their pleas made them so angry that they threatened to stone the two faithful spies.

> The traitors had done their work. If only the two men had brought the evil report, and all the ten had encouraged them to possess the land in the name of the Lord, they would still have taken the advice of the two in preference to the ten, because of their wicked unbelief. But there were only two advocating the right, while ten were on the side of rebellion.

---

13. See Numbers 13:28-33.
14. Numbers 14:1-10.
15. *Ibid.*, p. 389.
16. Numbers 14:6-10.

The unfaithful spies were loud in denunciation of Caleb and Joshua, and the cry was raised to stone them.[17]

Called a Rebellion

Deuteronomy 1:25-28: "And they took of the fruit of the land in their hands, and brought it down unto us, and brought us word again, and said, It is a good land which the LORD our God doth give us. Notwithstanding ye would not go up, but rebelled against the commandment of the LORD your God: And ye murmured in your tents, and said, Because the LORD hated us, he hath brought us forth out of the land of Egypt, to deliver us into the hand of the Amorites, to destroy us. Whither shall we go up? our brethren have discouraged our heart, saying, The people is greater and taller than we; the cities are great and walled up to heaven; and moreover we have seen the sons of the Anakims there."

They sat around their firesides and in their tents and murmured and criticized. In their refusing to follow God's leadership through Moses, the Psalmist declared that they "despised the pleasant land, they believed not His word; but murmured in their tents, and hearkened not unto the voice of the Lord. Therefore He lifted up His hand against them, to overthrow them in the wilderness."[18]

The rebellious hosts of Israel did four things that brought on them the wrath of God according to this Scripture. Their murmuring brought a "a slander upon the land" of promise.[19] The appointing of a captain to head them back to Egypt was paramount to the rejection of God's leadership. They had rejected the messages of God's prophets and therefore the spirit of prophecy.

The Divine Sentence

Deuteronomy 1:34-40: "And the LORD heard the voice of your words, and was wroth, and sware, saying, Surely there shall not one of these men of this evil generation see that good land, which I sware to give unto your fathers, Save Caleb the son of Jephunneh; he shall see it, and to him will I give the land that he hath trodden upon, and to his children, because he hath wholly followed the LORD. Also the LORD was angry with me for your sakes, saying, Thou also shalt not go in thither. But Joshua the son of Nun, which standeth before thee, he shall go in thither: encourage him: for he shall cause Israel to inherit it. Moreover your little ones, which ye said should be a prey, and your children, which in that day had no knowledge between good and evil, they shall go in thither, and unto them will I give it, and they shall possess it. But as for you, turn you, and take your journey into the wilderness by the way of the Red sea."

17. Ellen White, *Patriarchs and Prophets* (1890), p. 390.
18. Psalm 106:24-26.
19. Numbers 14:36.

Numbers 14:22-29: “Because all those men which have seen my glory, and my miracles, which I did in Egypt and in the wilderness, and have tempted me now these ten times, and have not hearkened to my voice; Surely they shall not see the land which I sware unto their fathers, neither shall any of them that provoked me see it: But my servant Caleb, because he had another spirit with him, and hath followed me fully, him will I bring into the land whereinto he went; and his seed shall possess it. (Now the Amalekites and the Canaanites dwelt in the valley.) To morrow turn you, and get you into the wilderness by the way of the Red sea.

“And the LORD spake unto Moses and unto Aaron, saying, How long shall I bear with this evil congregation, which murmur against me? I have heard the murmurings of the children of Israel, which they murmur against me. Say unto them, As truly as I live, saith the LORD, as ye have spoken in mine ears, so will I do to you: Your carcases shall fall in this wilderness; and all that were numbered of you, according to your whole number, from twenty years old and upward, which have murmured against me.”

They had expressed the wish that they might die in the wilderness and again the Lord gave them their request. As the rebels were in the act of stoning Caleb and Joshua for telling the truth, the Lord interposed in their behalf.

> The glory of His presence, like a flaming light, illuminated the tabernacle. All the people beheld the signal of the Lord. A mightier one than they had revealed Himself, and none dared continue their resistance. The spies who brought the evil report, couched terrorstricken, and with bated breath sought their tents. … In their rebellion the people had exclaimed, ‘Would God we had died in the wilderness.’ Now their prayer was to be granted.[20]

The Lord then sentences them to an additional forty years stay in the wilderness until their wish was fulfilled.

Sentence Rejected

Numbers 14:39-45: “And Moses told these sayings unto all the children of Israel: and the people mourned greatly. And they rose up early in the morning, and gat them up into the top of the mountain, saying, Lo, we be here, and will go up unto the place which the LORD hath promised: for we have sinned. And Moses said, Wherefore now do ye transgress the commandment of the LORD? but it shall not prosper. Go not up, for the LORD is not among you; that ye be not smitten before your enemies. For the Amalekites and the Canaanites [are] there before you, and ye shall fall by the sword: because ye are turned away from the LORD, therefore the LORD will not be with you.

---

20. Ellen White, *Patriarchs and Prophets* (1890), p. 390-391.

"But they presumed to go up unto the hill top: nevertheless the ark of the covenant of the LORD, and Moses, departed not out of the camp. Then the Amalekites came down, and the Canaanites which dwelt in that hill, and smote them, and discomfited them, even unto Hormah."

Deuteronomy 1:41-46: "Then ye answered and said unto me, We have sinned against the LORD, we will go up and fight, according to all that the LORD our God commanded us. And when ye had girded on every man his weapons of war, ye were ready to go up into the hill. And the LORD said unto me, Say unto them, Go not up, neither fight; for I am not among you; lest ye be smitten before your enemies.

"So I spake unto you; and ye would not hear, but rebelled against the commandment of the LORD, and went presumptuously up into the hill. And the Amorites, which dwelt in that mountain, came out against you, and chased you, as bees do, and destroyed you in Seir, even unto Hormah. And ye returned and wept before the LORD; but the LORD would not hearken to your voice, nor give ear unto you. So ye abode in Kadesh many days, according unto the days that ye abode there."

When Moses revealed to the rebels the sentence of God they expressed their dissatisfaction with it. Realizing what they had lost they decided that they would reject the sentence and fight their way into the promised land whether led by the Lord or not. Their utter defeat brought more discouragement than ever.

> "The night was spent in lamentation; but with the morning came a hope. They resolved to redeem their cowardice. When God had bidden them go up and take the land, they had refused; and now when He directed them to retreat, they were equally rebellious. They determined to seize upon the land and possess it; it might be the Lord would accept their work, and change His purpose toward them—'We have sinned against the Lord', they cried; 'We will go up and fight, according to all that the Lord our God commanded us.' So terribly blinded had they become by transgression. The Lord had never commanded them to 'go up and fight'. It was not His purpose that they should gain the land by warfare, but by strict obedience to His commands."[21]

God's Plan Altered

Numbers 14:32-34: "But as for you, your carcases, they shall fall in this wilderness. And your children shall wander in the wilderness forty years, and bear your whoredoms, until your carcases be wasted in the wilderness. After the number of the days in which ye searched the land, even forty days, each day for a year, shall ye bear your iniquities, even forty years, and ye shall know my breach of promise."

---

21. Ellen White, *Patriarchs and Prophets* (1890). p. 392.

> Altering of my purpose.—Margin.
> Ye shall know my alienation.—R.V.
> The revoking of my promise.—Margin.

What was God's purpose that had to be altered, and His promise that had to be revoked because of the rebellion of Israel at Kadesh-Barnea? It was God's promise and purpose to lead them directly into the promised land from Mount Horeb through the gateway of Kadesh. That this was the Lord's purpose and plan there can be no question. That this was the Lord's purpose and plan there can be no question.[22]

> God had made it their privilege and their duty to enter the land at the time of His appointment; but through their willful neglect that permission had been withdrawn. Satan had gained his object in preventing them from entering Canaan.[23]

Because of Unbelief

Hebrews 3:16-19: "For some, when they had heard, did provoke: howbeit not all that came out of Egypt by Moses. But with whom was he grieved forty years? was it not with them that had sinned, whose carcases fell in the wilderness? And to whom sware he that they should not enter into his rest, but to them that believed not? So we see that they could not enter in because of unbelief."

> It was not the will of God that Israel should wander forty years in the wilderness. He desired to lead them directly to the land of Canaan, and establish them there a holy, happy people. But they could not enter in because of unbelief.[24]

After the forty years of wandering were over and the city of Jericho had miraculously fallen into their hands, of God's original purpose we read:

> Long had God designed to give the city of Jericho to His favored people, and magnify His name among the nations of the earth. Forty years before, when He led Israel out of bondage, He had purposed to give them the land of Canaan.[25]

Unconsecrated Leaders

A few unconsecrated leaders who depended on human strength and numbers instead of the Lord turned the Exodus Movement back into the wilderness for a forty

22. See Hebrews 3:17-19.
23. Ellen White, *Patriarchs and Prophets* (1890), p. 392.
24. Ellen White, *Great Controversy* (1911), p. 458.
25. Ellen White, "The Taking of Jericho," *Signs of the Times*, April 14, 1881 par. 12.

year delay in reaching their goal. There were some who had faith enough to go directly in but they had to remain with the movement which was under divine leadership.

Through no fault of their own Caleb and Joshua had to share the sentence of the rebellious and faithless hosts of Israel to wander forty years in a barren wilderness. However, they did not die in the wilderness as did the rebels.

19

KADESH-BARNEA IN ANTITYPE

Recorded For Us

1 Corinthians 10:11 "Now all these things happened unto them for ensamples: and they are written for our admonition, upon whom the ends of the world are come."

{Of this Ellen White wrote:}

> The apostle Paul plainly states that the experience of the Israelites in their travels has been recorded for the benefit of those living in this age of the world, those upon whom the ends of the world are come. We do not consider that our dangers are any less than those of the Hebrews but greater. There will be temptations to jealousies and murmurings, and there will be outspoken rebellion, as are recorded of ancient Israel.[1]

> We are following the same path as did ancient Israel. ... Modern Israel are fast following in their footsteps. ... We are repeating the history of that people.[2]

Their Failures

> Call rebellion by its right name, and then consider that the experience of the ancient people of God with all its objectional features was faithfully chronicled to pass into history. The Scripture declares, 'These things were written for our admonition upon whom the end of the world are come.[3]

> We need ever to keep in mind the experience of the children of Israel, and learn the lesson that the record of their failures is intended to teach us.[4]

The greatest mistake of ancient Israel was their failure to go in and possess the promised land from Kadesh-Barnea as God had purposed for them. Their refusing

---

1. Ellen White, *Testimonies for the Church*, vol. 3 (1875), p. 358.
2. Ellen White, *Testimonies for the Church*, vol. 5 (1889), p. 75, 94, 160.
3. Leaflet Series, "Apostasies", Numbers 3.
4. Loma Linda Messages, p. 117.

to follow His leadership is divinely called a rebellion and resulted in the "altering" of God's purpose and the decree that they should wander in the wilderness for forty years before they could inherit Canaan.

The Advent Movement

We are definitely told that it was the Lord's will and plan to lead the Advent Movement into the heavenly Canaan soon after the 1844 disappointment when they had learned the lessons of the law and the sanctuary.[5]

It was a number of years before the movement got under headway toward the completion of their world task and their journey towards the heavenly Canaan. There was a tendency to remain camped around the Mount of the Law. What is known as the message of 1888 brought the Advent Movement to the very borders of the heavenly kingdom where was enacted the scenes which constitute the antitype of the Kadesh-Barnea experience of ancient Israel.

Laodicean Wilderness

Between the Mount of the Law and Kadesh-Barnea ancient Israel passed through a dreadful wilderness. Also between 1844 and 1888 the Advent Movement passed through a dreadful spiritual wilderness. It was the Laodicean wilderness. During this time however they learned many valuable lessons in obedience to divine leadership. They also greatly strengthened their organization and received the instruction in the principles of health reform.

In the early fifties the Lord, through the prophet of the Advent Movement, began to bear testimony that the church was in the deplorable Laodicean condition and that there must be a revival and reformation before His people could receive the latter rain and finish their task. Through the spirit of prophecy these messages continued to come with greater frequency and increasing urgency.

However, they received but little attention until at the Minneapolis General Conference in 1888. At that notable meeting the Laodicean message was more fully given with special emphasis upon the remedy found in the imputed and imparted righteousness of Christ.

Spiritual Desert

That modern Israel as in a barren spiritual wilderness previous to 1888 is evident from the following statements which are but a few of those which might be quoted:

In the latter sixties the following was written:

---

5. See *Great Controversy* (1911), p. 457-458.

> Many have for years made no advancement in knowledge and true holiness. They are spiritual dwarfs. Instead of going forward to perfection, they are going back to the darkness and bondage of Egypt.[6]

In 1888 appeared the following testimonies:

> As a people we are not advancing in spirituality as we near the end." "My heart aches day after day and night after night for our churches. Many are progressing, but in a back track.[7]

> A formal round of religious services is kept up; but where is the love of Jesus? Spirituality is dying. ... Shall we meet the mind of the Spirit of God? Shall we dwell more upon practical godliness, and far less upon mechanical arrangements?[8]

Further Rebukes

The following statement shows that great emphasis had been placed on the law to the neglect of the preaching of Christ and that this was one reason for their spiritual barrenness.

> As a people we have preached the law until we are as dry as the hills of Gilboa, that had neither dew or rain. We must preach Christ in the law, and there will be sap and nourishment in the preaching that will be as food for the famishing flock of God.[9]

The condition that demanded a reformation is further emphasized in the following which was published in the Review and Herald of March 22, 1887.

> What is our condition in this fearful and solemn time? Alas, what pride is prevailing in the church, what hypocrisy, what deception, what love of dress, frivolity, and amusement, what desire for the supremacy! ... We must no longer remain upon the enchanted ground. ... We have not the first reason for self-congratulation.[10]

Retreating Spiritually

{Ellen White penned these sad words:}

---

6. Ellen White, *Testimonies for the Church*, vol. 2 (1871), p.124.
7. Ellen White, *Testimonies for the Church*, vol. 5 (1889), p. 11, 93.
8. *Ibid.*, p. 538.
9. Ellen White, "Christ Prayed for Unity Among His Disciples," *Review and Herald*, March 11, 1890, par. 13; cited in *Christ Our Righteousness*, p. 64,
10. Ellen White, "The Church's Great Need," *Review and Herald*, March 22, 1887; cited in *Christ Our Righteousness*, p. 150, 151.

> I am filled with sadness when I think of our condition as a people. The Lord has not closed heaven to us, but our own course of continual backsliding has separated us from God. Pride, covetousness, and love of the world have lived in the heart without fear of banishment or condemnation. Grievous and presumptuous sins have dwelt among us. Yet the general opinion is that the church is flourishing, and that peace and spiritual prosperity are in all her borders. The church has turned back from following Christ her Leader, and is steadily retreating toward Egypt. Yet few are alarmed or astonished at their want of spiritual power. Doubt and even unbelief of the testimonies of the Spirit of God is leavening our churches everywhere.[11]

No person can read Vol. 5, without knowing that God's people were in deplorable spiritual condition previous to 1888. The same message applies to us again now and this volume should be carefully and prayerfully read by all our people. They should also read and study the book of *Christ Our Righteousness*, which explains the significance of the 1888 crisis.

Calls For Revival

Previous to the 1888 General Conference the Lord, through the spirit of prophecy, sent message after message calling for a revival of true and primitive godliness that His people might be prepared to enter the heavenly kingdom. This call was equivalent to that given to Israel at Mount Sinai;

> Ye have dwelt long enough in this Mount. … go in and possess the land which the Lord sware unto your father.[12]

The most outstanding and urgent of these heaven-sent messages appeared in the Review and Herald of March 22, 1887:

> A revival of true godliness among us is the greatest and most urgent of all our needs. To seek this should be our first work. … A revival need be expected only in answer to prayer. … There is nothing that Satan fears so much as that the people of God shall clear the way by removing every hindrance, so that the Lord can pour out His Spirit upon a languishing church and an impenitent congregation. If Satan had his way, there would never be another awakening, great or small, to the end of time.[13]

---

11. Ellen White, *Testimonies for the Church*, vol. 5 (1889), p. 217.
12. Deuteronomy 1:6, 8.
13. Ellen White, "The Church's Great Need," *Review and Herald*, March 22, 1887. See also, *Christ Our Righteousness*, p. 146-152; 40-48.

On the Borders

That the Advent Movement was on the very borders of the heavenly Canaan in those momentous days is evident from the following: In 1879 came the cheering message:

> We are now on the very borders of the eternal world.[14]

In 1881 the prophet of the movement said: "The end of all things is at hand", and "I have been shown that we are standing upon the threshold of the eternal world."[15]

During the next few years appeared the following statement:

> We are standing as it were, on the borders of the eternal world.[16]
> Eternity stretches before us. The curtain is about to be lifted.[17]

In the Review and Herald of June 18, 1889 was another statement to the same effect:

> What place have we for jesting and levity right here on the borders of the eternal world.

God's remnant people were told that the end was nearer than any of them realized. There is only one explanation for these and many other statements and that is that the end was then at hand and the Lord planned to quickly finish His work. His purpose for the Advent Movement was just as clear and definite as for the Exodus Movement when He led them to Kadesh-Barnea.

Minneapolis Conference

This General Conference began October 17, 1888, and before the conference proper started there was a week's ministerial institute. During this historic gathering the message of righteousness by faith was preached with power. Sister White placed her approval upon it at the conference and ever afterwards. She recognized it as the answer to the many calls for a revival and reformation. It was indeed a heaven-sent message to lead this movement out of the barren Laodicean wilderness into the heavenly Canaan. The message as given at this conference is clearly set forth in C.O.R., p. 56-71.

One cannot read these quotations without recognizing their tremendous import and that a new day had dawned.

---

14. Ellen White, *Testimonies for the Church*, vol. 4 (1881), p. 306.
15. Ellen White, *Testimonies for the Church*, vol. 5 (1889), p. 16, 17.
16. *Ibid.*, p. 382.
17. *Ibid.*, p. 460, 464.

Divine Credentials

Over and over again we are assured that this message was from heaven and bore the divine credentials.

> The present message—justification by faith—is a message from God; it bears the divine credentials, for its fruit is unto holiness.[18]

> Messages bearing the divine credentials have been sent to God's people; the glory, the majesty, the righteousness of Christ, full of goodness and truth have been presented; the fulness of the Godhead in Christ Jesus has been set forth among us with beauty and loveliness, to charm all whose hearts are not closed with prejudice. We know God has wrought among us. We have seen souls turn from sin to righteousness; we have seen faith revived in the hearts of the contrite ones.[19]

Further Testimony

{Ellen White gave further testimony at this time:}

> We thank the Lord with all the heart that we have precious light to present before the people, and we rejoice that we have a message for this time which is present truth. The tidings that Christ is our righteousness has brought relief to many, many souls, and God says to his people, 'Go forward.' The message to the Laodicean church is applicable to our condition. How plainly is pictured the position of those who think they have all the truth, who take pride in their knowledge of the word of God, while its sanctifying power has not been felt in their lives. The fervor of the love of God is wanting in their hearts, but it is this very fervor of love that makes God's people the light of the world.[20]

Burden of Message

> In every meeting since the General Conference, souls have eagerly accepted the precious message of the righteousness of Christ. We thank God that there are souls who realize that they are in need of something which they do not possess,—gold of faith and love, white raiment of Christ's righteousness, eye-salve of spiritual discernment. If you possess these precious gifts, the temple of the human soul will not be like a desecrated shrine. Brethren and sisters, I call upon you in the name of Jesus Christ of Nazareth to work where God works. Now is the day of gracious opportunity and privilege.[21]

---

18. Ellen White, "Campmeeting at Rome NY," *Review and Herald*, September 3, 1889.
19. Ellen White, "Living Channels of Light," *Review and Herald*, May 27, 1890, par. 6; cited in *Christ Our Righteousness*, p. 59-60.
20. Ellen White, "Camp-Meeting at Ottawa Kansas," *Review and Herald*, July 23, 1889, par. 12.
21. *Ibid.*

A Meeting Described

In an article in the Review and Herald of March 5, 1889, Sister White described a meeting in South Lancaster as follows:

> I have never seen a revival go forward with such thoroughness, and yet remain so free from all undue excitement. There was no urging or inviting. The people were not called forward, but there was a solemn realization that Christ came not to call the righteous but sinners to repentance. The honest in heart were ready to confess their sins, and to bring forth fruit to God by repentance and restoration as far as it lay in their power. We seemed to breathe in the very atmosphere of heaven. Angels were indeed hovering around. Friday evening the social service began at five, and it was not closed until nine. …
>
> There were many who testified that as the searching truths had been presented, they had been convicted in the light of the law as transgressors. They had been trusting in their own righteousness. Now they saw it as filthy rags, in comparison with the righteousness of Christ, which is alone acceptable to God. While they had not been open transgressors, they saw themselves depraved and degraded in heart. They had substituted other gods in the place of their heavenly Father. They had struggled to refrain from sin, but had trusted in their own strength. We should go to Jesus just as we are, confessing our sins, and cast our helpless souls upon our compassionate Redeemer. This subdues the pride of the heart, and is a crucifixion of self.[22]

In Battle Creek

In the Review and Herald of February 12, 1889, God's servant described a revival in Battle Creek as follows:

> The principal topic dwelt upon was justification by faith and this truth came as meet in due season to the people of God. The living oracles of God were presented in a new and precious light. …
>
> As one after another of these students of Battle Creek College, hitherto ignorant of the truth of the saving grace of God, espoused the cause of Christ, what joy was there in the heavenly courts. …
>
> [I]t made my heart glad to see those who had been connected with the publishing work for a period of thirty years rejoice as young converts rejoice in their first love. They expressed their gladness and gratitude of heart for the sermons that had been preached by Brother A.T. Jones; and saw the truth, goodness, mercy and love of God as they never before had

22. Ellen White, "Meetings at South Lancaster, Mass," *Review and Herald*, March 5, 1889, par. 10-11; cited in *Christ Our Righteousness*, p. 62.

seen it. They humbled their hearts, confessed their sins, and removed everything that had separated their souls from God and the Lord had put a new song in their mouth, even praise to His name. It was manifest that a renovation had taken place; for they expressed their determination of soul to work earnestly to counteract the evil influence they had exerted in the past. ... Will any of these who have tasted the Bread of Life ever loathe the manna that has been so sweet to their souls at these meetings?[23]

Great Power

I have traveled from place to place attending meetings where the message of the righteousness of Christ was preached. I considered it a privilege to stand by the side of my brethren and give my testimony with the message for the time; and I say that the power of God attended the message wherever it was spoken.[24]

When we went to Potterville, Mich., Bro. Van Horn said, 'I am so glad this meeting is not like the meetings we had in the past. There seems to be so much more weight to the truth. There is not so much levity and jesting. The people seem to have a realization of the solemn importance of the truth.' Why should we not have a solemn realization of the truth at this time? What place have we for jesting and levity right here on the borders of the eternal world?[25]

Purpose of Message

The purpose of the heaven-sent message that came to this people in 1888 and onward was described by the servant of the Lord in the R.H. of Nov. 24, 1904, as follows:

The Lord in His great mercy sent a most precious message to His people through Elders Waggoner and Jones. This message was to bring more prominently before the world the uplifted Saviour, the sacrifice for the sins of the world. It presented justification through faith in the Surety; it invited the people to receive the righteousness of Christ, which is made manifest in obedience to all the commandments of God. Many had lost sight of Jesus. They needed to have their eyes directed to His divine person, His merits, and His changeless love for the human family. All power is given into His hands, that He may dispense rich gifts unto man, imparting the priceless gift of His own righteousness to the helpless human agent. This is the message that God commanded to be given to the world. It is the third

23. Ellen White, "Revival Work in the Battle Creek Church," *Review and Herald*, February 12, 1889, par. 1-7.
24. Ellen White, "The Present Message" *Review and Herald*, March 18, 1890, par. 7.
25. Ellen White, "The Necessity of Dying to Self" *Review and Herald*, June 18, 1889, par. 15.

angel's message, which is to be proclaimed with a loud voice, and attended with the outpouring of His Spirit in large measure.[26]

Third Angel's Message

The message of the gospel of His grace was to be given to the church in clear and distinct lines that the world should no longer say that Seventh-day Adventists talk the law, but do not teach or believe in Christ.

The efficacy of the blood of Christ was to be presented to the people with freshness and power, that their faith might lay hold upon its merits....

For years the church has been looking to man, and expecting much from man, but not looking to Jesus, in whom our hopes of eternal life are centered. Therefore God gave to His servants a testimony that presented the truth as it is in Jesus, which is the third angel's message, in clear distinct lines.[27]

Several have written me, inquiring if the message of justification by faith is the third angel's message, and I have answered, 'It is the third angel's message in verity.'[28]

Therefore those who do not preach the third angel's message in the setting of righteousness by faith are not preaching it at all, that is, in its fullness. At best theirs is only a partial message with the salvation part left out. The Expectations For a decade or more this message went forward with power and wherever it was preached the Lord was present by His Spirit to witness that it was a message from heaven. The text was often quoted "Ye have dwelt long enough in this mount."

God's remnant people recognized it as a definite call to leave the wilderness of sin and enter the goodly land of the heavenly Canaan. They believed that it would bring the latter rain and a quickly finished work. Those who accepted the message and entered into the experience it demanded were jubilant because they believed their earthly pilgrimage was about ended. Like the Israelites they did not know that their hopes were to be blasted at the very borders of their goal because of the unbelief of a few of the leaders who gave a false report of the message given by God's servants.

---

26. Ellen White, *Testimonies to Ministers and Gospel Workers,* (1923), p. 92-93.
27. *Ibid.*
28. Ellen White, "Repentance the Gift of God," *Review and Herald,* April 1, 1890, par. 8.

20

OPPOSITION TO THE MESSAGE

A Crisis

Just as Kadesh Barnea brought ancient Israel to the greatest crisis of their journey, so the message of 1888 brought modern Israel to the parting of the ways and the greatest crisis of our history. That the Lord intended to pour out the latter rain and quickly finish His work is abundantly evident.

> The time of test is just upon us, for the loud cry of the third angel has already begun in the revelation of the righteousness of Christ, the sin-pardoning Redeemer. This is the beginning of the light of the angel whose glory shall fill the whole earth.[1]

> If you would stand through the time of trouble, you must know Christ and appropriate the gift of His righteousness, which He imputes to the repentant sinner.[2]

Quick Work

Romans 9:28: "And we know that all things work together for good to them that love God, to them who are the called according to his purpose."

It is through the preaching of the message of righteousness by faith that the latter rain comes and this text is fulfilled.

> Yet the work will be cut short in righteousness. The message of Christ's righteousness is to sound from one end of the earth to the other to prepare the way of the Lord. This is the glory of God which closes the work of the third angel.[3]

> A work is to be accomplished in the earth similar to that which took place at the outpouring of the Holy Spirit in the days of the early disciples,

---

1. Ellen White, "The Perils and Privileges of the Last Days," *Review and Herald*, November 22, 1892, par. 7.
2. *Ibid.*
3. Ellen White, *Testimonies for the Church*, vol. 6 (1901), p. 19; written during the nineties.

when they preached Jesus and Him crucified. Many will be converted in a day; for the message will go with power.[4]

What Might Have Been

That the Lord fully intended to lead the Advent Movement to a quick and glorious triumph following the Minneapolis Conference is evident from the following statements.

> If those who claimed to have a living experience in the things of God had done their appointed work as the Lord ordained, the whole world would have been warned ere this[5]

> Had the purpose of God been carried out by His people in giving to the world the message of mercy, Christ would, ere this, have come to the earth, and the saints would have received their welcome into the city of God.[6]

> If the people of God had gone to work as they should have gone to work right after the Minneapolis meeting in 1888, the world would have been warned in a few years and the Lord would have come.[7]

The Message Opposed

> God has raised up men to meet the necessity of this time who will 'cry aloud and spare not', who will lift up their 'voice like a trumpet, and show My people their transgression, and the house of Jacob their sins'. Their work is not only to proclaim the law, but to preach the truth for this time,—the Lord our righteousness. ... But there are those who see no necessity for a special work at this time. While God is working to arouse the people, they seek to turn aside the message of warning, reproof, and entreaty. Their influence tends to quiet the fears of the people, and to prevent them from awaking to the solemnity of this time. Those who are doing this, are giving the trumpet an uncertain sound. They ought to be awake to the situation, but they have become ensnared by the enemy. If they do not change their course, they will be recorded in the books of heaven as stewards who are unfaithful in the sacred trust committed to them, and the same reward will be apportioned to them as to those who are at enmity and in open rebellion against God.[8]

---

4. Ellen White, "The Perils and Privileges of the Last Days," *Review and Herald*, November 22, 1892.
5. Ellen White, "Whosoever Will, Let Him Come," *Review and Herald*, October 6, 1896, par. 7.
6. Ellen White, *Testimonies for the Church*, vol. 6 (1901), p. 450; published in 1900. First appeared in the "Australian Union Record" Oct. 15, 1898. See "Brown Leaflet" No. 1.
7. A statement attributed to Sister White and corroborated by a letter to the writer from Elder W. C. White. See also *Desire of Ages.*, p. 633, 634; *Testimonies*, vol. 9, p. 29.
8. Ellen White, "Camp-Meeting at Williamsport, Pa" *Review and Herald*, August 13, 1889, par. 17.

Preach the Law

> You will meet those who will say, 'You are too much excited over the matter. You are too much in earnest. You should not be reaching for the righteousness of Christ, and making so much of that. You should preach the law.' As a people we have preached the law until we are as dry as the hills of Gilboa, that had neither dew nor rain. We must preach Christ in the law, and there will be sap and nourishment in the preaching that will be as food to the famishing flock of God. We must not trust in our own merits at all, but in the merits of Jesus of Nazareth.[9]

Fully Two Thirds

According to some who attended the Minneapolis meeting fully two thirds of those present either opposed the message of righteousness by faith or were afraid of it. They felt that it was a form of fanaticism, a departure from the good old method of preaching the message. The teaching sounded new and strange and seemed to cast a reflection upon the message as it had been preached in the past and upon those who preached it.

The opposition of some became very bitter and they not only ridiculed and criticized those who led out in preaching the message of righteousness by faith, but they even accused Sister White for standing with them. Scenes were enacted at the Minneapolis Conference and afterwards that were very similar to those enacted by the faithless Israelites at Kadesh-Barnea.

Good Old Doctrines

> Some of our brethren are not receiving the message of God upon this subject. They appear to be anxious that none of our ministers shall depart from their former manner of teaching the good old doctrines. We inquire, is it not time that fresh light should come to the people of God, to awaken them to greater earnestness and zeal? The exceeding great and precious promises given us in the Holy Scriptures have been lost sight of to a great extent, just as the enemy of all righteousness designed that they should be. He has cast his own dark shadow between us and God, that we may not see the true character of God.[10]

Contempt and Reproach

> O, the soul poverty is alarming! And those who are most in need of the gold of love, feel rich and increased with goods, when they lack every

---

9. Ellen White, "Christ Prayed for Unity Among His Disciples" *Review and Herald*, March 11, 1890, par. 13.

10. Ellen White, "Repentance the Gift of God," *Review and Herald*, April 1, 1890, par. 7.

grace. Having lost faith and love, they have lost everything.

The Lord has sent a message to arouse His people to repent and do the first works; but how has His message been received? While some have heeded it others have cast contempt and reproach upon the message and the messenger. Spiritually deadened, humility and child-like simplicity gone, a mechanical, formal profession of faith has taken the place of love and devotion. Is this mournful condition of things to continue?—Why will you try to rekindle a mere fitful fire, and walk in the sparks of your own kindling?[11]

Criticized Messengers

The ten unfaithful spies centered their criticism upon Caleb and Joshua and finally they bade the people stone them. Because Moses stood with these two faithful men he shared the criticism and reproach heaped upon them.

God has sent to His people testimonies of truth and righteousness, and they are called to lift up Jesus, and to exalt His righteousness.

Those whom God has sent with a message are only men, but what is the character of the message they bear? Will you dare to turn from, or make light of the warnings, because God did not consult you as what would be preferred? God calls men who will speak, who will cry aloud and spare not. God has raised up His messengers to do His work for this time. Some have turned from the message of the righteousness of Christ to criticize the men and their imperfections. They have too much zeal, are too much in earnest, speak with too much positiveness, and the message that would bring healing and life and comfort to many weary and oppressed souls, is, in a measure, excluded; for just in proportion as men of influence close their own hearts and set up their own wills in opposition to what God has said, they will seek to take away the ray of light from those who have been longing and praying for light and for vivifying power. Christ has registered all the hard, proud, sneering speeches spoken against His servants as against Himself.[12]

Called False Light

The third angel's message will not be comprehended, the light which will lighten the earth with its glory will be called a false light, by those who refuse to walk in its advancing glory. The work that might have been done, will be left undone by the rejecters of truth, because of their unbelief. We entreat of you who oppose the light of truth, to stand out of the way of God's people. Let Heaven-sent light shine forth upon them in clear and

11. Ellen White, "'Be Zealous and Repent,'" *Review and Herald*, December 23, 1890.
12. Ellen White, "'Be Zealous and Repent,'" *Review and Herald*, May 27, 1890, par. 4-5.

steady rays. God holds you to whom this light has come responsible for the use you make of it. Those who will not hear will be held responsible; for the truth has been brought within their reach, but they despised their opportunities and privileges.[13]

Think Dangerous

There is to be in the churches a wonderful manifestation of the power of God, but it will not move upon those who have not humbled themselves before the Lord, and opened the door of their heart by confession and repentance. In the manifestation of that power which lightens the earth with the glory of God, they will see only something which in their blindness they think dangerous, something which will arouse their fears, and they will brace themselves to resist it. Because the Lord does not work according to their expectations and ideal, they will oppose the work. 'Why' they say,' should we not know the Spirit of God, when we have been in the work so many years? Because they did not respond to the warnings, the entreaties, of the message of God, but persistently said, 'I am rich, and increased with goods, and have need of nothing. Talent, long experience, will not make men channels of light unless they place themselves under the bright beams of the Son of Righteousness. [14]

Own Ideas

For nearly two years, we have been urging the people to come up and accept the light and the truth concerning the righteousness of Christ, and they do not know whether to come and take hold of this precious truth or not. They are bound about with their own ideas. They do not let the Saviour in.[15]

This statement shows that it is the acceptance of the Laodicean message with its complete remedy that brings Jesus into the heart. Those who reject this message refuse to let the Saviour in. The hesitant attitude on the part of the people generall was due to the attitude of many of the leaders toward the new preaching. They interposed themselves between the people and God's message.

Just as the whole camp of Israel was affected by the faithless and rebellious attitude of the ten princes who "brought an evil report," so Adventists in general were made cautious and hesitant and many were led to openly reject the message because of the attitude of men of long years experience in whom they had confidence.

---

13. *Ibid.*
14. Ellen White, "'Be Zealous and Repent,'" *Review and Herald*, December 23, 1890.
15. Ellen White, "'Christ Prayed for Unity Among His Disciples,'" *Review and Herald*, March 11, 1890, par 11.

Very Stones Cry Out

There is sadness in heaven over the spiritual blindness of many of our brethren. …

The Lord has raised up messengers and endued them with His Spirit, and has said, 'Cry aloud, spare not, lift up the voice like a trumpet, and show My people their transgression, and the house of Jacob their sins.' Let no one run the risk of interposing himself between the people and the message of Heaven. The message of God will come to the people; and if there were no voice among men to give it, the very stones would cry out. I call upon every minister to seek the Lord, to put away pride, to put away strife after supremacy, and humble the heart before God. It is the coldness of heart, the unbelief of those who ought to have faith, that keeps the churches in feebleness.[16]

Criticism in Rooms

Just as the Israelites "murmured in their tents" at Kadesh-Barnea, so those who opposed the message of righteousness by faith at Minneapolis murmured and criticized in their rooms.

> I shall never again, I think, be called to stand under the direction of the Holy Spirit as I stood at Minneapolis. The presence of Jesus was with me. All assembled at that meeting had an opportunity to place themselves on the side of truth by receiving the Holy Spirit, which was sent by God in such a rich current of love and mercy. But in the rooms occupied by some of our people were heard ridicule, criticism, jeering, laughter. The manifestations of the Holy Spirit were attributed to fanaticism. … The scenes which took place at that meeting made the God of heaven ashamed to call those who took part in them His brethren. All this the heavenly Watcher noticed, and it was written in the book of God's remembrance.[17]

Could there be a more striking antitype to what happened at Kadesh-Barnea? Testimony of Witnesses Several ministers who attended the Minneapolis Conference have testified to their personal knowledge of what happened in the rooms of some of the delegates. The following is from one who stayed in the same house with a group of workers:

> In our lodging house we were hearing a good many remarks about Sister White favoring Elder Waggoner, and that he was one of her pets. The spirit of controversy was up, and when the delegates came in from the last meeting of the day there was simply babble, with much laughter and

16. Ellen White, ""Search the Scriptures" *Review and Herald*, July 26, 1892, par. 8-9.
17. Special testimony to the Review and Herald Office, p. 16, 17, written in 1896.

joking and some very disgusting comments were being made, no spirit of solemnity prevailing. A few did not engage in the hilarity. No worship hour was kept, and anything but solemnity that should have been felt and manifested on such an occasion was present.—Written by Elder C. McReynolds in 1931.

Satan in Control

Just as Satan got control of the ten spies whose false report kept Israel from entering the promised land at the time of God's appointment, and led them to bitterly denounce and persecute the two men of faith, so Satan's spirit controlled those who rejected the message of 1888 and criticized, ridiculed and persecuted the men of faith who gave it. In T.M. pp. 77-81, is a testimony from God's servant entitled "A Faithful Message", and written from Hobart, Tasmania, May 1, 1895.

After speaking of Cain's hatred for Abel which led to murder, the following statement is made:

> Just as soon as man separates from God so that his heart is not under the subduing power of the Holy Spirit, the attributes of Satan will be revealed, and he will begin to oppress his fellow men. ... Men who are entrusted with weighty responsibilities, but who have no living connection with God, have been and are doing despite to His Holy Spirit. They are indulging the very same spirit as did Korah, Dathan, and Abiram, and as did the Jews in the time of Christ. (See Matthew 12:22- 29, 31-37.) Warnings have come from God again and again for these men, but they have cast them aside, and ventured on in the same course.

Persecutors of Christ

After repeating many of the woes pronounced by Christ upon the Scribes and Pharisees as recorded in Matthew 23, with the prediction that other prophets and teachers would be sent them in future against whom they would manifest the same persecuting spirit of their fathers, the application is then made to the rejectors of the message at Minneapolis and the persecution of the messengers:

> This prophecy was literally fulfilled by the Jews in their treatment of Christ and of the messengers whom God sent to them. Will men in these last days follow the example of those whom Christ condemned?[18]
>
> These terrible predictions they have not as yet carried out to the full; but if God spares their lives, and they nourish the same spirit that marked their course of action both before and after the Minneapolis meeting,

18. Ellen White, *Testimonies to Ministers and Gospel Workers,* (1923), p. 79.

they will fill up to the full of deeds of those whom Christ condemned when He was upon the earth.[19]

A Satanic Work

Continuing we read:

> Satan takes control of every mind that is not decidedly under the control of the spirit of God. Some have been cultivating hatred against the men whom God has commissioned to bear a special message to the world. They began this satanic work at Minneapolis. Afterward, when they saw and felt the demonstration of the Holy Spirit, testifying that the message was of God, they hated it the more, because it was a testimony against them. They would not humble their hearts to repent, to give God the glory, and vindicate the right. They went on in their own spirit, filled with envy, jealousy, and evil-surmisings, as did the Jews. They opened their hearts to the enemy of God and man. Yet these men have been holding positions of trust, and have been molding the work after their own similitude, as far as they possibly could. . . .
>
> Those who are now first, who have been untrue to the cause of God, will soon be last, unless they repent. Unless they speedily fall upon the Rock and be broken, and be born again, the spirit that has been cherished will continue to be cherished. Mercy's sweet voice will not be recognized by them. Bible religion, in private and in public, is with them a thing of the past. They have been zealously declaiming against enthusiasm and fanaticism. Faith that calls upon God to relieve human suffering, faith that God has enjoined upon His people to exercise, is called fanaticism. But if there is anything upon the earth that should inspire men with sanctified zeal, it is the truth as it is in Jesus. It is the grand, great work of redemption. It is Christ, made unto us wisdom, and righteousness, and sanctification, and redemption.[20]

Called A Rebellion

I question whether genuine rebellion is ever curable. Call rebellion by its right name and apostasy by its right name, and then consider that the experience of the ancient people of God with all its objectional features was faithfully chronicled to pass into history. The Scripture declares, 'These things were written for our admonition, upon whom the ends of the world are come.' And if men and women who have the knowledge of the truth are so far separated from their Great Leader that they will take the great leader of apostasy and name him Christ our Righteousness, it is

19. Ellen White, *Pamphlet 154*, p. 21.
20. Ellen White, *Testimonies to Ministers and Gospel Workers*, (1923), p. 79-80.

because they have not sunk deep into the mines of truth. They are not able to distinguish the precious ore from the base material.[21]

21. Leaflet Series, Number 3, "Apostasies."

21

THE ALTERING OF GOD'S PURPOSE

In Type

Numbers 14:32-34: "But as for you, your carcases, they shall fall in this wilderness. And your children shall wander in the wilderness forty years, and bear your whoredoms, until your carcases be wasted in the wilderness. After the number of the days in which ye searched the land, even forty days, each day for a year, shall ye bear your iniquities, even forty years, and ye shall know my breach of promise."

> Altering of My purpose. – Margin.
> Ye shall know My alienation. – R.V.
> The revoking of My promise. – Margin R.V.

> Ever since they left Egypt, Satan had been steadily at work to throw hindrances and temptations in their way, that they might not inherit Canaan. And by their own unbelief they had repeatedly opened the door for him to resist the purpose of God.[1]

> God had made it their privilege and their duty to enter the land at the time of His appointment; but through their willful neglect that permission had been with-drawn. Satan had gained his object in preventing them from entering Canaan.[2]

Through the ten unfaithful spies Satan succeeded in turning Israel back into the wilderness.

God Dishonored

> Moses faithfully set before them their errors, and the transgression of their fathers. They had often felt impatient and rebellious because of their long wandering in the wilderness; but the Lord had not been chargeable with this delay in possessing Canaan; He was more grieved than they because He could not bring them into immediate possession of the prom-

1. Ellen White, *Patriarchs and Prophets,* (1890), p. 423.
2. *Ibid.*, p. 392.

ised land, and thus display before all nations His mighty power in the deliverance of His people. With their distrust of God, with their pride and unbelief, they had not been prepared to enter Canaan. They would in no way represent that people whose God is the Lord; for they did not bear His character of purity, goodness, and benevolence. Had their fathers yielded in faith to the direction of God, being governed by His judgments, and walking in His ordinances, they would long before have been settles in Canaan, a prosperous, holy, happy people. Their delay to enter the goodly land dishonored God, and detracted from His glory in the sight of surrounding nations.[3]

God Insulted

Of the capture of Jericho we read:

> Long had God designed to give the city of Jericho to His favored people, and magnify His name among the nations of the earth. Forty years before, when he led Israel out of bondage, He had proposed to give them the land of Canaan. But, by their wicked murmurings and jealousy, they had provoked His wrath, and He had caused them to wander for weary years in the wilderness, till all those who had insulted Him with their unbelief were no more. In the capture of Jericho, God declared to the Hebrews that their fathers might have possessed the city forty years before, had they trusted in Him as did their children.[4]

God's Promise Revoked

> God had declared that He would give them the country, and they should have fully trusted Him to fulfill His word. ... In their unbelief they were limiting the work of God, and distrusting the hand that had hitherto safely guided them. ...
>
> They distorted the truth in order to carry their baneful purpose. ...
>
> Thus they manifested their disrespect for God and the leaders He had appointed to conduct them. ...
>
> Moses prevailed with God to spare the people; but because of their arrogance and unbelief, the Lord could not go with them to work in a miraculous manner in their behalf. Therefore, in His divine mercy He bade them adopt the safest course, to turn back into the wilderness toward the Red Sea. He also decreed that, as a punishment for their rebellion, all the adults who left Egypt, with the exception of Caleb and Joshua, should be forever excluded from Canaan. They had utterly failed to keep their promise of obedience to God, and this released Him from the covenant that they had so repeatedly violated.[5]
>
> God had purposed better things for them.[6]

---

3. Ellen White, *Patriarchs and Prophets*, (1890), p. 464.
4. Ellen White, *Testimonies for the Church*, vol. 4 (1881), p. 162.
5. *Ibid.*, p. 149-153.
6. Ellen White, *Patriarchs and Prophets*, (1890), p. 428.

Modern Application

1 Corinthians 10:11: "Now all these things happened unto them for ensamples: and they are written for our admonition, upon whom the ends of the world are come."

> The history of the report of the twelve spies has an application to us as a people. The scenes of cowardly complaining and drawing back from action when there are risks to be encountered, are re-enacted among us today. The same unwillingness is manifested to heed faithful reports and true counsel as in the days of Caleb and Joshua. …
>
> Satan is wide awake, and working warily in these last days, and calls for men of spiritual nerve and stamina to resist his artifices. …
>
> The church needs faithful Calebs and Joshuas, who are ready to accept eternal life on God's simple condition of obedience.[7]

History Repeated

{Ellen White explains how history so easily repeats:}

> The history of ancient Israel is written for our benefit. …
>
> Many who, like ancient Israel, profess to keep God's commandments, have hearts of unbelief while outwardly observing the statues of God. Although favored with great light and privileges, they will nevertheless lose the heavenly Canaan that God had promised them as the reward of their obedience.
>
> As a people we lack faith. In these days few would follow the directions given through God's chosen servant as obediently as did the armies of Israel at the taking of Jericho. …
>
> Faith is the living power that presses through every barrier, overrides all obstacles, and plants its banner in the heart of the enemy's camp.
>
> God will do marvelous things fo those who trust in Him. It is because His professed people trust so much in their own wisdom, and do not give the Lord an opportunity to reveal His power in their behalf, that they have no more strength. …
>
> God works mightily for a faithful people, who obey His word without questioning or doubt.[8]

Kadesh-Barnea Repeated

Speaking of the Kadesh-Barnea experience of ancient Israel, Sister White said:

> The lesson of this record is for us. The Lord had prepared the way before His people. They were very near the promised land. A little while and

---

7. Ellen White, *Testimonies for the Church,* vol. 4 (1881), p. 154-156.
8. *Ibid.*, p. 162-164.

they would have entered Canaan. They themselves delayed the entering. In the first place, it was they who requested that spies should be sent into Canaan showed a lack of faith; for God had told the people plainly that they were to take possession of the land. Why then did they need to send spies to search it? Had they put their trust in God, they could have gone straight in. God would have gone before them. ... Brethren and Sisters, from the light given me, I know that if the people of God had preserved a living connection with Him, if they had obeyed His word, they could today be in the heavenly Canaan.[9]

Work of Satan

{Of the work of Satan, Ellen White penned these words:}

> Satan's snares are laid for us as verily as they were laid for the children of Israel just prior to their entrance into the land of Canaan. We are repeating the history of that people.[10]

> As we approach the close of time, as the people of God stand upon the borders of the heavenly Canaan, Satan will, as of old, redouble his efforts to prevent them from entering the goodly land. He lays his snares for every soul.[11]

Many times did the servant of the Lord declare that the spirit of opposition to the message of 1888 was inspired by Satan. See T.M. pp.77-81. Because the Advent Movement was at the borders of the heavenly Canaan, Satan worked desperately to defeat the purpose of God.

At Minneapolis

Through the efforts of Satan the glorious message that began in 1888 at the Minneapolis General Conference was made of none effect. It was rejected and despised by many, and while others acknowledged it to be true they failed to take it to heart and enter into the experience of righteousness by faith. This is paramount to a rejection.

> Has not the Lord Jesus sent message after message of rebuke, of warning, of entreaty to these self-satisfied ones? Have not His counsels been despised and rejected? Have not His delegated messengers been treated with scorn, and their words been received as idle tales? Christ sees that which man does not see. He sees the sins which, if not repented of, will

9. Ellen White, "Lessons from the Sending Out of the Spies," *General Conference Bulletin*, March 30, 1903, par. 23.
10. Ellen White, *Testimonies for the Church*, vol. 5 (1889), p. 160.
11. Ellen White, *Patriarchs and Prophets*, (1890), p. 457.

exhaust the patience of a longsuffering God. Christ cannot take up the names of those who are satisfied with their own self sufficiency. He cannot importune in behalf of a people who feel no need of His help, who claim to know and possess everything. …

In every meeting since the General Conference, souls have eagerly accepted the precious message of the righteousness of Christ. We thank God that there are souls who realize that they are in need of something which they do not possess,—gold of faith and love, white raiment of Christ's righteousness, eye-salve of spiritual discernment. … Now is the day of gracious opportunity and privilege. Let us not be a traitor to holy, sacred trusts, as were the Jews. Resist not grace, abuse not privileges, smother not in your human pride the convictions of the Spirit of God. Despise not warnings, settle not down in hardness of heart, in confirmed impenitence, as did Pharaoh, the rebellious king of Egypt. Let every one listen to the voice of the True Shepherd, and not only hear but obey, and it will be well with your soul.[12]

Ridiculed and Rejected

The prejudices and opinions that prevailed at Minneapolis are not dead by any means; the seeds sown there in some hearts are ready to spring into life and bear a like harvest. The tops have been cut down, but the roots have never been eradicated, and they still bear their unholy fruit to poison the judgment, pervert the perceptions, and blind the understanding of those with whom you connect, in regard to the message and the messengers. When by thorough confession, you destroy the root of bitterness, you will see light in God's light. Without this thorough work you will never clear your souls. …

There has been a departure from God among us, and the zealous work of repentance and return to our first love essential to restoration to God and regeneration of heart, has not yet been done. … The true religion, the only religion of the Bible, that teaches forgiveness only through the merits of a crucified and risen Saviour, that advocates righteousness by faith of the Son of God, has been slighted, spoken against, and rejected.[13]

Persecution

To accuse and criticize those whom God is using, is to accuse and criticize the Lord, who has sent them. All need to cultivate their religious faculties that they may have a right discernment of religious things. Some have failed to distinguish between pure gold and mere glitter, between the substance and the shadow.

---

12. Ellen White, "'Camp-Meeting at Ottawa, Kansas," *Review and Herald*, July 23, 1889, par. 13-16.
13. Ellen White, *Life Sketches*, (1915), p. 326-327; Vision of November 3, 1890.

We should be the last people on earth to indulge in the slightest degree the spirit of persecution against those who are bearing the message of God to the world. This is the most terrible feature of unchristlikeness that has manifested itself among us since the Minneapolis meeting. Sometime it will be seen in its true bearing, with all the burden of woe that has resulted from it.[14]

False Ideas and Standards

False ideas that were largely developed at Minneapolis have not been entirely uprooted from some minds. Those who have not made thorough work of repentance 81 under the light God has been pleased to give to His people since that time, will not see things clearly, and will be ready to call the messages God sends, a delusion.[15]

There are those who have prided themselves on their great caution in receiving 'new light', as they term it; but they are blinded by the enemy, and cannot discern the works and ways of God. Light, precious light comes from heaven, and they array themselves against it. What next? These very ones will accept messages that God has not sent, and thus will become even dangerous to the cause of God because they set up false standards.[16]

Only Assented To

I feel a special interest in the movements and decisions that shall be made at this conference regarding the things that should have been done years ago, and especially ten years ago, when we were assembled in Conference, and the Spirit and power of God came into our meeting testifying that God was ready to work for this people if they would come into working order. The brethren assented to the light God had given, but there were those connected with our institutions, especially with the Review and Herald office and the Conference, who brought in elements of unbelief, so that the light that was given was not acted upon. It was assented to, but no special change was made to bring about such a condition of things that the power of God could be revealed among His people. ...

Year after year the same acknowledgment was made, but the principles which exalt a people were not woven into the work. We are living in the last time. We are standing as it were on the very borders of the final conflict.[17]

---

14. Ellen White, Special Testimony, "Danger of Adopting a Worldly Policy in the Work of God." Quoted in *General Conference Bulletin*, February 7, 8, 1893, p. 184.
15. *Ibid.*
16. Ellen White, Special Testimony, "To Brethren in Responsible Positions", p. 12. Quoted in *General Conference Bulletin*, February 7, 8, 1893, p. 182.
17. Ellen White, "Address by E.G. White," *General Conference Bulletin*, April 3, 1901, p. 23.

To assent to the truthfulness of a message and not act upon it is equivalent to a rejection. A message that is not accepted is rejected even thought it may be acknowledged as the truth.

Rejected Light

In the chapter entitled "Rejecting the Light," in *Testimonies to Ministers*, is the following:

> God says to His servants, 'Cry aloud, spare not, lift up they voice like a trumpet, and show My people their transgression, and the house of Jacob their sins.' But when the plain, straight testimony comes from lips under the moving of the Spirit of God, there are many who treat it with disdain....
>
> I inquire of those in responsible positions in Battle Creek, what are you doing? You have turned your back, and not your face, to the Lord. ... What is the message to be given at this time? It is the third angel's message. But that light which is to fill the whole earth with its glory, has been despised by some who claim to believe the present truth. Be careful how you treat it. Take off the shoes from your feet; for you are on holy ground. Beware how you indulge the attributes of Satan, and pour contempt upon the manifestation of the Holy Spirit. I know not but some have even now gone too far to return and repent.
>
> I state the truth. The souls who love God, who believe in Christ, and who eagerly grasp every ray of light, will see light, and rejoice in the truth. They will communicate the light. They will grow in holiness. Those who receive the Holy Spirit will feel the chilling atmosphere that surrounds the souls of other by whom these great and solemn realities are unappreciated and spoken against.[18]

Holy Spirit Departing

> The Spirit of God is departing from many among His people. Many have entered into dark, secret paths, and some will never return. They will continue to stumble to their ruin. They have tempted God, they have rejected light. All the evidence that will ever be given them they have received, and have not heeded. They have chosen darkness rather than light. These men are parties to the ruin of souls. They have interposed themselves between the heaven-sent light and the people. They have trampled upon the Word of God, and are doing despite to His Holy Spirit.[19]

---

18. Ellen White, *Testimonies to Ministers and Gospel Workers* (1923), p. 89-90.
19. Ellen White, *Testimonies to Ministers and Gospel Workers* (1923), p. 90-91.

Then follows a description of the message by justification by faith as presented at the Minneapolis Conference in 1888.

Intercepting Light

The charge that the men who rejected the message of righteousness by faith were intercepting the light and keeping from God's people, was also made in a letter written by Sister White to the Miller Brothers, July 23, 1889:

> The very men who ought to be on the alert to see what the people of God need that the way of the Lord may be prepared, are intercepting the Light God would have come to His people and rejecting the message of His healing grace.

Surely no one can read or hear these statements from divine inspiration regarding the crisis that came to the Advent Movement as the result of the Minneapolis Conference and the message of righteousness by faith, without knowing that it was indeed the antitype of the Kadesh-Barnea experience of ancient Israel that delayed their entrance into the Canaan land for many years and turned them back to wander in the wilderness. Here is the real cause of the tarrying time.

22

THE REWARD OF UNBELIEF

Cause of Failure

Hebrews 3:16-19; 4:1: "For some, when they had heard, did provoke: howbeit not all that came out of Egypt by Moses. But with whom was he grieved forty years? was it not with them that had sinned, whose carcases fell in the wilderness? And to whom sware he that they should not enter into his rest, but to them that believed not? So we see that they could not enter in because of unbelief. Let us therefore fear, lest, a promise being left us of entering into his rest, any of you should seem to come short of it."

There can be no question but these verses have special reference to the Kadesh-Barnea experience when the majority of the hosts of Israel "did provoke" God. In verse 8 this experience is called "the provocation" and "the day of temptation in the wilderness." Not only did this great manifestation of unbelief and rebellion "provoke" God, but He was "grieved" for forty years while they were wandering in the wilderness "under the divine rebuke."

It was because of what happened at Kadesh-Barnea that the Lord decreed that their "carcasses" should fall "in the wilderness." It was at that place they tried to "enter in" to the promised inheritance but "could not" because of unbelief. We are told that there were "some" or a few who did not provoke and grieve God. Caleb, Joshua, Moses, Aaron and doubtless many others did not take part in the rebellion. Then follows an admonition to those who have part in the Advent Movement to follow their example.

God's Plan Altered

We have already produced the evidence that the Lord was compelled to alter His plan and purpose to lead ancient Israel directly into the promised land by way of Kadesh-Barnea because of their unbelief and insubordination. But the Kadesh-Barnea experience of the Exodus Movement has had its antitype in the Advent Movement. There has been a long delay because of our unbelief. The Lord purposed to finish the work long ago and especially soon after the 1888 revival began. In 1898 the prophet of the Advent people wrote:

> Had the church of Christ done her appointed work as the Lord ordained, the whole world would before this have been warned, and the Lord Jesus would have come to our earth in power and great glory.[1]

Several similar statements have been previously quoted.

A Long Delay

> The history of ancient Israel is a striking illustration of the past experience of the Adventist body. God led His people in the advent movement, even as He led the children of Israel from Egypt. In the great disappointment their faith was tested as was that of the Hebrews at the Red Sea. Had they still trusted to the guiding hand that had been with them in their past experience, they would have seen the salvation of God. If all who had labored unitedly in the work in 1844, had received the third angel's message and proclaimed it in the power of the Holy Spirit, the Lord would have wrought mightily with their efforts. A flood of light would have been shed upon the world. Years ago the inhabitants of the earth would have been warned, the closing work completed, and Christ would have come for the redemption of His people.
>
> It was not the will of God that Israel should wander forty years in the wilderness; He desired to lead them directly to the land of Canaan and establish them there, a holy, happy people. But "they could not enter in because of unbelief." Hebrews 3:19. Because of their backsliding and apostasy they perished in the desert, and others were raised up to enter the Promised Land. In like manner, it was not the will of God that the coming of Christ should be so long delayed and His people should remain so many years in this world of sin and sorrow. But unbelief separated them from God. As they refused to do the work which He had appointed them, others were raised up to proclaim the message. In mercy to the world, Jesus delays His coming, that sinners may have an opportunity to hear the warning and find in Him a shelter before the wrath of God shall be poured out.[2]

This delay was foretold in the parable of the ten virgins and the tarrying time during which "they all slumbered and slept."

Because of Insubordination

When the calls came, through the spirit of prophecy, to move the college out of Battle Creek, some of the leaders were perplexed. They felt that the end was so near that it was too late to try to establish another college, and in fact would be a denial of

1. Ellen White, *Desire of Ages* (1898), p. 633-634.
2. Ellen White, *Great Controversy* (1911), p. 457-458.

their faith in the soon coming of Christ. Dr. P. T. Magan had these convictions and wrote them to Sister White and asked for counsel. Her reply was dated December 7, 1901, and its number in the files is—184-1901.

In the letter were the following statements:

> The hand of providence is holding the machinery. When that hand starts the wheel then all things will begin to move. How can finite men carry the burden of responsibility for this time. His people have been far behind. Human agencies under the divine planning may recover some thing of what is lost because the people who had great light did not have corresponding piety, sanctification, and zeal in working out God's specified plans. They have lost to their own disadvantages what they might have gained to the advancement of the truth if they had carried out the plans and will of God. Man cannot possibly stretch over the gulf that has been made by the workers who have not been following the divine Leader.

Many More Years

The letter continues:

> We may have to remain here in this world because of insubordination many more years, as did the children of Israel, but for Christ's sake, His people should not add sin to sin by charging God with the consequences of their own wrong course of action. Now, have men who claim to believe the Word of God learned their lesson that obedience is better than sacrifice? 'He hath showed thee (this rebellious people) O man, what is good, and what doth the Lord require of thee but to do justly, and to love mercy, and to walk humbly with thy God.' You, nor any other agency, can not heal the hurt that has come to God's people by neglect to lift up His standard, and occupy new territory. But if all now would only see and confess and repent of their own course of action in departing from the truth of God, and following human devisings then the Lord would pardon. Warnings have been coming, but they have been unheeded, but a few who may now seek to bridge the gulf that stands so offensively before God must make haste slowly, else the standard bearers will fail, and who will take their place?

Plan Delayed But Not Disannulled

Isaiah 14:24, 27: "The LORD of hosts hath sworn, saying, Surely as I have thought, so shall it come to pass; and as I have purposed, so shall it stand... For the LORD of hosts hath purposed, and who shall disannul it? and his hand is stretched out, and who shall turn it back?"

The Lord's purpose for Israel was finally fulfilled and He led them into the promised land. Satan was able only to delay the carrying out of God's purpose; he could not disannul it. The same is true of the Advent Movement. Satan has succeeded in delaying the finishing of the work but it will be finished triumphantly and the eternal purpose of God will be fulfilled.

> Not by any temporary failure of Israel, however, was the plan of the ages for the redemption of mankind to 84 be frustrated. Those to whom the prophet was speaking, might not heed the message given; but the purposes of Jehovah were nevertheless to move steadily forward to their complete fulfillment.[3]

> Thus God's purpose for Israel will meet with literal fulfillment. That which God purposes, man is powerless to disannul. Even among the working of evil, God's purposes have been moving steadily forward to their accomplishment. It was thus with the house of Israel; it is thus with spiritual Israel today.[4]

A Remarkable Letter

Neither the retiring or the newly elected General Conference president was present at the Minneapolis Conference in 1888. Elder George T. Butler was unable to be present because of sickness, and Elder O. A. Olsen was in Europe. Under date of September 1, 1892, Sister White wrote Elder O. A. Olsen a very remarkable letter regarding the crisis that began in 1888, at which time he was elected president. From this long letter I will quote quiet freely. Its file number in the vault at Elmshaven is O. 19 d' 92.

> I wish that all would see that the very same spirit which refused to accept Christ, the light that would dispel the moral darkness, is far from being extinct in this age of the world. There are those in our day who are no more ready to recognize and acknowledge light than were the people when the prophets and the apostles came with the message from God, and many rejected the message and despised the messenger. Let us beware that this spirit is not entertained by us.

Then follows the quoting of the message of Christ to the church of Ephesus and its application to us.

A Long Journey

After quoting 1 John 1:5-10; 2:9-11, Sister White continued:

3. Ellen White, *Prophets and Kings* (1917), p. 705-706.
4. *Ibid.*, p. 720.

> Could any description be more sharp and clear than John has given us? These things are written for us; they are applicable to the churches of Seventh-day Adventists. Some may say, 'I do not hate my brother; I am not so bad as that.' But how little they understand their own hearts. They may think they have a zeal for God in their feelings against their brother if his ideas seem in any way to conflict with theirs; feelings are brought to the surface that have no kinship with love. They show no disposition to harmonize with him; they would as leave be at swords point with their brother as not, and yet he may be bearing a message from God to the people, just the light we need for this time.

Why do not brethren of like precious faith consider that in every age, when the Lord has sent a special message to His people, all powers of the confederacy of evil are set at work to prevent the word of truth from coming to those who should receive it. If Satan can impress the mind and stir up the passions of those who claim to believe the truth, and thus lead them to unite with the forces of evil, he is well pleased.

If once he can get them to commit themselves to the wrong side, he has laid his plans to lead them on a long journey. Through his deceptive wiles he will cause them to act upon the same principle he adopted in his disaffection in heaven. They take step after step in the false way, until there seems to be no other course than for them to go on, believing they are right in their bitterness of feeling against their brethren. Will the Lord's messenger bear the pressure brought against him? If so, it is because God bids him stand in His strength, and vindicate the truth that he is sent of God."

Message From Heaven

{Ellen White continues in her letter:}

> When men listen to the Lord's message, but through temptation allow prejudice to bar the mind and heart against the reception of truth, the enemy has the power to present the most precious things in a distorted light. Looking through the medium of prejudice and passion, they feel too indignant to search the Scriptures in a Christlike spirit, but repudiate the whole matter because points are presented that are not in accordance with their own ideas. When a new view is presented, the question is often asked, 'Who are its advocates? What is the position or influence of the one who would teach us, who have been students of the Bible for many years?' God will send His words of warning by whom He will send. And the question to be settled is not what person it is who brings the message; this does not in any way affect the word spoken. … In regard to the testimony that has come to us through the Lord's messengers we can say, 'We know in whom we have believed; we know that Christ is our righteousness, not alone because He is so described in the Bible, but because we have felt His transforming power in our hearts.

Determined Opposition

> Now although there has been a determined effort to make of no effect the message God has sent, its fruits have been proving that it was from the source of light and truth. Those who have cherished unbelief and prejudice, who in place of helping to do the work the Lord would have them do, have stood to bar the way against all evidence, cannot be supposed to have clearer spiritual eyesight for having so long closed their eyes to the light God sent to the people. If we are to bear a part in this work to its close, we must recognized the fact that there are good things to come to the people of God in a way that we have not discerned; and that there will be resistance from the very ones we expected to engage in such a work.

Messengers May Fail

Then follows a statement indicating that the men who preached that message under such great opposition might not be able to stand up under the pressure but become discouraged and fail. If so, it would not effect in the least the truthfulness of the message they preached.

> How long will the Lord have patience with men in their blindness, how long will He wait before leaving them to grope their way to final darkness, we cannot determine. Should the Lord's messengers, after standing manfully for the truth for a time, fall under temptation, and dishonor Him who has given them their work, will that be proof that the message is not true? No, because the Bible is true. ... Sin on the part of the messenger of God would cause Satan to rejoice, and those who have rejected the message and the messenger would triumph; but it would not at all clear the men who are guilty of rejecting the message of God.

It seems that God's servant was given foreknowledge regarding what happened twelve or thirteen years later to Elder Jones and Waggoner, of whom these statements were written.

Laodicean Condition

> If ever a people needed true and faithful watchmen, who will not hold their peace, who will cry day and night, sounding the warnings God has given, it is Seventh-day Adventists. ... I wish to plead with our brethren who shall assemble at the General Conference to heed the message given to the Laodiceans. What a condition of blindness is theirs; this subject has been brought to your notice again and again; but your dissatisfaction with your spiritual condition has not been deep and painful enough to work a reform. 'Thou sayest I am rich, and increased with goods, and have need of nothing, and knowest not that thou art wretched, and miserable, and poor, and blind, and naked.' The guilt of self-deception is upon our

churches. The religious life of many is a lie. Jesus has presented to them the precious jewels of truth, the riches of His grace and salvation, the glistening white vesture of His own righteousness, woven in heaven's loom, and containing not one thread of human invention. Jesus is knocking; open the door of the heart and buy of Him the precious heavenly treasure. Shall His pleadings fall upon ears that are dull of hearing if not entirely closed? Shall Jesus knock in vain?

Unchristlike Spirit

{Ellen White continues to write of the condition of God's people at this time:}

I ask, what means the contention and strife among us? What means this hard, iron spirit, which is seen in our churches, in our institutions, and which is so utterly 86 unchristlike? I have deep sorrow of heart because I have seen how readily a word or action of Elder Jones or Elder Waggoner is criticized. How readily many minds overlook all the good that has been done by them in the few years past, and see no evidence that God is working through these instrumentalities. They hunt for something to condemn, and their attitude toward these brethren who are zealously engaged in doing a good work, shows that feelings of enmity and bitterness are in the heart. What is needed is the converting power of God upon hearts and minds. ... Cease watching your brethren with suspicion. There are many in the ministry who have no love for God or for their fellow men. They are asleep, and while they sleep, Satan is sowing his tares. The flock of God is in need of help from heaven, and the sheep and lambs are perishing for food.

Demand Evidence

Many have been convinced that they have grieved the Spirit of God by their resistance of light, but they hated to die to self, and deferred to do the work of humbling their hearts and confessing their sins. They would not acknowledge that the reproof was sent of God, or the instruction was given from heaven until every shadow of uncertainty was removed. They did not walk out in the light. They hoped to get out of difficulty in some easier way than by confession of sin, and Satan has kept hold of them and tempted them, and they have had but feeble strength to resist him. Evidence has been piled upon evidence, but they have not been willing to acknowledge it. By their stubborn attitude they have revealed the soul-malady that was upon them, for no evidence could satisfy them. Doubt, unbelief, prejudice, and stubbornness killed all love from their souls. They demanded perfect assurance, but this was not compatible with faith.

What Might Have Been

If the rays of light which shone at Minneapolis were permitted to exert their convincing power upon those who took their stand against light, if all had yielded their ways, and submitted their will to the Spirit of God at that time, they would have received the richest blessings, disappointed the enemy, and stood as faithful men, true to their convictions. They would have had a rich experience; but self said, No. Self was not willing to be bruised; self struggled for the mastery, and everyone of those souls will be tested again on the points where they failed then. They will have less clearness of judgment, less submission, less genuine love for God or their brethren now than before the test and trial at Minneapolis.

In the books of heaven they are registered as wanting. Self and passion developed hateful characteristics. Since that time, the Lord has given abundance of evidence in messages of light and salvation. No more tender calls, no better opportunities could be given them in order that they might do that which they ought to have done at Minneapolis.

Forsaken of God

The light has been withdrawing from some, and ever since they have been walking in the sparks of their own kindling. No one can tell how much may be at stake when neglecting to comply with the call of the Spirit of God. The time will come when they will be willing to do anything and everything possible in order to have a chance of hearing the call which they rejected at Minneapolis. God moved upon hearts, but many yielded to another spirit which was moving upon their passions from beneath. O that these poor souls would make thorough work before it is everlastingly too late. Better opportunities will never come, deeper feelings they will not have. … God will not be trifled with.

A Terrible Sin

The sin committed in what took place at Minneapolis remains on the record books of heaven, registered against the names of those who resisted light, and it will remain upon the record until full confession is made, and the transgressors stand in full humility before God. The levity of some, the free speeches of others, the manner of treating the messenger and the message when in their private stopping places, the spirit that stirred action from beneath, all stand registered in the books of heaven. And when these persons are tried, and brought over the ground again, the same spirit will be revealed. When the Lord has sufficiently tried them, if they do not yield to them, He will withdraw His Holy Spirit. …

Those who are commanded to bear a message must move out although obstacles of a forbidding character are in the way. Those who claim to know the truth, and yet lay every obstacle in the way, so that light shall not come to the people, will have an account to settle with God that they will not be pleased to meet. God manages His own work, and woe to the man who puts his hand to the ark of God.[5]

5. All from the letter to Elder O.A. Olsen, September 1, 1892, file number at Elmshaven is O. 19 d' 92.

23

THE REJECTION OF DIVINE LEADERSHIP

Rebellious Attitude

Deuteronomy 1:45, 46: "And ye returned and wept before the LORD; but the LORD would not hearken to your voice, nor give ear unto you. So ye abode in Kadesh many days, according unto the days that ye abode there."

Ancient Israel spent many days at Kadesh-Barnea on the borders of the promised land before they turned back into the wilderness. Deuteronomy 2:1. The length of their stay at the gateway to Canaan is not given, but a number of important events took place before the retreat began, events of far-reaching consequences in the history of the Exodus Movement.

Because of the Lord's sentence that the rebels must die in the wilderness, the camp was in a rebellious attitude. Their defeat by the Amalakites and Canaanites when they tried to force their way into the promised land, after the Lord had revoked His promise and altered His purpose, filled them with murmurings and the spirit of revolt.

The Provocation

In Hebrews 3:8 the rebellion at Kadesh-Barnea is divinely called "the provocation" and "the day of temptation in the wilderness." Here they tempted, provoked and grieved God and hardened their own hearts. In no way was this more strikingly fulfilled than in their rejection of God's leadership through the gift of prophecy.[1]

At Kadesh-Barnea they rejected the spirit of prophecy and attempted to follow their own counsel.[2] They did not return back to Egypt in person but "in their hearts they turned back again into Egypt." The Israelites refused to obey the prophet of the Exodus Movement, but "thrust him from him", and rejected his counsel. In doing this they rejected God and His divine leadership. See 1 Samuel 8:7, 19.

New Leadership

1. Hosea 12:13.
2. Acts 7:37-39.

Numbers 14:1-4: "And all the congregation lifted up their voice, and cried; and the people wept that night. And all the children of Israel murmured against Moses and against Aaron: and the whole congregation said unto them, Would God that we had died in the land of Egypt! or would God we had died in this wilderness! And wherefore hath the LORD brought us unto this land, to fall by the sword, that our wives and our children should be a prey? were it not better for us to return into Egypt? And they said one to another, Let us make a captain, and let us return into Egypt."

Nehemiah 9:16,17: "So it was alway: the cloud covered it by day, and the appearance of fire by night. And when the cloud was taken up from the tabernacle, then after that the children of Israel journeyed: and in the place where the cloud abode, there the children of Israel pitched their tents."

This was fulfilled in the great apostasy that took place at Kadesh under the leadership of Korah, Dathan, and Abiram. 250 princes joined them in their revolt against divine leadership through the spirit of prophecy and before this offshoot movement came to an end 14,700 lay-members were led astray and destroyed. The Lord vindicated His appointed leadership by the destruction of the rebels and the bringing to an ignominious end their movement. The three leaders of this false movement were swallowed up by the earth, and 250 princes were burned with fire, and the 14,700 who joined in the apostasy were destroyed by a terrible plague.

The Real Issue

That the real issue in this apostasy was the gift of prophecy is evident from the record in Numbers 16:1-3. The claim of the offshoots was that Moses and Aaron lifted themselves up above the congregation of the Lord and assumed too much authority. They declared that "all the congregation are holy, everyone of them." It was a plea that all share equally in the authority and responsibility of leadership regardless of the Lords' appointments. Moses had previously showed his bigness in saying:

> Would God that all the Lord's people were prophets, and that the Lord would put His spirit upon them.[3]

All members of God's church are not equally holy or qualified for leadership. To forever settle the question of divine call to leadership through the instruments of God's own choosing He demanded the demonstration of the rods recorded in Numbers 17. The miracle of the budding, blossoming, and fruit-bearing of Aaron's rod closed the mouths of the critics and vindicated the leadership of the movement.

Mistake of Moses

Korah was the new captain who was to supercede Moses. He declared

3. Numbers 11:29.

that Moses was an overbearing ruler; that he had reproved the people as sinners, when they were a holy people, and the Lord was among them. … His hearers thought they saw clearly that their troubles might have been prevented if Moses had pursued a different course. They decided that all their disasters were chargeable to him, and that their exclusion from Canaan was in consequence of the mismanagement of Moses and Aaron; that if Korah would be their leader, and would encourage them by dwelling upon their good deeds instead of reproving their sins, they would have a very peaceful, prosperous journey; instead of wandering to and fro in the wideness, they would proceed directly to the promised land.[4]

Deceived by Flattery

They had been flattered by Korah and his company until they really believed themselves to be a very good people, and that they had been wronged and abused by Moses. Should they admit that Korah and his company were wrong, and Moses right, then they would be compelled to receive as the Word of God the sentence that they must die in the wilderness. They were not willing to submit to this, and they tried to believe that Moses had deceived them. They had fondly cherished the hope that a new order of things was about to be established, in which praise would be substituted for reproof, and ease for anxiety and conflict. The men who had perished had spoken flattering words, and had professed great interest and love for them, and the people had concluded that Korah and his companions must have been good men, and that Moses had by some means been the cause of their destruction. It is hardly possible for men to offer greater insult to God than to despise and reject the instrumentalities He would use for their salvation.[5]

The Antitype

Just as ancient Israel remained at Kadesh "many days" before being led back into the wilderness, so the Advent people remained for a number of years at the borders of the heavenly Canaan before the message that brought them there was rejected and ceased to be preached. It is impossible to state just when the message ceased to do its work and the Advent Movement was turned back into the wilderness. The message of righteousness by faith was preached with power for more than ten years during which time the Minneapolis crisis was kept before the leaders. This message brought the beginning of the latter rain.

The time of test is just upon us, for the loud cry of the third angel has already begun in the revelation of the righteousness of Christ, the

4. Ellen White, *Patriarchs and Prophets* (1890), p. 397-398.
5. *Ibid.*, p. 401-402.

sin-pardoning Redeemer. This is the beginning of the light of the angel whose glory shall fill the whole earth.[6]—R.H. Nov. 22, 1892.

Why did not the latter rain continue to fall? Because the message that brought it ceased to be preached. It was rejected by many and it soon died out of the experience of the Advent people and the loud cry died with it. It can begin again only when the message that brought it then is revived and accepted.

World Revival

During the period when this revival message was being preached in this movement with such wonderful results, the Holy Spirit was being poured out all over the world. A great revival swept through the Christian world and God's people everywhere heard the call to prepare for the soon coming of Christ and in view of that event to evangelize the world. These were the days of D. L. Moody and his great revivals, and of A. T. Pierson and his message to arouse Christendom to its duty in giving the gospel to the whole world.

In 1886 Mr. Moody called together 251 students from 89 colleges and universities of the United States and Canada, and conducted a four week's institute during which time the Holy Spirit was present with power. At the close, 21 students dedicated their lives to foreign missions. At a meeting held later the number of volunteers was increased to 100. At that meeting A. T. Pierson coined the phrase: "All should go and go to tell." All of the colleges and universities of the United States were then visited and the foreign mission recruits increased to 2,500.

Important Date

1888 is not alone an important date to Seventh-day Adventists. In that year was organized "The Student Volunteer Movement of Foreign Missions", with the watchcry, "The Evangelization of the World in this Generation." John R. Mott, one of the founders, wrote an article in the "Missionary Review" of November, 1889, in which he declared that the movement was the beginning of "the greatest missionary revival since the days of the apostles."

The Holy Spirit was being poured out on all flesh preparatory to the great ingathering of souls under the latter rain. In our own movement there were many evidences that we were on the borders of the heavenly Canaan and that the end was near. Many miracles were wrought especially in the healing of the sick. Persecution also started and it looked as if the prophecy of Revelation 13 was about to be fulfilled.

In 1883 the Blair Sunday Bill was introduced into Congress. During the years 1889

6. Ellen White, "The Perils and Priveleges of the Last Day," *Review and Herald*, November 22, 1892, par. 7.

and 1890 many of our people in the South were fined and imprisoned and placed in chain-gangs for working on Sunday. There was every evidence that the end was at hand.

A Great Apostasy

But the spirit of revival died out and the Christian world entered the greatest apostasy since the great Reformation had broken the power of the Papal apostasy. The leadership of the Holy Spirit was substituted with the ideas and opinions of men. The great evangelical denominations rejected divine leadership and appointed other captains to lead them. Most of their leaders today are modernists headed toward Egypt.

With the rejection of the message of righteousness by faith in the Advent Movement came the greatest apostasy in our history. The crisis was precipitated by disbelief of the instruction the Lord sent through the spirit of prophecy, the divine agency by which the movement is led and preserved. When the crisis was past it was evident to all who remained loyal that the Lord had abundantly vindicated His leadership through His chosen instrument. The passing of time continues to prove that "by a prophet" the Lord is leading and preserving the Advent Movement, as He did the Exodus Movement.[7]

Gift Made Void

Just as Israel "would not obey" the messages of their prophet, so modern Israel manifested the same spirit of doubt and unbelief in God's chosen instrument and thus made the testimonies of His Spirit of none effect. The rejection of the message from heaven was virtually a rejection of the spirit of prophecy.

> The testimonies of His Spirit call your attention to the Scriptures, point out your defects of character, and rebuke your sins; therefore you do not heed them. And to justify your carnal, ease-loving course, you begin to doubt whether the testimonies are from God. If you would obey their teachings, you would be assured of their divine origin. Remember, your unbelief does not effect their truthfulness. If they are from God, they will stand. Those who seek to lessen the faith of God's people in these testimonies are fighting against God. It is not the instrument whom you fight and insult, but God, who has spoken to you in these warnings and reproofs.[8]

Thus even before 1888 the spirit of doubt and unbelief was developing which ripened into a virtual revolt against the divine leadership of the movement.

Attitude Before 1888

---

7. Hosea 12:13.
8. Ellen White, *Testimonies for the Church*, vol. 5 (1889), p. 234-235.

Before the Minneapolis Conference the spirit of unbelief in the spirit of prophecy had been developing so that when the crisis came it was but the natural consequence of a former attitude that led many to reject the heaven-sent message and the divinely given counsel.

> I am filled with sadness when I think of our condition as a people. The Lord has not closed heaven to us, but our own course of continual backsliding has separated us from God. Pride, covetousness, and love of the world have lived in the heart without fear of banishment or condemnation. And yet the general opinion is that the church is flourishing and that peace and spiritual prosperity are in all her borders. The church has turned back from following Christ her Leader, and is steadily retreating toward Egypt. Yet few are alarmed or astonished at their want of spiritual power. Doubt and even disbelief of the testimonies of the Spirit of God is leavening our churches everywhere. Satan would have it thus. Ministers who preach self instead of Christ would have it thus. The testimonies are unread and unappreciated. God has spoken to you. Light has been shining from His word and from the testimonies, and both have been slighted and disregarded.[9]

Result of Crisis

The message that brought the 1888 crisis ripened into a harvest this spirit of disbelief in the spirit of prophecy. On Nov. 3, 1890, the following testimony was given:

> What reserve power has the Lord with which to reach those who have cast aside His warnings and reproofs, and have accredited the testimonies of the Spirit of God to no higher source than human wisdom? In the judgment, what can you who have done this offer to God as an excuse for turning from the evidence that He has given you that God was in the work? 'By their fruits ye shall know them.' I would not now rehearse before you the evidences given in the past two years of the dealings of God by His chosen servant.[10]

Two years previous to this testimony was at the very time of the Minneapolis meeting.

Of No Effect

At the General Conference early morning meeting of Feb. 27, 1893, a testimony was read from Sister White which contained the following:

9. Ellen White, *Testimonies for the Church*, vol. 5 (1889), p. 217.
10. Quoted in "General Conference Bulletin", February 7, 8, 1893.

"The Lord designed that the messages of warning and instruction given through the Spirit to His people should go everywhere. But the influences that grew out of the resistance of light and truth at Minneapolis tended to make of no effect the light God had given to His people through the Testimonies. ... Some of those who occupy responsible positions were leavened with the spirit that prevailed at Minneapolis, a spirit that clouded the discernment of the people of God.[11]

The rejection of the heaven-sent message which began in 1888 was also a rejection of the spirit of prophecy. The same is true today as that message is being repeated. To disregard the present call for a revival and reformation is to reject the counsel of God through the Spirit of Prophecy.

Spirit of Satan

The spirit that opposed the message of 1888 was divinely called "the spirit of Satan." Knowing the results that would follow the acceptance of that message, Satan became desperate in his efforts to destroy its influence. As many as he could, he lead to openly oppose the message and thus reject the spirit of prophecy. Others who assented to the message were led into extremes that brought a reproach upon the work of God.

One of these was the "Holy Flesh" movement which began in the year 1900. This was a perversion of the doctrine of righteousness by faith and was inspired by Satan to cast a reproach upon it. Even to this day, some who are opposed to the repetition of the 1888 message attempt to use the "holy flesh" scare as an argument against it. There is absolutely nothing related to the idea of "holy flesh" in the genuine message of righteousness by faith.

Another effort of Satan to defeat God's purpose was the teaching that God was naturally in all of us and in every living thing; that all life is a manifestation of God and is therefore God. This Pantheistic teaching was accepted by many and destroyed the necessity of bringing Christ into the heart and life by faith for according to the spiritualistic philosophy He was already there in both the good and the bad.

Offshoot Movements

During the two decades following the crisis of 1888, there were many "offshoot" movements and they were all related to the message from heaven and the attitude towards it. Some openly rejected and fought the spirit of prophecy and others used it to a wrong purpose by attempting to prove that their false movement was of God.

---

11. Ellen White, "February 28, 1893 Testimony Dated Jan. 9, 1893," *General Conference Daily Bulletin*, February 28, 1893, par 4.

This has been true of every offshoot movement to the present time. Statements made by the servant of God during this crisis period, and especially those strongly reproving leaders because of their attitude toward God's message and messengers, are taken out of their natural and historical setting and used in an effort to support a false and counterfeit movement inspired by Satan. Most false movements begin with much pretended reverence for the spirit of prophecy but usually end in its repudiation because of the impossibility of proving that its teachings are in accord with their doctrines and practices.

Chief Argument

The basic argument of most offshoot movements originated in 1893 when an effort was made to prove from the messages of the spirit of prophecy that the Seventh-day Adventist Church had become Babylon. Misguided men gathered out of the writings of Sister White the strongest statements of reproof to the church and its leaders and drew from them a false conclusion which deceived many. To correct this grievous error Sister White wrote four articles which appeared in the *Review and Herald* of August 22 and 29, and September 5 and 12. This series was later printed in *Testimonies to Minsters*, pp. 32-62. We shall quote a few extracts from these articles which were entitled, "The Remnant Church Not Babylon:"

Movement Condemned

> In the pamphlet published by Brother S. and his associates, he accuses the church of God of being Babylon and would urge a separation from the church. This is a work that is neither honorable nor righteous. In compiling this work they have used my name and writings for the support of that which I disapprove and denounce as error. ... I have no hesitancy in saying that those who are urging on this work are greatly deceived. For years I have borne my testimony to the effect that when any arise claiming to have great light and yet advocating the tearing down of that which the Lord through His human agents has been building up, they are greatly deceived, and are not working along the lines where Christ is working. Those who assert that the Seventh-day Adventist Churches constitute Babylon, or any part of Babylon, might better stay at home.

Inspired by Satan

> In place of working with divine agencies to prepare a people to stand in the day of the Lord, they have taken their stand with him who is the accuser of the brethren, who accuses them before God day and night. Satanic agencies have been moved from beneath, and they have inspired men to unite with a confederacy of evil, that they may perplex, harass, and cause the people of God great distress."

To claim that the Seventh-day Adventist Church is Babylon, is to make the same claim as does Satan." "Is it possible that men will arise among us, who speak perverse things, and give voice to the very sentiments that Satan would have disseminated in the world in regard to those who keep the commandments of God, and have the faith of Jesus?

Are Dishonest

It will be found that those who bear false messages will not have a high sense of honor and integrity. They will deceive the people, and mix up with their error the 'Testimonies' of Sister White, and use her name to give influence to their work. They take such selections from the 'Testimonies' as they think they can twist to support their positions, and place them in a setting of falsehood, so that their error may have weight, and be accepted by the people. They misinterpret and misapply that which God has given to the church to warn, counsel, reprove, comfort, and encourage those who will make up the remnant people of God. These same dishonest practices are still being used by offshoot movements who attempt to deceive by trying to prove that they are in accord with the 'Testimonies'.

24

THE RETREAT TOWARD EGYPT

The Retreat

Deuteronomy 2:1: "Then we turned, and took our journey into the wilderness by the way of the Red sea, as the LORD spake unto me: and we compassed mount Seir many days."

According to verses 14 and 15, the "many days" the Israelites encamped around Mount Seir in the wilderness of Zin was almost 38 years. During this time "the hand of the Lord was against them, to destroy them from among the host until they were consumed." This of course is speaking of those who rebelled and "provoked the Lord" at Kadesh.

During the whole period of their wilderness wandering they were under the disfavor of God. A study of the map reveals the fact that the hosts of Israel practically retraced their steps as far as the Elanatic Gulf, the western arm of the Red Sea. This return into the wilderness from Kadesh was a retreat and was so considered by the nations of Canaan who had trembled at their reproach.

Went Backwards

Jeremiah 7:22-24: "For I spake not unto your fathers, nor commanded them in the day that I brought them out of the land of Egypt, concerning burnt offerings or sacrifices: But this thing commanded I them, saying, Obey my voice, and I will be your God, and ye shall be my people: and walk ye in all the ways that I have commanded you, that it may be well unto you. But they hearkened not, nor inclined their ear, but walked in the counsels and in the imagination of their evil heart, and went backward, and not forward."

At the very threshold of their goal the Israelites refused to hearken to divine counsel, but walked "in the stubbornness of their evil heart, (margin) and retreated backward toward Egypt instead of going forward toward Canaan." The rebellion at Kadesh made it necessary for them to turn their backs upon the promised land and face again toward the land of their bondage.

"In their hearts" they had "turned back again into Egypt", and had even "appointed a captain to return to their bondage", so now they were compelled to start an ignominious retreat toward the place of their heart's desire where they could obtain the things their souls lusted after. They did not return all of the way to Egypt. The next 38 years were spent wandering about in the desert of Zin. They did not return to Egypt, nor did they go forward to the promised land. They were practically at a standstill.

Wilderness Wandering

Numbers 14:32-34: "But as for you, your carcases, they shall fall in this wilderness. And your children shall wander in the wilderness forty years, and bear your whoredoms, until your carcases be wasted in the wilderness. After the number of the days in which ye searched the land, even forty days, each day for a year, shall ye bear your iniquities, even forty years, and ye shall know my breach of promise."

Numbers 32:13 "And the LORD'S anger was kindled against Israel, and he made them wander in the wilderness forty years, until all the generation, that had done evil in the sight of the LORD, was consumed."

The wilderness wandering of Israel was the fulfillment of a divine decree or sentence because at Kadesh they "had done evil in the sight of the Lord"[1] and had kindled His anger.There was not even a highway for them to travel on but they drifted or wandered aimlessly about in a desert of "void place." -Margin.

Psalm 107:4, 5: "They wandered in the wilderness in a solitary way; they found no city to swell in. Hungry and thirsty, their soul fainted in them."

It was indeed a solitary and desolate way over which they traveled during their wilderness wanderings. "Wander" means ramble here and there, without any certain course or object in view; to rove, range, or roam about; to stray; to depart or stray from any settled course or path; to deviate." During this period they made no progress toward their final goal. Their punishment was very severe, but their sin at Kadesh was very grievous. They must learn lessons of faith and obedience in the hard school of experience. The Lord could not take rebels into the promised land {because} they "Loved to wander."[2]

Material Prosperity

"He blessed them also, so that they multiplied greatly." Psalm 107:38.

While this was doubtless spoken of the experience of the Israelites in Egypt, there can be no question but the Exodus Movement continued to increase in membership during the entire course of their journey. See Nehemiah 9:23. Material prosperity in

1. Psalm 107:40.
2. Jeremiah 14:10.

increasing numbers did not cease during their wilderness wanderings. During this time they doubtless also increased in efficiency of their organization and from a material viewpoint they appeared to be a prosperous people. This sort of prosperity, however, did not lead them toward the promised land. Increased equipment and numbers is not the prosperity that counts with God. Spiritual progress alone could bring success to the movement and lead them out of the wilderness and into the promised land.

Advent Movement

While the heaven-sent message that began at the Minneapolis Conference in 1888 led the Advent Movement out of the wilderness of sin to the very borders of the heavenly Canaan, the rejection of that message resulted in a retreat back into the wilderness again. The movement itself has not gone all the back to Egypt or the world, but like Israel of old has only retreated "toward Egypt."

It is true, however, that many thousands of individual members have completed the journey all the way back to the world. Their retreat has taken them back to Babylon, the place of their former bondage. It is also true that thousands of Adventists are dangerously near the world and will soon sever all connections with God's people and return to spiritual Egypt.

But the Advent Movement itself has never completed the retreat and never will. Its final triumph is just as certain as was that of the Exodus Movement, and all who remain in the movement to the end will reach the heavenly goal.

Hearts in Egypt

The long delay of the Exodus Movement was due to the fact that the Israelites did not sever all connections with Egypt and the things in Egypt. "In their hearts they turned back again into Egypt." They continued to think of and lust after the things of the land of their bondage. This is also the cause of the long delay of the triumph of the Advent Movement. Those whose hearts are in the world, and whose affections are set upon the things of the world, will eventually follow their hearts and return to the world.

Only those who make a complete separation from the world, and who "Seek those things which are above" and set their 'affections on things above, and not on things on the earth'[3] will eventually triumph with the Advent Movement. It is dangerous to retreat toward the world and to have our interests centered on the things of the world. Those who are living on the very borders of the world are courting tragic failure and eternal ruin. They constitute the "mixed multitude" of the Advent Movement.

3. Colossians 3:1, 2.

Previous Retreat

The retreat worldward after the rejection of the 1888 message was only the repetition of a spiritual retreat that had been in progress previous to the giving of that heaven-sent message. In fact a growing conformity to the world was the reason why the Lord sent the message calling for a spiritual revival and reformation. The following are a few of many statements regarding the spiritual condition of God's people before 1888:

> Many have for years made no advancement in knowledge and true holiness. They are spiritual dwarfs. Instead of going forward to perfection, they are going back to the darkness and bondage of Egypt.[4]

> As a people we are not advancing in spirituality as we near the end.[5]

> "My heart aches day after day and night after night for our churches. Many are progressing, but in a back track.[6]

Retreating

> I am filled with sadness when I think of our condition as a people. The Lord has not closed heaven to us, but our own course of continual backsliding has separated us from God. Pride, covetousness, and love of the world have lived in the heart without fear of banishment or condemnation. Grievous and presumptuous sins have dwelt among us. And yet the general opinion is that the church is flourishing, and that peace and spiritual prosperity are in all her borders. The church has turned back from following Christ her Leader, and is steadily retreating toward Egypt. Yet few are alarmed or astonished at their want of spiritual power.[7]

Just as the Israelites were in the wilderness before they reached Kadesh at the borders of the promised land, so the Advent people were in the wilderness of sin before they reached the borders of the heavenly Canaan in 1888.

A Worse Retreat

The worst spiritual retreat in the history of the Advent Movement has come as the result of rejecting the 1888 message.

> Since the time of the Minneapolis meeting, I have seen the state of the Laodicean church as never before. I have heard the rebuke of God spoken

---

4. Ellen White, *Testimonies for the Church*, vol. 2 (1871), p. 214.
5. Ellen White, *Testimonies for the Church*, vol. 5 (1889), p. 11.
6. *Ibid.*, p. 93.
7. *Ibid.*, p. 217.

to those who feel so well satisfied, who know not their spiritual destitution. ...

Like the Jews, many have closed their eyes lest they should see; but there is as great peril now, in closing the eyes to light, and walking apart from Christ, feeling need of nothing, as there was when He was upon earth. I have been shown many things which I have presented before our people in solemnity and earnestness, but those whose hearts have been hardened through criticism, jealously, and evil surmisings, knew not that they were poor, and miserable, and blind, and naked. ...

I feel sad when I think how for long years there has been a gradual lowering of the standard. ... This great spiritual destitution is not caused by any failure on the part of Christ doing all that is possible for the church.[8]

The movement retreated back into the terrible Laodicean wilderness out of which the 1888 message endeavored to lead them.

Spiritual Weakness

The Lord has sent a message to arouse His people to repent and do the first works; but how has His message been received? While some have heeded it, others have cast contempt and reproach upon the message and the messenger. Spiritually deadened, humility and child-like simplicity gone, a mechanical, formal profession of faith has taken the place of love and devotion. Is this mournful condition of things to continue?. ... Why will you try to rekindle a mere fitful fire, and walk in the sparks of your own kindling?. ...

The church is like the unproductive tree which, receiving the dew and the rain and the sunshine, should have produced an abundance of fruit, but on which the Divine Searcher discovers nothing but leaves. Solemn thought for our churches. Solemn, indeed for every individual. Marvelous is the patience and forbearance of God; but 'except thou repent', it will be exhausted. The churches and our institutions will go from weakness to weakness, and from cold formality to deadness, while they are saying, 'I am rich and increased with goods, and have need of nothing.' The True Witness says, 'And knowest not that thou art wretched, and miserable, and poor, and blind, and naked.' Will they ever see clearly their true condition?[9]

Christless Experience

There are many, many professed Christians who are waiting uncon-

8. Ellen White, "The Righteousness of Christ," *Review and Herald*, August 26, 1890.
9. Ellen White, "Be Zealous and Repent," Review and Herald, Extra, December 23, 1890. Republished in the R.H. November 7, 1918.

cernedly for the coming of the Lord. They have not on the garment of His righteousness. They may profess to be children of God, but they are not cleansed from sin. They are selfish and self-sufficient. Their experience is Christless. They neither love God supremely nor their neighbor as themselves. They have no true idea of what constitutes holiness. They do not see the defects in themselves. So blinded are they that they are not able to detect the subtle working of pride and iniquity. They are clad in the rags of self-righteousness, and stricken with spiritual blindness. Satan has cast his shadow between them and Christ, and they have no wish to study the pure and holy character of the Saviour.[10]

Half-dead Christianity

In many hearts there seems to be scarcely a breath of spiritual life. This makes me very sad. I fear that aggressive warfare against the world, the flesh, and the devil has not been maintained. Shall we cheer on, by a half-head Christianity, the selfish, covetous spirit of the world, sharing its ungodliness and smiling on its falsehood? Nay! …

God brings against ministers, and people the heavy charge of spiritual feebleness, saying, 'I know thy works, that thou art neither cold nor hot: I would thou wert cold or hot. So then because thou are lukewarm, and neither cold nor hot, I will spue thee out of My mouth. … God calls for a spiritual revival and a spiritual reformation. Unless this takes place, those who are lukewarm will continue to grow more abhorrent to the Lord, until He will refuse to acknowledge them as His children.[11]

Church Converted to World

It is a solemn and terrible truth that many who have been zealous in proclaiming the third angel's message are now becoming listless and indifferent. The line of demarcation between worldlings and many professed Christians is almost indistinguishable. Many who were once earnest Adventists are conforming to the world,—to its practices, its customs, its selfishness. Instead of leading the world to render obedience to God's law, the church is uniting more and more closely with the world in transgression. Daily the church is becoming converted to the world.[12]

This statement indicates that not only many individuals but the entire church or movement has made a retreat world-ward. There are scores of other similar statements that might be read.

---

10. Ellen White, "The Influence of the Truth," *Review and Herald*, February 26, 1901.
11. Ellen White, "The Need of Revival and Reformation," *Review and Herald*, February 25, 1902.
12. Ellen White, *Testimonies for the Church*, vol. 8 (1904), p. 118-119.

Material Prosperity

Just as Israel increased in numbers and enjoyed a degree of material prosperity during their retreat and wilderness wandering, so the Advent Movement likewise steadily increased its membership, improved its organization, extended its influence, expanded its mission borders, and multiplied its institutions, evangelists and finances, even while it was retreating toward the world and wandering about in the wilderness of sin. But material prosperity is not always an evidence of spiritual progress. It is possible to experience the former without the latter. If material progress constitutes a sure evidence of the blessing and approval of God, what conclusion would be inevitable regarding the growth of the Papacy, Mohammedanism, Christian Science, and many other false religions?

Spiritual Retreat

The retreat is in regard to spiritual and not material things.

> The work has been extended so that it now covers a large territory, and the number of believers has increased. Still there is a great deficiency, for a larger work might have been accomplished had the same missionary spirit been manifested as in earlier days. Without this spirit the laborer will only mar and deface the cause of God. The work is really retrograding instead of advancing as God designs it should. Our present members are not to be compared with what they were in the beginning. We should consider what might have been done had every worker consecrated himself, in soul, body, and spirit, to God as he should have done.[13]

> But in some respects the work has deteriorated. While it has grown in extent and facilities, it has waned in piety.[14]

True Prosperity

> If numbers were an evidence of success, Satan might claim the pre-eminence; for, in this world his followers are largely in the majority. It is the degree of moral power pervading the college, that is the test of its prosperity. It is the virtue, intelligence, and piety of the people composing our churches, not their numbers, that should be a source of joy and thankfulness.[15]

Following a description of material prosperity and display in religious worship when godliness is lacking, we read:

---

13. Ellen White, *Testimonies for the Church*, vol. 6 (1901), p. 420.
14 *Ibid.*, vol. 7 (1902), p. 217.
15. *Ibid.*, vol. 5 (1889), p. 31-32.

> But in all this God is not honored. He values His church, not for its external advantages, but for the sincere piety which distinguishes it from the world. He estimates it according to the growth of its members in the knowledge of Christ, according to their progress in spiritual experience. He looks for the principles of love and goodness. …
>
> A congregation may be the poorest in the land. It may be without attractions of any outward show; but if the members possess the principles of the character of Christ, angels will unite with them in their worship.[16]

Cause of Deception

Here is the reason for the Laodicean deception. The church has mistaken material prosperity for spiritual progress; as the evidence of the presence of God and the favor of heaven. The purpose of the Laodicean message is to correct this false impression and to show that God reckons prosperity from the viewpoint of spiritual life and growth. Material prosperity will of course follow the presence and blessing of God as in apostolic days, but it is the result and not the cause of the Divine favor. The history of many ancient and modern false religious movements prove that material prosperity of itself is meaningless. To learn this lesson is one of the greatest needs of the Advent people for on it depends our eternal destiny.

16. Ellen White, *Prophets and Kings*, (1917), p. 564-566.

25

UNDER THE DIVINE REBUKE

Sad Spiritual State

Notwithstanding the fact that the children of Israel greatly increased their membership and improved their organization during their wilderness wandering, they were in a deplorable spiritual condition. This is evident from many Scriptures of which the following are samples:

Deuteronomy 9:7, 8, 23, 24: "Remember, and forget not, how thou provokedst the LORD thy God to wrath in the wilderness: from the day that thou didst depart out of the land of Egypt, until ye came unto this place, ye have been rebellious against the LORD. Also in Horeb ye provoked the LORD to wrath, so that the LORD was angry with you to have destroyed you. ...

"Likewise when the LORD sent you from Kadeshbarnea, saying, Go up and possess the land which I have given you; then ye rebelled against the commandment of the LORD your God, and ye believed him not, nor hearkened to his voice. Ye have been rebellious against the LORD from the day that I knew you."

Psalm 78:17, 18, 36-41: "And they sinned yet more against him by provoking the most High in the wilderness. And they tempted God in their heart by asking meat for their lust. ...

"Nevertheless they did flatter him with their mouth, and they lied unto him with their tongues. For their heart was not right with him, neither were they stedfast in his covenant. But he, being full of compassion, forgave their iniquity, and destroyed them not: yea, many a time turned he his anger away, and did not stir up all his wrath. For he remembered that they were but flesh; a wind that passeth away, and cometh not again. How oft did they provoke him in the wilderness, and grieve him in the desert! Yea, they turned back and tempted God, and limited the Holy One of Israel."

Their entire journey was marked by disobedience and rebellion.

> Yet the only records of their wilderness life are instances of rebellion against the Lord. The revolt of Korah had resulted in the destruction of fourteen thousand of Israel. And there were isolated cases that showed the same spirit of contempt for the divine authority.[1]

1. Ellen White, *Patriarchs and Prophets*, (1890), p. 407.

Destitute of Faith

Deuteronomy 31:27: "For I know thy rebellion, and thy stiff neck: behold, while I am yet alive with you this day, ye have been rebellious against the LORD; and how much more after my death?"

Deuteronomy 32:16-20: "They provoked him to jealousy with strange [gods], with abominations provoked they him to anger. They sacrificed unto devils, not to God; to gods whom they knew not, to new gods that came newly up, whom your fathers feared not. Of the Rock that begat thee thou art unmindful, and hast forgotten God that formed thee. And when the LORD saw it, he abhorred them, because of the provoking of his sons, and of his daughters. And he said, I will hide my face from them, I will see what their end shall be: for they are a very froward generation, children in whom is no faith."

The secret of their backslidden spiritual state is found in the statement that they were "children in whom is no faith." In Hebrews 3:17-19 we are told that unbelief or lack of faith was the reason for their failure to enter Canaan and was the thing that especially grieved and provoked God. Between the crossing of the Red Sea and the capture of Jericho there was no exhibition of faith that was worthy of mention in the divine record. Hebrews 11:29,30. The very purpose of the wilderness sojourn was to teach them lessons of faith and obedience but they were slow to learn.

Divine Rebuke

During the wilderness wandering, Israel was not only under the divine rebuke but they were a partially rejected people.

Numbers 32:13: "And the LORD'S anger was kindled against Israel, and he made them wander in the wilderness forty years, until all the generation, that had done evil in the sight of the LORD, was consumed."

Deuteronomy 2:14, 15: "And the space in which we came from Kadeshbarnea, until we were come over the brook Zered, was thirty and eight years; until all the generation of the men of war were wasted out from among the host, as the LORD sware unto them. For indeed the hand of the LORD was against them, to destroy them from among the host, until they were consumed."

> For nearly forty years the children of Israel were lost to view in the obscurity of the desert. ... During these years the people were constantly reminded that they were under the divine rebuke. In the rebellion of Kadesh they had rejected God; and God had, for the time, rejected them. Since they had proved unfaithful to His covenant they were not to receive the sign of the covenant, the rite of circumcision. Their desire to return to the land of slavery had shown them to be unworthy of freedom, and the ordi-

nance of the Passover, instituted to commemorate the deliverance from bondage, was not to be observed.[2]

Period of Rejection

The divine rebuke or partial rejection continued till the crossing of the Jordan into the promised land.

Joshua 5:7-10: "And their children, whom he raised up in their stead, them Joshua circumcised: for they were uncircumcised, because they had not circumcised them by the way. And it came to pass, when they had done circumcising all the people, that they abode in their places in the camp, till they were whole. And the LORD said unto Joshua, This day have I rolled away the reproach of Egypt from off you. Wherefore the name of the place is called Gilgal unto this day. And the children of Israel encamped in Gilgal, and kept the passover on the fourteenth day of the month at even in the plains of Jericho."

On that day the "reproach of Egypt" was rolled away, the divine rebuke removed, the period of rejection ended, and the covenant of grace renewed. Here Joshua "circumcised the children of Israel", and "the children of Israel encamped at Gilgal, and kept the Passover."

Since the rebellion at Kadesh the Lord had forbidden the Israelites the privilege of celebrating these two ordinances because their rebellion had made them void of meaning. Their desire to return to Egypt and the fact that in their hearts they did return to Egypt made the Passover of none effect. The Passover also pointed forward to Calvary and that event also was lost sight of. Circumcision was a symbol of the cutting off of sins from the heart and was therefore a sign of righteousness by faith. Rom. 2:28, 29; 4:11. Without this inward experience circumcision was a farce.

Jeremiah 4:4; 9:26: "Circumcise yourselves to the LORD, and take away the foreskins of your heart, ye men of Judah and inhabitants of Jerusalem: lest my fury come forth like fire, and burn that none can quench it, because of the evil of your doings."

"Egypt, and Judah, and Edom, and the children of Ammon, and Moab, and all that are in the utmost corners, that dwell in the wilderness: for all these nations are uncircumcised, and all the house of Israel are uncircumcised in the heart."

Ezekiel 44:7: "In that ye have brought into my sanctuary strangers, uncircumcised in heart, and uncircumcised in flesh, to be in my sanctuary, to pollute it, even my house, when ye offer my bread, the fat and the blood, and they have broken my covenant because of all your abominations."

---

2. Ellen White, *Patriarchs and Prophets*, (1890), p. 406.

Meaningless Ordinances

The rejection of divine leadership through the prophet of the Exodus Movement together with the abundance of evidence that the Israelites were not separated from their sins, knew nothing of righteousness by faith as an experience, and were still lusting after the things of Egypt and were not therefore delivered from their former bondage, made the rite of circumcision and the ordinance of the Passover meaningless.

> The suspension of the rite of circumcision since the rebellion at Kadesh had been a constant witness to Israel that their covenant with God, of which it was the appointed symbol, had been broken. And the discontinuance of the Passover, the memorial of their deliverance from Egypt, had been an evidence of the Lord's displeasure at their desire to return to the land of bondage. Now, however, the years of rejection were ended. Once more God acknowledged Israel as His people, and the sign of the covenant was restored.[3]

Reminded of Sins

There are many texts that indicate that Moses constantly reminded the Israelites of their sins during their period of partial rejection and he especially did not permit them to forget their rebellion at Kadesh-Barnea.

> Moses faithfully set before them their errors, and the transgression of their fathers. They had often felt impatient and rebellious because of their long wandering in the wilderness; but the Lord had not been chargeable with this delay in possessing Canaan. He was more grieved than they because He could not bring them into immediate possession of the promised land, and thus display before all nations His mighty power in the deliverance of His people. ... Had their fathers yielded in faith to the direction of God, being governed by His judgments, and walking in His ordinances, they would long before have been settled in Canaan, a prosperous, holy, happy people. Their delay to enter the goodly land dishonored God, and detracted from His glory in the sight of surrounding nations.[4]

Reproof Disagreeable

> It was the design of God that Moses should frequently remind Israel of their transgressions and rebellion, that they might humble their hearts before God in view of their sins. The Lord would not have them forget the errors and sins which had provoked His anger against them. The rehearsal of their transgressions, and of the mercies and goodness of God to them,

3. Ellen White, *Patriarchs and Prophets*, (1890), p. 485.
4. *Ibid.*, p. 464.

which they had not appreciated, was not agreeable to their feelings. Nevertheless, God directed that this should be done.[5]

We are told that Korah flattered the people and criticized Moses for being too pessimistic. He declared that the people should not be constantly reminded of their sins because they were really a good people and that their leader should talk courage and cheer them along. This was the reason for the large following of Korah and his fellow rebels.[6]

Their Enemies Mocked

Numpers 14:13-16: "And Moses said unto the LORD, Then the Egyptians shall hear it, (for thou broughtest up this people in thy might from among them;) And they will tell it to the inhabitants of this land: for they have heard that thou LORD art among this people, that thou LORD art seen face to face, and [that] thy cloud standeth over them, and that thou goest before them, by day time in a pillar of a cloud, and in a pillar of fire by night. Now if thou shalt kill all this people as one man, then the nations which have heard the fame of thee will speak, saying, Because the LORD was not able to bring this people into the land which he sware unto them, therefore he hath slain them in the wilderness."

This is exactly what happened when Israel was turned back into the wilderness from Kadesh, the gateway into the promised land.

> Heathen nations had reproached the Lord and His people because the Hebrews had failed to take possession of Canaan, as they expected, soon after leaving Egypt. Their enemies had triumphed because Israel had wandered so long in the wilderness, and they had mockingly declared that the God of the Hebrews was not able to bring them into the promised land.[7]

> Their delay to enter the goodly land dishonored God and detracted from His glory in the sight of surrounding nations.[8]

It was at this time that the heathen said: "Where is their God?"

The Advent Movement

Notwithstanding the fact that the Advent Movement has steadily increased its membership, improved its organization, extended its influence, and has prospered in material things along all lines, God's remnant people are in a sad spiritual state. They

5. Ellen White, *Testimonies for the Church*, vol. 3 (1875), p. 320.
6. See *Patriarchs and Prophets* (1890), p. 349.
7. Ellen White, *Patriarchs and Prophets*, (1890), p. 486.
8. *Ibid.*, p. 464.

have lost their first love and are lukewarm and are spiritually wretched, miserable, poor, blind, and naked.[9] We are said to be under the divine forbearance.

> I saw that at present we are under divine forbearance; but no one can say how long this will continue. No one knows how great the mercy that has been exercised toward us. But few are heartily devoted to God. There are only a few who, like the stars in a tempestuous night, shine here and there among the clouds. Many who complacently listen to the truth from God's word are dead spiritually, while they profess to live. For years they have come and gone in our congregation, but they seem only less and less sensible of the value of revealed truth. They do not hunger and thirst after righteousness. They have no relish for spiritual or divine things. They assent to the truth, but are not sanctified through it. Neither the word of God nor the testimonies of His Spirit make any lasting impression upon them. ... The entreaties of the Spirit of God, like divine melody, the promises of His word so rich and abundant, its threatenings against idolatry and disobedience, —all are powerless to melt the world-hardened heart.[10]

The Divine Rebuke

Revelation 3:19: "As many as I love, I rebuke and chasten: be zealous therefore, and repent."

"As many as I love I rebuke and chasten", indicates that the Laodicean church is under the divine rebuke because of her spiritual state. The Laodicean message is a divine rebuke. It is evidence of a partial rejection or separation. The union between Christ and the church is not complete as is evident from the fact that He is outside the door knocking and pleading to be invited in. He is not in the innermost sanctuary of the hearts of His people and He does not have full possession of His churchtemple.

> Since the time of the Minneapolis meeting, I have seen the state of the Laodicean church as never before. I have heard the rebuke of God spoken to those who feel so well satisfied, who know not their spiritual destitution. ...
>
> Like the Jews, many have closed their eyes lest they should see; but there is a great peril now, in closing the eyes to light and in walking apart from Christ, feeling need of nothing as there was when He was upon earth.[11]

The Laodicean message is here called "the rebuke of God" and Laodiceans are said to be "walking apart from Christ."

---

9. Revelation 2:1-5; 3:14-22.
10. Ellen White, *Testimonies for the Church*, vol. 5 (1889), p. 76.
11. Ellen White, "The Righteousness of Christ," *Review and Herald*, August 26, 1890, par. 4-5.

The Rebuke of God

The rebuke of God is upon us because of our neglect of solemn responsibilities. His blessings have been withdrawn because the testimonies He has given have not been heeded by those who profess to believe them. O, for a religious awakening! The angels of God are going from church to church, doing their duty; and Christ is knocking at the door of your hearts for entrance. But the means that God has devised to awaken the church to a sense of their spiritual destitution, have not been regarded.

The voice of the True Witness has been heard in reproof, but has not been obeyed. Men have chosen to follow their own way, instead of God's way, because self was not crucified in them. Thus the light has had but little effect upon their minds and hearts. ... If you wait for light to come in a way that will please everyone, you will wait in vain. If you wait for louder calls or better opportunities, the light will be withdrawn, and you will be left in darkness.[12]

Not in Midst

The following statement is a comment on Revelation 3:20 and shows that as long as Christ is kept outside the door, He is not in the midst of Zion and He is excluded from His own temple:

> The church is in the Laodicean state. The presence of God is not in her midst. ... What a terrible thing it is to exclude Christ from His own temple! What a loss to the church! Our Redeemer sends His messengers to bear a testimony to His people. He says, 'Behold, I stand at the door and knock. If any man hear my voice, and open the door, I will come in to him and will sup with him and he with Me.' But many refuse to receive Him, because they fear that He will be an expensive guest. The Holy Spirit waits to soften and subdue hearts, but they are not willing to open the door and let the Saviour in; for they fear that He will require something of them. And so Jesus of Nazareth passes by. He longs to bestow on them His rich blessings and gifts of grace, but they refuse to accept them.[13]

Cause of Weakness

The cause of the present spiritual weakness of God's remnant people is declared to be their Laodicean condition which makes the church "a place whence the divine presence and glory have departed! For this cause there is weakness, and strength is lacking. Unless the church, which is now being leavened with her own backsliding, shall repent and be converted, she will eat of the fruit of her own doing, until she

---

12. Ellen White, *Testimonies for the Church*, vol. 5 (1889), p. 719-720.
13. Brown Leaflet Series, Education, No. 6, 1898.

shall abhor herself." That the situation is not hopeless is indicated by the promise of a revival:

> When purification shall take place in our ranks, we shall no longer rest at ease, boasting of being rich and increased with goods, in need of nothing.[14]

Aimlessly Drifting

Just as Israel of old wandered aimlessly about in the wilderness during the time of their partial rejection while they were under the divine rebuke, so modern Israel is said to be "drifting" as though they were "without chart or compass."

> The solemn question should come home to every member of our churches, How are we standing before God, as the professed followers of Jesus Christ?. ... Spiritual death has come upon the people that should be manifesting life and zeal, purity and consecration by the most earnest devotion to the cause of the truth. The facts concerning the real condition of the professed people of God, speak more loudly than their profession, and make it evident that some power has cut the cable that anchored them to the Eternal Rock, and that they are drifting away to sea, with chart or compass.[15]

Ministration Hindered

While we are in the Laodicean condition the ministration of Christ in the heavenly sanctuary is being hindered and retarded.

> To those who are indifferent at this time Christ's warning is, 'Because thou art lukewarm, and neither cold or hot, I will spew thee out of my mouth.' The figure of spewing out of His mouth means that He cannot offer up your prayers or your expressions of love to God. He cannot endorse your teaching of His word or your spiritual work in any wise. He cannot present your religious exercises with the request that grace be given you.[16]

Our Laodicean attitude has brought the priestly ministration of Christ to virtually a standstill which has delayed His return. The Bridegroom tarries while the church slumbers and sleeps.

Constantly Reminded

Through the spirit of prophecy the Lord has constantly reminded the Advent peo-

---

14. Ellen White, *Testimonies for the Church*, vol. 8 (1904), p. 250.
15. Ellen White, "How Do We Stand," *Review and Herald*, July 24, 1888, par. 1.
16. Ellen White, *Testimonies for the Church*, vol. 6 (1901), p. 408.

ple of their sins and especially of their Laodicean condition and the great sin of rejecting the message of 1888.

> The Lord directed Moses to recount to the children of Israel His dealings with them in their deliverance from Egypt and their wonderful preservation in the wilderness. He was to call to mind their unbelief and murmurings when brought into trial, and the Lord's great mercy and loving-kindness, which had never forsaken them. …
> It is just as essential that the people of God in this day should bear in mind how and when they have been tested, and where their faith has failed; where they have imperiled His cause by their unbelief, and also by their selfconfidence. … As God's people thus review the past, they should see that the Lord is ever repeating His dealings. They should understand the warnings given, and should beware not to repeat their mistakes.[17]

Reproof Not Agreeable

But this reproof and reminding of their mistakes has been no more acceptable to modern Israel during their wilderness wanderings than to ancient Israel while they were under the divine rebuke.

> The apostle Paul plainly states that the experience of the Israelites in their travels has been recorded for the benefit of those living in this age of the world, upon whom the ends of the world are come. We do not consider that our dangers are any less than those of the Hebrews, but greater. There will be temptations to jealousies and murmurings, and there will be outspoken rebellion, as are recorded of ancient Israel. There will ever be a spirit to rise up against reproof of sins and wrongs. But shall the voice of reproof be hushed because of this?. …
> There will be men and women who despise reproof, and whose feelings will ever rise up against it. It is not pleasant to be told of our wrongs.[18]

This prophecy was fulfilled following the 1888 meeting when year after year the prophet of the Advent Movement reminded the church and her leaders of what happened at Minneapolis and the terrible consequences of that rebellion against heavenly light and divine leadership.

Conflicting Attitudes

During all the years the church has been boasting of her progress and prosperity in increased members, facilities, institutions and world-wide mission enterprises, the Lord through the spirit of prophecy has been rebuking the members of the

---

17. Ellen White, *Testimonies for the Church*, vol. 7 (1902), p. 210.
18. Ellen White, *Testimonies for the Church*, vol. 3 (1875), p. 358-359.

church for their sins and backsliding, for the loss of their first love which has resulted in lukewarmness and spiritual poverty.

The reproof has not been understood or appreciated by those under the Laodicean deception, and therefore the Testimonies have been practically set aside and by many virtually rejected. Not being able to understand the manifest contradiction between the attitude of the church and the prophetic agency of the movement through whom God speaks, the tendency has been to question the authority of the latter and conclude that God's prophet was altogether too pessimistic.

26

GOD'S LOVE AND LEADERSHIP

Not Forsaken

While the children of Israel rejected God at Kadesh-Barnea and had to be led back into the wilderness to fulfill the sentence of a provoked and offended God, they were not forsaken or cast off. They were under the divine rebuke and a partial or temporary rejection, but God still claimed them as His own people. Even though the records of their wilderness sojourn reveal little else save murmurings and rebellions against the Lord, yet He loved them above all people on the earth, and He kept them "as the apple of His eye."[1] No person can read these statements and doubt God's love, or claim that He had entirely rejected or cast off His people.

Divine Leadership

Even during the retreat of Israel toward Egypt and their wilderness wanderings under the divine rebuke, God continued to be their Leader. It was under the divine leadership that they returned into the wilderness and God's presence continued with them during the entire period of their alienation.

Deuteronomy 2:7: "For the LORD thy God hath blessed thee in all the works of thy hand: he knoweth thy walking through this great wilderness: these forty years the LORD thy God hath been with thee; thou hast lacked nothing."

Nehemiah 9:15-23: "And on the day that the tabernacle was reared up the cloud covered the tabernacle, [namely], the tent of the testimony: and at even there was upon the tabernacle as it were the appearance of fire, until the morning. So it was alway: the cloud covered it [by day], and the appearance of fire by night. And when the cloud was taken up from the tabernacle, then after that the children of Israel journeyed: and in the place where the cloud abode, there the children of Israel pitched their tents. At the commandment of the LORD the children of Israel journeyed, and at the commandment of the LORD they pitched: as long as the cloud abode upon the tabernacle they rested in their tents. And when the cloud tarried long upon the tabernacle many days, then the children of Israel kept the charge of the LORD, and journeyed not.

"And so it was, when the cloud was a few days upon the tabernacle; according to the commandment of the LORD they abode in their tents, and according to the

1. Deuteronomy 33:2, 3; 32:10; Isaiah 63:8, 9.

commandment of the LORD they journeyed. And so it was, when the cloud abode from even unto the morning, and that the cloud was taken up in the morning, then they journeyed: whether it was by day or by night that the cloud was taken up, they journeyed. Or whether it were two days, or a month, or a year, that the cloud tarried upon the tabernacle, remaining thereon, the children of Israel abode in their tents, and journeyed not: but when it was taken up, they journeyed. At the commandment of the LORD they rested in the tents, and at the commandment of the LORD they journeyed: they kept the charge of the LORD, at the commandment of the LORD by the hand of Moses."

The Israelites moved only when the pillar of cloud or fire went before them. That the occupant of the pillar of cloud and fire was Christ, has already been proven. See 1 Corinthians 10:4. God's love and tender care for His people during this period is beautifully illustrated in Acts 13:18.

> And about the time of forty years bore, or fed them as a nurse beareth, or feedeth her child. —Margin.

They were spiritually sick and God exercised toward them the tender love or care of a nurse toward her patient. A nurse never spurns or rejects a patient because of sickness which produces an unnatural and irritable and rebellious disposition. The Lord is more patient, kind, and considerate of His sick church than a nurse can be of a sick child.

No New Movement

Because the Exodus Movement failed at Kadesh-Barnea to enter the promised land "at the time of His appointment", the Lord did not start a new movement under new leadership. Caleb, Joshua, Moses and doubtless many others did not take part in the rebellion and were ready to enter the promised land, but they too, were divinely led back into the wilderness.

They did not start a new or offshoot movement and attempt to enter the promised land by themselves. They knew that God remained with the original movement even though it contained the rebels and that if they ever reached the promised land they too must go into the wilderness with the movement that God was leading and patiently await His own pleasure as to the time they would enter Canaan.

Korah, Dathan and Abiram attempted to start an offshoot movement and go directly in, but it ended in failure as did other similar efforts. The only hope of success was to remain loyal to the original organization or movement that God led out of Egypt and was still leading.

Advent Movement

Notwithstanding the return of modern Israel into the same dreadful Laodicean wilderness out of which the Lord attempted to lead them in 1888, the Advent Movement is still under divine leadership. Although under the divine rebuke of the Laodicean message and the alienation that excludes Christ from complete possession of His church-temple and that keeps Him outside the door of the inner chamber of the heart-temples of His people, He continues to claim the Laodicean church as His own and to love His remnant people above all others of the earth.

In Deuteronomy 7:6-9 we are told why the Lord love ancient Israel above all other people and chose them as His own, and for the same reason the Lord has chosen and set His love upon modern Israel even while she is in the Laodicean state. Laodiceans are the most obedient and loyal people in the world.

The Rebuke of Love

Revelation 3:19: "As many as I love, I rebuke and chasten: be zealous therefore, and repent."

> All whom I hold dear I reprove and chastise. —Weymouth

The Laodicean message is the most scathing rebuke contained in Holy Writ and comparable only to that administered to ancient Israel and recorded in the first chapter of Isaiah. The picture would be hopeless and discouraging if it were not for the fact that the rebuke is the rebuke of love.

The Laodicean message is a love-message and is not spoken in anger to wound and destroy, but in love to save and restore. Jesus reproves and chastises the remnant of His people because He loves them very dearly and He longs to have His love awaken a response of love in our hearts. One reason for His love is because His people are honestly deceived. This is indicated by the statement, "And knowest not that thou art wretched, and miserable, and poor, and blind, and naked."[2]

> The message of the True Witness finds the people of God in a sad condition, yet honest in that deception. They know not that their condition is deplorable in the sight of God.[3]

There is always hope for an honest person even though he be deceived, for "Every truly honest soul will come to the light of truth."[4] The Laodiceans who are honest will accept the rebuke and repent of their lukewarmness and reform their lives.

---

2. Revelation 3:17.
3. Ellen White, *Testimonies for the Church*, vol. 3 (1875), p. 252.
4. Ellen White, *Great Controversy* (1911), p. 522.

Supreme Regard

{Of God's care for His church, Ellen White writes:}

> Nothing else in this world is so dear to God as His church. Nothing is guarded by Him with such jealous care. Nothing so offends God as an act that injures the influence of those who are doing His service. He will call to account all who aid Satan in his work of criticizing and discouraging.[5]
>
> Enfeebled and defective, needing constantly to be warned and counseled, the church is nevertheless the object of Christ's supreme regard.[6]
>
> God has a people in which all heaven is interested, and they are the one object on earth dear to the heart of God.[7]
>
> Although there are evils existing in the church, and will be until the end of the world, the church in these last days is to be the light of the world that is polluted and demoralized by sin. The church, enfeebled and defective, needing to be reproved, warned, and counseled, is the only object upon earth which Christ bestows His supreme regard.[8]

Divine Leadership

The Laodicean church is not a fully rejected and forsaken church but is still the object of Christ's supreme affection and is the church He claims as His own because it is the best on earth at the present time. The original Advent Movement that started in the early part of the nineteenth century under divine leadership is still under the same guidance and control.

> God has a church and she has a divinely appointed ministry. ...
>
> God has a church upon the earth, who are His chosen people, who keep His commandments. He is leading, not stray offshoots, not one here and one there, but a people. The truth is a sanctifying power, but the church militant is not the church triumphant. There are tares among the wheat. ... The gospel net draws not only good fish, but bad ones as well, and the Lord only knows who are His.[9]

The Church Imperfect

Ancient Israel was a very imperfect people during the period of their partial rejec-

5. Ellen White, *Testimonies for the Church*, vol. 6 (1901), p. 42.
6. *Ibid*, vol. 7 (1902), p. 16.
7. Ellen White, *Testimonies to Ministers and Gospel Workers* (1923), p. 41.
8. *Ibid.*, p. 49.
9. *Ibid.*, p. 52, 61.

tion but this did not prevent God from loving and leading them. That the people of the Advent Movement are very imperfect no person can deny, but that this imperfection gives evidence that they are cast off by Christ and wholly rejected we must most emphatically deny.

> The church of Christ on earth will be imperfect, but God does not destroy His church because of its imperfection.[10]

> I know that the Lord loves His church. It is not to be disorganized or broken up into independent atoms. There is not the least consistency in this, there is not the least evidence that such a thing will be. Those who shall heed this false message, and try to leaven others will be deceived, and prepared to receive advanced delusions, and they will come to naught. There is in some of the members of the church pride, selfsufficiency, stubborn unbelief, and a refusal to yield their ideas although evidence may be piled upon evidence which makes this message to the Laodicean church applicable. But that will not blot out the church that it will not exist.[11]

Tares with Wheat

Matthew 13:30,37-43: "Let both grow together until the harvest: and in the time of harvest I will say to the reapers, Gather ye together first the tares, and bind them in bundles to burn them: but gather the wheat into my barn. ... He answered and said unto them, He that soweth the good seed is the Son of man; the field is the world; the good seed are the children of the kingdom; but the tares are the children of the wicked one; the enemy that sowed them is the devil; the harvest is the end of the world; and the reapers are the angels. As therefore the tares are gathered and burned in the fire; so shall it be in the end of this world. The Son of man shall send forth his angels, and they shall gather out of his kingdom all things that offend, and them which do iniquity; and shall cast them into a furnace of fire: there shall be wailing and gnashing of teeth. Then shall the righteous shine forth as the sun in the kingdom of their Father. Who hath ears to hear, let him hear."

> The tares and the wheat are to grow together until the harvest; and the harvest is the end of probationary time. … False brethren will be found in the church till the 103 close of time.[12]

> Those who train the mind to seize upon everything which they can use as a peg to hang a doubt upon, and suggest these thoughts to other minds, will always find occasion to doubt. They will question and criticize

10. *Ibid.*, p. 46.
11. Letter 16, 1893.
12. Ellen White, *Christ's Object Lessons* (1900), p. 72-73.

everything that arises in the unfolding of truth, criticize the work and position of others, criticize every branch of the work in which they have not themselves a part. They will feed upon the errors and mistakes and faults of others, 'until', said the angel, 'the Lord Jesus shall rise up from His mediatorial work in the heavenly sanctuary, and shall clothes Himself with the garments of vengeance, and surprise them at their unholy feast; and they will find themselves unprepared for the marriage supper of the Lamb.[13]

Not Disorganized

That the Advent Movement will not be disorganized and replaced by a new movement and organization is evident from many statements in the Spirit of Prophecy.

> Those who know the waymarks that have pointed out the right path are not to permit the banner of the third angel to be taken from their hand. ... We cannot now step off the foundation that God has established. We cannot now enter into any new organization; for this would mean apostasy from the truth.[14] —

The same movement that started from Babylon will go through to the heavenly Canaan. The rebels will be purged out but the movement will triumph for it will be under divine leadership to the end of the journey.

> I am encouraged and blessed as I realize that the God of Israel is still guiding His people, and that He will continue to be with them even to the end.[15]

Not Babylon

> My brother, I learn that you are taking the position that the Seventh-day Adventist Church is Babylon, and that all that would be saved must come out of her. You are not the only man the devil has deceived in this matter. For the last forty years, one man after another has arisen, claiming that the Lord has sent him with the same message; but let me tell you, as I have told them, that this message you are proclaiming is one of the satanic delusions designed to create confusion among the churches. My brother, you are certainly off the track.[16]

> We are not to think that the chosen ones of God who are trying to walk in the light compose Babylon. The fallen denominational churches are

---

13 Ellen White, *Testimonies for the Church,* vol. 5 (1889), p. 690.

14. MS-129-1905.

15 Ellen White, *Life Sketches* (1889), p. 437-438.

16 Ellen White, *Testimonies to Ministers and Gospel Workers* (1923), p. 58-59.

Babylon. Babylon has been fostering poisonous doctrines, the wine of error. This wine of error is made up of false doctrines, such as the natural immorality of the soul, the eternal torment of the wicked, the denial of the pre-existence of Christ prior to His birth in Bethlehem, and advocating and exalting the first day of the week above God's holy and sanctified day.[17]

Offshoots Not of God

Those who start up to proclaim a message on their individual responsibility, who, while claiming to be taught of God, still make it their special work to tear down that which God has been for years building up, are not doing the will of God. Be it known that these men are on the side of the great deceiver. Believe them not. They are allying themselves with the enemies of God and the truth. They will deride the order of the ministry as a system of priestcraft. From such turn away, have no fellowship with their message, however much they may quote the 'Testimonies' and seek to entrench themselves behind them. Receive them not; for God has not given them this work to do.[18]

Separatists Condemned

There are little companies continually arising who believe that God is only with the very few, the very scattered, and their influence is to tear down and scatter that which God's servants build up. Restless minds who want to be seeing and believing something new continually, are constantly arising, some in one place and some in another, all doing a special work for the enemy, yet claiming to have the truth. They stand separate from the people whom God is leading out and prospering, and through whom He is to do His great work. They are continually expressing their fears that the body of Sabbath-keepers are becoming like the world; but there are scarcely two of these whose views are in harmony.[19]

To Be Shunned

When men arise, claiming to have a message from God, but instead of warring against principalities and powers, and the rulers of the darkness of this world, they form a hollow square, and turn the weapons of warfare against the church militant. Be afraid of them. They do not bear the divine credentials. God has not given them any such burden of labor. They would tear down that which God would restore by the Laodicean message. He wounds only that He may heal, not cause to perish. The Lord lays upon no man a message that will discourage and dishearten the church. He re-

---

17. *Ibid.*, p. 61.
18. *Ibid.*, p. 51.
19. Ellen White, *Testimonies for the Church*, vol. 1 (1868), p. 417-418.

> proves, He rebukes, He chastens; but it is only that He may restore and approve at last.[20]

The Laodicean message is here declared to be given for the purpose of restoring the church and not to condemn and destroy it.

Will Come to Naught

Just as all the offshoot movements of the past have come to naught, those of the present and future will likewise end in failure and ignominiously perish. There are no shortcuts to the heavenly Canaan by the new movement route. The only way to reach the kingdom is to remain with and loyal to the original movement for that is the only one God is leading.

All offshoots are inspired and led by the devil in an effort to defeat the purpose of God for modern Israel. Only those who "wholly followed the Lord" and remained loyal to the Exodus Movement reached the promised land.[21] Only those who wholly follow the Lord and obey His instructions through the gift of prophecy and follow His leadership and maintain their loyalty to the Advent Movement will triumph with the movement and enter the heavenly Canaan.

20. Ellen White, *Testimonies to Ministers and Gospel Workers* (1923), p. 22-23.
21. Numbers 32:10-12; Joshua 14:6-14.

27

THE TEST OF FAITH REPEATED

Message Repeated

Deuteronomy 2:1-3: "Then we turned, and took our journey into the wilderness by the way of the Red sea, as the LORD spake unto me: and we compassed mount Seir many days. And the LORD spake unto me, saying, Ye have compassed this mountain long enough: turn you northward."

After almost 40 years of wandering around the mountains of Seir, the call to enter the promised land was repeated. The message was almost identical with the one given at Mount Horeb more than 38 years before.[1] It is evident that the Lord intended to cut short the 40 years sentence He had given at Kadesh-Barnea, hoping that His people had learned their lesson.

During these years of sojourn in the wilderness no heaven-sent message came to the Israelites for the purpose of leading them out of the wilderness and into Canaan. The message was one of good tidings to he weary pilgrims who had wandered so long in "the great and terrible wilderness." It must have filled the camp with rejoicing to know that the long delay or tarrying time was about ended.

School of Experience

The wilderness sojourn had been for the benefit of God's people. It was a school of experience to prepare them for entrance into the promised land. It took Moses 40 years in the wilderness to become qualified for the leadership of the Exodus Movement.

> Such was the experience that Moses gained by his forty years of training in the desert. To impart such experience, Infinite Wisdom counted not the period too long or the price too great.[2]

This experience doubtless helped Moses to be more patient and sympathetic with the Israelites during their wilderness term in the desert school of experience.

Deuteronomy 8:1-3: "All the commandments which I command thee this day shall

1. See Deuteronomy 1:6-8.
2. Ellen White, *Education* (1903), p. 64.

ye observe to do, that ye may live, and multiply, and go in and possess the land which the LORD sware unto your fathers. And thou shalt remember all the way which the LORD thy God led thee these forty years in the wilderness, to humble thee, and to prove thee, to know what was in thine heart, whether thou wouldest keep his commandments, or no. And he humbled thee, and suffered thee to hunger, and fed thee with manna, which thou knewest not, neither did thy fathers know; that he might make thee know that man doth not live by bread only, but by every word that proceedeth out of the mouth of the LORD doth man live."

> The varied experiences of the Hebrews was a school of preparation for their promised home in Canaan.[3]

Now the message comes that they had spent "long enough" in this school of training and preparation.

Back to Kadesh

Numbers 20:1-3: "Then came the children of Israel, even the whole congregation, into the desert of Zin in the first month: and the people abode in Kadesh; and Miriam died there, and was buried there. And there was no water for the congregation: and they gathered themselves together against Moses and against Aaron. And the people chided with Moses, and spake, saying, Would God that we had died when our brethren died before the LORD!"

That this is the same Kadesh where Israel had failed 38 years before is evident. It is located in or near "the wilderness of Paran" and "the desert of Zin."[4] "The wilderness of Zin which is Kadesh."[5] In Numbers 21:1 the Kadesh to which they returned is called "the way of the spies" which definitely identifies it as the same Kadesh from which the 12 spies entered the promised land 38 years before. We are told that Kadesh was the "appointed route to Canaan."[6]

The "popular and Critical Bible Encyclopedia" declares that Kadesh is the place

> at which the Israelites twice encamped with the intention of entering Palestine, and from which they were twice sent back.

Further Evidence

In proving that there was but one Kadesh the above mentioned authority continues:

---

3. Ellen White, *Patriarchs and Prophets* (1890), p. 293.
4. Numbers 13:26; 20:1.
5. Numbers 33:36.
6. Ellen White, *Patriarchs and Prophets* (1890), p. 414.

> It was left for Dr. Kitto to show that one Kadesh would sufficiently answer all the conditions required. According to this view, Kadesh was laid down in the map prepared under his direction, in the same line, and not far from the place which has since been assigned to it from actual observations by Dr. Robinson. This concurrence of different lines of research in the same result is curious and valuable, and the position of Kadesh will be regarded as now scarcely open to dispute.[7]

The authors of "The Pulpit Commentary" also contend that there was but one Kadesh to which Israel came and encamped twice. Sir. Wm. Smith in his "Dictionary of the Bible" says of Kadesh:

> This place, the scene of Miriam's death, was the farthest point to which the Israelites reached in their direct road to Canaan; it was also that whence the spies were sent, and where, on their return, the people broke out into murmuring, upon which their strictly penal term of wandering began.

Spirit of Prophecy

While Bible students have only recently come to the conclusion that there was but one Kadesh, the Spirit of Prophecy gave us the same information years ago and at a time when most of the authorities were contending that there were two.

> Again the congregation of Israel was brought into the wilderness, to the very place where God proved them soon after their leaving Egypt. The Lord brought them water out of the rock, which had continued to flow until just before they came again to the rock, when the Lord caused that living stream to cease, to prove His people again, to see if they would endure the trial of their faith, or would again murmur against Him.[8]

Test Repeated

The Lord led Israel back to the same place where they had failed 38 years before and again tested their faith to see if they would follow His leadership into the promised land. To bring this test the Lord caused the miraculous flow of water to cease.[9]

> Just before the Hebrew host reached Kadesh, the living stream ceased that for so many years has gushed out beside their encampment. It was the Lord's purpose again to test His people. He would prove whether they would trust His providence or imitate the unbelief of their fathers.

---

7. *Ibid.*
8. Ellen White, *Spirit of Prophecy* vol. 1 (1870), p. 309.
9. See Numbers 20:2.

They were now in sight of the hills of Canaan. A few days march would bring them to the borders of the promised land. …

Before God permitted them to enter Canaan, they must show that they believed His promise. The water ceased before they reached Edom. Here was an opportunity for them for a little time, to walk by faith instead of sight. But the first trial developed in them the same turbulent, unthankful spirit that had been manifested by their fathers.[10]

The Second Failure

Numbers 20:3-13: "And the people chode with Moses, and spake, saying, Would God that we had died when our brethren died before the LORD! And why have ye brought up the congregation of the LORD into this wilderness, that we and our cattle should die there? And wherefore have ye made us to come up out of Egypt, to bring us in unto this evil place? it is no place of seed, or of figs, or of vines, or of pomegranates; neither is there any water to drink.

"And Moses and Aaron went from the presence of the assembly unto the door of the tabernacle of the congregation, and they fell upon their faces: and the glory of the LORD appeared unto them. And the LORD spake unto Moses, saying, Take the rod, and gather thou the assembly together, thou, and Aaron thy brother, and speak ye unto the rock before their eyes; and it shall give forth his water, and thou shalt bring forth to them water out of the rock: so thou shalt give the congregation and their beasts drink. And Moses took the rod from before the LORD, as he commanded him.

"And Moses and Aaron gathered the congregation together before the rock, and he said unto them, Hear now, ye rebels; must we fetch you water out of this rock? And Moses lifted up his hand, and with his rod he smote the rock twice: and the water came out abundantly, and the congregation drank, and their beasts also. And the LORD spake unto Moses and Aaron, Because ye believed me not, to sanctify me in the eyes of the children of Israel, therefore ye shall not bring this congregation into the land which I have given them. This is the water of Meribah; because the children of Israel strove with the LORD, and he was sanctified in them."

The Israelites displayed the same spirit of unbelief and murmuring as they did at the same place 38 years before. What was intended to be the gateway to Canaan became "the water of Meribah" or "Strife."[11] The command "turn you northward" together with the cessation of the flow of water should have strengthened the faith and courage of the Israelites.

Deuteronomy 2:2-6: "And the LORD spake unto me, saying, Ye have compassed this mountain long enough: turn you northward. And command thou the people, saying, Ye are to pass through the coast of your brethren the children of Esau, which

10. Ellen White, *Patriarchs and Prophets* (1890), p. 413-414.
11. Margin.

dwell in Seir; and they shall be afraid of you: take ye good heed unto yourselves therefore: meddle not with them; for I will not give you of their land, no, not so much as a foot breadth; because I have given mount Seir unto Esau for a possession. Ye shall buy meat of them for money, that ye may eat; and ye shall also buy water of them for money, that ye may drink."

> "These directions should have been sufficient to explain why their supply of water had been cut off; they were about to pass through a well-watered, fertile country, in a direct course to the land of Canaan. God had promised them an unmolested passage through Edom and an opportunity to purchase food, and also water sufficient to supply the host. The cessation of the miraculous flow of water should therefore have been a cause of rejoicing, a token that the wilderness wandering was ended. Had they not been blinded by their unbelief, they would have understood this. ... The people seemed to have given up all hope that God would bring them into possession of Canaan, and they clamored for the blessings of the wilderness.[12]

Because of this second failure at Kadesh the Exodus Movement had to make a long detour around Edom and thus entrance into the promised land was further delayed.

The Antitype

Because modern Israel rejected the message that began in 1888, the Lord declared that He would "lead them on a long journey" and that they would be "brought over the ground again" and "will be tested again on the same points where they failed then" in "the test and trial at Minneapolis."[13] We are also told that many who failed the first time will not stand the test when it is repeated, but will oppose the message again and that "the same spirit will be revealed."

It is an interesting fact that in the 1920's the same message that was given at Minneapolis began to be repeated to God's remnant people. The Advent Movement was brought back to the same issues and therefore back again to the very borders of the heavenly Canaan. It is also an interesting fact that during our wilderness wanderings between the two Kadesh-Barnea antitypes, the Laodicean message was not preached and justification by faith was virtually forgotten as a doctrine and largely unknown as an experience.

The Same Spirit

The repetition of the Laodicean message with its remedy was met with the same spirit of opposition on the part of many as was manifested at Minneapolis. Some of

---

12. Ellen White, *Patriarchs and Prophets* (1890), p. 414.
13. See Lesson 22.

the same leaders who fought the message and criticized the messengers in 1888 have manifested the same bitter spirit as the message has been repeated.

Many others who did not pass through the 1888 crisis have shown a passive resistance if not an open opposition to the heaven-sent message that is to bring the latter rain and prepare the remnant people of God to enter the heavenly Canaan. To them it has sounded new and strange and has aroused their fears of fanaticism and that we are in danger of departing from the good old methods of preaching the law and the doctrines. Exactly the same arguments used by the opposition of the 1888 message have been and are still being repeated by those who resist the same message in its second presentation.

Spirit of Prophecy

> It is thus that God still tests His people. And if they fail to endure the trial, He brings them again to the same point, and the second time the trial will come closer, and be more severe than the preceding. This is continued till they bear the test, or, if they are still rebellious, God withdraws His light from them, and leaves them in darkness.[14]

> To accuse and criticize those whom God is using, is to accuse and criticize the Lord, who has sent them. …
>
> The prejudices and opinions that prevailed at Minneapolis are not dead by any means; the seeds sown there in some hearts are ready to spring into life and bear a like harvest. The tops have been cut down, but the roots have never been eradicated, and they still bear their unholy fruit to poison the judgment, pervert the perceptions, and blind the understanding of those with whom you connect; in regard to the message and the messengers.[15]

The truthfulness of this statement has been abundantly demonstrated during the last few years.

Heaven-Sent Message

The Lord has given abundance of evidence that He is again speaking to His people. The same blessed fruits are seen in the lives of those who accept this heaven-sent message as were manifested in the lives of those who accepted it forty years ago. It has the same definite ring of certainty and brings its hearers to the same conviction. It convinces God's remnant people that the end is near and that our wilderness wanderings are about over. It virtually says,

14. Ellen White, *Patriarchs and Prophets* (1890), p. 427.
15. Ellen White, *Testimonies to Ministers and Gospel Workers* (1923), p. 466-467.

You have compassed this mountain long enough: turn you northward.

In fact this statement is often used as a text in the giving of the message of which it was the type. As the message is being repeated the Holy Spirit bears witness to its divine origin and truthfulness. The fact that the 1888 message is being repeated is one of the greatest evidences that the coming of Christ is near and that the Lord has set His hand to lead the Advent Movement into the heavenly Canaan.

Waters of Strife

The very message and experience that should have brought unity and joy and faith to the members of the Exodus Movement, resulted in strife, confusion and defeat. "And the people choked with Moses." Choked means to "scold, reprove, rebuke, blame or censure; to make a rough clamorous roaring noise." The entire camp seems to have been thrown into strife and confusion, and some of the scenes and experiences of 38 years before were at least partially re-enacted.

The repeating of the 1888 message to the Advent people brought the movement back to the same crisis and created the same opposition. The message should have brought increased unity and faith to the whole movement and filled the camp of the modern Israel with joy and rejoicing. While it has accomplished this for the thousands who accepted the message and entered into the spiritual experience demanded by it. The opposition to the message is the same and the criticism of the messengers have created much strife and confusion and brought the Advent Movement to "the waters of Meribah." Some of the scenes and experiences of the 1888 crisis have been at least partially re-enacted. It is significant that Kadesh means "the judging of the people" or "the church of the judgment of the people."

Test of Patience

The second experience at Kadesh was not only a test of faith to the Israelites, but it was also a test of patience to the leaders who were seeking to bring the wilderness wandering to an end by leading the Exodus Movement into the promised land. For almost 40 years Moses, who was declared to be "the meekest man on earth", had borne with a faithless and rebellious people. Had it not been for their failures he could have entered the promised land years before.

During these long and weary years in the wilderness he and his loyal associates had looked forward to the time when the divine sentence would terminate and Israel could be led to their final destination in Canaan. Now when that cherished goal was again in sight and their long deferred hopes were about to be realized, the second failure of Israel to enter the promised land through unbelief seemed to be more than the great leaders could stand. The patience of Moses gave way under the strain and he was provoked to anger and lost control of His tongue and "spake unadvisedly with his lips."[16]

The Sad Result

This one act of impatience which produced a few hasty and ill-spoken words deprived 108 Moses of the privilege of leading Israel into the land of promise.

> Moses manifested distrust of God. 'Shall we bring water?' he questioned, as if the Lord would not do what He promised. 'Ye believed Me not', the Lord declared to the two brothers 'to sanctify Me in the eyes of the children of Israel.' At the time when the water failed, their own faith in the fulfillment of God's promise had been shaken by the murmuring and rebellion of the people. The first generation had been condemned to perish in the wilderness because of their unbelief, yet the same spirit appeared in their children. Would these also fail of receiving the promise?...
>
> All who profess godliness are under the most sacred obligation to guard the spirit, and to exercise self-control under the greatest provocation. The burdens placed upon Moses were very great; few men will ever be so severely tried as he was; yet this was not allowed to excuse his sin. The strongest temptation cannot excuse sin. However great the pressure brought to bear upon the soul, transgression is our own act. ... However severe or unexpected the assault, God has provided help for us, and in His strength, we may conquer.[17]

If one sin of impatience in the leaders of the Exodus Movement was so severely dealt with, what will happen to leaders in the Advent Movement who continue in the same sin without victory?

The Advent Movement. Patience is also one of the chief qualifications for leadership in the Advent Movement. Those who triumph with the movement will have "the patience of the saints."[18] This patience will give them complete control of their tongues for in their mouths will be "found no guile."[19] It is impatience that produces anger and causes people to speak "unadvisedly" with their lips. The use we make of our words constitutes an evidence of the condition of the heart and character and will therefore determine our fate in the judgment.[20] The perfect control of our tongues as the result of patience is also the evidence of the perfection of character.[21]

> We must subdue a hasty temper, and control our words; and in this we

16. See Psalm 106:32, 33; Deuteronomy 3:23-27.
17. Ellen White, *Patriarchs and Prophets* (1890), p. 417-421.
18. Revelation 14:12.
19. Revelation 14:5.
20. Matthew 12:24-27.
21. James 1:2-4; 3:2-18.

> shall gain great victories. Unless we control our words and temper, we are slaves of Satan. We are in subjection to him. He leads us captive. All jangling, and unpleasant, impatient, fretful words are an offering presented to his Satanic majesty.[22]

Cause of Failure

There can be no greater test of patience than that which comes to those who proclaim a heaven-sent message that is rejected by the professed people of God, especially when the acceptance of that message is the only means by which God's work can be finished and the eternal rewards obtained. The acceptance of the Laodicean message with its remedy of the imputed and imparted righteousness of Christ received by faith, is the only means of obtaining the outpouring of the Holy Spirit in the showers of the early and latter rain which will cut short God's work and lead modern Israel into the heavenly Canaan.

The failure of some of the leaders who proclaimed the 1888 message was due chiefly to a loss of patience because of the strife and opposition and even persecution produced by their preaching which finally resulted in its rejection and the turning of the Advent Movement back into the Laodicean wilderness causing a long delay of the coming of Christ. In the letter to O.A. Olsen, previously quoted from, the servant of the Lord intimated that the pressure and persecution brought against the preachers of righteousness might cause them to give way and fail in their personal experience, and this is what did happen. The same danger faces all who proclaim the same message at the present time. Their greatest need is to develop and maintain "the patience of the saints."

Live by Faith

The cutting off of the water supply at Kadesh was the final test by which the Lord attempted to teach the children of Israel to walk and live by faith instead of sight. Only a people of faith could triumph and enter the promised land and therefore during the last part of the journey they must learn to walk and live by faith. The same is true in the Advent Movement.

> In the last great conflict of the controversy with Satan those who are loyal to God will see every earthly support cut off.[23]

This will be the Lord's last lesson to teach His remnant people to walk and live by faith. While many will fail to meet this test as in ancient Israel, and will cast away their confidence and lose the promised reward, God will have a people whose faith and patience will cause them to triumph with the triumphant movement. Then "the just shall live by faith."[24]

---

22. Ellen White, *Testimonies for the Church,* vol. 1 (1868), p. 310.
23. Ellen White, *Desire of Ages* (1898), p. 122.
24 See Hebrews 10:35-39.

28

THE DETOUR AROUND EDOM

Second Defeat

The second time at Kadesh-Barnea, "the gateway to the promised land", Israel was defeated in their effort to enter Canaan. At the waters of Meribah Satan had again triumphed in his plan to thwart the purpose of God for His people.

> Ever since they left Egypt, Satan had been steadily at work to throw hindrances and temptations in their way, that they might not inherit Canaan. And by their own unbelief they had repeatedly opened the door for him to resist the purpose of God.[1]

The cause of the failure was the same that kept them out 38 years before. "They could not enter in because of unbelief."[2]

Lessons Unlearned

The chief design of the wilderness sojourn was to teach the Israelites lessons of faith and patience to prepare them for the promised land. Their conduct at Kadesh-Barnea indicated that these lessons were not yet learned.

> In Rephidim when the people thirsted for water, they were again proud, and showed that they still possessed an evil heart of unbelief, of murmuring, of rebellion, which revealed the fact that it would not yet be safe to establish them in the land of Canaan.[3]

The Israelites and their leaders failed to meet the tests of faith and patience and were turned back into the wilderness again.

God's Purpose

It was God's purpose to lead His people through the land of Edom in a triumphant march to Canaan. The Lord would have given them favor with the Edomites who

---

1. Ellen White, *Patriarchs and Prophets* (1890), p. 423.
2. Hebrews 3:19.
3. Ellen White, *Testimonies for the Church*, vol. 2 (1871), p. 107.

were the descendants of Esau and therefore their relatives.

> Had they in this manner passed though Edom, as God had purposed, the passage would have proved a blessing, not only to themselves, but to the inhabitants of the land. ... But all this the unbelief of Israel had prevented. God had given the people water in answer to their clamors, but He permitted their unbelief to work out its punishment. Again they must traverse the desert and quench their thirst from the miraculous spring, which, had they but trusted in Him, they would no longer have needed.[4]

A Detour

Numbers 20:21,22; 21:4: "Thus Edom refused to give Israel passage through his border: wherefore Israel turned away from him. And the children of Israel, even the whole congregation, journeyed from Kadesh, and came unto mount Hor."

Numbers 21:4: "And they journeyed from mount Hor by the way of the Red sea, to compass the land of Edom: and the soul of the people was much discouraged because of the way."

The second journey into the wilderness was not so much a retreat as a detour around Edom, through which God had purposed to lead them.

> The Hebrews were forbidden to resort to force. They must make the long journey around the land of Edom. Had the people, when brought into trial, trusted in God, the Captain of the Lord's host would have led them through Edom, and the fear of them would have rested upon the inhabitants of the land, so that, instead of manifesting hostility, they would have shown them favor. But the Israelites did not act promptly upon God's word, and while they were complaining and murmuring, the golden opportunity passed.[5]
>
> Accordingly the hosts of Israel again turned toward the south, and made their way over sterile wastes, that seemed even more dreary after a glimpse of the green spot among the hills and valleys of Edom.[6]

Sad Experience

We can well imagine the gloom that settled over the hosts of Israel as they again turned their backs on the promised land with no knowledge of the length of their second wilderness sojourn or of the difficulties of their journey. Moses and Aaron

---

4. Ellen White, *Patriarchs and Prophets* (1890), p. 424.
5. *Ibid.* (1890), p. 422-423.
6. *Ibid.* (1890), p. 424.

must have been almost broken-hearted at the thought of the blighted anticipations and especially of their own failure to meet the tests of patiences. Then too, Miriam, their sister, had died at Kadesh-Barnea. The first encampment seems to have been at Mount Hor, one of the mountain peaks of Seir.

Here at God's command, Aaron's priestly garments were taken from him and given to his son, Eleazar, and Aaron, with Moses and Eleazar, climbed to the top of the mountain and there he died and was buried by his brother and son. It may be that the bitter disappointment together with the remorse of his own failure hastened Aaron's death. The combination of events and circumstances together with the knowledge of his own approaching death without the privilege of leading Israel into the promised land doubtless saddened the life of Moses.

A Dreary March

Numbers 21:4: "And they journeyed from mount Hor by the way of the Red sea, to compass the land of Edom: and the soul of the people was much discouraged because of the way."

This text indicates that the journey around Edom was very dreary and discouraging. We are told that the route was over a stony, sandy, almost barren plain shut in by mountain walls on either side, and subject to sand-storms.[7]

> As they continued their journey toward the south, their route lay through a hot, sandy valley, destitute of shade or vegetation. The way seemed long and difficult, and they suffered from weariness and thirst. Again they failed to endure the test of their faith and patience. By continually dwelling on the dark side of their experiences, they separated themselves farther and farther from God. They lost sight of the fact that but for their murmuring when the water ceased at Kadesh, they would have been spared the journey around Edom.[8]

Self-Confidence

During the journey around Edom the Israelites had an experience that constituted a warning against boasting and self-confidence. They were attacked and defeated by a nation of the Canaanites. They were in retreat from Canaan at the time and were doubtless too discouraged to put up to a good fight, and too faithless to trust in God. Humbled by this defeat they sought God for divine aid and their enemies were defeated. Then they became over-confident and boastful and took the glory to themselves.

---

7. See Pulpit Commentary.
8. Ellen White, *Patriarchs and Prophets* (1890), p. 428.

This victory, instead of inspiring gratitude, and leading the people to feel their dependence upon God, made them boastful and self-confident. Soon they fell into the old habit of murmuring. They were now dissatisfied because the armies of Israel had not been permitted to advance upon Canaan immediately after their rebellion at the report of the spies nearly forty years before. They pronounced their long sojourn in the wilderness an unnecessary delay, reasoning that they might have conquered their enemies as easily heretofore as now.[9]

Tarrying Time

The second defeat of Israel at Kadesh did not annul the plan and purpose of God, but it did delay its fulfillment. The first failure resulted in a long delay or tarrying time which lasted almost forty years while Israel was wandering about in the wilderness. The second failure at the same place and for the same cause resulted in another delay or tarrying in the fulfillment of the purpose of God for Israel. This delay however was of brief duration compared to the first. It was the result of a detour rather than a retreat.

Advent Movement

The hesitancy of the Advent people to fully accept the 1888 message as it is being repeated is defeating the purpose of God to pour out the Holy Spirit in the latter rain and "finish the work, cut it short in righteousness." Not only have God's remnant people been hesitant about accepting the heaven-sent message that is to prepare them for translation, but many have manifested decided and even in some cases bitter opposition.

As predicted, some of the opposers of the same message in 1888 have revealed "the same spirit" again and have manifested the same "hateful characteristics" as led them to reject the message and despise the messengers in that eventful crisis. For more than twelve years now the message to the Laodicean church has been preached with emphasis on the need of the imputed and imparted righteousness of Christ, and thus far the acceptance has been half-hearted and the rich spiritual experience called for has been received by but few.

God's Purpose

There can be no question but the repetition of the message that brought the Advent Movement to the borders of the heavenly Canaan in 1888, led God's remnant people back to the same place again. The same message also brought us face to face with the same issues and test of faith. It was therefore the purpose of God to quickly finish His work and lead the Advent Movement triumphantly into the heavenly rest. Those who preached the message and those who accepted it were confident that the work would be finished in a very few years.

---

9. *Ibid.* See Numbers 21:1-3.

The Laodicean message so completely explained the spiritual state of the church and the reasons for the long delay in the coming of Christ, and the Laodicean remedy so adequately meets the spiritual needs of God's remnant people, that no true Seventh-day Adventist can doubt that it is Christ's last call to His people.

Spiritual Revivals

The repetition of the message of 1888 brought a repetition of the blessed results in the lives of those who accepted it and entered into the experience of the imputed and imparted righteousness of Christ. The recognition of our wretched Laodicean condition and the acceptance by faith of the gold of faith and love and truth, the garments of Christ's righteousness, and the anointing of the Holy Spirit, brought great revivals in all parts of the world where the message was preached.

The message brought new hope and cheer to the weary Advent pilgrims, many of whom were becoming "much discouraged because of the way" and were casting away their confidence. The call for "a spiritual revival and a spiritual reformation" on the basis of the Laodicean message clears away doubts, explains many puzzling questions, and shows the way out of the dreadful wilderness of sin in which the Advent Movement has so long been wandering in a "wretched, and miserable, and poor, and blind, and naked" spiritual state.

Waters of Strife

We are told that the Laodicean message and the call for a revival and reformation will stir up the wrath of the enemy who will make every effort to stop it by causing it to be opposed and rejected.

> There is nothing that Satan fears so much as that the people of God shall clear the way by removing every hindrance, so that the Lord can pour out His Holy Spirit upon a languishing church and an impenitent congregation. If Satan had his way, there would never be another awakening, great or small, to the end of time. But we are not ignorant of his devices. It is possible to resist his power. When the way is prepared for the Spirit of God, the blessings will come. Satan can no more hinder a shower of blessings from descending upon God's people than he can close the windows of heaven that rain cannot come upon the earth.[10]

> Satan will do his utmost to keep them in a state of indifference and stupor.[11]

---

10. Ellen White, "The Church's Greatest Need," *Review and Herald,* March 22, 1887, par. 7; quoted in *Christ our Righteousness*, p. 149, 160.

11. Ellen White, "The Perils and Privileges of the Last Days," *Review and Herald,* November 22, 1892, par. 4; quoted in *Christ our Righteousness*, p. 149, 160.

The Laodicean message therefore always brings God's people to "the waters of strife."

The Shaking

It is opposition to the Laodicean message that produces the shaking among God's people and separates the chaff from the wheat.

> I asked the meaning of the shaking I had seen, and was shown that it would be caused by the straight testimony called forth by the counsel of the True Witness to the Laodiceans. This will have its effect upon the heart of the receiver, and will lead him to exalt the standard and pour forth the straight truth. Some will not bear this straight testimony. They will rise up against it, and this is what will cause a shaking among God's people. I saw that the testimony of the True Witness has not been half heeded. The solemn testimony upon which the destiny of the church hangs has been lightly esteemed, if not entirely disregarded. This testimony must work deep repentance; all who truly receive it will obey it, and be sanctified.[12]

Satan Desperate

Satan knows that his time is short and he is therefore becoming desperate in his efforts to delay the final triumph of the Advent Movement. He knows that the acceptance of the Laodicean message with its complete remedy is the only means by which God's remnant people can receive the latter rain and enter the heavenly Canaan. He therefore hates the Laodicean message and all who accept and preach it, and especially the latter.

> Satan's snares are laid for us as verily as they were laid for the children of Israel just prior to their entrance into the land of Canaan. We are repeating the history of that people.[13]

Is it any wonder that the repetition of the message of 1888 brought the Advent Movement to "the waters of strife?"

Dislike Division

There is nothing that genuine Christians dislike more than strife and division, and this is especially true of church leaders. While we know that there must be a shaking in the church before the latter rain can come and the work be completed, and that this shaking is the result of the preaching of the Laodicean message, it is only natural that we should dread to see it come. There is therefore a strong temptation to avoid that which produces opposition and strife, or to tame down the "straight testimony" so as

---

12. Ellen White, *Early Writings* (1882), p. 270.
13. Ellen White, *Testimonies for the Church*, vol. 5 (1889), p. 160.

to appease the wrath of the enemy and soothe the ruffled waters of strife and opposition. This temptation is so great that many cease preaching the message altogether, or, seeing what happens to those who do preach it, they never begin.

One of the most discouraging features of the present situation is that hundreds and even thousands of our ministers acknowledge that the Laodicean message is the only hope of God's remnant people, but they do not preach it, or if they do, it is only occasionally and then with great timidity and with an apologetic attitude. Our leaders and ministers need courage commensurate with their convictions. Pray for Courage It is for this reason that ministers are told to pray earnestly for courage to preach the Laodicean message.

> Will you not seek God most humbly, that you may give the Laodicean message, with clear, distinct utterance? Where are God's watchmen who will see the peril, and give the warning? Be assured that there are messages to come from human lips, under the inspiration of the Holy Spirit. 'Cry aloud, spare not, … show my people their transgressions, and the house of Jacob their sins.' Yet they seek Me daily, … as a nation that did righteousness, and forsook not the ordinances of their God.[14]

This statement indicates that the great "transgression" of God's remnant people is the Laodicean condition, and that it is the preachers of the Laodicean message who "cry aloud" and "spare not" in revealing to them their sins.[15] The acceptance of this message will bring the blessings predicted in verse 8. This is the latter rain.

Must be Preached

The Laodicean message is absolutely essential and must be proclaimed. It is the message "upon which the destiny of the church hangs." We dare not neglect our duty as God's watchmen.

> I was shown that the pointed testimony must live in the church. This alone will answer to the message to the Laodiceans. Wrongs must be reproved, sin must be called sin, and iniquity must be met promptly and decidedly, and put away from us as a people.[16]

> The plain, straight testimony must live in the church, or the curse of God will rest upon His people as surely as it did upon ancient Israel because of their sins. … If the leaders of the church neglect to diligently search out the sins which brings the displeasure of God upon the body, they become responsible for these sins.[17]

---

14. Ellen White, *Testimonies to Ministers and Gospel Workers* (1923), p. 296.
15. See Isaiah 58:1,2.
16. Ellen White, *Testimonies for the Church*, vol. 3 (1875), p. 260.
17. *Ibid.*, p. 296.

> Ministers who are preaching present truth should not neglect the solemn message to the Laodiceans. The testimony of the True Witness is not a smooth message. … The True Witness declares that when you suppose you are really in a good condition of prosperity, you are in need of everything.[18] —Id. 257.

Further Delay

The hesitancy of both leaders and people of the Advent Movement to accept the second call for a revival and reformation, has resulted in a second delay or tarrying time. The rejection has not been so complete nor the crisis so great as that which took place forty years ago. The result could hardly be called a retreat, but it is at least a detour that temporarily defeats God's purposes and delays the triumph of the movement.

We may be cheered by the fact that in the type the delay was not long and that the journey around Edom brought experiences to ancient Israel that prepared them for a triumphant march to the promised land. The Laodicean message is again being sounded and is gaining headway throughout the Advent Movement and we may be assured that brighter days are ahead; that soon "there will be delay no longer" and in 'a little while, He that shall come will come, and will not tarry, or, will not longer tarry.' Cheer up weary Advent pilgrim "for you redemption draweth nigh."

18. *Ibid.*, p. 257.

29

THE VISION OF CHRIST AND CALVARY

Discouragement

Numbers 21:4: "And they journeyed from mount Hor by the way of the Red sea, to compass the land of Edom: and the soul of the people was much discouraged because of the way."

> This people grew impatient over the route. —Moffatt.

The further delay of the Exodus Movement to enter the promised land because of the second failure at Kadesh and the consequent detour around the land of Edom, produced discouragement and impatience among the Israelites. Impatience is one of the chief fruits of discouragement. Moses and Aaron became impatient at the waters of Meribah because of their disappointment and discouragement over the murmurings and rebellion of Israel which resulted in their second failure to meet the test of faith and enter the promised land through Kadesh-Barnea, "the appointed route to Canaan."

Spiritual Depression

The second retreat from the borders of the promised land produced a spiritual depression resulting in an impatient and irritable temper.

> It was not merely the heat and drought and ruggedness of the route which depressed them, but the fact that they were marching directly away from Canaan, and knew not how they were ever to reach it.[1]

It was "the soul of the people" that was "much discouraged because of the way." The depression was not so much physical as spiritual. They were depressed in spirit which is the most serious of all depressions. The great economic depression through which the world has been passing has effected only for their good the souls of those whose hearts have been filled with faith, hope and courage. Physical or financial depressions do not discourage the souls of those who maintain their union with God. The Israelites were "much discouraged" because they had committed a great sin in

1. Pulpit Commentary.

rejecting the call and leadership of God. Sin is the root of discouragement and impatience. Jesus was never discouraged or impatient because He knew no sin.

The Result

Numbers 21:5: "And the people spake against God, and against Moses, Wherefore have ye brought us up out of Egypt to die in the wilderness? for there is no bread, neither is there any water; and our soul loatheth this light bread."

Discouragement leads to criticism especially of leaders. The Israelites laid their failures onto Moses and charged him with the cause of their defeat and depression. Unjustified criticism is always an excuse for personal defects and failings. Adam attempted to excuse his disobedience by accusing Eve of leading him into sin and criticizing God for creating her.

It is human nature to try to escape the responsibility for our own acts. It is for this reason that discouraged and disgruntled persons are always severe critics and their criticism is especially directed towards leaders. They are what and where they are because of some real or imagined mistake on the part of leaders. This was one of the chief sins that delayed the final triumph of the Exodus Movement, and it is also the principal sin that has kept back the refreshing showers of the early and latter rain and thus delayed the final triumph of the Advent Movement.

Criticism of leaders is the chief stock in trade of apostates and their divergent movements. They live on the putrefying flesh of the dead. This is one of the distinguishing characteristics of false teachers and counterfeit religious movements.

The Serpents

Numbers 21:6: "And the LORD sent fiery serpents among the people, and they bit the people; and much people of Israel died."

These serpents were permitted to visit the camp of Israel because of their criticism and complaining. In criticizing Moses and murmuring against the human leadership of the movement the Israelites were tempting Christ, their Divine Leader. This was the reason for the visitation of the deadly serpents.

1 Corinthians 10:9,10: "For it is written in the law of Moses, Thou shalt not muzzle the mouth of the ox that treadeth out the corn. Doth God take care for oxen? Or saith he it altogether for our sakes? For our sakes, no doubt, this is written: that he that ploweth should plow in hope; and that he that thresheth in hope should be partaker of his hope."

Criticism and murmuring are terrible sins which lead to destruction. They caused the downfall of Lucifer and his angels and turned them into serpents whose sting of sin produces eternal death. The Lord endeavored to teach Israel and His people in all future generations that severe and unjust criticism is like the sting of an adder. It injects poison into the system of its victims and especially does it bring destruction to those who indulge in it. The apostle James declares that the critical and untamed tongue is "a world of iniquity" that "defileth the whole body, and setteth on fire the course of nature, and is set on fire of hell;" that is it is "an unruly evil, full of deadly poison."[2]

Fiery Serpents

Later Moses declared that this experience took place in "a great and terrible wilderness" not only infested with "fiery serpents" but also with "scorpions." Deut. 8:15. The serpents were called "fiery" first of all because of the result of their sting.

> The poisonous serpents that infested the wilderness were called fiery serpents, on account of the terrible effects produced by their sting, it causing violent inflamation and speedy death.[3]

The poison produced fiery red inflamation and a burning fever which was fatal. It is also believed that the serpents were called "fiery" because of their color which resembled the "copper snakes" of Australia and other countries. The fact that Moses made the metallic serpent of brass or copper might also indicated that they were of that color.

The Sting of Death

The serpents were symbolic of Satan and his angels whose sting of sin brings death. In Revelation 12:9, Satan is called "that old serpent" who "deceiveth the whole world." In the garden of Eden the fallen angel used the instrumentality of a serpent to deceive Eve and lead her into sin and thus deprive our first parents of their paradise home. The experience that came to the Israelites just after they had failed the second time to enter Canaan was doubtless designed to teach them that their sins were keeping them out of the promised land.

The lesson is also for us "upon whom the ends of the world are come," for this tragic experience was recorded "for our admonition." All through the camp of Israel the deadly serpents crawled and from every direction came the cry of pain and the wail of woe. The dying and dead were everywhere and there was no remedy. Because they had been "much discouraged" and indulged in much criticism, "much people of Israel died." The same stinging criticism in the Advent Movement has opened the way for the great serpent to enter the camp or church with the deadly poison of sin and as the result "much people" of modern Israel are dying spiritually and falling out

---

2. James 3:6, 8.
3. Ellen White, *Patriarchs and Prophets* (1890), p. 429.

by the way. Back-biting serpents are infesting the camp of modern Israel with tragic consequences to many.

Repentance

Numbers 21:7: "Therefore the people came to Moses, and said, We have sinned, for we have spoken against the LORD, and against thee; pray unto the LORD, that he take away the serpents from us. And Moses prayed for the people."

The fearful results of sin brought confession and repentance. The Israelites acknowledged that in speaking against Moses they had also "spoken against the Lord" and had "sinned." They asked Moses to pray for them and "Moses prayed for the people." When they were in trouble they asked for the prayers of the very one they had so severely and unjustly criticized. Moses showed a fine Christian spirit and interceded for them and the Lord heard his prayer and instructed him how to provide a remedy that would at the same time test the faith of the victims of the serpents sting of death. They had twice failed to enter the promised land "because of unbelief" and they must learn the lesson of faith before they could succeed.

The Remedy

Numbers 21:8, 9: "And the LORD said unto Moses, Make thee a fiery serpent, and set it upon a pole: and it shall come to pass, that every one that is bitten, when he looketh upon it, shall live. And Moses made a serpent of brass, and put it upon a pole, and it came to pass, that if a serpent had bitten any man, when he beheld the serpent of brass, he lived."

Jesus declared that this brazen serpent lifted up on the pole in the wilderness was symbolic of Himself lifted up on the cross of Calvary.[4] Brass is made of a mixture of copper and zinc, so Jesus was a combination of the divine and human. He was the God-man, or "God manifest in the flesh." The serpent was symbolic of sin, and Christ came "in the likeness of sin." He was therefore represented by symbol of sin. Jesus was made "to be sin for us, who knew no sin, that we might be made the righteousness of God in Him."[5] "By man came death" and therefore Jesus must come "in the likeness of sinful flesh" in order to destroy the author of sin and death and "deliver them who through fear of death were all their lifetime subject to bondage."[6] The Deliverer must come in the likeness of the Destroyer.

Antidote of Poison

It was His coming to earth in "sinful flesh" and "in the likeness of sin" that made it possible for Christ to counteract the poison of sin and destroy "that old serpent, the

---

4. John 3:14-17.
5. 2 Corinthians 5:21.
6. See Hebrews 2:14,15.

devil and Satan." There was no deadly poison in the brazen serpent and there was no sin in Christ. He was lifted up on the cross "in the likeness of sinful flesh" in order that He might save from the deadly virus of sin and eternal death all who behold Him through the eyes of faith. Jesus is the great antitoxin for the poison of sin which is injected into out characters by the sting of the great serpent. A vision of Christ on the cross of Calvary is the only remedy for sin. "Whosoever" looks and believes shall "not perish, but have everlasting life." Beholding Christ is the antidote for death and the elixir of eternal life.

Israel's Great Need

For almost forty years the Israelites had so far lost sight of Christ and Calvary that the celebration of the Passover was denied them. Unlike Moses, they had not "endured as seeing Him who is invisible." The pillar of fire by night and cloud by day, which represented the visible presence of Christ, meant nothing to them. This was the cause of their failure both times at Kadesh-Barnea.

Now Israel is brought to the place where they are compelled to look to Christ as their only hope. The only requirement of the serpent-bitten victims was to look, and the look of faith brought life. Doubtless many in the camp had no faith in the remedy and they died in hopeless agony. The remedy may have seemed unscientific and unreasonable to them and therefore useless. It took faith to apply the remedy.

Glad Tidings

The announcement of the remedy for the venom of the serpents was glad tidings to the hopeless victims.

> The joyful news sounded throughout the encampment that all who had been bitten might look upon the brazen serpent and live. Many had already died, and when Moses raised the serpent upon the pole, some would not believe that merely gazing upon the metallic image would heal them; these perished in their unbelief. Yet there were many who had faith in the provision which God had made. Fathers, mothers, brothers, and sisters were anxiously engaged in helping their suffering, dying friends to fix their languid eyes upon the serpent. If these, though faint and dying, could only once look, they were perfectly restored. …
>
> They could not help themselves from the fatal effect of the poison of their wounds. God alone was able to heal them. Yet they were required to show their faith in the provision which He had made. They must look in and by looking upon the serpent their faith was shown. They knew that there was no virtue in the serpent itself, but it was a symbol of Christ, and the necessity of faith in His merits was thus presented to their minds. …
>
> That look implied faith. They lived because they believed God's word,

and trusted in the means provided for their recovery.[7]

The Advent Movement

The Advent Movement is now making its anti-typical journey around Edom and the experiences of ancient Israel are being repeated. Again "we are repeating the history of that people." The message of 1888 and its repetition in recent years brought us to the very borders of the heavenly Canaan but we "could not enter in because of unbelief." As a people we have failed to behold Christ and Calvary. We are told that the message of 1888 was given because "many had lost sight of Jesus," and "they needed to have their eyes directed to His divine person, His merits, and His changeless love for the human family." We are told that this is "the third angel's message, which is to be proclaimed with a loud voice, and attended with the outpouring of the Holy Spirit in a large measure."[8]

Calvary Forgotten

{That we have forgotten Calvary, Ellen White writes:}

> Do not try to draw the attention of the people to yourselves. Let them lose sight of the instrument, while you exalt Jesus. Talk of Jesus; lose self in Jesus. There is too much bustle and stir about our religion, while Calvary and the cross are forgotten.[9]

> A spirit of worldliness and selfishness has deprived the church of many a blessing. … A clear, steady view of the cross of Christ would counteract their worldliness, and fill their souls with humility, penitence and gratitude. … A deadly spiritual malady is upon the church. Its members are wounded by Satan, but they will not look to the cross of Christ, as the Israelites looked to the brazen serpent, that they may live. The world has so many claims upon them that they have not time to look to the cross of Calvary long enough to see its glory or to feel its power.[10]

Our Only Hope

Revelation 3:20: "Behold, I stand at the door, and knock: if any man hear my voice, and open the door, I will come in to him, and will sup with him, and he with me."

Christ is outside the door of the church-temple and the individual hearts of modern Israel, and He calls for us to "behold" Him and let Him in. We are as helpless of ourselves as were the Israelites in the wilderness when they were bitten by the ser-

---

7. Ellen White, *Patriarchs and Prophets* (1890), p. 430-431.
8. See *Testimonies to Ministers and Gospel Workers* (1923), p. 92.
9. Ellen White, *Testimonies for the Church,* vol. 5 (1889), p. 133.
10. *Ibid.*, p. 202.

pents. Our only hope is in Christ.

> Nothing but the righteousness of Christ can entitle us to one of the blessings of the covenant of grace. There are many who have long desired and tried to obtain these blessings, but have not received them, because they have cherished the idea that they could do something to make themselves worthy of them. … Let none look to self, as though they had power to save themselves. Jesus died for us because we are helpless to do this. In Him is our hope, our justification, our righteousness. … Look and Live. Jesus has pledged His word. He will save all who come to Him. Though millions who need to be healed will reject His offered mercy, not one who trusts in His merits will be left to perish. … It is our duty, first, to look, and the look of faith will give us life.[11]s

It is just as hard to us to learn the lesson that there is life in a look at Christ and Calvary as it was for the Israelites. We desire to do something to merit eternal life.

Result of Beholding

2 Corinthians 3:18: "But we all, with open face beholding as in a glass the glory of the Lord, are changed into the same image from glory to glory, [even] as by the Spirit of the Lord."

John 6:40: "And this is the will of him that sent me, that every one which seeth the Son, and believeth on him, may have everlasting life: and I will raise him up at the last day."

John 12:31, 32: "Now is the judgment of this world: now shall the prince of this world be cast out. And I, if I be lifted up from the earth, will draw all men unto me."

> Holy men of old were saved by faith in the blood of Christ. As they saw the dying agonies of the sacrificial victims they looked across the gulf of ages to the Lamb of God that was to take away the sins of the world.[12]

> At the gate of Damascus the vision of the Crucified One changed the whole current of Paul's life.[13]

> As the sinner, drawn by the power of Christ, approaches the uplifted cross, and prostrates himself before it, there is a new creation. A new heart is given him. He becomes a new creature in Christ Jesus. Holiness

11. Ellen White, *Patriarchs and Prophets* (1890), p. 431-432.
12. Ellen White, *Sketches from the Life of Paul* (1883), p. 242.
13. Ellen White, *Education* (1903), p. 65.

finds that it has nothing more to require.[14]

Pride and selfesteem cannot flourish in the hearts that keep fresh in memory the scenes of Calvary." "Reflections of Calvary will awaken tender, sacred, and lively emotions in the Christian's heart. It will fill the mind, touch and melt the soul, refine and elevate the affections, and completely transform the whole character.[15]

Power of the Cross

1 Corinthians 2:2: "For I determined not to know any thing among you, save Jesus Christ, and him crucified."

Galatians 2:20: "I am crucified with Christ: nevertheless I live; yet not I, but Christ liveth in me: and the life which I now live in the flesh I live by the faith of the Son of God, who loved me, and gave himself for me."

Galatians 6:14: "But God forbid that I should glory, save in the cross of our Lord Jesus Christ, by whom the world is crucified unto me, and I unto the world."

If sinners can be led to give one earnest look at the cross, if they can obtain a full view of the crucified Saviour, they will realize the depth of God's compassion and the sinfulness of sin.[16]

The existence of sin is unexplainable, therefore not a soul knows what God is until he sees himself in the light reflected from the cross of Calvary and detests himself as a sinner, in the bitterness of his soul.[17]

To remove the cross from the Christian would be like blotting the sun from the sky. Without the cross, man would have no union with the Father. On it depends our only hope. From it shines the light of the Saviour's love, and when at the foot of the cross the sinner looks up to the One who died to save him, he may rejoice with fulness of joy for his sins are pardoned. Kneeling in faith at the cross, he has reached the highest place to which man can attain.[18]

Laodicean Message

The very crux of the remedy for the Laodicean condition of modern Israel is to be-

14. Ellen White, *Christ's Object Lessons* (1900), p. 163.
15. Ellen White, *Testimonies for the Church* vol. 2 (1871), p. 212.
16. Ellen White, *Acts of the Apostles* (1911), p.209.
17. Ellen White, *Testimonies to Ministers and Gospel Workers* (1923), p.254.
18. Ellen White, *Acts of the Apostles* (1911), p.209, 210.

hold Christ and Him crucified. While the Israelites were making their detour around Edom they were given a vision of Christ and Calvary which marked the beginning of a victorious march toward the promised land.

While the Advent people are experiencing the antitype of Israel's detour they too will get a vision of Christ on the cross and it will mark the beginning of a triumphant march to the heavenly Canaan. The spiritual barrenness of their wilderness journey will drive them to Christ as their only hope, and to Calvary as the only remedy for the ravages and poison of sin. When the message to behold Christ as man's only hope is being given to God's remnant people it will be evident that our journey is about over and we will soon reach our heavenly home.

Just as Moses had to send a message throughout the camp of Israel announcing the remedy for the poison of the serpents, so likewise a message will be given the Advent people announcing the remedy for the Laodicean condition. This message will center in the uplifted Christ and His righteousness. This message is now being given and it will soon swell into the loud cry.

30

THE TRIUMPHS OF FAITH

Secret of Victory

1 John 5:4, 5: "For whatsoever is born of God overcometh the world: and this is the victory that overcometh the world, even our faith. Who is he that overcometh the world, but he that believeth that Jesus is the Son of God?"

The Exodus Movement had twice been turned back from the borders of the promised land through lack of faith. "They could not enter in because of unbelief." The serpent experience gave them a vision of Christ and the cross and through faith they conquered the serpent-enemies and were saved. This lesson of faith was the beginning of a new experience for Israel. It was the starting place of a victorious march toward Canaan. The vision of the cross marked the turning point in the detour around Edom when the Israelites turned their backs toward Egypt and their faces toward Canaan for the last time. Faith was the victory that led them onward toward their long sought goal.

Triumphant March

The journey from the wilderness infested with poisonous reptiles to the banks of the Jordan and the victorious campaigns along the way is described in Numbers 21:10-35, and Deuteronomy 2:17-3:17. The Israelites were no longer "much discouraged because of the way," but were filled with hope and faith and courage.

> After passing to the south of Edom, the Israelites turned northward, and again set their faces toward the promised land. Their route now lay over a vast, elevated plain, swept by cool, fresh breezes from the hills. It was a welcome change from the parched valley through which they had been traveling, and they pressed forward, buoyant and hopeful.[1]

The time had come in the history of the Exodus Movement when there should be delay no longer in the fulfillment of God's purpose and the fruition of their hopes.

Conquered Giants

1. Ellen White, *Patriarchs and Prophets* (1890), p.433.

The ten spies had lost hope and courage because of the giants that possessed the promised land.

Numbers 13:25-28, 31-33: "And they returned from searching of the land after forty days. And they went and came to Moses, and to Aaron, and to all the congregation of the children of Israel, unto the wilderness of Paran, to Kadesh; and brought back word unto them, and unto all the congregation, and showed them the fruit of the land. And they told him, and said, We came unto the land whither thou sentest us, and surely it floweth with milk and honey; and this is the fruit of it. Nevertheless the people be strong that dwell in the land, and the cities are walled, and very great: and moreover we saw the children of Anak there. ...

"But the men that went up with him said, We be not able to go up against the people; for they are stronger than we. And they brought up an evil report of the land which they had searched unto the children of Israel, saying, The land, through which we have gone to search it, is a land that eateth up the inhabitants thereof; and all the people that we saw in it are men of a great stature. And there we saw the giants, the sons of Anak, which come of the giants: and we were in our own sight as grasshoppers, and so we were in their sight."

While this report was somewhat exaggerated it was partly true. Anak was the father of a race of giants called Anakim. There were three tribes of them and they possessed Hebron, Debir and Anak. Goliath was of the race of Anak. These giants so frightened the ten spies that they rendered "an evil report" and threw the whole camp into discouragement and confusion. The fear of giants delayed the entrance of Israel into the promised land for forty years. In the meantime the giants multiplied and strengthened their fortification. Now they are conquered by faith the courageous Israelites. Impregnable fortresses were captured and nothing could stand before them. God's Message As the Israelites faced these giants and fortresses the Lord sent them the message:

Deuteronomy 3:22: "Ye shall not fear them, for the Lord your God shall fight for you."

One of the great nations that attempted to block the progress of the Exodus Movement was Bashan which was ruled over by giant king Og whose bed was 13 feet long and 6 feet wide. The Lord fought for them and the hosts of Israel captured every stronghold and overcame every obstacle.

> It was the Captain of the Lord's host who vanquished the enemies of His people, and He would have done the same thirty eight years before, had Israel trusted in Him. Filled with hope and courage, the army of Israel eagerly pressed forward, and, still journeying northward, they soon reached a country that might well test their courage and faith in God. Before them

lay the powerful and populous kingdom of Bashan, crowded with great stone cities that to this day excite the wonder of the world, … 'threescore cities … with high walls, gates, and bars, besides unwalled towns a great many.[2]

Impregnable Fortresses

The houses were constructed of huge black stones, of such stupendous size as to make the buildings absolutely impregnable to any force that in those times could have been brought against them. It was a country filled with wild caverns, lofty precipices, yawning gulfs, and rocky strong-holds. The inhabitants of this land, descendants of a giant race, were themselves of marvelous size and strength, and so distinguished for violence and cruelty as to be the terror of all surrounding nations. …

The hearts of many in Israel quaked with fear. But Moses was calm and firm. …

The calm faith of the leader inspired the people with confidence in God. They trusted all to His omnipotent arm, and He did not fail them. Not mighty giants nor walled cities, armed hosts nor rocky fortresses, could stand before the Captain of the Lord's host. The Lord led the army, the Lord discomfited the enemy, the Lord conquered in behalf of Israel.[3]

Past Mistakes Seen

For the first time the Israelites were able to see and acknowledge their past mistakes and those of their fathers.

In the conquest of Gilead and Bashan there were many who recalled the events which nearly forty years before, had, in Kadesh, doomed Israel to the long desert wandering. They saw that the report of the spies concerning the promised land was in many respects correct. The cities were walled and very great, and were inhabited by giants, in comparison with whom the Hebrews were mere pygmies. But they could now see that the fatal mistake of their fathers had been in distrusting the power of God. This alone had prevented them from at once entering the goodly land.[4]

During their wilderness wanderings the Israelites had been irritated by being reminded of the crisis and failure at Kadesh- Barnea and they refused to assume the blame for the long delay. With the rebirth of faith and its consequent deepening spiritual experience, the past was seen in a new light and the true significance of the Kadesh-Barnea crisis was clearly understood. It was doubtless explained to them in the light of their new experience.

---

2. Ellen White, *Patriarchs and Prophets* (1890), p. 435.
3. *Ibid.*, p. 435-436.
4. *Ibid.*, p. 436.

Result of Delay

The long delay had given the enemies of Israel opportunity to strengthen their defense and prepare to make a strong resistance.

> When they were at first preparing to enter Canaan, the undertaking was attended with far less difficulty than now. God had promised His people that if they would only obey His voice He would go before them and fight for them; and He would also send hornets to drive out the inhabitants of the land. The fears of the nations had been greatly aroused, and little preparation had been made to oppose their progress. But when the Lord now bade Israel go forward, they must advance against alert and powerful foes, and must contend with large and well-trained armies that had been preparing to resist their approach....
>
> The difficulties in the way had greatly increased since they refused to advance when bidden to do so in the name of the Lord.[5] —P.P. 436, 437.

The Advent Movement

The serpent experience of ancient Israel during their detour of the land of Edom helps to determine where we are in the journey of the Advent people. We are making the turn of the last detour of our pilgrimage to the heavenly Canaan. The great and terrible spiritual wilderness through which we have been passing has produced a great deal of murmuring, complaining and criticism and many have been "much discouraged because of the way," and have cast away their confidence in the movement and its leadership. The great serpent and his fellow demons have been infecting God's remnant people with the deadly virus of sin.

Christ is now being exalted in modern Israel and pointed to as the only remedy for sin and the only hope of salvation. A heaven-sent message is now sounding through the church calling attention to the uplifted cross and its dying sacrificial Victim. The antitype of the uplifted brazen serpent will be more fully met as the vision of Christ and Calvary is increased and the message to behold the Lamb of God swells into the loud cry.

Time Located

Our location in the journey toward the heavenly Canaan is further identified by the following quotations:

> When the children of Israel were journeying through the wilderness, the Lord protected them from venomous serpents, but the time came when, because of Israel's transgression, impenitence, and stubbornness, the Lord removed His restraining power from these reptiles, and many of

---

5. Ellen White, *Patriarchs and Prophets* (1890), p. 436-437.

> the people were bitten and died. Then it was that the brazen serpent was uplifted, that all who repented and looked to it in faith might live. In the time of confusion and trouble before us, a time of trouble such as has not been since there was a nation, the uplifted Saviour will be presented to the people in all lands, that all who look to Him in faith may live.[6]

This is the time of trouble that immediately precedes the close of probation and the falling of the seven last plagues. The uplifting of Christ is one of the greatest of all signs that the end is near and the journey is about over. We are certainly now entering "the time of confusion and trouble" mentioned in this quotation and it is time to lift up the crucified Saviour before the church and the world.

Our Message

The message at this time must center in Christ and the cross.

> It is the work of every one to whom the message of warning has come, to lift up Jesus, to present Him to the world as revealed in types, as shadowed in symbols, as manifested in the revelations of the prophets, as unveiled in the lessons given to His disciples and in the wonderful miracles wrought for the sons of men. …
>
> The theme that attracts the heart of the saints is Christ and Him crucified. On the cross of Calvary, Jesus stands revealed to the world in unparalleled love. Present Him thus to the hungering multitudes, and the light of His love will win men from darkness to light, from transgression to obedience and true holiness. Beholding Jesus upon the cross of Calvary arouses the conscience to the heinous character of sin as nothing else can do.[7]

No Human Glory

Not until the Israelites learned to distrust self and give all glory to Christ, their Leader, did their march of triumph begin. We are unprepared for the evil days ahead until we humble ourselves and exalt Christ and appropriate His righteousness.

> The days in which we live are eventful and full of peril. The signs of the coming of the end are thickening around us, and events are to come to pass that will be of a more terrible character than any the world has yet witnessed. … If you would stand through the time of trouble, you must know Christ, and appropriate the gift of His righteousness, which He imputes to the repentant sinner. Human wisdom will not avail to devise a

---

6. Ellen White, *Testimonies for the Church*, vol. 8 (1904), p. 50.
7. Ellen White, "The Perils and Privileges of the Last Days," *Review and Herald*, November 22, 1892, par. 7-9.

plan of salvation. Human philosophy is vain, the fruits of the loftiest powers of man are worthless, aside from the great plan of the divine Teacher. No glory is to redound to man ; all human help and glory lies in the dust; for the truth as it is in Jesus is the only available agent by which man may be saved. Man is privileged to connect with Christ, and then the divine and human combine; and in this union the hope of man must rest alone.[8] —Id. Quoted from the R.H. Nov. 22, 29, 1892.

Message Accepted

That the message of the uplifted Saviour and His imputed and imparted righteousness will soon be accepted and the Advent Movement turned Zionward for the last time is evident from many statements in the Spirit of Prophecy.

> The Lord will work to purify His church. I tell you the truth, the Lord is about to turn and overturn in the institutions called by His name. Just how soon this refining process will begin, I cannot say, but it will not be long deferred.[9]

> The purging and cleansing will surely pass through every church in our land that has had great opportunities, and has passed then by unheeded.[10]

> The power which stirred the people so mightily in the 1844 movement will again be revealed. The third angel's message will go forth, not in whispered tones, but with a loud voice.[11]

A Great Revival

Acts. 3:19-21: "Repent ye therefore, and be converted, that your sins may be blotted out, when the times of refreshing shall come from the presence of the Lord; and he shall send Jesus Christ, which before was preached unto you: whom the heaven must receive until the times of restitution of all things, which God hath spoken by the mouth of all his holy prophets since the world began."

> Repent, therefore, and reform your lives, so that the record of your sins may be cancelled, and that there may come seasons of revival from the Lord. —Weymouth

This great heaven-sent revival will come just before the close of probation and the return of Christ.

---

8. Ellen White, "The Perils and Privileges of the Last Days," *Review and Herald*, November 22, 1892, par. 5, 9.
9. Ellen White, *Testimonies to Ministers and Gospel Workers*, (1923), p. 373.
10. *Ibid.*, p. 414.
11. Ellen White, *Testimonies for the Church*, vol. 5 (1889), p. 252.

> I have been deeply impressed by scenes that have recently passed before me in the night season. There seemed to be a great movement—a work of revival— going forward in many places. Our people were moving into line, responding to God's call.[12]

> Before the final visitation of god's judgments upon the earth, there will be, among the people of the Lord, such a revival of primitive godliness as has not been witnessed since apostolic times. The Spirit and power of God will be poured out upon His children....Many, both of ministers and people, will gladly accept those truths which God has caused to be proclaimed at this time. to prepare a people for the Lord's second coming.[13]

Reformation Movement

A genuine revival is always accompanied by a reformation.

> In visions of the night representations passed before me of a great reformatory movement among God's people. Many were praising God. The sick were healed, and other miracles were wrought. A spirit of intercession was seen, even as manifested before the great day of Pentecost. Hundreds of thousands were seen visiting families, and opening before them the Word of God. Hearts were convicted by the power of the Holy Spirit, and a spirit of genuine conversion was manifest.[14]

That this reformation will save our institutions which are now called "prisoners of hope" is also stated.

> Though in many respects our institutions of learning have swung into worldly conformity, though step by step have advanced toward the world, they are prisoners of hope. Fate has not so woven its meshes about their working that they need to remain helpless and in uncertainty. If they will listen to His voice and follow His ways, God will correct and enlighten them, and bring them back to their upright position of distinction from the world.[15]

In F.E. p. 290, we are told that "God will bring them back." What is said of these institutions is also true of the entire movement. God will bring us back to Himself and lead us into the heavenly Canaan. The movement will triumph gloriously.

---

12. Ellen White, *Testimonies to Ministers and Gospel Workers,* (1923), p. 515.
13. Ellen White, *Great Controversy,* (1911), p. 464.
14. Ellen White, *Testimonies for the Church,* vol. 9 (1909), p. 126.
15. Ellen White, *Testimonies for the Church,* vol. 6 (1901), p. 145.

A Divine Visitation

Isaiah 52:1-10: "Awake, awake; put on thy strength, O Zion; put on thy beautiful garments, O Jerusalem, the holy city: for henceforth there shall no more come into thee the uncircumcised and the unclean. Shake thyself from the dust; arise, and sit down, O Jerusalem: loose thyself from the bands of thy neck, O captive daughter of Zion. For thus saith the LORD, Ye have sold yourselves for nought; and ye shall be redeemed without money. For thus saith the Lord GOD, My people went down aforetime into Egypt to sojourn there; and the Assyrian oppressed them without cause.

"Now therefore, what have I here, saith the LORD, that my people is taken away for nought? they that rule over them make them to howl, saith the LORD; and my name continually every day is blasphemed. Therefore my people shall know my name: therefore they shall know in that day that I am he that doth speak: behold, it is I. How beautiful upon the mountains are the feet of him that bringeth good tidings, that publisheth peace; that bringeth good tidings of good, that publisheth salvation; that saith unto Zion, Thy God reigneth!

"Thy watchmen shall lift up the voice; with the voice together shall they sing: for they shall see eye to eye, when the LORD shall bring again Zion. Break forth into joy, sing together, ye waste places of Jerusalem: for the LORD hath comforted his people, he hath redeemed Jerusalem. The LORD hath made bare his holy arm in the eyes of all the nations; and all the ends of the earth shall see the salvation of our God."

Here is pictured the divine visitation that turns the captivity of modern Israel.

> When Jehovah returneth to Zion. —R.V.

> When the Lord shall convert Zion. —Douay.

> All your sentinels are shouting in a triumph song, for they see the Eternal face as He returns to Zion. —Moffatt.

This is a description of the Laodicean message and the blessed results of its acceptance. Zion is asleep and without the garments of Christ's righteousness. God calls for her to awake and arise from the dust and "sit on my throne." —R.V. The church is unconverted and unready for the coming of the Bridegroom. The glory of the Lord had departed because of the Laodicean condition, but now the Lord "returns" with Pentecostal power and the latter rain is poured out and the work finished. This glorious visitation of the divine power and work of revival and reformation is also pictured in Micah 7:15-10 and Joel 2:1, 12-32.

When the Advent people turn to the Lord with all our hearts, "He will return and repent and leave a blessing behind Him."

The Lord in Control

Even though many will oppose the message calling for a revival and reformation and will manifest a lack of faith, the Lord has promised to take control of the Advent Movement and lead it to victory.

> Unless those who can help in … are aroused to a sense of their duty, they will not recognize the work of God when the loud cry of the third angel's message shall be heard. When light goes forth to lighten the earth, instead of coming up to the help of the Lord, they will want to bind about His work to meet their narrow ideas. Let me tell you that the Lord will work in this last work in a manner very much out of the common order of things, and in a way that will be contrary to any human planning. There will be those among us who will always want to control the work of God, to dictate even what movements shall be made when the work goes forward under the direction of the angel who joins the third angel in the message to be given to the world. God will use ways and means by which it will be seen that He is taking the reins into His own hands. The workers will be surprised by the simple means that He will use to bring about and perfect His work in righteousness.[16]

Result of Delay

The long delay occasioned by the lack of faith of the Advent people has resulted in a great increase in the strength and strongholds of the enemy. The finishing of the work forty years ago would have been much easier in many ways than at the present time. Every form of evil has experienced a mighty growth. Catholicism, Spiritism, Modernism, and Atheism, and scores of other isms and enemy institutions have greatly fortified their positions during the wilderness wanderings of the Advent Movement. They now seem as impregnable as the fortifications and walled cities before the children of Israel.

> The work which the church has failed to do in a time of peace and prosperity, she will have to do in a terrible crisis, under most discouraging, forbidding circumstances. The warnings that worldly conformity has silenced or with-held, must be given under the fiercest opposition from enemies of the faith.[17]

An Important Date

1888 is not only an important date in the history of the Advent Movement because of the message that began at that time, but also because it marked the beginning of Satan's greatest efforts to strengthen his positions and thwart the purpose of God through His remnant people. In Oklahoma City a group of men and women have

16. Ellen White, *Testimonies to Ministers and Gospel Workers,* (1923), p. 300.
17. Ellen White, *Testimonies for the Church,* vol. 5 (1889), p. 463.

been meeting weekly to worship the Devil. They receive communications from "The Masters," an invisible army of teachers. One who left the group reported the following message from the spirit world:

> Preach anything except salvation by grace. Ridicule the efficacy of the blood of Christ. Emphasize the wonderful teaching of Jesus, always stressing that He was no more divine than any other man.
>
> Preach self-righteousness, for, 'know ye not that ye are gods in the making and no soul is ever lost?'
>
> In 1888 Satan changed his plan and prepared to take advantage of the Age of Intellectual Egotism, which is now in full bloom. Orders were given to appeal to Intellect and Reason in high places. Christian churches are to be changed into synagogues of Satan.
>
> The Devil desires a Federation of Churches. This Federation eventually will merge into a Brotherhood of Religion and finally into a Universal Religion.[18]

Invincible Army

But notwithstanding the fact that the enemy has greatly strengthened his position since 1888, when the Lord returns to Zion and takes the reins of the Advent Movement into His own hand, His remnant people will become an invincible army that goes forth conquering and to conquer.

> Then will the church of Christ appear fair as the moon, clear as the sun, and terrible as an army with banners.[19]

Great giants of evil and apparently impregnable fortifications will fail to stop the progress of the people of God who have had a vision of Christ and Calvary. Freely acknowledging and confessing the sins and mistakes of the past that have delayed the coming of Christ and the triumphs of His message, the members of the Advent Movement will march forward victoriously toward their heavenly goal.

18. From an article in the "Sunday School Times" of May 7, 1932, by Dr. Arthur I. Brown, entitled "Facing the Atheists - In college and outside."
19. Ellen White, *Testimonies for the Church*, vol. 5 (1889), p. 82.

31

SATAN'S FINAL EFFORTS TO DEFEAT ISRAEL

Satan Desperate

From the very beginning of the Exodus Movement Satan had made every possible effort to defeat the purpose of God in the triumph of Israel. He had twice succeeded in turning the movement back into the wilderness from the borders of the promised land. He had triumphed through their unbelief. "They could not enter in because of unbelief." But the serpent experience which gave Israel a vision of Christ and Calvary also greatly increased their faith and turned their retreat into a victorious march toward Canaan. Faith made them invincible in warfare and nothing could stop them. With Christ as their Captain "not mighty giants nor walled cities, armed hosts nor rocky fortresses, could stand before" them. This alarmed Satan and in his desperation he used other weapons in a final effort to stop the movement and defeat Israel.

Banks of Jordan

Numbers 22:1: "And the children of Israel set forward, and pitched in the plains of Moab on this side Jordan by Jericho."

After the conquest of Bashan the Israelites marched to the banks of the Jordan on the very border of the promised land and began to make "preparation for the immediate invasion of Canaan."[1] The success of Israel filled the Moabites with fear and they appealed to the Midianites to cooperate with them in an effort to defeat the invaders. Knowing that the weapons of war could not avail, the two nations sent messengers into Mesopotamia to persuade Balaam, a false prophet and magician, to come and curse Israel. Balaam had been a true prophet but through covetousness had apostatized. Rich gifts and offers of princely rewards finally persuaded the false prophet to attempt to stop the progress of Israel by placing them under a curse.

A Blessing

But the attempted curse was turned into a blessing. It was impossible for man to curse those "whom the Lord hath not cursed", and to defy those "whom the Lord hath not defied." Israel paid not the least attention to the efforts of their enemies to curse them. They were "as a great lion" lying down in fearless confidence knowing

1. Ellen White, *Patriarchs and Prophets* (1890), p. 438.

that no other creature could "stir him up" with fear by threatening his security. The false prophet was helpless before the perfect order and organization of the Exodus Movement which he was compelled to admire and even commend.[2] The prosperity of Israel was like "fertile valleys covered with abundant harvests" and "flourishing gardens watered by never-failing springs and the stately cedar of Lebanon", the mightiest tree of the forests of the East. Against such a prosperous movement the cursing of enemies is useless.

Acknowledgments

The apostate prophet was compelled to acknowledge that God was with Israel, "and the shout of a King is among them." God had pronounced a blessing upon His people and no man could "reverse it." The false leader also found out that "There is no enchantment against Jacob, neither is there any divination against Israel," and that because of the progress and triumph of the movement even the enemies of Israel would be compelled to say, "What hath God wrought!" Balaam found out by experience that "blessed is he that blesseth" Israel, "and cursed is he that curseth" Israel. It is a terrible thing to criticize and curse the only people upon whom Christ "bestows His supreme regard." Those who fight against the people of God are fighting against God and are therefore engaged in a losing cause. Of Balaam we read:

"His wisdom had become foolishness; his spiritual vision was beclouded; he had brought blindness upon himself by yielding to the power of Satan." —P.P. 444.

No Perverseness

During the attempt to curse Israel, there was written under inspiration one of the most wonderful statements ever recorded: Numbers 23:21. It seems impossible that this could be said of a people who had been so faithless and rebellious as the Israelites had been during most of their journey from Egypt. They had certainly been filled with iniquity and perverseness all along the way.

But a change had come since their vision of Christ and Calvary. They had experienced a new birth of faith and spiritual life that made them victorious over all their enemies. Faith was the victory by which they had overcome their foes and would continue to conquer. The Israelites, encamped in the plains of Moab in preparation to enter the promised land, were under divine favor and protection because their sins had been forgiven and covered until even the penetrating eye of God could see no iniquity or perverseness in them.

Still Defective

And yet we know from what happened in the near future that Israel was not yet a perfected people. The characters of many were very defective and thousands of

---

2. See Numbers 24:2-5.

those very people had to be shaken out of the movement in order to purify it for final victory. Many of them were of the rebels who had rejected God's leadership at Kadesh-Barnea and upon whom had been pronounced the sentence of an offended God that they must die in the wilderness and could not enter the promised land. But notwithstanding this condition, when an attempt was being made by their enemies to place them under a curse, the Lord overlooked those who were perverse among them and declared the movement to be without iniquity or perverseness. The Lord did not permit the perverseness of individuals in the camp of Israel to blind His vision of the movement as a whole and of what it would finally be under His leadership. The statement was doubtless partly prophetic, but even the false prophet saw such a contrast between the people he was trying to curse and himself that he cried out:

> Let me die the death of the righteous, and let my end be like his![3]

All apostate enemies would say this if they could get a real vision of the future and could see their final doom. Balaam died the death of the wicked and will share in the sinner's reward. He never repented and re-united with God and His people.

The Advent Movement

Revelation 12:12, 13: "Therefore rejoice, ye heavens, and ye that dwell in them. Woe to the inhabiters of the earth and of the sea! for the devil is come down unto you, having great wrath, because he knoweth that he hath but a short time. And when the dragon saw that he was cast unto the earth, he persecuted the woman which brought forth the man child."

The Advent Movement will soon experience to the full the antitype of Satan's effort to stop the Exodus Movement through the attempted curses of Balaam, the false prophet. Many false and apostate teachers have already attempted to stop he progress of the Advent Movement through their stinging criticism and threatened curses. But the worst is yet to come. We cannot help but think of the fruitless efforts of Balaam when we hear or read the bitter denunciations of the apostate leaders of offshoot movements in their attempt to scatter God's remnant people and stop the progress of the Advent Movement. Their burden is to "call out the faithful" into a new movement under their own leadership. Their gathering of the followers to themselves is a scattering of souls from Christ. Their message instead of being a gathering call is a scattering call. Instead of gathering to Christ they scatter abroad, because they are not with Christ but against Him.

Warnings

It is impossible to know exactly what will take place in the future by way of apos-

3. Numbers 23:10.

tasies and denunciations but many warnings have been given through the Spirit of Prophecy that they will increase as we near the end. Through this means Satan will make one of his last efforts to hinder the work of God.

> There will be messages of accusation against the people of God, similar to the work done by Satan in accusing God's people, and these messages will be sounding at the very time when God is saying to His people, "Arise, shine; for thy light is come, etc.[4]

> Those who start up to proclaim a message on their own responsibility, who, while claiming to be taught and led of God, still make it their special work to tear down that which God has been for years building up, are not doing the will of God. Be it known that these men are on the side of the great deceiver. Believe them not. They are allying themselves with the enemies of God and the truth.[5]

Other Predictions

> Every phase of fanaticism and erroneous theories claiming to be the truth will be brought in among the remnant people of God. ...
>
> Fanaticism will appear in the very midst of us. Deception will come, and of such a character that if it were possible they would mislead the very elect. ...
>
> The very last deception of Satan will be to make of none effect the testimony of the Spirit of God. ... Satan will work ingeniously, in different ways and through different agencies, to unsettle the confidence of God's remnant people in the true testimony. He will bring in spurious visions, to mislead and mingle the false with the true, and so disgust people that they will regard everything that bears the name of visions as a species of fanaticism. ... New and strange things will continually arise to lead God's people into false excitement, religious revivals, and curious developments. ...
>
> If Satan sees that the Lord is blessing His people and preparing them to discern his delusions, he will work with his master power to bring in fanaticism on the one hand, and cold formalism on the other. ...
>
> As the end draws near, the enemy will work with all his power to bring in fanaticism among us.[6]

Nothing to Fear

But God's remnant people have no more to fear from the rantings and curses of

4. Ellen White, *Testimonies to Ministers and Gospel Workers,* (1923), p. 42.
5. *Ibid.,* p. 51.
6. "Instructions for the Church Regarding Past and Future Manifestations of Fanaticism and Deceptive Teachings", p. 6, 8, 9, 13, 21.

these accusers of the brethren than ancient Israel feared the efforts of Balaam. God will likewise turn their curses into blessings for it is still impossible to curse that which God has blessed or bless that which God has cursed. "Blessed is he that blesseth, and cursed is he that curseth" modern Israel. If we will always remember the following texts we will never worry or become disturbed over denunciations or oppositions:

Psalm 76:10: "Surely the wrath of man shall praise Thee: the remainder of wrath shalt thou restrain."

2 Corinthians 13:8: "For we can do nothing against the truth, but for the truth."

To become agitated or even worried over false doctrines or offshoot movements is evidence of a lack of faith in the Advent Movement, its divine leadership, and ultimate triumph.

Help Bring Shaking

That false teachings and counterfeit movements will play an important part in the final shaking and therefore in the purifying of the church for translation is evident from the following statements:

> When the shaking comes, by the introduction of false theories, these surface readers, anchored no where, are like shifting sand. They slide into any position to suit the tenor of their feelings of bitterness.[7]

> God will arouse His people; if all other means fail, heresies will come in among them, which will sift them, separating the chaff from the wheat.[8]

This last statement indicates that heresies gather out of the Advent Movement only worthless chaff and is therefore a blessing in disguise to the church. It is one of the "all things" that "work together for good to them that love God, to them who are the called according to His purpose."[9]

Sees No Iniquity

While these attacks are being made we may rejoice to know that the Lord is not centering His attention on the iniquities of His people and the perverse among them, as do the false prophets, for "he hath not beheld iniquity in Jacob, neither hath He seen perverseness in Israel", for "the Lord his God is with him, and the shout of a king is among them." The attacks and curses of false teachers will doubtless be the

7. Ellen White, *Testimonies to Ministers and Gospel Workers,* (1923), p. 112.
8. Ellen White, *Testimonies for the Church,* vol. 5 (1889), p. 707.
9. Romans 8:28.

greatest during the latter rain which they "shall not recognize" or "discern". They will still be searching for evil and finding it because "there are evils existing in the church and will be until the end of the world."[10] The tares are not all separated from the wheat until the harvest which is "the end of the world", or "the end of probationary time."[11]

> False brethren will be found in the church till the close of time.[12]

> When the work of the gospel is completed, there immediately follows the separation between the good and the evil, and destiny of each class is forever fixed.[13]

Sees His Own

We are told that in the time of separation "those who have joined the church, but who have not joined Christ, will be manifest."[14] Christ does not reckon the rebels and hypocrites among His remnant people as His own, for His spiritual body is made up only of those who are in union with Him. This invisible body within the visible body will be perfect when probation closes even though the tares or chaff has not all been separated from among them. He therefore see no iniquity or perverseness in those who are Israelites indeed because their iniquities have been forgiven and covered by the imputed and imparted righteousness of Christ. Many texts describe the perfect church that will be waiting for Christ when He returns.[15] We too should learn to look at the church from this viewpoint and see God's people as they will be when the plan of redemption has completed its work in them. With such a vision, we will pay no more attention to the attacks of apostates than did Israel to the efforts of Balaam.

Motive of Balaam

The real motive that controlled Balaam in his attempts to curse Israel was his love for gain and position. Peter declared that Balaam "loved the wages of unrighteousness."[16] He was covetous and we are told that a "covetous man" is "an idolater" and will have no "inheritance in the Kingdom of Christ and of God."[17]

> Balaam was once a good man and a prophet of God; but he had apostatized, and had given himself up to covetousness; yet he still professed to be a servant of the Most High. … The bribe of costly gifts and prospective exaltation excited his covetousness.[18]

10. Ellen White, *Testimonies to Ministers and Gospel Workers,* (1923), p. 49.
11. Ellen White, *Christ's Object Lessons,* (1900), p. 72.
12. *Ibid.,* p. 73.
13. *Ibid.,* p. 123.
14. *Ibid.,* p. 74.
15. See Ephesians 5:25-27; Philippians 2:15; 1 Thessalonians 5:23; Revelation 14:5, 12.
16. 2 Peter 2:15.
17. Ephesians 5:5.
18. Ellen White, *Patriarchs and Prophets* (1890), p. 439.

The love of position and leadership and the desire for personal gain and honor led Balaam to sell himself to the service of the enemies of God and His people.

Modern Balaam

This same motive plays an important part in the work of modern Balaams. Most of those who apostatize and start offshoot movements are controlled by covetousness and are therefore idolaters. They "love the pre-eminence" and crave positions of leadership. Feeling that their talents and abilities have not been appreciated in the movement proper, they start something of their own and thus become leaders of their own choosing. They are also often dominated by the love of gain and they make merchandise of the gospel by selling their heretical literature and by collecting tithes and offerings for personal use. The more members of the Advent Movement they can poison with their false teachings and lead away from the fold into their own little camp, the more prominent their position of leadership and the greater their income in tithes and offerings. This accounts for much of their earnestness and zeal.

Written For Us

1 Corinthians 10:11: "Now all these things happened unto them for ensamples: and they are written for our admonition, upon whom the ends of the world are come."

> The great magician had tried his power of enchantment, in accordance with the desire of the Moabites; but concerning this very occasion it should be said of Israel, 'What hath God wrought!' While they are under the divine protection, no people or nation, though aided by all the power of Satan, should be able to prevail against them. All the world should wonder at the marvelous work of God in behalf of His people,—that a man determined to pursue a sinful course, should be so controlled by divine power as to utter, instead of imprecations, the richest and most precious promises, in the language of sublime and impassioned poetry. And the favor of God at this time manifested toward Israel, was to be an assurance of His protecting care for His obedient, faithful children in all ages. When Satan should inspire evil men to misrepresent, harass, and destroy God's people, this very occurrence would be brought to the remembrance, and would strengthen their courage and their faith in God.[19]

19. Ellen White, *Patriarchs and Prophets* (1890), p. 449.

32

THE IDOLATRY OF WORLDLINESS

Another Attack

Satan had utterly failed in his attack on the Exodus Movement through Balaam the false prophet. His attempted curses were turned into blessings and he was compelled to acknowledge that "there is no enchantment against Jacob, neither is there any divination against Israel." His predictions of the success of the movement he was trying to curse included "the increase and prosperity of the true Israel of God to the close of time."[1] But our wily foe is not easily defeated. When one plan fails he tries another. He has many weapons of warfare and his long experience has made him an expert in their use. His next attempt to keep Israel out of the promised land was by leading them into sin through the idolatry of worldliness.

Curse of God

The only curse that can affect God's people is the curse of sin. The transgressors of God's law place themselves under a divine curse.[2] Peter declares that those who follow "the way of Balaam" are under a curse.[3] It was at the suggestion of Balaam that Balak pursued a course that would bring the curse of God on Israel.

> Balaam knew that the prosperity of Israel depended upon their obedience to God, and that there was no way to cause their overthrow but by seducing them into sin. He now decided to secure Balak's favor by advising the Moabites of the course to be pursued to bring a curse upon Israel....The Moabites themselves were convinced that so long as Israel remained true to God, He would be their shield. The plan proposed by Balaam was to separate them from God by enticing them into Idolatry.[4]

A Separate People

The success and prosperity of Israel depended on their remaining an entirely separate people from all other nations. As long as they remained distinct and separate

---

1. Ellen White, *Patriarchs and Prophets* (1890), p. 447.
2. See Deuteronomy 27:15-26; Jeremiah 11:3; Malachi 3:9; Matthew 25:41.
3. 2 Peter 2:14,15.
4. Ellen White, *Patriarchs and Prophets* (1890), p. 451.

from the world they could not be cursed or defied.[5] Moses warned the Israelites that worldly associations would lead to intermarriage and idolatry which would bring upon them the curse of God and final destruction.[6] The promised blessing of God upon Abraham depended upon his making a complete separation from the world.[7] The favor of God and the blessings of the promised land depended on Israel's maintaining their complete separation from all other people.[8] Satan knew that if he could lead the children of Israel into worldly associations with the Moabites and Midianites he could bring upon them the curse of God and thus accomplish what he had failed to do through the curses of a false prophet.

Plan Succeeded

> Balaam witnessed the success of his diabolical scheme. He saw the curse of God visited upon His people, and thousands falling under His judgments; but the divine justice that punished sin in Israel, did not permit the tempters to escape. In the war of Israel against the Midianites, Balaam was slain.[9]

Numbers 25:1-3: "And Israel abode in Shittim, and the people began to commit whoredom with the daughters of Moab. And they called the people unto the sacrifices of their gods: and the people did eat, and bowed down to their gods. And Israel joined himself unto Baalpeor: and the anger of the LORD was kindled against Israel."

This experience happened on the banks of the Jordan when the Exodus Movement was on the very borders of the promised land when they were preparing to enter and take possession of Canaan.

> Only the river Jordan lay between them and the promised land. …
>
> During the time of their encampment beside Jordan, Moses was preparing for the occupation of Canaan. In this work the great leader was fully employed; but to the people this time of suspense and expectation was most trying, and before many weeks had elapsed, their history was marred by the most frightful departures from virtue and integrity.[10]

Worldly Influences

> But amid these attractive surroundings they were to encounter an evil more deadly than mighty hosts of armed men or the wild beasts of the

---

5. See Numbers 23:8, 9.
6. Deuteronomy 7:2-6.
7. Genesis 12:1-3.
8. Exodus 33:16; Leviticus 20:24.
9. Ellen White, *Patriarchs and Prophets* (1890), p. 451.
10. *Ibid.*, p. 453-454.

> wilderness. That country, so rich in natural advantages, had been defiled by the inhabitants. ... On every side were places noted for idolatry and licentiousness, the very names being suggestive of the vileness and corruption of the people. These surroundings exerted a polluting influence upon the Israelites. Their minds became familiar with the vile thoughts constantly suggested; their life of ease and inaction produced its demoralizing effect; and almost unconsciously to themselves, they were departing from God, and coming into a condition where they would fall an easy prey to temptation.[11]

Worldly Gatherings

> At first there was little intercourse between the Israelites and their heathen neighbors. ... At Balaam's suggestion, a grand festival in honor of their gods was appointed by the King of Moab, and it was secretly arranged that Balaam should induce the Israelites to attend. ... Great numbers of the people joined him in witnessing the festivities. They ventured upon the forbidden ground, and were entangled in the snare of Satan. Beguiled with music and dancing, and allured by the beauty of the heathen vestals, they cast off their fealty to Jehovah. As they united in mirth and feasting, indulgence in wine beclouded their senses, and broke down the barriers of self-control. Passion had full sway; and having defiled their consciences by lewdness, they were persuaded to bow down to idols.[12]

Dangerous Course

In taking the first step toward the world the Israelites started on a dangerous course that led to tragedy for thousands. Doubtless the leaders in this apostasy were of the "mixed multitude" who had always been the first to transgress.

> One cherished sin will, little by little, debase the character, bringing all its nobler powers into subjection to the evil desire. The removal of one safe-guard from the conscience, the indulgence of one evil habit, one neglect of the high claims of duty, breaks down the defenses of the soul, and opens the way for Satan to come in and lead us astray. The only safe course is to let our prayers go forth daily from a sincere heart, as did David, 'Hold up my goings in Thy paths, that my footsteps slip not.'[13]

One step led to another until many of the Israelites had gone too far to return.

---

11. Ellen White, *Patriarchs and Prophets* (1890), p. 453-454.
12. *Idid.*
13. *Ibid.*, p. 452.

The Antitype

1 Corinthians 10:6-8, 11: "Now these things were our examples, to the intent we should not lust after evil things, as they also lusted. Neither be ye idolaters, as were some of them; as it is written, The people sat down to eat and drink, and rose up to play. Neither let us commit fornication, as some of them committed, and fell in one day three and twenty thousand. ... Now all these things happened unto them for ensamples: and they are written for our admonition, upon whom the ends of the world are come."

One of the last attacks of Satan on the Advent Movement will be with the same effective weapon. On the borders of the heavenly Canaan he will seek to defeat the purpose of God for modern Israel by leading them into the idolatry of worldliness.

> It was by association with the idolaters and joining in their festivities that the Hebrews were led to transgress Gods law, and bring His judgments upon the nation. So now it is by leading the followers of Christ to associate with the ungodly and unite in their amusements, that Satan is most successful in alluring them into sin. … God requires of His people now as great a distinction from the world, in customs, habits, and principles, as He required of Israel anciently. If they faithfully follow the teachings of His Word, this distinction will exist; it cannot be otherwise. The warnings given to the Hebrews against assimilating with the heathen were not more direct or explicit than are those forbidding Christians to conform to the spirit and customs of the ungodly.[14]

Timely Warning

> Many of the amusements popular in the world today, even with those who claim to be Christians, tend to the same end as did those of the heathen. There are indeed few among them that Satan does not turn to account in destroying souls. Through the drama he has worked for ages to excite passion and glorify vice. The opera, with its fascinating display and bewildering music, the masquerade, the dance, the cardtable, Satan employs to break down the barriers of principle, and open the door to sensual indulgence. In every gathering for pleasure, where pride is fostered or appetite indulged, where one is led to forget God and lose sight of eternal interests, there Satan is binding his chains about the soul. …
>
> Those who would not fall a prey to Satan's devices must guard well the avenues of the soul; they must avoid reading, seeing, hearing that which will suggest impure thoughts. The mind should not be left to wander at random upon every subject that the adversary of souls may suggest. … This will require earnest prayer and unceasing watchfulness. We must be

14. Ellen White, *Patriarchs and Prophets* (1890), p. 458.

aided by the abiding influences of the Holy Spirit, which will attract the mind upward, and habituate it to dwell on pure and holy things. And we must give diligent study to the Word of God.[15]

Here is set forth the sound Christian principles which should guide us in choosing our reading, music, and amusements and which should regulate the conduct of our social gatherings.

Form of Idolatry

That worldliness or worldly conformity is a species of idolatry is evident. Worshiping and serving "the creature more than the Creator" is idolatry as set forth in Romans 1:25.

> Idolatry is every worship that stops short of the Supreme. —New Standard Dictionary.

"Creature" includes any object or person made by the Creator.

> Man is forbidden to give to any other object the first place in his affections or his service. Whatever we cherish that tends to lesson our love for God or to interfere with the service due Him, of that do we make a god.[16]

Anything that is permitted to come between us and our Lord Jesus Christ is an idol. It may be a person whom we love more than we love God, or it may be other things, interests, objectives, or purposes which has first place in our service and affections and therefore constitutes idolatry. Covetousness is called idolatry in Ephesians 5:5.

Warning to Us

1 Corinthians 10:7, 11, 14: "Neither be ye idolaters, as were some of them; as it is written, The people sat down to eat and drink, and rose up to play. ... Now all these things happened unto them for ensamples: and they are written for our admonition, upon whom the ends of the world are come. ... Wherefore, my dearly beloved, flee from idolatry."

Pleasure seeking is here called idolatry from which the members of the Advent Movement "upon whom the ends of the world are come" are told to "flee". The idols of the idolatry mentioned here are identified in the following statement in the Spirit of Prophecy:

15. Ellen White, *Patriarchs and Prophets* (1890), p. 459-460.
16. *Ibid.*, p. 305.

> The apostle's words of warning to the Corinthian church are applicable to all time, and are especially adapted to our day. By idolatry he means not only the worship of idols, but self-serving, love of ease, the gratification of appetite and passion. A mere profession of faith in Christ, a boastful knowledge of the truth, does not make a man a Christian.[17]
>
> Anything that men love and trust in instead of loving the Lord and trusting wholly in Him, becomes an idol, and is thus registered in the books of Heaven.[18]

Thus when we look at at the command of God, "Thou shalt have no other gods before Me", we must respond with the Psalmist, "They commandment is exceeding broad."

Complete Separation

The very purpose of the Advent Movement is to call God's people out of modern Babylon, which embraces the whole world.[19] The acceptance of this call makes them a separate and distinct people from all nations; a people who "dwell alone, and shall not be reckoned among the nations." Just before the final decree goes forth against God's remnant people who have gathered "together" out of Babylon they will be reckoned as "a nation not desired".[20] They are "the meek of the earth" who have sought God's "righteousness" and "have kept His ordinances", and therefore they are "hid in the day of the Lord's anger." The final decree of death goes forth against the Advent people because they have "separated themselves from the people of the lands unto the law of God,"[21] and are therefore a peculiar and separate people.

Cause of Persecution

Being "not of the world" because different from the world is the chief cause of persecution.[22] Jesus was persecuted because He was not of the world and was therefore different. His godly life was a constant rebuke to sinners and it made them angry. He was hated, maligned, reproached, persecuted, and finally murdered, not because His enemies could find any fault in Him, but because they could not. It was because He was different and separate from them that they nailed Him to the cross. The same is true of His genuine disciples. If we are like Christ we will be different from the world and differences always arouses opposition.

A genuine Christian is a constant rebuke to the selfish and proud hearted and

17. Ellen White, *Acts of the Apostles* (1911), p. 317.
18. Ellen White, *Testimonies for the Church,* vol. 5 (1889), p. 250.
19. Revelation 18:1-5.
20. See Zephaniah 2:1-3.
21. Nehemiah 10:28.
22. John 15:18-20.

makes them feel uncomfortable. His unselfish life offends them and stirs up their hatred and enmity which ends in persecution. Jesus prayed that His disciples be "not of the world" even as He was "not of the world" and while they remained in the world that they should be kept "from the evil", and "sanctified by the truth".[23]

Condition of Discipleship

2 Corinthians 6:14-18: "Be ye not unequally yoked together with unbelievers: for what fellowship hath righteousness with unrighteousness? and what communion hath light with darkness? And what concord hath Christ with Belial? or what part hath he that believeth with an infidel? And what agreement hath the temple of God with idols? for ye are the temple of the living God; as God hath said, I will dwell in them, and walk in them; and I will be their God, and they shall be my people. Wherefore come out from among them, and be ye separate, saith the Lord, and touch not the unclean thing; and I will receive you, and will be a Father unto you, and ye shall be my sons and daughters, saith the Lord Almighty."

Without a complete separation from the world we cannot be God's people or enjoy His family of sons and daughters. He will not receive into His family those who are conformed to the world and to its customs. Only those who are "transformed by the renewing" of their minds and the cleansing of their hearts and habits can enter the Kingdom of God.[24] We are told that all who experience the new birth and become new creatures in Christ Jesus will "overcome the world" through faith.[25] "The world" here represents "the sum of all the forces antagonistic to the spiritual life." It includes all of the worldly temptations and influences that lead to sin. For our encouragement Jesus said:

John 16:33: "Be of good cheer; I have overcome the world."

Our Eternal Destiny

The question of our relation to the world involves our eternal destiny.

1 John 2:14- 17: "I have written unto you, fathers, because ye have known him that is from the beginning. I have written unto you, young men, because ye are strong, and the word of God abideth in you, and ye have overcome the wicked one. Love not the world, neither the things that are in the world. If any man love the world, the love of the Father is not in him. For all that is in the world, the lust of the flesh, and the lust of the eyes, and the pride of life, is not of the Father, but is of the world. And the world passeth away, and the lust thereof: but he that doeth the will of God abideth for ever."

23. See John 17:15-17.
24. Romans 12:1, 2.
25. 1 John 5:4, 5.

We cannot love both God and the world, nor can we "serve two masters." In overcoming the world we must overcome "the wicked one" who is the prince, god and ruler of the world. All of the worldly lusts and temptations are embraced in the three here mentioned. Before these three the first Adam fell, but the second Adam met the same threefold temptation and conquered. Getting the victory over worldliness is a life and death question.

> There must be far greater humility, a much greater distinction from the world, among Seventh-day Adventists, else God will not accept us, whatever our position or the character of the work in which we are engaged.[26]

The Seal of God

Ezekiel 9:1-7: "He cried also in mine ears with a loud voice, saying, Cause them that have charge over the city to draw near, even every man with his destroying weapon in his hand. And, behold, six men came from the way of the higher gate, which lieth toward the north, and every man a slaughter weapon in his hand; and one man among them was clothed with linen, with a writer's inkhorn by his side: and they went in, and stood beside the brazen altar. And the glory of the God of Israel was gone up from the cherub, whereupon he was, to the threshold of the house. And he called to the man clothed with linen, which had the writer's inkhorn by his side;

"And the LORD said unto him, Go through the midst of the city, through the midst of Jerusalem, and set a mark upon the foreheads of the men that sigh and that cry for all the abominations that be done in the midst thereof. And to the others he said in mine hearing, Go ye after him through the city, and smite: let not your eye spare, neither have ye pity: Slay utterly old [and] young, both maids, and little children, and women: but come not near any man upon whom is the mark; and begin at my sanctuary. Then they began at the ancient men which were before the house. And he said unto them, Defile the house, and fill the courts with the slain: go ye forth. And they went forth, and slew in the city."

> The leaven of godliness has not entirely lost its power. At the time when the danger and depression of the church are greatest, the little company who are standing in the light will be sighing and crying for the abominations that are done in the land. But more especially will their prayers arise in behalf of the church, because its members are doing after the manner of the world.[27]

> Those who are uniting with the world, are receiving the worldly mold, and preparing for the mark of the beast. Those who are distrustful of self, who are humbling themselves before God and purifying their souls by

26. Ellen White, *Testimonies for the Church,* vol. 7 (1902), p. 296-297.
27. Ellen White, *Testimonies for the Church,* vol. 5 (1889), p. 219.

obeying the truth,—these are receiving the heavenly mold, and preparing for the seal of God in their foreheads. When the decree goes forth, and the stamp is impressed, their characters will remain pure and spotless for eternity. Now is the time to prepare. The seal of God will never be placed upon the forehead of an impure man or woman. It will never be placed upon the forehead of the ambitious, worldloving man or woman. It will never be placed upon the forehead of men and women of false tongues or deceitful hearts. All who receive the seal of God must be without spot before God—candidates for heaven.[28]

Satan's Last Attack

Infecting ancient Israel with the spirit of worldliness was one of Satan's last efforts to thwart the purpose of God to lead them into the promised land. It will also be one of his last attacks against modern Israel to defeat the Advent Movement and delay the entrance of God's remnant people into the heavenly Canaan. It will be one of the means by which the chaff will be separated from the wheat in the final shaking that will purify the church for translation. The modern world is defiled by its inhabitants.

Isaiah 24:5: "The earth also is defiled under the inhabitants thereof; because they have transgressed the laws, changed the ordinance, broken the everlasting covenant."

The newspapers, magazines and billboards contain names and pictures and suggestions of that which is impure and which leads to idolatry. Only the power of God can protect His remnant people during Satan's last and most desperate attempts to keep them from entering the heavenly kingdom.

28. Ellen White, *Testimonies for the Church,* vol. 5 (1889), p. 210, 216.

33

THE IDOLATRY OF IMMORALITY

Satan's Last Attack

Numbers 25:1-5, 9: "And Israel abode in Shittim, and the people began to commit whoredom with the daughters of Moab. And they called the people unto the sacrifices of their gods: and the people did eat, and bowed down to their gods. And Israel joined himself unto Baalpeor: and the anger of the LORD was kindled against Israel. And the LORD said unto Moses, Take all the heads of the people, and hang them up before the LORD against the sun, that the fierce anger of the LORD may be turned away from Israel. And Moses said unto the judges of Israel, Slay ye every one his men that were joined unto Baalpeor. ... And those that died in the plague were twenty and four thousand."

The last attack of Satan on the Exodus Movement just before the crossing of the Jordan into the promised land was an appeal to the indulgence of sexual passion which led to the terrible sin of Baal-Peor effecting 24,000 members including many leaders. Immorality is the climax and ultimate consequences of worldly conformity. It is the greatest of all the sins of worldliness and the final goal of the enemy of our souls in leading God's people worldward. The lord gave ancient Israel many warnings against licentiousness and immorality as the worst forms of idolatry.[1]

Form of Immorality

That immorality is a form of idolatry is evident from many scriptures. In Ephesians 5:3-5 and Colossians 3:5, fornication, uncleanness, filthiness, inordinate affection, and evil concupiscence are enumerated among the lusts of the flesh which constitutes idolatry. In Psalm 106:28, 35-38 we are told that when the Israelites "joined themselves to Baal-Peor" they "sacrificed their sons and daughters unto devils" and "sacrificed unto the idols of Canaan" and "served their idols which were a snare unto them." Idolatry is defined as "inordinate love and admiration." False worship and moral corruption have always gone hand in hand. The friendship of the world or worldliness is called adultery in James 4:4. This is not only because union with the world constitutes spiritual fornication, but also because physical licentiousness has always been the climax of abandonment to the spirit worldliness. The most worldly

1. See Deuteronomy 22:20-24; 23:14-17; 24:1-4.

and idolatrous ages of human history have also been the most immoral and corrupt.

Satanic Religion

Satan's religion is pictured in Revelation 17 as a "harlot" with whom "the kings of the earth have committed fornication", because apostasy from the religion of the true God and fornication have always been linked together.

> Harlotry is the standing symbol in the word of God of a debauched worship, idolatry, and false devotion. When people worship for God what is not God, and given their hearts to idols, or institute systems, doctrines, rites, or administrations, to take the place of what God has revealed or appointed, the Scriptures call it whoredom, adultery, fornication. The reason is obvious. The breaking down of the divine laws and ordinances necessarily carries with it the breaking down of the marriage institution, and hence all supports of godly chastity and pureness. Accordingly all false religions are ever attended with lewdness, even in connection with their most sacred rites.[2]

This figure is appropriate because fornication and adultery are forms of false affection which prostitutes the most sacred part of the nature to alien purposes. The alienation of the heart's affection and allegiance from Christ is a violation of the most sacred ties that bind a Christian to Christ and is therefore designated as spiritual fornication.

Paganism Corrupt

Romans 1:21-32: "Because that, when they knew God, they glorified [him] not as God, neither were thankful; but became vain in their imaginations, and their foolish heart was darkened. Professing themselves to be wise, they became fools, and changed the glory of the uncorruptible God into an image made like to corruptible man, and to birds, and fourfooted beasts, and creeping things. Wherefore God also gave them up to uncleanness through the lusts of their own hearts, to dishonour their own bodies between themselves: who changed the truth of God into a lie, and worshipped and served the creature more than the Creator, who is blessed for ever. Amen.

"For this cause God gave them up unto vile affections: for even their women did change the natural use into that which is against nature: and likewise also the men, leaving the natural use of the woman, burned in their lust one toward another; men with men working that which is unseemly, and receiving in themselves that recompense of their error which was meet. And even as they did not like to retain God in [their] knowledge, God gave them over to a reprobate mind, to do those things which are not convenient; being filled with all unrighteousness, fornication, wickedness, covetousness, maliciousness; full of envy, murder, debate, deceit, malignity;

---

2. Seiss, *The Apocalypse*. vol. 3, p. 113. See Isaiah 1:21; Jeremiah 3:1,3, 6-9; Ezekial 16:32.

whisperers, backbiters, haters of God, despiteful, proud, boasters, inventors of evil things, disobedient to parents, without understanding, covenantbreakers, without natural affection, implacable, unmerciful: who knowing the judgment of God, that they which commit such things are worthy of death, not only do the same, but have pleasure in them that do them."

One cannot read this description of idolatry without knowing that it is inseparably connected with licentiousness.

> All paganism is at bottom a worship of nature in some form or other. … The mystery of birth was the deepest mystery of nature; it lay at the root of all thoughtful paganism, and appeared in various forms, some of a more innocent, others a more debasing type. To ancient pagan thinkers, as well as modern men of science, the key and the hidden secret of the origin and preservation of the universe lay in the mystery of sex. … Upon such basis as this rested almost all the Polytheistic worship of the old civilization; and to it may be traced back stage by stage the separation of divinity into male and female gods, the deification of distinct powers of nature, and the idealization of man's own faculties and desires and lusts; where every power of his understanding was embodied as an object of adoration, and every impulse of his will became an incarnation of deity.[3]

Mount Peor

Numbers 23:28: "And Balak brought Balaam unto the top of Peor, that looketh toward Jeshimon."

Mount Peor was on the east side of the Jordan over against Jericho, and was one of the mountains from which Balaam attempted to curse Israel. Baal-Peor was an idol whose worship was attended with the most degrading and licentious rites. A great temple crowned the summit of Mount Peor which was dedicated to the worship of Baal and Ashtaroth, the chief god and goddess of the Moabites and Midianites. It was to a great religious festival in this temple on Mount Peor that Balaam invited the Israelites, and those who attended were beguiled and led into worldliness and licentiousness and thus into idolatry.

> Having defiled their consciences by lewdness, they were persuaded to bow down to the idols. They offered sacrifices upon heathen altars, and participated in the most degrading rites. It was not long before the poison had spread, like a deadly infection, through the camp of Israel. Those who would have conquered their enemies in battle, were overcome by the wiles of heathen women. The people seemed to be infatuated. The rulers and the leading men were among

3. Encyclopedia Britannica.

the first to transgress, and so many of the people were guilty that the apostasy became national.[4]

Moses Aroused

When Moses was aroused to perceive the evil, the plots of their enemies had been so successful that not only were the Israelites participating in the licentious worship at Mount Peor, but the heathen rites were coming to be observed in the camp of Israel. The aged leader was filled with indignation, and the wrath of God was kindled. Their iniquitous practices did that for Israel which all the enchantments of Balaam could not do—they separated them from God. By swift coming judgments the people were awakened to the enormity of their sin. A terrible pestilence broke out in the camp, to which tens of thousands speedily fell a prey. God commanded that the leaders in this apostasy be put to death by the magistrates. This order was quickly obeyed. The offenders were slain, then their bodies were hung up in the sight of all Israel, that the congregation, seeing the leaders so severely dealt with, might have a deep sense of God's abhorrence of their sin, and the terror of His wrath against them.[5]

Leader's Executed

Numbers 25:3-5: "And Israel joined himself unto Baalpeor: and the anger of the LORD was kindled against Israel. And the LORD said unto Moses, Take all the heads of the people, and hang them up before the LORD against the sun, that the fierce anger of the LORD may be turned away from Israel. And Moses said unto the judges of Israel, Slay ye every one his men that were joined unto Baalpeor."

This divine sentence was pronounced against the leaders who were guilty. The guilty leaders were hanged and the others who had committed fornication were slain with the sword and by the plague. The Lord did not simply remove the guilty officials from their positions, nor did He move them to another part of the camp in an effort to cover up their sins. The example of leadership must be of the highest order and they must be clean who bear the vessels of the Lord. This prompt execution of the divine sentence brought a revival and reformation into the camp.

With tears and deep humiliation" the Israelites confessed their sins and wept before God "at the door of the tabernacle. … The priests and leaders had prostrated themselves in grief and humiliation, weeping 'between the porch and the altar', and entreating the Lord to spare His people, and give not His heritage to reproach.[6]

---

4. Ellen White, *Patriarchs and Prophets* (1890), p. 454.
5. *Ibid.*, p. 455.
6. *Ibid.*

Final Cleansing

This earnest work of repentance and confession on the part of the leaders and members of the Exodus Movement, when they were made aware of their spiritual destitution, brought about a spiritual revival and reformation that purged out the last of the rebels and cleansed the movement for entrance into the promised land.

> The judgments visited upon Israel for their sin at Chittim, destroyed the survivors of that vast company, who, nearly forty years before, had incurred the sentence, 'They shall surely die in the wilderness.' The numbering of the people by divine direction, during their encampment on the plains of Jordan, showed that 'of them whom Moses and Aaron the priest numbered, when they numbered the children of Israel in the wilderness of Sinai, … there was not left a man of them, save Caleb the son of Jephunneh, and Joshua the son of Nun.[7]

This last attack of Satan proved a blessing in disguise to the movement as a whole by shaking out the last of the rebels and in giving the others a vision of the sinfulness of sin which led to godly sorrow and repentance.

Advent Movement

1 Corinthians 10:8, 11, 12: "Neither let us commit fornication, as some of them committed, and fell in one day three and twenty thousand. ... Now all these things happened unto them for ensamples: and they are written for our admonition, upon whom the ends of the world are come. Wherefore let him that thinketh he standeth take heed lest he fall."

After quoting these verses the servant of the Lord wrote:

> All along through the ages there are strewn wrecks of character that have been stranded upon the rocks of sensual indulgence. As we approach the close of time, as the people of God stand upon the borders of the heavenly Canaan, Satan will, as of old, redouble his efforts to prevent them from entering the goodly land.[8]

> Satan's snares are laid for us as verily as they were laid for the children of Israel just prior to their entrance into the land of Canaan. We are repeating the history of that people.[9]

> I was pointed back to ancient Israel. But two of the adults of the vast

7. Ellen White, *Patriarchs and Prophets* (1890), p. 456.
8. *Ibid.*, p. 457.
9. Ellen White, *Testimonies for the Church*, vol. 5 (1889), p. 160.

army that left Egypt entered the land of Canaan. Their dead bodies were strewn in the wilderness because of their transgressions. Modern Israel is in greater danger of forgetting God and being led into idolatry than were His ancient people. Many idols are worshiped, even by professed Sabbath-keepers.[10]

Worldly Associations

Satan is continually seeking to overcome the people of God by breaking down the barriers which separate them from the world. Ancient Israel was enticed into sin when they ventured into forbidden association with the heathen. In a similar manner modern Israel is led astray.[11] —G.C. 508.

[Satan] lays his snare for every soul. It is not the ignorant and uncultured merely that need to be guarded; he will prepare his temptations for those in the highest positions, in the most holy office; if he can lead them to pollute their souls, he can through them destroy many. And he employs the same agents now as he employed three thousand years ago. By worldly friendships, by the charms of beauty, by pleasure-seeking, mirth, feasting, or the wine-cup he tempts to the violation of the seventh commandment.[12]

The God of Passion

Many today are worshiping the god of lustful passion.

Satan seduced Israel into licentiousness before leading them into idolatry. Those who will dishonor God's image and defile His temple in their own persons will not scruple at any dishonor to God that will gratify the desire of their depraved hearts. Sensual indulgence weakens the mind and debases the soul. The moral and intellectual powers are benumbed and paralyzed by the gratification of the animal propensities; and it is impossible for the slave of passion to realize the sacred obligation of the law of God, to appreciate the atonement, or to place a right value upon the soul. Goodness, purity, and truth, reverence for God, and love for sacred things,—all those holy affections and noble desires that link men with the heavenly world,—are consumed in the fires of lust. The soul becomes a blackened and desolate waste, the habitation of evil spirits, and 'the cage of every unclean and hateful bird.' Beings formed in the image of God are dragged down to a level with the brutes.[13]

---

10. Ellen White, *Testimonies for the Church,* vol. 1 (1868), p. 609.
11. Ellen White, *Great Controversy* (1911), p. 508.
12. Ellen White, *Patriarchs and Prophets* (1890), p. 457-458.
13. *Ibid.,* p. 458.

A Gradual Moral-Decline

> A long preparatory process, unknown to the world, goes on in the heart before the Christian commits open sin. The mind does not come down at once from purity and holiness to depravity, corruption, and crime. It takes time to degrade those formed in the image of God to the brutal or the satanic. By beholding, we become changed. By the indulgence of impure thoughts, man can so educate his mind that sin which he once loathed will become pleasant to him. Satan is using every means to make crime and debasing vice popular. We cannot walk the streets of our cities without encountering flaring notices of crime presented in some novel, or to be acted at some theater. The mind is educated to familiarity with sin. The course pursued by the base and vile is kept before the people in the periodicals of the day, and everything that can excite passion is brought before them in exciting stories. They hear and read so much of debasing crime, that the once tender conscience, which would have recoiled with horror from such scenes, becomes hardened, and they dwell upon these things with greedy interest.[14]

An Immoral Age

Genesis 6:5: "And God saw that the wickedness of man was great in the earth, and that every imagination of the thoughts of his heart was only evil continually."

This same condition will again prevail just before the return of Christ.

Matthew 24:37-39: "But as the days of Noe [were], so shall also the coming of the Son of man be. For as in the days that were before the flood they were eating and drinking, marrying and giving in marriage, until the day that Noe entered into the ark, and knew not until the flood came, and took them all away; so shall also the coming of the Son of man be."

> The growing compromise with the world on the part of the large proportion of the membership of our churches, the neglect of real prayer and the inactivity in real soul-winning work, cannot but fill any intelligent and properly instructed Christian with a sorrow that almost breaks the heart. ... Conditions in our universities, colleges, high schools and grade schools, not merely the religious conditions, but the moral conditions, are terrible beyond expression. I could not put into print things that have come under my observation as to the slump, not only in the modesty, but in the moral decency, not only among our young men and boys, but among our young women and girls.[15]

---

14. Ellen White, *Patriarchs and Prophets* (1890), p. 459.
15. "Moody Bible Institute Monthly." July, 1927.

Antitype of Baal-Peor

No person can read the following named characters from the Spirit of Prophecy regarding the terrible sin or immorality in the church without knowing that we have come to the antitype of the Baal-peor experience of ancient Israel, and that we are therefore on the very borders of the heavenly Canaan:

> Agents of Satan.[16]
>
> The Appearance of Evil.[17]
>
> Moral Pollution.[18]
>
> An Appeal to the Church.[19] —Id. 439-489.

These references and many others picture conditions of worldliness and immorality among church members just before the end that is sad to contemplate. We are told that many leaders will fall through this last attack of Satan. These conditions will result in the message that brings the shaking and purifies the Advent Movement.

Joel 2:1, 12-17: "Blow ye the trumpet in Zion, and sound an alarm in my holy mountain: let all the inhabitants of the land tremble: for the day of the LORD cometh, for it is nigh at hand; ... Therefore also now, saith the LORD, turn ye even to me with all your heart, and with fasting, and with weeping, and with mourning: and rend your heart, and not your garments, and turn unto the LORD your God: for he is gracious and merciful, slow to anger, and of great kindness, and repenteth him of the evil. Who knoweth if he will return and repent, and leave a blessing behind him; even a meat offering and a drink offering unto the LORD your God?

"Blow the trumpet in Zion, sanctify a fast, call a solemn assembly: gather the people, sanctify the congregation, assemble the elders, gather the children, and those that suck the breasts: let the bridegroom go forth of his chamber, and the bride out of her closet. Let the priests, the ministers of the LORD, weep between the porch and the altar, and let them say, Spare thy people, O LORD, and give not thine heritage to reproach, that the heathen should rule over them: wherefore should they say among the people, Where is their God?"

This is the Laodicean message and the same language is used in describing the consternation of the loyal 135 leaders in connection with the Baal-peor experience. The final execution will begin with the "ancient men" or "elders" who minister in the Lord's house.[20]

---

16. Ellen White, *Testimonies for the Church,* vol. 5 (1889), p. 137-148.
17. *Ibid.,* p. 591-603.
18. Ellen White, *Testimonies for the Church,* vol. 2 (1871), p. 346-353.
19. *Ibid.,* p. 439-489.
20. See Exodus 9:4-9.

Day of Execution

The day of execution in modern Israel will come and the Lord will cleanse the church of all moral pollution.

Ephesians 5:25-27: "Husbands, love your wives, even as Christ also loved the church, and gave himself for it; that he might sanctify and cleanse it with the washing of water by the word, that he might present it to himself a glorious church, not having spot, or wrinkle, or any such thing; but that it should be holy and without blemish."

> Cleanse the camp of this moral corruption, if it takes the highest men in the highest positions. God will not be trifled with. Fornication is in our ranks. I know it, for it has been shown me to be strengthening and extending its pollutions. There is much we will never know; but that which is revealed makes the church responsible and guilty unless they show a determined effort to eradicate the evil. Cleanse the camp, for there is an accursed thing in it.[21]

> The time has come for earnest and powerful efforts to rid the church of the slime and filth which is tarnishing her purity.[22]

Idol Worship

> Shall the sacred vessel, whom God is to use for a high and holy work, be dragged from its lofty, controlling sphere to minister to debasing lust? Is not this idol worship of the most degrading kind?—The lips uttering praises and adoring a sinful human being, pouring forth expressions of ravishing tenderness and adulation which belong alone to God,—the powers given to God in solemn consecration administering to a harlot; for any woman who will allow the addresses of another man than her husband, who will listen to his advances, and whose ears will be pleased with the outpouring of lavish words of affection, of adoration, or endearment, is an adulteress and a harlot.[23]

The Church Purged

> Israel's sin at Baal-peor brought the judgments of God upon the nation, and though the same sins may not now be punished as speedily, they will as surely meet retribution.[24]

---

21. Ellen White, *Testimonies to Ministers and Gospel Workers,* (1923), p. 428.
22. *Ibid.,* p. 450.
23. *Ibid.,* p. 434-435.
24. Ellen White, *Patriarchs and Prophets* (1890), p. 461.

The church is corrupt because of her members who defile their bodies, and pollute their souls. ... But the days of purification of the church are hastening on apace. God will have a people pure and true. In the mighty sifting soon to take place, we shall be better able to measure the strength of Israel. The signs reveal that the time is near when the Lord will manifest that His fan is in His hand, and that He will thoroughly purge His floor. ...

In this time, the gold will be separated from the dross in the church. True godliness will be clearly distinguished from the appearance and tinsel of it. Many a star that we have admired for its brilliancy, will then go out in darkness. Chaff like a cloud will be borne away on the wind, even from places where we see only floors of rich wheat. All who assume the ornaments of the sanctuary, but are not clothed with Christ's righteousness, will appear in the shame of their own nakedness. ... Then will the church of Christ appear 'fair as the moon, clear as the sun, and terrible as an army with banners.[25]

This is a description of the church during the latter rain and loud cry.

The Shaking Time

That the shaking time will also be the result of the preaching of the Laodicean message is evident from the following:

I asked the meaning of the shaking I had seen, and was shown that it would be caused by the straight testimony called forth by the counsel of the True Witness to the Laodiceans. This will have its effect upon the heart of the receiver, and will lead him to exalt the standard and pour forth the straight truth. Some will not bear this straight testimony. They will rise up against it, and this is what will causes a shaking among God's people. I saw that the testimony of the True Witness has not been half heeded. The solemn testimony upon which the destiny of the church hangs, has been lightly esteemed, if not entirely disregarded. This testimony must work deep repentance; all who truly receive it will obey it, and 136 be purified.[26]

Then follows a description of the latter rain. The immoral conditions in the church will give emphasis to the need of the Laodicean message.

A Cleansed Church

When the church militant becomes the church triumphant it will have been cleansed from all pollution and will be "holy and without blemish." Revelation 14:1-5.

---

25. Ellen White, *Testimonies for the Church,* vol. 5 (1889), p. 79-82.
26. Ellen White, *Early Writings* (1882), p. 270.

> They are as pure as virgins. —Weymouths.

Christ's loyal and pure church is symbolized by a "virgin" and the individual members as "virgins."[27] Dean Alfred believes that the language should be taken literally, that the 144,000 get complete victory over impurity of mind and body during the most licentious and immoral age of all history. They pass triumphantly through the antitype of the Baal-peor experience of ancient Israel.

> 'They are virgins,' in that they lived chaste lives, both as to faithfulness to God in their religion, and as to their pureness from all bodily lewdness.[28]

The sealed 144,000 will be pure in both soul and body, mind and spirit.

---

27. See 2 Corinthians 11:2; Matthew 25:1.
28. Seiss, *The Apocalypse*, vol. 3, p. 22.

34

LEST WE FORGET

History Repeated

Deuteronomy 1:1, 3: "These be the words which Moses spake unto all Israel on this side Jordan in the wilderness, in the plain over against the Red sea, between Paran, and Tophel, and Laban, and Hazeroth, and Dizahab. And it came to pass in the fortieth year, in the eleventh month, on the first day of the month, that Moses spake unto the children of Israel, according unto all that the LORD had given him in commandment unto them."

Deuteronomy is a Greek name given by Alexandrian Jews to the fifth book of Moses when they translated the Old Testament from Hebrew into Greek and thus produced the Septuagint Version,—the one used by Christ and the apostles. The name means "repetition" or "repetition of the law", because it is a repetition of all of the instruction given to Israel during their forty years of wandering as well as a review of their experiences while they were "under the divine rebuke." The book of Deuteronomy was given by Moses in a series of discourses on the banks of the Jordan in the plains of Moab just before the Israelites entered the promised land.

> Moses gave the whole book of Deuteronomy in discourses to the people.[1]

Kadesh-Barnea Crisis

The series of sermons began with the heaven-sent message given at Mount Sinai that led the Israelites to Kadesh-Barnea, the gateway to the promised land.

Deuteronomy 1:5-8: "On this side Jordan, in the land of Moab, began Moses to declare this law, saying, The LORD our God spake unto us in Horeb, saying, Ye have dwelt long enough in this mount: turn you, and take your journey, and go to the mount of the Amorites, and unto all the places nigh thereunto, in the plain, in the hills, and in the vale, and in the south, and by the sea side, to the land of the Canaanites, and unto Lebanon, unto the great river, the river Euphrates. Behold, I have set the land before you: go in and possess the land which the LORD sware unto your

1. Ellen White, *Patriarchs and Prophets* (1890), p. 503.

fathers, Abraham, Isaac, and Jacob, to give unto them and to their seed after them."

Moses then dwells at great length on the Kadesh-Barnea crisis resulting in the divine sentence that sent them back into the wilderness for a forty year delay. The period of wandering is now over and Moses delivers his message in the eleventh month of the fortieth year. Throughout the entire series of discourses, Moses lays special emphasis on the Kadesh-Barnea experiences as the cause of their failure to inherit the promised land "at the time of God's appointment."

During their wilderness wanderings while they were "under the divine rebuke" the Israelites resented being reminded of their mistakes and rebellions, but now as they are repeated near the end of their journey they see them in a new light. As they look back over the forty years from the banks of the Jordan their past history takes on a new significance. At last they are willing to freely acknowledge their mistakes and confess them.

Forget Not

Deuteronomy 8:2-5: "And thou shalt remember all the way which the LORD thy God led thee these forty years in the wilderness, to humble thee, and to prove thee, to know what was in thine heart, whether thou wouldest keep his commandments, or no. And he humbled thee, and suffered thee to hunger, and fed thee with manna, which thou knewest not, neither did thy fathers know; that he might make thee know that man doth not live by bread only, but by every word that proceedeth out of the mouth of the LORD doth man live. Thy raiment waxed not old upon thee, neither did thy foot swell, these forty years. Thou shalt also consider in thine heart, that, as a man chasteneth his son, so the LORD thy God chasteneth thee."

Deuteronomy 9:7: "Remember, and forget not, how thou provokedst the LORD thy God to wrath in the wilderness: from the day that thou didst depart out of the land of Egypt, until ye came unto this place, ye have been rebellious against the LORD."

"Remember and forget not" seems to be the key-note of this series of sermons that closed the career of their great leader. It was his farewell message and was delivered with great earnestness and power. He told them to "ask now of the days that are past" and never to forget the divine leadership of the Exodus Movement and the purpose and love of God in leading them from Egyptian bondage to the land of promise and freedom.[2]

> Moses stood before the people to repeat his last warnings and admonitions. His face was illumined with a holy light. His hair was white with age, but his form was erect, his countenance expressed the unabated vigor

2. See Deuteronomy 4:32-40.

of health, and his eye was clear and undimmed. It was an important occasion, and with deep feeling he portrayed the love and mercy of their Almighty Protector. …

The people of Israel had been ready to ascribe their troubles to Moses; but now their suspicions that he was controlled by pride, ambition, or selfishness, were removed, and they listened with confidence to his words.[3]

Emphasized Mistakes

Moses faithfully set before them their errors, and the transgressions of their fathers. They had often felt impatient and rebellious because of their long wandering in the wilderness; but the Lord had not been chargeable with this delay in possessing Canaan. He was more grieved than they because He could not bring them into immediate possession of the promised land, and thus display before all nations His mighty power in the deliverance of His people. With their distrust of God, with their pride and unbelief, they had not been prepared to enter Canaan. They would in no way represent that people whose God is the Lord, for they did not bear His character of purity, goodness, and benevolence. Had their fathers yielded in faith to the direction of God, being governed by His judgments, and walking in His ordinances, they would long before have been settled in Canaan, a prosperous, holy, happy people. Their delay to enter the goodly land dishonored God, and detracted from His glory in the sight of the surrounding nations.[4] —P.P. 464.

Commemorated in Song

Not only did Moses repeat the experiences of Israel's past history and urge them to "remember" and "forget not," but they were to talk about them and repeat them to their children. It was of vital importance that they see the past in the proper light and never forget their mistakes and experiences. To help them remember, Moses commemorated the history of the past in a song which he composed under divine direction and inspiration.

Deuteronomy 31:19-22: "Now therefore write ye this song for you, and teach it the children of Israel: put it in their mouths, that this song may be a witness for me against the children of Israel. For when I shall have brought them into the land which I sware unto their fathers, that floweth with milk and honey; and they shall have eaten and filled themselves, and waxen fat; then will they turn unto other gods, and serve them, and provoke me, and break my covenant. And it shall come to pass, when many evils and troubles are befallen them, that this song shall testify against

3. Ellen White, *Patriarchs and Prophets* (1890), p. 463-464.
4. *Ibid.*, p. 464.

them as a witness; for it shall not be forgotten out of the mouths of their seed: for I know their imagination which they go about, even now, before I have brought them into the land which I sware. Moses therefore wrote this song the same day, and taught it the children of Israel."

This song is found in Chapter 32 and is called "The Song of Moses" as was the one he composed and Israel sang on the shores of the Red Sea following their deliverance from Egypt. The 105th, 106th, and 107th Psalms are other songs composed for the same purpose and these too may have been written by Moses who was the author of some of the Psalms. In all of these songs the Israelites were especially reminded of the mistakes that caused the long delay in reaching their goal.

Essential Preparation

It is evident that one of the most essential parts of the preparation of the Israelites to enter the earthly Canaan was a clear view of the history of the past and especially of the errors and mistakes of their fathers. They could not enter into the promised land until they recognized these mistakes and confessed them. Therefore their last study was concentrated on their past history in the light of God's love and leadership. On the banks of the Jordan they must look backward before they could go forward. This was the final lesson in the school of experience and training that would prepare them to triumph gloriously. This review would strengthen their faith for the crossing of the Jordan and the conquest of Canaan.

The Advent Movement

Since "we are repeating the history of that people," we too must get a vision of the past just before our pilgrim journey is ended. Just before the end, the Advent people will review their past history and see it in a new light. We must study and understand the antitypes of the two Kadesh-Barnea experiences of ancient Israel and profit by the mistakes of our fathers especially during the 1888 crisis. We must acknowledge and confess the mistakes of our fathers and see to it that we do not repeat them and thus further delay the final triumph of the Advent Movement.

The history of the past must be reviewed and studied in the light of these mistakes and their consequence in a long delay of the coming of Christ. Such a vision will explain many puzzling questions and will greatly strengthen our faith in the divine leadership of the Advent Movement. It is for this purpose that this series of studies are being given and published. It is evident that the end is near and that such a vision of the past is an essential part of the preparation for entrance into the heavenly Canaan.

Review Exodus Movement

The best way to review our past history in the light of God's purpose and leadership is through the study of the Exodus Movement of which it is the antitype.

The history of the wilderness life of Israel was chronicled for the benefit of the Israel of God to the close of time. The record of God's dealings with the wanderers of the desert in all their marchings to and fro, in their exposure to hunger, thirst, and weariness, and in the striking manifestations of His power for their relief, is fraught with warning and instruction for His people in all ages. The varied experience of the Hebrews was a school of preparation for their promised home in Canaan. God would have his people in these days review with a humble heart and teachable spirit the trials through which ancient Israel passed, that they may be instructed in their preparation for the heavenly Canaan.[5]

Lest We Forget

In {*Testimonies*} Vol. 8, p. 107 is the beginning of a chapter entitled "Forgetfulness" which starts as follows:

> All who profess to be children of God, I would invite to consider the history of the Israelites, as recorded in the one hundred and fifth, the one hundred and sixth, and the one hundred and seventh Psalms. By carefully studying these Scriptures, we may be able to appreciate more fully the goodness, mercy, and love of God.

After quoting these Psalms the servant of the Lord continues:

> These things ... are written for our admonition, upon whom the ends of the world are come. ... The record of Israel's forgetfulness has been preserved for our enlightenment. In this age God has set His hand to gather unto Himself a people from every nation, kindred, and tongue. In the Advent Movement He has wrought for His heritage, even as He wrought for the Israelites in leading them from Egypt.[6]

The Chief Lesson

The chief lesson to be learned from the study of the Exodus Movement as a type of the Advent Movement is the reason for the long delay in the coming of Christ. That too was the chief reason why Moses reviewed the past history of the Israelites just before their final triumph. Continuing, the same writer said:

> Had the Adventists in the early days still trusted to the guiding hand that had been with them in their past experience, they would have seen the salvation of God. If all who had labored unitedly in the work of 1844 and received the third angel's message, and proclaimed it in the power of

5. Ellen White, *Patriarchs and Prophets* (1890), p. 293.
6. Ellen White, *Testimonies for the Church,* vol. 8 (1904), p. 115.

> the Holy Spirit, the Lord would have wrought mightily with their efforts. A flood of light would have been shed upon the world. Years ago the inhabitants of the earth would have been warned, the closing work would have been completed, and Christ would have come for the redemption of His people.[7]

> It was not the will of God that Israel should wander forty years in the wilderness. He desired to lead them directly to the land of Canaan, and establish them there a holy, happy people. But 'they could not enter in because of unbelief.' Because of their backsliding and apostasy, they perished in the desert, and others were raised up to enter the promised land. In like manner, it was not the will of God that the coming of Christ should be so long delayed and His people should remain so many years in this world of sin and sorrow. But unbelief separated them from God.[8]

Nothing explains this long delay like the study of the two movements.

Our Only Safety

Our only safety as we face the future is to remember that God has been the Leader of the Advent Movement from the beginning, and that He will continue to lead till the church militant becomes the church triumphant.

> We have nothing to fear for the 139 future, except as we shall forget the way the Lord has led us, and His teaching in our past history.[9]

> In reviewing our past history, having traveled over every step of advance to our present standing, I can say, Praise God! As I see what God has wrought, I am filled with astonishment, and in confidence in Christ as Leader. We have nothing to fear for the future, except as we shall forget the way the Lord has led us.[10]

We are told that the same divine leadership that has guided the Advent Movement in the past will continue to the end and nothing proves this more conclusively than the study of the two movements. It is therefore high time that God's remnant people are making a thorough study of this subject.

Law Repeated

Deuteronomy 4:1-9: "Now therefore hearken, O Israel, unto the statutes and unto

---

7. Ellen White, *Testimonies for the Church,* vol. 8 (1904), p. 116.
8. Ellen White, *Great Controversy* (1911), p. 458.
9. Ellen White, *Life Sketches* (1915), p. 196.
10. Ellen White, *Testimonies to Ministers and Gospel Workers* (1923), p. 31.

the judgments, which I teach you, for to do them, that ye may live, and go in and possess the land which the LORD God of your fathers giveth you Ye shall not add unto the word which I command you, neither shall ye diminish ought from it, that ye may keep the commandments of the LORD your God which I command you. Your eyes have seen what the LORD did because of Baalpeor: for all the men that followed Baalpeor, the LORD thy God hath destroyed them from among you.

"But ye that did cleave unto the LORD your God are alive every one of you this day. Behold, I have taught you statutes and judgments, even as the LORD my God commanded me, that ye should do so in the land whither ye go to possess it. Keep therefore and do them; for this is your wisdom and your understanding in the sight of the nations, which shall hear all these statutes, and say,

"Surely this great nation is a wise and understanding people. For what nation is there so great, who hath God so nigh unto them, as the LORD our God is in all things that we call upon him for? And what nation is there so great, that hath statutes and judgments so righteous as all this law, which I set before you this day? Only take heed to thyself, and keep thy soul diligently, lest thou forget the things which thine eyes have seen, and lest they depart from thy heart all the days of thy life: but teach them thy sons, and thy sons' sons."

Moses also called attention in his farewell sermons to the binding claims of the law given at Mount Sinai. The law is referred to in practically every chapter of Deuteronomy being mentioned no less than fifty times. The discourses of Moses therefore constituted a call to God's great standard of righteousness and conduct. It was a lifting up of the standard in preparation for entrance into the promised land.

> Before relinquishing his position as the visible leader of Israel, Moses was directing to rehearse to them the history of their deliverance from Egypt and their journeyings in the wilderness, and also to recapitulate the law spoken from Sinai. When the law was given, but few of the present generation were old enough to comprehend the awful solemnity of the occasion. As they were soon to pass over Jordan and take possession of the promised land, God would present before them the claims of His law, and enjoin upon them obedience as the condition of prosperity.[11]

Moses gave directions that the law be repeated or reread to all Israel every 7 years.

Deuteronomy 31:10-13: "And thou shalt stone him with stones, that he die; because he hath sought to thrust thee away from the LORD thy God, which brought thee out of the land of Egypt, from the house of bondage. And all Israel shall hear, and fear, and shall do no more any such wickedness as this is among you. If thou shalt hear say in one of thy cities, which the LORD thy God hath given thee to dwell

11. Ellen White, *Patriarchs and Prophets* (1890), p. 463.

there, saying, Certain men, the children of Belial, are gone out from among you, and have withdrawn the inhabitants of their city, saying, Let us go and serve other gods, which ye have not known."

Joshua repeated the necessity of strict obedience to the law of God as the basis of prosperity.

Joshua 1:7, 8: "The same came for a witness, to bear witness of the Light, that all men through him might believe. He was not that Light, but was sent to bear witness of that Light."[12]

The Antitype

Isaiah 62:10-12: "Go through, go through the gates; prepare ye the way of the people; cast up, cast up the highway; gather out the stones; lift up a standard for the people. Behold, the LORD hath proclaimed unto the end of the world, Say ye to the daughter of Zion, Behold, thy salvation cometh; behold, his reward is with him, and his work before him. And they shall call them, The holy people, The redeemed of the LORD: and thou shalt be called, Sought out, A city not forsaken."

Just before the Advent Movement reaches its destination "the way of the people" will be prepared by casting or lifting "up the highway" of holiness, gathering "out the stones" or stumbling blocks, and lifting "up a standard for the people." We are told that those who preach the Laodicean message "upon which the destiny of the church hangs" and which brings the shaking and the latter rain, will "exalt the standard and pour forth the straight truth."[13] The Laodicean message with its complete remedy which embraces the imputed and imparted righteousness of Christ, call for a high standard. Its standard is perfection as revealed in the character of Christ of which the law is the transcript. The lifting up of the standard of righteousness by which we will be measured in the judgment will take place just before the latter rain and the entrance of God's remnant people into the heavenly Canaan.

Price of Victory

Reaching the high standard demanded by the Laodicean message is the price of the seal of God, the latter rain, and triumph with the movement.

> Not one of us will ever receive the seal of God while our characters have one spot or stain upon them. It is left with us to remedy the defects in our characters, to cleanse the soul temple of every defilement. Then the latter rain will fall upon as as the early rain fell upon the disciples on the day of Pentecost.[14]

---

12. See also Deuteronomy 28-30.
13. See *Early Writings*, p. 270.
14. Ellen White, *Testimonies for the Church*, vol. 5 (1890), p. 214.

> If the professed people of God find their hearts opposed to this straight work, it should convince them that they have a work to do to overcome, if they would not be spewed out of the mouth of the Lord. … Some are willing to receive one point, but when God brings them to another testing point, they shrink from it and stand back, because they find that it strikes directly at some cherished idol. Here they have opportunity to see what is in their hearts that shuts out Jesus. … Those who come up to every point, and stand every test, and overcome, be the price what it may, have heeded the counsel of the True Witness, and they will receive the latter rain, and thus be fitted for translation.[15]

Death of Moses

Deuteronomy 34: "And Moses went up from the plains of Moab unto the mountain of Nebo, to the top of Pisgah, that is over against Jericho. And the LORD shewed him all the land of Gilead, unto Dan, And all Naphtali, and the land of Ephraim, and Manasseh, and all the land of Judah, unto the utmost sea, And the south, and the plain of the valley of Jericho, the city of palm trees, unto Zoar. And the LORD said unto him, This is the land which I sware unto Abraham, unto Isaac, and unto Jacob, saying, I will give it unto thy seed: I have caused thee to see it with thine eyes, but thou shalt not go over thither.

"So Moses the servant of the LORD died there in the land of Moab, according to the word of the LORD. And he buried him in a valley in the land of Moab, over against Bethpeor: but no man knoweth of his sepulchre unto this day. And Moses was an hundred and twenty years old when he died: his eye was not dim, nor his natural force abated. And the children of Israel wept for Moses in the plains of Moab thirty days: so the days of weeping and mourning for Moses were ended.

"And Joshua the son of Nun was full of the spirit of wisdom; for Moses had laid his hands upon him: and the children of Israel hearkened unto him, and did as the LORD commanded Moses. And there arose not a prophet since in Israel like unto Moses, whom the LORD knew face to face, In all the signs and the wonders, which the LORD sent him to do in the land of Egypt to Pharaoh, and to all his servants, and to all his land, And in all that mighty hand, and in all the great terror which Moses shewed in the sight of all Israel."

The prophet of the Exodus Movement did not live to see the final triumph of the movement. After giving all of the instruction necessary to take Israel into the promised land, and after being given a vision of the future home of his people which embraced the new earth, Moses died and was buried in the land of Moab on the east side of the Jordan. The leadership of the movement was placed upon Joshua who in the strictest sense was not a prophet but one chosen to carry into effect the instructions given through Moses. After his death the instruction given through Moses was

15. Ellen White, *Testimonies for the Church*, vol. 1 (1868), p. 187.

appreciated more fully and obeyed more implicitly than during his lifetime.

> The Israelites deeply mourned for their departed leader. … Never till he was taken from them had they so fully realized his unswerving faith. With a new and deeper appreciation, they recalled the precious lessons he had given while still with them.[16]

No prophet has ever been fully accepted or his work appreciated till after his or her death. Passing time always enhances the value of the writings of a prophet in the estimation of God's people.

The Antitype

The prophet of the Advent Movement did not live to witness the final triumph of the cause she loved and served so long and faithfully. But before she died all of the instruction necessary to the finishing of the work was given in detail so that there is no need of another such instrument. Many have attempted to take her place but their claims have been so weak and the attempt to imitate her methods and messages so apparent that they have been unable to get a following. It is the duty of the leaders of the Advent Movement to carry out the instructions given in such detail through the gift of prophecy. Many visions of the heavenly Canaan cheer the Advent people along their march through the desert of sin toward the promised land.

Greater Appreciation

Every passing year since the death of Mrs. E.G. White makes her counsels and instructions to be more greatly appreciated. It has always been hard to accept a living prophet because they are human like their fellows and their many rebukes and corrections produce prejudices and even enmity. Now the instruction can be read the studied for what it is worth without the interference of personal feelings and prejudices. As the years go by the divine origin of the prophetic gift in the Advent Movement becomes more apparent. The permanency and success of the various lines of work established through the Spirit of Prophecy as well as the fulfillment of the many predictions made are piling up proof of the genuineness of this spiritual gift among God's remnant people.

This gift has been the greatest of all factors in the guiding, controlling, preserving and unifying of the Advent people in their world-wide gospel enterprise. It has held the movement together and made it in many ways the marvel of the religious world in this generation. If time should last long enough Sister White would be accorded a place among the leading prophets of the church by the religious world.

As in the case of the other prophets centuries would be required to bring about this

16. Ellen White, *Patriarchs and Prophets* (1890), p. 481.

result. But God's remnant people do not need centuries or even decades to establish their confidence. We have had experiences and demonstrations enough to prove that the work is of the Lord and that the stability and prosperity of the Advent Movement depends upon our attitude toward it.

2 Chronicles 20:30: "Believe in the Lord your God, so shall ye be established; believe His prophets, so shall ye prosper."

35

VICTORY AND RIGHTEOUSNESS BY FAITH

Triumph of Faith

Psalm 44:3: "For they got not the land in possession by their own sword, neither did their own arm save them: but thy right hand, and thine arm, and the light of thy countenance, because thou hadst a favour unto them."

Deuteronomy 9:1-6: "Hear, O Israel: Thou art to pass over Jordan this day, to go in to possess nations greater and mightier than thyself, cities great and fenced up to heaven, A people great and tall, the children of the Anakims, whom thou knowest, and of whom thou hast heard say, Who can stand before the children of Anak! "Understand therefore this day, that the LORD thy God is he which goeth over before thee; as a consuming fire he shall destroy them, and he shall bring them down before thy face: so shalt thou drive them out, and destroy them quickly, as the LORD hath said unto thee. Speak not thou in thine heart, after that the LORD thy God hath cast them out from before thee, saying, For my righteousness the LORD hath brought me in to possess this land: but for the wickedness of these nations the LORD doth drive them out from before thee.

"Not for thy righteousness, or for the uprightness of thine heart, dost thou go to possess their land: but for the wickedness of these nations the LORD thy God doth drive them out from before thee, and that he may perform the word which the LORD sware unto thy fathers, Abraham, Isaac, and Jacob. Understand therefore, that the LORD thy God giveth thee not this good land to possess it for thy righteousness; for thou art a stiffnecked people."

One of the last messages that came of the Israelites before they entered the promised land was that their success would not be the result of their "own sword" or their "own arm" or their own "righteousness," but by the faith and through the righteousness of their great Leader. Moses then reminded them of their rebellion at Kadesh-Barnea when "they would not enter in because of unbelief."[1] At Kadesh-Barnea they had attempted to enter in their own strength and miserably failed.

They had rebelled against His commands when He bade them to go up

1. See Deuteronomy 9:7, 8, 23, 24.

and take the land that He had promised them, and now, when He directed them to retreat from it, they were equally insubordinate, and declared that they would go to battle with their enemies. They arrayed themselves in warriors dress and armor, and presented themselves before Moses, in their own estimation prepared for conflict, but sadly deficient in the sight of God and His sorrowful servant.[2]

Hard Lesson

That victory and righteousness are obtainable alone through faith was a hard lesson for Israel to learn and it is equally hard for modern Israel. Failure to learn this lesson delayed the triumph of the Exodus Movement for forty years, and the same failure has delayed the final triumph of the Advent Movement for many years. At last Israel learned the lesson and the Lord led them into the promised land. We are told that this might have been done forty years before if they had exercised faith.

The Advent people will also eventually learn this lesson and enter the heavenly Canaan. The final messages of the prophet of the Exodus Movement just before his death centered in victory, justification and righteousness by faith in Christ, their Leader, and this too was the great burden of the prophet of the Advent Movement just before her death. Her final messages are filled with reminders of the failure of the Advent people to accept the message of 1888 and enter the heavenly Canaan, and with earnest appeals to accept by faith the victory and righteousness of Christ as the only hope of salvation.

> We may achieve victories which our own erroneous and misconceived opinions, our own defects of character, our own smallness of faith, have made to seem impossible. Faith! We scarcely know what it is.[3]

The message now being given is restoring faith in the hearts of God's remnant people and soon they will march in triumph into the heavenly kingdom.

Crossing the Jordan

The message of victory and righteousness by faith was soon followed by the crossing of the Jordan. This was a wonderful manifestation of faith such as had not been seen among them since the crossing of the Red Sea.[4] This event is recorded in Joshua 1:11; 3:7-17.

> All watched with deep interest as the priests advanced down the banks of the Jordan. They saw them with the sacred ark move steadily forward

2. Ellen White, *Testimonies for the Church,* vol. 4 (1881), p. 153-154.
3. Ellen White, *Testimonies to Ministers and Gospel Workers* (1923), p. 187.
4. Hebrews 11:29.

> toward the angry, surging stream, till the feet of the bearers were dipped into the waters. Then suddenly the tide above was swept back, while the current below flowed on, and the bed of the river was laid bare. At the divine command, the priests advanced to the middle of the channel, and stood there, while the entire host descended, and crossed to the farther side. Thus was impressed upon the minds of all Israel the fact that the power that stayed the waters of Jordan was the same that had opened the Red Sea to their fathers forty years before.[5]

A Memorial

As a memorial of this great miracle twelve men chosen from the twelve tribes took each a stone from the bed of the river and set up a monument on the western bank.

> The people were bidden to repeat to their children the story of the deliverance that God has wrought for them, as Joshua said, 'that all the people of the earth might know the hand of he Lord, that it is mighty, that ye might fear the Lord your God forever.' The influence of this miracle, both upon the Hebrews and upon their enemies, was of a great importance. It was an assurance to Israel of God's continued presence and protection. …
>
> Such an assurance was needed to strengthen their hearts as they entered upon the conquest of the land,—the stupendous task that had staggered the faith of their fathers forty years before.[6]

Reproach of Egypt

Joshua 5:2-10: "At that time the LORD said unto Joshua, Make thee sharp knives, and circumcise again the children of Israel the second time. And Joshua made him sharp knives, and circumcised the children of Israel at the hill of the foreskins. And this is the cause why Joshua did circumcise: All the people that came out of Egypt, that were males, even all the men of war, died in the wilderness by the way, after they came out of Egypt.

"Now all the people that came out were circumcised: but all the people that were born in the wilderness by the way as they came forth out of Egypt, them they had not circumcised. For the children of Israel walked forty years in the wilderness, till all the people that were men of war, which came out of Egypt, were consumed, because they obeyed not the voice of the LORD: unto whom the LORD sware that he would not shew them the land, which the LORD sware unto their fathers that he would give us, a land that floweth with milk and honey.

"And their children, whom he raised up in their stead, them Joshua circumcised: for they were uncircumcised, because they had not circumcised them by the way. And it came to pass, when they had done circumcising all the people, that they abode

5. Ellen White, *Patriarchs and Prophets* (1890), p. 484.
6. *Ibid.*, p. 484-485.

in their places in the camp, till they were whole. And the LORD said unto Joshua, This day have I rolled away the reproach of Egypt from off you. Wherefore the name of the place is called Gilgal unto this day. And the children of Israel encamped in Gilgal, and kept the passover on the fourteenth day of the month at even in the plains of Jericho."

Sin is the reproach of Egypt.[7] True circumcision is the cutting off of sin.

Colossians 2:11: "In whom also ye are circumcised with the circumcision made without hands, in putting off the body of the sins of the flesh by the circumcision of Christ."

It is also a sign of righteousness by faith.

Romans 4:11: "And he received the sign of circumcision, a seal of the righteousness of the faith which he had yet being uncircumcised: that he might be the father of all them that believe, though they be not circumcised; that righteousness might be imputed unto them also."

The acceptance of victory over sin and the righteousness of Christ by faith rolled away the reproach of Egypt and thus ended the period of their rejection which began at Kadesh-Barnea and during which they "were under the divine rebuke."

> The suspension of the rite of circumcision since the rebellion at Kadesh had been a constant witness of Israel that their covenant with God, of which it was the appointed symbol, had been broken. And the discontinuance of the Passover, the memorial of their deliverance from Egypt, had been an evidence of the Lord's displeasure at their desire to return to the land of bondage. Now, however, the years of rejection were ended. Once more God acknowledged Israel as His people, and the sign of the covenant was restored.[8]

Because the "reproach of Egypt" was rolled away from Israel at their first encampment after crossing the Jordan, the name of the place was called Gilgal which means "a rolling away" or "rolling off." The crossing of the Jordan by faith after the final shaking, sealed Israel as God's covenant-keeping people. The reproach was removed and the Lord returned to Zion to work with power among them.

Spiritual Baptism

In 1 Corinthians 10:1, 2, we are told that the crossing of the Red Sea was a baptism.

7. See Numbers 15:30; Proverbs 13:34; Ezekiel 20:5-8.
8. Ellen White, *Patriarchs and Prophets* (1890), p. 485.

Then the crossing of River Jordan would also be a baptism. In an individual sense the former probably symbolized our water baptism at the beginning of our Christian experience and the other the Spirit baptism at the close. In relation to the movement they probably represent the two great outpourings of the Holy Spirit at the beginning and close of the Advent Movement, which might be called the early and latter rain. The Holy Spirit was poured out during the 1844 experience at the beginning of the Advent Movement, and there will be another baptism of the Spirit during the latter rain at the close. The crossing of the Jordan by faith and the restoration of the rite of circumcision and the ordinance of the Passover were the evidences of restoration to divine favor and full acceptance which was the necessary preparation for entrance of the promised land.

The Latter Rain

Just as the crossing of the Jordan was the result of the acceptance of the message of victory and righteousness by faith, so the preaching and acceptance of the same message will bring the latter rain.

> The time of test is just upon us, for the loud cry of the third angel has already begun in the revelation of the righteousness of Christ, the sin pardoning Redeemer. This is the beginning of the light of the angel whose glory shall fill the whole earth.[9]

> The message of Christ's righteousness is to sound from one end of the earth to the other to prepare the way of the Lord. This is the glory of God, which closes the work of the third angel.[10]

> Clad in the armor of Christ's righteousness, the church is to enter upon her final conflict.[11]

The latter rain will be the chief evidence to the Advent people of the restoration of the divine favor and acceptance and that they are sealed for the kingdom. It will indicate that the Laodicean rebuke has been removed and the Laodicean message and remedy accepted and applied. It will be the evidence that the reproach of sin and the world has been removed and that the Lord has returned to Zion to complete the work of redemption.

Capture of Jericho

Joshua 5:13-15: "And it came to pass, when Joshua was by Jericho, that he lifted up

---

9. Ellen White, "The Perils and Privileges of the Last Days," *Review and Herald,* November 22, 1892, par. 7.
10. Ellen White, *Testimonies for the Church,* vol. 6 (1901), p. 19.
11. Ellen White, *Prophets and Kings* (1917), p. 725.

his eyes and looked, and, behold, there stood a man over against him with his sword drawn in his hand: and Joshua went unto him, and said unto him, Art thou for us, or for our adversaries?

"And he said, Nay; but as captain of the host of the LORD am I now come. And Joshua fell on his face to the earth, and did worship, and said unto him, What saith my lord unto his servant? And the captain of the LORD'S host said unto Joshua, Loose thy shoe from off thy foot; for the place whereon thou standest is holy. And Joshua did so."

Joshua 6: "Now Jericho was straitly shut up because of the children of Israel: none went out, and none came in. And the LORD said unto Joshua, See, I have given into thine hand Jericho, and the king thereof, and the mighty men of valour. And ye shall compass the city, all ye men of war, and go round about the city once. Thus shalt thou do six days. And seven priests shall bear before the ark seven trumpets of rams' horns: and the seventh day ye shall compass the city seven times, and the priests shall blow with the trumpets. And it shall come to pass, that when they make a long blast with the ram's horn, and when ye hear the sound of the trumpet, all the people shall shout with a great shout; and the wall of the city shall fall down flat, and the people shall ascend up every man straight before him.

"And Joshua the son of Nun called the priests, and said unto them, Take up the ark of the covenant, and let seven priests bear seven trumpets of rams' horns before the ark of the LORD. And he said unto the people, Pass on, and compass the city, and let him that is armed pass on before the ark of the LORD. And it came to pass, when Joshua had spoken unto the people, that the seven priests bearing the seven trumpets of rams' horns passed on before the LORD, and blew with the trumpets: and the ark of the covenant of the LORD followed them. And the armed men went before the priests that blew with the trumpets, and the rereward came after the ark, the priests going on, and blowing with the trumpets.

"And Joshua had commanded the people, saying, Ye shall not shout, nor make any noise with your voice, neither shall any word proceed out of your mouth, until the day I bid you shout; then shall ye shout.

"So the ark of the LORD compassed the city, going about it once: and they came into the camp, and lodged in the camp. And Joshua rose early in the morning, and the priests took up the ark of the LORD. And seven priests bearing seven trumpets of rams' horns before the ark of the LORD went on continually, and blew with the trumpets: and the armed men went before them; but the rereward came after the ark of the LORD, the priests going on, and blowing with the trumpets.

"And the second day they compassed the city once, and returned into the camp: so they did six days. And it came to pass on the seventh day, that they rose early about the dawning of the day, and compassed the city after the same manner seven times: only on that day they compassed the city seven times.

"And it came to pass at the seventh time, when the priests blew with the trumpets, Joshua said unto the people, Shout; for the LORD hath given you the city. And the city shall be accursed, even it, and all that are therein, to the LORD: only Rahab the harlot shall live, she and all that are with her in the house, because she hid the messengers that we sent. And ye, in any wise keep yourselves from the accursed thing, lest ye make yourselves accursed, when ye take of the accursed thing, and make the camp of Israel a curse, and trouble it. But all the silver, and gold, and vessels of brass and iron, are consecrated unto the LORD: they shall come into the treasury of the LORD.

"So the people shouted when the priests blew with the trumpets: and it came to pass, when the people heard the sound of the trumpet, and the people shouted with a great shout, that the wall fell down flat, so that the people went up into the city, every man straight before him, and they took the city. And they utterly destroyed all that was in the city, both man and woman, young and old, and ox, and sheep, and ass, with the edge of the sword.

"But Joshua had said unto the two men that had spied out the country, Go into the harlot's house, and bring out thence the woman, and all that she hath, as ye sware unto her. And the young men that were spies went in, and brought out Rahab, and her father, and her mother, and her brethren, and all that she had; and they brought out all her kindred, and left them without the camp of Israel.

"And they burnt the city with fire, and all that was therein: only the silver, and the gold, and the vessels of brass and of iron, they put into the treasury of the house of the LORD. And Joshua saved Rahab the harlot alive, and her father's household, and all that she had; and she dwelleth in Israel even unto this day; because she hid the messengers, which Joshua sent to spy out Jericho.

"And Joshua adjured them at that time, saying, Cursed be the man before the LORD, that riseth up and buildeth this city Jericho: he shall lay the foundation thereof in his firstborn, and in his youngest son shall he set up the gates of it. So the LORD was with Joshua; and his fame was noised throughout all the country."

The capture of Jericho is placed in the great chapter of faith as one of the two greatest exhibitions of faith during the Exodus Movement.

Hebrews 11:29, 30: "By faith they passed through the Red sea as by dry land: which the Egyptians assaying to do were drowned. By faith the walls of Jericho fell down, after they were compassed about seven days."

The movement began and ended in victory by faith even though there were few demonstrations of faith between the two events. Faith is absolute dependence on the Word of God without any evidence in sight.

Hebrews 11:1: "Now faith is the substance of things hoped for, the evidence of things not seen."

> Now faith is a wellgrounded assurance of that for which we hope, and

a conviction of the reality of things which we do not see. —Weymouths.

Implicit obedience to the Lord's directions for the capture of Jericho, when they were seemingly so unreasonable, was a wonderful manifestation of faith. The capture of this fortified stronghold just after the crossing of the Jordan was a type of the conquest of the entire promised land and thus ends the events of the Exodus Movement as typical of the Advent Movement.

Victory by Faith

> The Israelites had not gained the victory by their own power; the conquest had been wholly the Lord's; and as the first-fruits of the land, the city with all that it contained, was to be devoted as a sacrifice to God. It was to be impressed upon Israel that in the conquest of Canaan they were not to fight for themselves, but simply as instruments to execute the will of God; not to seek for riches or selfexaltation, but the glory of Jehovah their king.[12]

After describing the encircling movements of Israel around the walls of Jericho the same author continues:

> The very plan of continuing this ceremony through so long a time prior to the final overthrow of the walls, afforded opportunity for the development of faith among the Israelites. It was to impress upon their minds that their strength was not in the wisdom of man, nor in his might, but only in the God of their salvation. They were thus to become accustomed to relying wholly upon their divine Leader. God will do great things for those who trust in Him.[13]

God the Victor

> How easily the armies of Heaven brought down the walls that had seemed so formidable to the spies who brought the false report! The word of God was the only weapon used. The mighty God of Israel had said, 'I have given Jericho into thine hand.' If a single warrior had brought his strength to bear against the walls, the glory of God would have been lessened and His will frustrated. But the work was left to the Almighty; and had the foundation of the battlements been laid in the center of the earth, and their summits reached the arch of heaven, the result would have been the same when the Captain of the Lord's host led His legions of angels to the attack.[14]

---

12. Ellen White, *Patriarchs and Prophets* (1890), p. 491.
13. *Ibid.*, p. 493.
14. Ellen White, *Testimonies for the Church,* vol. 4 (1881), p. 161-162.

"The majesty of Heaven, with His army of angels, leveled the walls of Jericho without human aid. The armed warriors of Israel had no cause to glory in their achievements. All was done through the power of God.[15]

Human Credit Excluded

Psalm 44:3: "For they got not the land in possession by their own sword, neither did their own arm save them: but thy right hand, and thine arm, and the light of thy countenance, because thou hadst a favour unto them."

> In the taking of Jericho the Lord God of hosts was the General of the army. He made the plan for the battle, and united heavenly and human agencies to act a part in the work, but no human hand touched the walls of Jericho. God so arranged the plan that man could take no credit to himself for achieving the victory. God alone is to be glorified. So it shall be in the work in which we are engaged. The glory is not to be given to human agencies; the Lord alone is to be magnified.[16]

> None but God can subdue the pride of man's heart. We cannot save ourselves. We cannot regenerate ourselves. In the heavenly courts there will be no song sung, 'To me that loved myself, and washed myself, redeemed myself, unto me be glory and honor, blessing and praise.' But this is the keynote of the song that is sung by many here in this world.[17]

What Might Have Been

> Long had God designed to give the city of Jericho to His favored people, and magnify His name among the nations of the earth. Forty years before, when He led Israel out of bondage, He had purposed to give them the land of Canaan. But, by their wicked murmurings and jealousy, they had provoked His wrath, and He had caused them to wander for weary years in the wilderness, till all those who had insulted Him with their unbelief were no more. In the capture of Jericho, God declared to the Hebrews that their fathers might have possessed the city forty years before, had they trusted in Him as did their children.[18]

Now the Israelites fully realize the cause of their previous failures to enter Canaan. "They could not enter in because of unbelief."

The Advent Movement

---

15. Ellen White, *Testimonies for the Church,* vol. 4 (1881), p. 164.
16. Ellen White, *Testimonies to Ministers and Gospel Workers,* (1923), p. 214.
17. *Ibid.*, p. 456.
18. Ellen White, *Testimonies for the Church,* vol. 4 (1881), p. 162.

Hebrews 4:1: "Let us therefore fear, lest, a promise being left us of entering into his rest, any of you should seem to come short of it."

> The history of ancient Israel is written for our benefit. … Many who, like ancient Israel, profess to keep God's commandments, have hearts of unbelief while outwardly observing the statutes of God. Although favored with great light and precious privileges, they will nevertheless lose the heavenly Canaan, even as the rebellious Israelites failed to enter the earthly Canaan that God had promised them as the reward of their obedience. As a people we lack faith. In these days few would follow the direction given through God's chosen servant as obediently as did the armies of Israel at the taking of Jericho. The Captain of the Lord's host did not reveal Himself to all the congregation.[19]

A Conquering Power

Faith is a conquering power that will bring triumph to the Advent Movement.

> Faith is the living power that presses through every barrier, overrides all obstacles, and plants its banner in the heart of the enemy's camp. God will do marvelous things for those who trust in Him. It is because His professed people trust so much in their own wisdom, and do not give the Lord an opportunity to reveal His power in their behalf, that they have no more strength. He will help His believing children in every emergency, if they will place their entire confidence in Him and implicitly obey Him. … God works mightily for a faithful people, who obey His work without questioning or doubt. … Let the people give up self and the desire to work after their own plans, let them humbly submit to the divine will, and God will revive their strength and bring freedom and victory to His children.[20]

The fact that the message of victory is one of the many evidences that we are on the very borders of the kingdom of Heaven.

Fruition of Hopes

We have come to wonderful days in the history of the Advent Movement, especially for the young men and women. Soon the final shaking will purify the movement of all rebels and the children of faith will be sealed and receive the latter rain. The reproach of Egypt or of the world will be rolled away, the Laodicean rebuke removed, the divine favor restored, and the Lord will return to Zion with Pentecostal power. Then will the remnant of the church go forth "fair as the moon, clear as the sun, and terrible as an army with banners."

---

19. Ellen White, *Testimonies for the Church,* vol. 4 (1881), p. 162.
20. *Ibid.*, p. 162-264. See 1 John 5:4, 5; 1 Corinthians 15:57; 2 Corinthians 1:10; 2:14.

36

THE PROMISED LAND

Hope of Reward

Matthew 19:27-29: "Then answered Peter and said unto him, Behold, we have forsaken all, and followed thee; what shall we have therefore? And Jesus said unto them, Verily I say unto you, That ye which have followed me, in the regeneration when the Son of man shall sit in the throne of his glory, ye also shall sit upon twelve thrones, judging the twelve tribes of Israel. And every one that hath forsaken houses, or brethren, or sisters, or father, or mother, or wife, or children, or lands, for my name's sake, shall receive an hundredfold, and shall inherit everlasting life."

Jesus did not rebuke Peter for inquiring about their future reward. In answer to his question He assured the disciples of a compensation that far exceeded their expectation and comprehension. In the kingdom of glory they would be kings ruling over the twelve nations of the saved. The "exceeding great and precious promises" of a "great recompense of reward" occupy a large place in the Scriptures and has been one of the chief factors in leading men and women to decisions for righteousness and against iniquity.

The promises of "the inheritance of the saints in light" have made buoyant the spirits of the Christian pilgrims in all ages as they have journeyed through the enemy's country toward their home land. Faith is declared to be "the substance of things hoped for, the evidence of things not seen." Most of the hopes of God's people center in the divine promises of rewards that are unseen because invisible except through the eye of faith.

Vision of Future

It was the promise of the restored dominion that buoyed up the drooping spirits of Adam and Eve after they were driven from Paradise. This was also the secret of Enoch's 300 year walk with God which ended in his translation.

> But Enoch's heart was upon his eternal treasures. He had looked upon the celestial city. He had seen the King in His glory in the midst of Zion. The greater the existing iniquity, the more earnest was his longing for the home of God. While still on earth, he dwealt, by faith, in the realms of light.[1]

1. Ellen White, *Testimonies for the Church,* vol. 8 (1904), p. 330-331.

The vision of the future reward was also one of the secrets of Christ's Calvary victory.

> What sustained the Son of God in His betrayal and trial?—He saw the travail of His soul and was satisfied. He caught a view of the expanse of eternity, and saw the happiness of those who through His humiliation should receive pardon and everlasting life....His eyes caught the sight of the redeemed. He heard the ransomed ones singing the song of Moses and the Lamb.[2]

The Exodus Movement

It was his "respect unto the recompense of the reward" that influenced Moses to make the momentous decisions that resulted in his being chosen by the Lord to become the visible leader of the Exodus Movement.[3] Moses was able to endure all the privations and hardships of the journey from Egypt to Canaan because he kept his eyes on "Him who is invisible" and his faith centered on the promised rewards that were out of sight. It was the promises regarding the land of Canaan that made it possible to persuade the Israelites to leave Egypt and make the long and weary journey through the barren wilderness. The oft repetition of these promises helped keep the movement together and furnished inspiration for the marching multitudes. In time of crisis and discouragement, the hope of reward prevented them from returning to the land of their bondage.

Goodly Land

Exodus 3:7, 8: "And the LORD said, I have surely seen the affliction of my people which are in Egypt, and have heard their cry by reason of their taskmasters; for I know their sorrows; And I am come down to deliver them out of the hand of the Egyptians, and to bring them up out of that land unto a good land and a large, unto a land flowing with milk and honey; unto the place of the Canaanites, and the Hittites, and the Amorites, and the Perizzites, and the Hivites, and the Jebusites."

The statement: "A land flowing with milk and honey" is a symbol of fertility and prosperity and is repeated twenty different times. The promised inheritance of the Hebrews is further described in Deuteronomy 6:10, 11; 11:10-12; Ezekiel 20:6. In Psalm 106:24 Palestine is called the "pleasant land" or "the land of desire." -Margin. The angel Gabriel describes the homeland of the Jews as "the glorious land" or "the goodly land."[4] When the twelve spies returned from a forty day tour of the promised land they reported that it was all that the Lord had promised and they brought samples of its fruit. Caleb and Joshua declared that it "is exceeding good land."

---

2. *Ibid.*, p. 43-44. See Hebrews 12:2.
3. See Hebrews 11:24-27.
4. See Daniel 11:16. —Margin.

An Inheritance

The Lord told the Israelites that the promised land would be an inheritance so they would not feel that they had obtained it on the basis of purchase or conquest. They were to inherit the land of promise.[5] The fact that the land was a gift on the basis of inheritance was commemorated in a song.[6] The size of this inheritance is given in Numbers 34:1-12. The territory of the two and one half tribes on the east side of the Jordan was to reach to the River Euphrates.

> To the heights of Lebanon in the far distance, to the shores of the Great Sea, and away to the banks of the Euphrates in the east,—all was to be theirs.[7]

The promise was that it would be "a good land and large." That the Lord planned to gradually expand the land of promise to embrace the whole earth is evident from the fact that when the promise was made to Abraham it embraced the whole earth.[8]

Vision of Moses

Just before his death Moses was given a vision of the promised land from which he was to be excluded because of his sin of impatience.

> And now a panoramic view of the land of promise was presented to him. Every part of the country was spread out before him, not faint and uncertain in the dim distance, but standing out clear, distinct, and beautiful to his delighted vision. In this scene it was presented, not as it then appeared, but as it would become, with God's blessing upon it, in possession of Israel. He seemed to be looking upon a second Eden. There were mountains clothed with cedars of Lebanon, hills gay with olives and fragrant with the odor of the vine, wide green plains bright with flowers and rich in fruitfulness, here the palm trees of the tropics, there waving fields of wheat and barley, sunny valleys musical with the ripple of brooks and the song of birds, goodly cities and fair gardens, lakes rich in 'the abundance of the seas,' grazing flocks upon the hillsides, and even among the rocks the wild bee's hoarded treasure. It was indeed such a land as Moses, inspired by the Spirit of God, had described to Israel.[9]

This vision of God's prophet was then merged into a view of the whole earth when restored to its Edenic beauty and inhabited by the redeemed.

---

5. See Exodus 6:4, 8; Numbers 34:2; Psalm 105:44.
6. See Psalm 44:1-3.
7. Ellen White, *Patriarchs and Prophets* (1890), p. 482.
8. See Romans 4:13.
9. Ellen White, *Patriarchs and Prophets* (1890), p. 472.

Land Occupied

The promised land was already occupied by thirty nations each of which was greater in numbers than that of the Hebrews. These nations had been given opportunity to know Jehovah but they had rejected Him for the worship of false gods and had sinned away their day of grace. The Lord could not give the promised land to His people till these nations and their inhabitants had filled up the cup of their iniquity. This would happen in a specified generation.[10] The nations and people occupying the promised land were to be "utterly" destroyed.[11] The destroying would be done by the Lord through His destroying angel who would "cut them off."[12] As weapons of destruction the Lord would use "hornets", "plagues", and "hailstones."[13]

Heavenly Canaan

The promised land of the Advent Movement is the heavenly Canaan which is the whole earth redeemed and restored to its original state.[14] The heavenly Canaan like the earthly comes to God's people by inheritance and is a gift of God received by faith. Just as Abraham, Isaac, and Jacob and the twelve patriarchs were pilgrims and strangers in a land which they "should after receive for an inheritance", so are all of God's people throughout the reign of sin, pilgrims and strangers in a world which will come to them by inheritance.

This promised land is now occupied by wicked nations who will have been given every opportunity to know the Lord and His truth. The complete rejection of God's last warning message under the latter rain will fill up their cup of iniquity. The Lord cannot give the earth to His chosen people till the inhabitants of the earth have sinned away their day of grace. When "the times of the Gentiles" are "fulfilled" probation will close and the final preparation will be made for the saints to inherit the earth.

Utterly Destroyed

The Lord has promised to destroy utterly all earthly nations and all sinners.

Daniel 2:34, 35, 44, 45: "Thou sawest till that a stone was cut out without hands, which smote the image upon his feet that were of iron and clay, and brake them to pieces. Then was the iron, the clay, the brass, the silver, and the gold, broken to pieces together, and became like the chaff of the summer threshingfloors; and the wind carried them away, that no place was found for them: and the stone that smote the image became a great mountain, and filled the whole earth. ...

"And in the days of these kings shall the God of heaven set up a kingdom, which

---

10. See Genesis 15:13-16.
11. See Deuteronomy 7:1, 2.
12. See Exodus 23:23; 33:1, 2.
13. See Exodus 23:28; Joshua 10:11.
14. Psalm 37:11; Matthew 5:5; Hebrews 11:12-16.

shall never be destroyed: and the kingdom shall not be left to other people, but it shall break in pieces and consume all these kingdoms, and it shall stand for ever. Forasmuch as thou sawest that the stone was cut out of the mountain without hands, and that it brake in pieces the iron, the brass, the clay, the silver, and the gold; the great God hath made known to the king what shall come to pass hereafter: and the dream is certain, and the interpretation thereof sure."

Zephaniah 1:2, 3, 14-18: "I will utterly consume all things from off the land, saith the LORD. I will consume man and beast; I will consume the fowls of the heaven, and the fishes of the sea, and the stumblingblocks with the wicked; and I will cut off man from off the land, saith the LORD. ...The great day of the LORD is near, it is near, and hasteth greatly, even the voice of the day of the LORD: the mighty man shall cry there bitterly. That day is a day of wrath, a day of trouble and distress, a day of wasteness and desolation, a day of darkness and gloominess, a day of clouds and thick darkness, A day of the trumpet and alarm against the fenced cities, and against the high towers. And I will bring distress upon men, that they shall walk like blind men, because they have sinned against the LORD: and their blood shall be poured out as dust, and their flesh as the dung. Neither their silver nor their gold shall be able to deliver them in the day of the LORD'S wrath; but the whole land shall be devoured by the fire of his jealousy: for he shall make even a speedy riddance of all them that dwell in the land."

Isaiah 13:9: "Behold, the day of the LORD cometh, cruel both with wrath and fierce anger, to lay the land desolate: and he shall destroy the sinners thereof out of it."

Isaiah 24:1-6: "Behold, the LORD maketh the earth empty, and maketh it waste, and turneth it upside down, and scattereth abroad the inhabitants thereof. And it shall be, as with the people, so with the priest; as with the servant, so with his master; as with the maid, so with her mistress; as with the buyer, so with the seller; as with the lender, so with the borrower; as with the taker of usury, so with the giver of usury to him.

"The land shall be utterly emptied, and utterly spoiled: for the LORD hath spoken this word. The earth mourneth and fadeth away, the world languisheth and fadeth away, the haughty people of the earth do languish. The earth also is defiled under the inhabitants thereof; because they have transgressed the laws, changed the ordinance, broken the everlasting covenant. Therefore hath the curse devoured the earth, and they that dwell therein are desolate: therefore the inhabitants of the earth are burned, and few men left."

This destruction will be accomplished by "plagues" and "great hailstones."

Ezekiel 38:18-22: "And it shall come to pass at the same time when Gog shall come against the land of Israel, saith the Lord GOD, that my fury shall come up in my face. For in my jealousy and in the fire of my wrath have I spoken, Surely in that day there shall be a great shaking in the land of Israel; So that the fishes of the sea, and the fowls of the heaven, and the beasts of the field, and all creeping things that creep upon the earth, and all the men that are upon the face of the earth, shall shake at my presence, and the mountains shall be thrown down, and the steep places shall fall, and every wall shall fall to the ground. And I will call for a sword against him throughout all my mountains, saith the Lord GOD: every man's sword shall be against his brother. And I will plead against him with pestilence and with blood; and I will rain upon him, and upon his bands, and upon the many people that are with him, an overflowing rain, and great hailstones, fire, and brimstone."

Revelation 16: "And I heard a great voice out of the temple saying to the seven angels, Go your ways, and pour out the vials of the wrath of God upon the earth. And the first went, and poured out his vial upon the earth; and there fell a noisome and grievous sore upon the men which had the mark of the beast, and upon them which worshipped his image.

"And the second angel poured out his vial upon the sea; and it became as the blood of a dead man: and every living soul died in the sea.

"And the third angel poured out his vial upon the rivers and fountains of waters; and they became blood. And I heard the angel of the waters say, Thou art righteous, O Lord, which art, and wast, and shalt be, because thou hast judged thus. For they have shed the blood of saints and prophets, and thou hast given them blood to drink; for they are worthy. And I heard another out of the altar say, Even so, Lord God Almighty, true and righteous are thy judgments.

"And the fourth angel poured out his vial upon the sun; and power was given unto him to scorch men with fire. And men were scorched with great heat, and blasphemed the name of God, which hath power over these plagues: and they repented not to give him glory.

"And the fifth angel poured out his vial upon the seat of the beast; and his kingdom was full of darkness; and they gnawed their tongues for pain, And blasphemed the God of heaven because of their pains and their sores, and repented not of their deeds.

"And the sixth angel poured out his vial upon the great river Euphrates; and the water thereof was dried up, that the way of the kings of the east might be prepared. And I saw three unclean spirits like frogs come out of the mouth of the dragon, and out of the mouth of the beast, and out of the mouth of the false prophet. For they are the spirits of devils, working miracles, which go forth unto the kings of the earth and of the whole world, to gather them to the battle of that great day of God Almighty.

"Behold, I come as a thief. Blessed is he that watcheth, and keepeth his garments, lest he walk naked, and they see his shame. And he gathered them together into a place called in the Hebrew tongue Armageddon.

"And the seventh angel poured out his vial into the air; and there came a great voice out of the temple of heaven, from the throne, saying, It is done. And there were voices, and thunders, and lightnings; and there was a great earthquake, such as was not since men were upon the earth, so mighty an earthquake, and so great. And the great city was divided into three parts, and the cities of the nations fell: and great Babylon came in remembrance before God, to give unto her the cup of the wine of the fierceness of his wrath. And every island fled away, and the mountains were not found. And there fell upon men a great hail out of heaven, every stone about the weight of a talent: and men blasphemed God because of the plague of the hail; for the plague thereof was exceeding great."

The wicked will be burned up root and branch and shall "be ashes under the soles" of the feet of the righteous who inhabit the land.[15] This destruction has been delayed in the mercy of God till the cup of iniquity is filled to the brim, and there is every evidence that the day of vengeance is at hand.

> Evil workers have been treasuring up wrath against the day of wrath; and when the time fully comes that iniquity shall have reached the stated boundary of God's mercy, his forbearance will cease. When the accumulated figures in heaven's record books shall mark the sum of transgression complete, wrath will come, unmixed with mercy.[16]

Goodly Land

The heavenly Canaan is indeed a goodly land. The earth will be completely restored to its original Edenic state.

Acts 3:20, 21: "And he shall send Jesus Christ, which before was preached unto you: whom the heaven must receive until the times of restitution of all things, which God hath spoken by the mouth of all his holy prophets since the world began."

"Restitution" means to bring back to a former state of condition. The earth will be made "like Eden" and "like the garden of the Lord."[17] Paul declared that "when the perfect state of things is come, all that is imperfect will be brought to an end."[18] This perfect state of things is described in many texts.[19]

After viewing the earthly Canaan from the summit of Mount Nebo Moses was given a vision of the new earth.

> Still another scene opens to his view,—the earth freed from the curse,

---

15. See Malachi 4:1-3.
16. Ellen White, *Testimonies for the Church,* vol. 5 (1889), p. 524.
17. Isaiah 51:3.
18. 1 Corinthians 13:10. Weymouth.
19. See Isaiah 11:4-9; 35:3-10; 60:18-21; 65:17-25; 66:22, 23; Revelation 21 and 22.

lovelier than the fair land of promise so lately spread out before him. There is no sin, and death cannot enter. There the nations of the saved find their eternal home. With joy unutterable, Moses looks upon the scene,—the fulfillment of a more glorious deliverance than his highest hopes have ever pictured. There earthly wanderings forever past, the Israel of God have at last entered the goodly land.[20]

Spiritual Purpose

In the heavenly Canaan God's original purpose will be carried out "as if man had never fallen." Eden, which means "a delightful region" will be restored, and we can again enter Paradise, "the garden of all delights."

> As the earth came from the hand of its Maker, it was exceedingly beautiful. Its surface was diversified with mountains, hills, and plains, interspersed with noble rivers and lovely lakes; but the hills and mountains were not abrupt and rugged, abounding in terrific steeps and frightful chasms, as they now do; the sharp ragged edges of earth's rocky framework were buried beneath the fruitful soil, which everywhere produced a luxuriant growth of verdure. There were no loathsome swamps or barren deserts. Graceful shrubs and delicate flowers greeted the eye at every turn. The heights were crowned with trees more majestic than any that now exist. The air, untainted by foul miasm, was clear and healthful. The entire landscape outvied in beauty the decorated grounds of the proudest palace.[21]

All this is to be restored.

Highest Ambitions Realized

> There are ever-flowing streams, clear as crystal, and beside them waving trees cast their shadows upon the paths prepared for the ransomed of the Lord. There the wide-spreading plains swell into hills of beauty, and the mountains of God rear their lofty summits. On these peaceful plains, beside those living streams, God's people, so long pilgrims and wanderers, shall find a home. ...
>
> There, immortal minds will contemplate with never failing delight the wonders of creative power, the mysteries of redeeming love. There will be no cruel, deceiving foe to tempt to forgetfulness of God. Every faculty will be developed, every capacity increased. The acquirement of knowledge will not weary the mind or exhaust the energies. There the grandest enterprises may be carried forward, the loftiest aspirations reached, the highest

20. Ellen White, *Patriarchs and Prophets* (1890), p. 477.
21. *Ibid.*, p. 44.

ambitions realized; and still there will arise new heights to surmount, new wonders to admire, new truths to comprehend, fresh objects to call forth the powers of mind and soul and body. All the treasures of the universe will be open to the study of the redeemed.[22]

Source of Encouragement

Just as contemplations and conversations concerning the promised land cheered the Hebrew pilgrims on their journey through the wilderness, so the Advent people are encouraged to press on and not cast away their confidence because of the glories of the heavenly Canaan at the end of their journey.

> There are revealed in these last days visions of future glory, scenes pictured by the hand of God, and these should be dear to His church. …
>
> We must have a vision of the future and of the blessedness of heaven.[23]

> Let your imagination picture the home of the saved, and remember that it will be more glorious than your brightest imagination can portray.[24]

The Home Land

Palestine was the homeland of the Hebrews as they were only sojourners in Egypt. As soon as they reached their homeland the Feast of Tabernacles was instituted to commemorate their deliverance from Egyptian bondage and "in memory of their pilgrim life in the wilderness."[25] This great festival was a home-coming celebration and was also known as The feast of home-coming." It was never celebrated while Israel was in bondage or captivity in a foreign land. It was instituted as soon as they reached their homeland from Egyptian bondage and was reinstituted after they returned from captivity in Babylon.

> The Feast of Tabernacles was the closing gathering of the year. It was God's design that at this time the people should reflect on His goodness and mercy. …
>
> The feast continued for seven days. … From far and near the people came, bringing in their hands a token of rejoicing. Old and young, rich and poor, all brought some gift as a tribute of thanksgiving to Him who had crowned the year with His goodness, and made His paths drop fatness. Everything that could please the eye, and give expression to the universal joy, was brought from the woods; the city bore the appearance of a beautiful forest.

---

22. Ellen White, *Great Controversy* (1911), p. 675, 677.
23. Ellen White, *Testimonies for the Church,* vol. 8 (1904), p. 43-44.
24. Ellen White, *Steps to Christ* (1893), p. 86. See 1 Corinthians 2:9.
25. Ellen White, *Patriarchs and Prophets* (1890), p. 540.

> The feast was not only the harvest thanksgiving, but the memorial of God's protecting care over Israel in the wilderness. In commemoration of their tent life, the Israelites during the feast dwelt in booths or tabernacles of green boughs. …
>
> With sacred song and thanksgiving the worshipers celebrated this occasion.[26]

The Final Home Coming

This home-coming celebration was typical of the home-coming of the redeemed of the earth to the heavenly Canaan.[27] The Revelator is given visions of the redeemed of earth in the heavenly land "clothed with white robes, and with palms in their hands" celebrating the antitypical Feast of Tabernacles or Ingathering.[28] The whole universe joins in the celebration of the greatest home-coming and thanksgiving celebration of all the ages.

> The Feast of Tabernacles was not only commemorative, but typical. It not only pointed back to the wilderness sojourn, but, as the feast of harvest, it celebrated the ingathering of the fruits of the earth, and pointed forward to the great day of final ingathering, when the Lord of the harvest shall send forth His reapers to gather the tares together in bundles for the fire, and to gather the wheat into His garner. … And every voice in the whole universe will unite in joyful praise to God. …
>
> The people of God praised God at the Feast of Tabernacles as they called to mind His mercy in their deliverance from the bondage of Egypt and His tender care for them during their pilgrim life in the wilderness. They rejoiced also in the consciousness of pardon and acceptance, through the service of the day of atonement, just ended. But when the ransomed of the Lord shall have been safely gathered into the heavenly Canaan,—forever delivered from the bondage of the curse, under which 'the whole creation groaneth and travileth in pain together until now,'—they will rejoice with joy unspeakable and full of glory. Christ's great work of atonement for men will then have been completed, and their sins will have been forever blotted out.[29]

Three-fold Doxology

It is during this great thanksgiving celebration of the final home-coming that the three-fold doxology of Revelation 5 is sung by the cherubim guardians of the throne

26. Ellen White, *Desire of Ages* (1898), p. 447-448.
27. See Revelation 14:1-5; 15:2-8; 19:1-9.
28. See Revelation 7:9-17.
29. Ellen White, *Patriarchs and Prophets* (1890), p. 541-542f.

of God with the twenty-four elders, the innumerable angelic host with their seven-fold ascription of praise to the Lamb, and ending with a mighty Hallelujah chorus of praise to God and the Lamb in which every creature in the universe participates. In the great home-coming celebration the triple doxology breaks out beyond the throne room of the celestial temple to all creation.

> Finally, all creation affected by the fall and embraced in the provisions of redemptive restoration reverberates with loyal praises to God and His Lamb, offering up unto them in thankful voice from all those spheres all 'blessing, and honor, and glory, and power.' We can well understand the thrill of rapturous anticipation that will at this time animate all the waiting creation when we read a passage like Rom. 8:18-21![30]

Waiting for Celebration

The apostle Paul describes the whole universe waiting in joyful anticipation for this great thanksgiving celebration when the Advent Movement completes its journey and all the saints enter the heavenly Canaan:

Romans 8:18-23: "Why, what we now suffer I count as nothing in comparison with the glory which is soon to be manifested in us. For all Creation, gazing eagerly as if with outstretched neck, is waiting and longing to see the manifestation of the sons of God. For the Creation fell into subjection to failure and unreality (not of its own choice, but by the will of him who so subjected it.) Yet there was always the hope that at last the Creation itself would also be set free from the thraldom of decay so as to enjoy the liberty that will attend the glory of the children of God. For we know that the whole Creation is groaning together in the pains of childbirth until this hour. And more than that, we ourselves, though we possess the Spirit as a foretaste and pledge of the glorious future, yet we ourselves inwardly sigh, as we wait and long for open recognition as sons through the deliverance of our bodies."[31]

30. Stevens, Revelation, the Crown Jewel of Biblical Prophecy, p. 126.
31. Weymouth.

More publications from Return of the Latter Rain Publishers...

The Third Angel's Message 1893 and 1897

The 1893 and 1897 sermons that A. T. Jones gave at the General Conferences Ellen White described in this way: "I have been instructed to use those discourses of yours printed in the General Conference bulletins of 1893, 1897 ... I was shown that many would be helped by the articles ... which were of the Holy Spirits framing" (9MR 278). In these sermons you will see for yourself Christ and His righteousness exalted.

The Third Angel's Message 1895

Just after the 1895 General Conference ended in April, Ellen White wrote the following in May of that year: "The Lord in His great mercy sent a most precious message to His people through Eld. Waggoner and Jones" (TM 91).

The Everlasting Covenant

Ellen White wrote to those who were opposing Waggoner on the Covenants: "Night before last I was shown that evidences in regard to the covenants were clear and convincing. Yourself, ... and others are spending your investigative powers for naught to produce a position on the covenants to vary from the position that Brother Waggoner has presented" (9MR 328). The Preface, written by Ron Duffield, covers the history of Waggoner's views on the *Everlasting Covenant*.

Ellen White and the Godhead

Read what Ellen White wrote concerning the Godhead— the Father, Son, and Holy Spirit. May it be a blessing in a time when many winds of Doctrine concerning the divinity of Christ and the person of the Holy Spirit are creeping into the church.

Ellen White and the Loud Cry

Read for yourself what Ellen White wrote about the message that came to us in 1888, as well as what she said about the messengers. It will bless your heart and give you confidence in the Loud Cry Message of God.

Preparing for the Latter Rain Series

Read select sermons taken from the 1893 *General Conference Bulletin,* where all the ministers joined together in proclaiming the message of preparation for the Loud Cry under the outpouring of the Latter Rain.

The Heart of the 1888 Message

In 1895 Ellen White penned these words: "The Lord in His great mercy sent a most precious message to His people through Elders Waggoner and Jones." (*1888 Materials*, 1336). What was the heart of that message that came to us as Seventh-day Adventists in 1888?

Forty Years in the Wilderness in Type and Antitype

In this small pamphlet Elder Taylor Bunch compares briefly the history of ancient Israel in their journeyings to the promised land with the history of the Adventist people. He wrote: "The time has come for the Advent people to carefully review their past history and profit by the mistakes made. Especially should we study the 1888 experience and learn the reasons for our wilderness wanderings." (*Forty Years in the Wilderness*, p. 31).

The Return of the Latter Rain, vol. 1

A historical review of Seventh-day Adventist History from 1844 through 1891.

The title itself implies that the latter rain must have been among us as a people once before. If so, what was it — and when did this occur? Is the latter rain what our Pentecostal friends describe as "being slain in the Spirit?" Or, is the latter rain a powerful message of the revelation of the righteousness of Christ? As Ron Duffield, a fifth generation Seventh-day Adventist, reviews our history, our hearts will be strangely warmed as we see, perhaps as never before, that his great second Advent movement was raised up by God to give the latter rain message.

Wounded in the House of His Friends

A summary volume, in *The Return of the Latter Rain* series, this book is a story of a time much closer to ours, then the time of the Jews, when Jesus came near to his people, bringing with Him the priceless gift—the full measure of the Holy Spirit in Latter Rain power—but was wounded again in the house of his friends. The Latter Rain that might have been was delayed—and waits even yet to resume.

Books published by Return of the Latter Rain Publishers may be obtained from the following sellers:

Amazon Books: www.amazon.com
Light Bearers Ministry: www.lbm.org
Orion Publishing: www.orion-publishing.org
Glad Tidings Publishers: www.1888msc.org

Or contact your local ABC: 1-800-765-6955

For bulk orders, questions or comments: returnofthelatterrain@gmail.com

Made in the USA
Coppell, TX
12 January 2026